OUR FAITHFUL ALLY,

THE NIZAM

OUR FAITHFUL ALLY,

THE NIZAM:

BEING

AN HISTORICAL SKETCH OF EVENTS,

SHOWING THE VALUE OF

THE NIZAM'S ALLIANCE TO THE BRITISH GOVERNMENT IN INDIA, AND HIS SERVICES DURING THE MUTINIES.

BY

CAPTAIN HASTINGS FRASER

GYAN

Published by

Gyan Publishing House
5, Ansari Road
Daryaganj, New Delhi-110002
Phone: 011-47034999, 9811692060
E-mail: books@gyanbooks.com

Distribution Network
gyanbooks.com
India, USA, Canada, UK, Australia

ISBN: 978-93-6208-291-6 (PB)
First Published, 1865

2nd Impression 2024

Printed at: Gyan Press, Delhi.

OUR FAITHFUL ALLY, THE NIZAM
Author: CAPTAIN HASTINGS FRASER

"OUR FAITHFUL ALLY,"

THE NIZAM:

BEING

AN HISTORICAL SKETCH OF EVENTS,

SHOWING THE VALUE OF

THE NIZAM'S ALLIANCE TO THE BRITISH GOVERNMENT IN INDIA, AND HIS SERVICES DURING THE MUTINIES.

BY

CAPTAIN HASTINGS FRASER,

MADRAS STAFF CORPS.

"AMONG THE FAITHLESS, FAITHFUL STILL."

LONDON:

SMITH, ELDER AND CO., 65, CORNHILL.

1865.

PREFACE.

THOUGH quite aware of the general indisposition in England to engage in the study of Indian politics, I have ventured to employ my leisure in preparing a continuous narrative of our connection with his highness the Sovereign of Hyderabad, from a conviction that such a work will at least be found useful for reference, and may possibly assist to excite some additional interest in the subject. This hope is not altogether an unreasonable one, for not only have Hyderabad politics been more frequently discussed of late years, both officially and by the press, than formerly, but through the rapidly increasing importance of the Valley of Berar as a cotton-producing district, our relations with the Nizam are seen to be fraught with consequences which the most practical of Englishmen may be expected to regard with interest. I have brought my history down to the period of the late Resident Colonel Davidson's death.

An author who has no professional object in view needs some encouragement to persevere with his self-imposed task, however humble it may be. It will not, therefore, be unbecoming in me to confess that a sense of justice to the Nizam's Government seemed to demand at the present time some such recognition of the faithfulness of his highness to the British alliance.

In recalling to mind the chain of events since we first sent a deputation to the Hyderabad Durbar, I could not but recognize the important advantages we have derived from time to time, through our relations with his highness. When the war broke out with Tippoo Sultan, brought about at the instigation of Meer Allum,[1] the Nizam not only assisted us by sending a considerable force to co-operate with the British army, but he forwarded immense quantities of supplies for the use of the British force. When we were engaged in hostilities with the Mahrattas, he was again at our side, and after the campaign against Tippoo he ceded to us nearly the whole of the country which had fallen to his share for the payment of the subsidiary force stationed near his capital. At other periods, too, during our long residence in India, when at war with the neighbouring states, the Nizam continued faithful

[1] Meer Allum was the first of Salar Jung's family who was Dewan or Minister.

to his engagements; but, above all, at a period when the least show of vacillation on his part would have sufficed to set the whole of Southern India in a blaze, he remained true to the alliance, not in a merely negative or doubtful manner, but in a spirit which deserves our warmest acknowledgment.

Within the limitations which I imposed on myself, it was impossible to enter into full details of all the occurrences alluded to. It will be seen, however, that some endeavour has been made to proportion the narrative to the relative importance of events. Thus, the period ending with the treaty of September 1st, 1798, is treated with considerable minuteness, as showing the successive steps by which we obtained a permanent footing at the Nizam's capital, though opposed by French intrigue in addition to native mistrust, and even menaced by the large forces which had been organized under French influence. Of subsequent events up to 1838, a brief recapitulation was deemed sufficient, but with my father's, General Fraser's, administration, extending to the critical period of Lord Dalhousie's advent in India, the necessity for a more detailed treatment of the subject again presented itself.

It will be seen that General Fraser exhibited remarkable foresight in urging upon the Government the removal of the foreign mercenaries, either employed by the Nizam or the warlike Zemindars of his dominions, and had his advice been fully acted upon, the numerous predatory bands who helped to swell the forces opposed to us in Central India in 1857, would have been dispersed years previously. It is a proof of the soundness of his policy, that Salar Jung, the present enlightened minister of the Nizam, has silently carried it out, and the Rohillas are no longer admitted into the Nizam's service, while the Government Arabs, who stood by Salar Jung in 1857, still form a portion of the Nizam's own forces.

Many instances of wise foresight and judicious promptitude on the part of General Fraser, in his character of Political Resident at Hyderabad, might be cited; as when, in 1847, by a timely demonstration of military force, he protected the Nizam against his own turbulent soldiery. His endeavours to secure the appointment of a responsible minister were as untiring as his advice for the amelioration of the abuses and other troubles of the Nizam's Government. Though his recommendations were not attended to by Lord Dalhousie, they were in fact adopted by Lord Canning's Government, who restored to the Nizam a considerable portion of the country which had been made over to our management by the treaty of 1853.

A fortunate star again ruled our relations with the Nizam in the memorable year of the great mutiny, which found Colonel Davidson, an officer of long political experience of the Nizam's Court, in the position of Resident at Hyderabad, and Salar Jung in the office of Dewan or Minister.[1] At Hyderabad the wise measures that were rendered possible by the mutual good understanding between the Resident and minister, added to the firmness of his highness the Nizam, prevented a rising in the city of Hyderabad, and threw the Nizam's contingent troops into the balance of our fortunes in Central India. Without relating in minute detail the incidents of the campaign, I have given such particulars as may enable the reader to appreciate the important services rendered by this force, especially in the capture of arms and ammunition at Rawul, with which the rebels before Neemuch would otherwise have been reinforced. Details of the honours and rewards afterwards conferred on the Nizam and the officers of his court are added, as being justly entitled to prominence in a narrative which has for one of its objects the demonstration of the steadfastness with which his highness has always adhered to his engagements.

The remission of the Nizam's debt, chiefly made up of interest on sums advanced from the British Treasury for the payment of the contingent, which had been

---

[1] Colonel Davidson was one of the four military officers who mainly stayed the rebellion in the South of India. They were, Davidson at Hyderabad, Durand at Indore, Elliot at Nagpore, and Wallace at Baroda. Prevention was better than cure.

retained on a war footing during a long course of years, requires little comment. Every Englishman must feel that Lord Canning took a most comprehensive view of the question, and in insisting on the entire remission it was declared that the Nizam had a fair claim on us for nearly the same amount, we having exceeded the sum which, according to the original understanding, was to be applied to the civil management of the Assigned Districts. This should have been restricted to the eighth, or two annas in every rupee collected, while the sum actually expended amounted to a quarter or four annas. The Nizam's debt therefore was accepted by Lord Canning as a set-off against the claim Colonel Davidson advocated on the Nizam's account.

Our administration of the districts assigned by the late Nizam for the regular payment of the Hyderabad Force is another subject on which I have deemed it necessary to enter into some detail. While the reader is gratified by observing the general improvement which has taken place in those portions of the Nizam's dominions under the management of British officers, he will also not fail to admire Sir Charles Wood's honesty of purpose in restoring to the Nizam a portion of his country, when he was informed by Lord Canning's Government that the Northern part of Berar was sufficient for the objects stipulated by treaty.

Finally, the details which I have been able to give concerning the cultivation of cotton in the Valley of Berar speak for themselves, and hardly need to be commended to the attention of persons who are interested in that important staple. I may here remark, however, that those parts of the Nizam's dominions only await the advent of enterprising capitalists, to convert what is still in some places a mere jungle and the abode of wild beasts, to fields yielding every description of grain and cotton, and otherwise developing the latent resources of one of the most fertile districts of the Peninsula.

Settlers in Berar, however, should distinctly understand that we have not the power to grant lands in perpetuity, but only on tenure for a limited number of years. The Nizam has not relinguished his sovereign rights. He has only assigned Berar to us for a special purpose, namely, as a national guarantee to ensure the regular payment of the contingent, and in the event of that purpose no longer existing, his highness would at once be entitled to claim his country, or that material guarantee might at any time be furnished by a deposit of cash in the British Treasury.

The opening up of the country by a railroad now in course of construction, and running through the entire length of Berar, will no doubt tend to increase the revenues considerably, and enable the British

Government yet to pay into the Nizam's coffers large sums now collected by our officials in excess of the amount required by us to meet treaty engagements, which surplus the treaty expressly provides shall be paid to his highness.

I cannot let this opportunity pass without bearing testimony to the just and equitable views entertained by the late Marquis of Dalhousie as regards our obligations to the Nizam, and at some future date I shall probably place on public record the views of his lordship. This I am not at liberty to do at present.

SUCCESSION OF NIZAMS.

1. Kumroodeen Khan Asuph Jah Nizam-ool-Moolk ascended the Musnud, 1713, died in the vicinity of Berhampore 1748
2. Nizam Ally Khan, died at Hyderabad 1803
3. Secunder Jah ditto 1829
4. Nasir-oo-Dowlah ditto .... May, 1857
5. Afzul-oo-Dowlah, ascended the Musnud in ..... May, 1857

SUCCESSION OF RESIDENTS.

	From	To
Mr. Grant resigned in 1784.		
Mr. R. Johnson	Feb. 1784	— 1785
Captain Kennaway (subsequently Sir J. Kennaway)	— 1788	— 1794
Captain W. Kirkpatrick	— 1794	— 1798
Captain J. A. Kirkpatrick	— 1798	— 1805
Mr. H. Russell (acting)	Oct. 1805	Dec. 1805
Captain Sydenham	— 1805	— 1810
Lieut. C. Russell (acting)	June 1810	March 1811
Mr. H. Russell	— 1811	Dec. 1820
Mr. Metcalfe	Dec. 1820	Aug. 1825
Mr. Martin	Sep. 1825	— 1830
Mr. Ravenshaw (officiating)	Aug. 1830	— 1830
Col. Stewart	Nov. 1830	Jany. 1838
Major Cameron (officiating)	Jan. 1838	May 1838
Col. Fraser	Sep. 1838	Jany. 1853
Col. Low	Mar. 1853	Sep. 1853
Mr. Bushby	Dec. 1853	Dec. 1856
Col. Davidson, C.B.	— 1857	

SUCCESSION OF MINISTERS.

1. Azim-ool-oomrah.
2. Meer Allum.
3. Mooneer-ool-Moolk.
4. Chundoo Lall.
5. Seraj-ool-Moolk.
6. Shumsh-ool-oomrah.
7. Salar Jung.

SUCCESSION OF GOVERNORS-GENERAL OF INDIA.

	From
Warren Hastings	13th April, 1772
Sir J. Macpherson	1st Febry., 1785
Lord Cornwallis	12th Sept., 1786
Sir John Shore	28th Octbr., 1793
Sir Alured Clarke	6th April, 1798
Lord Mornington	17th May, 1798
Marquis Cornwallis	30th July, 1805
Sir G. H. Barlow	10th Octbr., 1805
Lord Minto	31st July, 1807
Earl of Moira	4th Octbr., 1813
Hon. J. Adam	13th Jany., 1823
Lord Amherst	1st August, 1823
Hon. W. B. Bayley	13th March, 1828
Lord W. Bentinck	4th July, 1828
Sir C. Metcalfe	20th March, 1835
Lord Auckland	4th March, 1836
Lord Ellenborough	28th Feby., 1842
W. Wilberforce Bird	15th June, 1844
Lord Hardinge	23rd July, 1844
Lord Dalhousie	12th Janry., 1848
Lord Canning	July, - 1855
Proclaimed Viceroy	1st Novmb., 1858
Lord Elgin	August, - 1861

CONTENTS.

CHAPTER III.

Asof Jah's Immediate Successors.

CHAPTER IV.

Nizam Ally and the Northern Circars.

CHAPTER V.

War with Tippoo Sultan.

CHAPTER VIII.

Complication with the Mahrattas—(*continued*).

CHAPTER IX.

Complication with the Mahrattas—(*continued*).

CHAPTER X.

The Hyderabad and Mahratta Armies in the Field.

CHAPTER XI.

The Arbitrament of War.

CHAPTER XII.

Progress of the French.

CHAPTER XIII.

POLITICAL INTRIGUES AT HYDERABAD.

CHAPTER XIV.

REBELLION OF THE NIZAM'S SON.

CHAPTER XV.

Ascendancy of the French.

CHAPTER XVI.

Our Opponents checkmated.

CHAPTER XVII.

The Rule of Order introduced.

CHAPTER XX.

Cession of Berar.

CHAPTER XXI.

The Nizam and the Great Rebellion.

CHAPTER XXII.

Recognition of the Nizam's Services.

CHAPTER XXIII.

The Ceded Districts and Public Works.

CHAPTER XXIV.

THE NIZAM, THE MINISTER, AND THE RESIDENT.

CHAPTER XXV.

BERAR AND RAICHORE AS COTTON-FIELDS.

CONTENTS OF APPENDICES.

OUR FAITHFUL ALLY,

THE NIZAM.

CHAPTER I.

THE DECCAN AND ITS RULERS.

Geography of the Deccan—the Great Rivers of India—the Nizam's Capital—Hindoo Principalities—Invasion of the Deccan by the Mohammedan Kings of Delhi—Complete Success of Mohammed Toghlak—Rebellion at Dowlatabad—Foundation of the Bahmani Dynasty—Change of the Seat of Government—The last King of the Deccan—The Independent Kingdoms of Berar, Beejapore, Ahmednuggur, Ahmedabad, and Golconda—Second Conquest of the Deccan by the Mogul Empire—Rise of the Mahratta Power under Sevaji—Career and Death of the Popular Chief.

An irregular line drawn across the map of India, from the Gulf of Cambay on the Western coast, to the mouth of the Hooghley on the Eastern, may be taken to represent the Northern boundary of the large tract of country called by the general name of the Deccan. This line is not altogether imaginary, but it represents, along a great part of its course, the range of the Vindhya mountains, northward of which lies the great valley of the Jumna and the Ganges, or Hindostan Proper. The mountain range forms the base of the triangle of Southern India; its highest point may be roughly estimated at 2,000 feet above the level of the Nerbudda, which flows from east to west, almost parallel with the mountains, and empties itself into the Gulf of Cambay.

South of the Nerbudda the land rises again, and forms another range of hills, to which succeeds a second deeply cut river valley—that of the Tapty—which falls into the Gulf of Cambay or Surat. This is the last great river that flows from east to west. A little beyond it is the commencement of the mountain chain, which extends to Cape Comorin at the point of the Peninsula, and forms the western embankment of the Deccan plateau.

The third side of the triangle is formed by the eastern or Coromandel coast, parallel to which there also runs a chain of mountains, inferior in height, and more broken in their aspect, than those of the Malabar coast. The average height of these Eastern Ghauts does not exceed 1,500 feet, while the average elevation of those on the Western side is about 4,000 feet. The area thus supported may be described as a vast water-shed, sloping from west to east, and intersected in that direction by numerous streams which have their outlet in the Bay of Bengal. Its highest part is in the south-western corner, say in Mysore, from which point the land falls by abrupt steps to the plains of Salem eastward, and by a succession of vast terraces to the valley of the Tapty northward.

From the summits of the rocky embankment on the western side we look down the rugged precipices and "ghauts" upon a narrow strip of country stretching over more than ten degrees of latitude, and so separated by the natural barrier of the mountains from the plateau of the Deccan, that each may be described as a separate world—so separate that scarcely any intercourse took place between the inhabitants of the Malabar coast and those of the Deccan, before the arrival of the British in India. On those heights, however, the robber-chiefs of the Deccan erected their *droogs* or fortresses, from which they issued forth upon the plains to visit with fire and sword the luckless inhabitants of the peaceful towns and villages with which the Deccan was studded. On the eastern coast the population from an early period assumed a different character. The fruitful plains of Tanjore, and of the Carnatic generally, invited a more peaceful settlement, and access to the sea was rendered easy by the broken character of the mountains and their inferior elevation.

Traders from other parts of the world were attracted to the coast, and towns flourished there even at the commencement of the Christian era.

It has been remarked above, that all the great rivers of India, south of the Tapty, flow from west to east, the fall of the land from the great embankment of the Malabar coast being in that direction. The first of these rivers, south of the Ganges, and therefore proper to the Deccan, is the Mahanuddy, a noble stream, navigable, between July and February, to a distance of 450 miles from its mouth, and no less than 4,500 feet wide as high up the stream as Sumbulpoor. Cuttack, at the head of the Delta formed by these waters, is the capital of a province of the same name. It has a population of 40,000 persons, and is a place of great commercial and political importance.

The next river of magnitude southward from the Mahanuddy is the great Godavery, which runs a course of more than 900 miles across the heart of the Deccan, partly through a rich alluvial soil, which is flooded in the season to a width of from three to six miles on either side of the river. The attention of the Madras Government has lately been called to the importance of the water communication formed by this river and its tributaries, between the eastern coast and the interior of the Nizam's dominions, especially the coffee and cotton-producing province of Berar, and large sums have been expended on the improvement of its navigation. Next to it is the Kistnah, which also passes through the territories of the Nizam in a course of 800 miles. On account of the declivity of its channel, this river is not navigable; but it supplies an extensive system of irrigation, and on one of its tributaries is situated Hyderabad, the Nizam's capital. The last of the southern rivers is the Cauvery, which runs a course of 472 miles from the western Ghauts to the Bay of Bengal, and fertilizes the plains of Tanjore. On an island in this river is situated the once celebrated capital of the Sultan of Mysore, Seringapatam. With these observations as a key to the map of India, the reader will find no difficulty of a geographical nature in understanding that the Deccan from remote ages has been the seat of several distinct kingdoms, and a field of contention, from generation to generation, between the Mohammedan and Hindoo occupants of the soil.

The general civilization of the Deccan can be traced back to a period of fabulous obscurity, ten centuries before Christ. In the fifth century B.C., four kingdoms are believed to have shared its territory; the most ancient of them being in the south, where the Tamul language prevailed. These kingdoms were in all probability broken up into many petty principalities ages before the Mohammedans ventured to cross the Nerbudda; but really so little is known about them that it is almost idle to speculate on the probabilities of the case. We come to the authentic history of the Deccan at the close of the thirteenth century, when the power of the Mohammedan Emperors of Delhi was at its zenith.

In the year 1294 (A. H. 693), according to Ferishta, the native historian, Alla-oo-deen, nephew of the Emperor of Delhi, and governor of Kurra, proposed an expedition against certain native princes who were reputed to be possessed of great wealth. The necessary permission having been given, Alla-oo-deen assembled his forces, and marched against Ram Deo of Deoghur, who is called by Ferishta the Rajah of the Deccan, but who, the translator of Ferishta remarks, was probably a king of Maharashtra, the country throughout which the Mahratta language prevailed. This invasion, being a surprise, was successful, and Deoghur being captured, was given up to pillage in the year 1295. All the rajahs of the Deccan took alarm, and the course of Mohammedan conquest having once taken this direction, one after another the native princes were subdued, until in 1325 the complete reduction of the Deccan was accomplished by Mohammed Toghlak. This prince, who deserves to rank with the most remarkable men of any age, then conceived the idea of translating the seat of his government from Delhi to Deoghur, and with his usual impetuosity, he compelled all the inhabitants of the capital to remove there. On this occasion he gave the name of Dowlatabad to Deoghur, and built the fort which still exists as a witness to the vastness of his undertakings. The design of making Deoghur the seat of his empire was, however, ultimately abandoned.

In 1347 Mohammed suppressed a rebellion in Guzerat, and some of the rebels having taken refuge in the Deccan, were protected by the Mogul chiefs, who were, thereupon, made prisoners by Mohammed. This led to a general rebellion against his authority, and Ismael Khan, an Affghan general, was proclaimed King at Dowlatabad, under the title of "Nazir-oo-deen." Under him, the rebellion was not successful, and while he was shut up in the capital, another leader, "Houssein Zuffur Khan," arose, who defeated and slew the imperial commander, and finally received the royal dignity, which was resigned in his favour by Nazir-oo-deen. The title he assumed was that of Sultan Alla-oo-deen Houssein Khan, of Bahmany, and by the success of the rebellion he became the first independent King of the Deccan, the founder of the Bahmani dynasty. He selected Koolburga as his capital, a town which was for many years a station of the forces of the Nizam, on the old route from Hyderabad to Poonah; he named it Ahsunabad, according to Ferishta, but the translator suggests that this is an error in the manuscript for Hassunabad.

The Bahmani dynasty reigned in the Deccan from the foundation of the kingdom in 1347 to 1526, and the last of the Kings retained the nominal title some years longer. Koolburga remained the capital till 1434, when the seat of government was transferred to Ahmedabad, built by Ahmed Shah Bahmany, on the site of Bidur, an ancient capital of the Hindoos. This prince was at Ahmedabad when he died in 1435, and his son (another Alla-oo-deen), according to his father's will, ascended the throne there. The last of this race of Kings fled from his capital to Ahmednuggur in 1526, and thus terminated the Bahmani dynasty of Mohammedan Kings.

A quarter of a century previous to this event the dissolution of the Deccan sovereignty had been virtually accomplished, and five independent kingdoms had been formed out of its ruins. In 1484 Imad Shah had declared his independence as King of Berar; in 1489 Adil Shah became in like manner King of Beejapore; in 1490 Nizam Shah established himself as King of Ahmednuggur; in 1492 Bereed Shah usurped the throne in the very capital of his Sovereign, and established his dynasty as Kings of

Bidur (Ahmedabad); and in 1512 Kootub Shah was declared King of Golconda. All these princes had risen to power in the service of the Bahmani dynasty, and had been tempted by the increasing imbecility of the Government to set up thrones for themselves. Only three of them—the Kings of Beejapore, Ahmednuggur, and Golconda—rose to any great power, and these were again absorbed in the Mogul Empire by Shah Jehan and his son Aurungzebe, the latter becoming master of all India in 1686. This, however, was not accomplished without a protracted struggle, in the course of which a new power and a popular hero arose, equally opposed to the rule of Delhi and that of the independent princes of the Deccan. As the establishment of the Nizam's dynasty was the consequence of events which would be unintelligible without some reference to this new disturbing cause, the following brief sketch is added of the locality in which it originated, and the objects at which it aimed.

From all that can be ascertained, Deoghur, captured by the Mussulmans in 1294, and afterwards named Dowlatabad, was, as we have previously remarked, the capital of that part of the Deccan in which the Mahratta language was spoken. The boundary of this territory on the north was the range of mountains lying south of the Nerbudda. On the south its limit would be described by a line drawn from Goa, through Colapore and Bidur to Chanda on the Warda; on the east that river is its boundary; on the west, the sea. The Western Ghauts, as far as Goa, were therefore included within the limits of Maharashtra, and rising abruptly to the height of from 3,000 to 5,000 feet, they formed natural fortresses, which were further strengthened by the erection of towers commanding every approach from the sea-coast. The table land of this region, looking eastward, commences with a broken tract of wild ravines, for the most part covered with dense forests: but at a distance of fifteen or twenty miles from the ridge, it terminates in fruitful plains which stretch eastward across the Deccan, far beyond the limits at present in question. Whether this large tract of country ever acknowledged a single ruler previous to the first Mohammedan invasion, may be open to doubt; but it is certain that the Mahrattas who inhabited it attracted but little attention at that period. In the middle of the sixteenth century we first hear of them as being employed by the King of Beejapore in a military capacity, and he adopted the Mahratta language about that time, instead of the Persian, for his official documents. From this period their importance increased; and when men arose capable of leading them to victory and organizing them as a people, the smouldering embers of their warlike qualities burst into sudden flame, and they acted a part in the history of the Deccan second to none of its rulers.

In 1586 the emperor Akber began to interfere in the disputes which naturally occurred between the kingdoms of the Deccan, and sent an expedition into Ahmednuggur, which failed in its object. In 1598 the attempt was renewed, and a great battle was fought on the banks of the Godavery, which ended in favour of the Moguls. Ahmednuggur was captured, and a creature of the Emperor's invested with the royal dignity in 1600. Finally, in 1637 the dynasty was extinguished and the kingdom subdued by Shah Jehan.

In the interval between the capture of Admednuggur and the subjugation of the kingdom, an Abyssinian named Malik Amber was entrusted by the feeble king with the conduct of the government. This clever minister, like the King of Beejapore, recognized the soldier-like qualities of the Mahrattas, and not only enlisted them in his army, but allowed them to attain military rank. One of these born soldiers, Yadu Rao, was entrusted with the command of 10,000 men; another, Mahadajee Bhonsla, after a notorious career as a partisan leader, commanded 5,000 horse, both in the service of the King of Ahmednuggur. These, perhaps, are only leading examples of the class of men who, like the vigorous German chiefs in the declining period of the Roman Empire, swayed the destinies of nations, according as they threw the weight of their influence into the one scale or the other.

It was amidst the struggles of the Mohammedans for power in the Deccan, that the fortunes of this predatory race grew to maturity. Yadu, the greatest of their chiefs, had a daughter who was married to Shahji, the son of Mahadajee Bhonsla. This Shahji himself was a conspicuous actor in the struggle between the kingdom of Ahmednuggur and its enemies; but his second son, born of the daughter of Yadu, ranks with heroes. Sevaji was a youth of sixteen in 1643, when he surprised one of the hill forts belonging to Beejapore, and within five years afterwards he became master of a province. In 1655-8 he made terms with Aurungzebe after plundering the Mogul territories, and immediately turned round to renew his attacks on the Beejapore Mohammedans (1657). His daring career had already made him the idol of the Hindu population and the army, when, in 1677, the people were attacked in their religion by the ruler of Delhi. Every Hindoo in the Deccan now regarded him with increased affection, and the Mahratta power was established more firmly than ever. His grand design to restore the religion of his country, and establish the absolute supremacy of the Mahrattas as a people, was cut short by his death, which took place, after a short illness, on the 5th of April, 1680, in the 53rd year of his age.

We are now approaching the period when the founder of the Asuphea dynasty appeared on the scene, of whom it will be convenient to trace a distinct, though necessarily brief, record.

CHAPTER II.

THE FIRST NIZAM.

Disorganized Condition of the Mahratta Power under the Son and Successor of Sevaji—Death of Aurungzebe and Contention for the Rule of Delhi—Ghazeer-oo-deen, the Father of the First Nizam—Prudence of Asof Jah in the Renewed Contest for Empire on the Death of Bahadoor Shah—Appointed Viceroy of the Deccan by Farokshir—Conciliation of the Mahrattas—is recalled to Delhi and appointed Vizier—Resigns office and retires to his Government at Hyderabad—the Independence of the Mahratta power secured by Balaji, the Founder of the Peishwa Dynasty—Asof Jah, virtually Independent, founds the Asuphea Dynasty—Hostilities with the Mahrattas—Invasion of India by Nadir Shah—Activity of Asof Jah in his own Government—Encroachments of the French on British Rights at Madras—Appeal to Asof Jah—He orders an Expedition against the French—His advanced Age and Death.

When Aurungzebe, in 1683, commenced his second invasion of the Deccan, Sevaji's son, Sambaji, occupied his father's seat, without possessing one of his virtues, except courage. Under his mismanagement the country became the prey of the disorganized Mahratta troops, who were unable indeed to prevent the conquest of Beejapore and Golconda, but were yet sufficiently daring and numerous to harass the imperial troops, and often to lay the country waste in their line of march. Sambaji himself was taken prisoner and put to a cruel death, but this event only excited the Mahrattas to greater ferocity in the guerilla warfare which ensued. The Mogul troops were so wasted by this harassing warfare, that Aurungzebe, in 1706, had no alternative but a disorderly retreat to Ahmednuggur, in the course of which the Emperor himself narrowly escaped falling into the hands of the enemy. He reached the city, however, from which years before he had marched at the head of a conquering army, and expired there in the 89th year of his age, at the commencement of the following year.

On the death of Aurungzebe his sons contended for the empire, and a bloody battle was fought near Agra, at which one of the brothers was killed.

Bahadoor Shah then became Emperor, and in 1716 he compounded for peace in the Deccan by admitting the claim of the Mahratta chief Saho to a fourth of the tribute levied through the whole of that territory. A viceroy was then appointed, and the peace of the empire was no more troubled by the Deccan rulers during the reign of Bahadoor, which was terminated by his death in 1712.

There was one man of note, a favourite officer of Aurungzebe's, who had kept himself aloof from all connection with either of the Emperor's sons in their contention for the empire. Ghazeer-oo-deen, the person alluded to, was Soobadar of Berar and Ellichpore, at the time of Aurungzebe's death, and had one son, afterwards known by his title of Asof Jah, whose future greatness was predicted by the Emperor. Asof Jah, unlike his father, tendered his allegiance to one of the competitors for the throne of Aurungzebe, Prince Azim, who conferred upon him the title of Soobadar of Boorhaunpore, and prevailed upon him to accompany him a few marches on his ill-fated expedition to Hindostan. The conduct of the Prince, at an early period of his march, appears to have alienated from him some of his principal followers; among others, Asof Jah quitted the army in open daylight at the head of his troops, and retraced his steps to Aurungabad. Here he remained an inactive spectator of events during the ensuing struggle, and when the result was known he was invited to court by Bahadoor Shah, and appointed Soobadar of Oude and Foujdar of Lucknow.

The prudence of Asof Jah was further shown by his conduct during this reign. Disgusted with the frivolity and incapacity of the Emperor, and with the manners of the Court, he took an early opportunity of relinquishing all his appointments, and retiring into private life.

In 1712 Bahadoor Shah died, and was succeeded by his eldest son Jehandar Shah, who began his career by putting to death all the princes of the blood within his reach. His brother Azim Shah, however, had left a son, Farokshir, who was living securely in Bengal, and who now claimed the friendship of his father's old adherents, and assembled an army at Allahabad, at the head of which he claimed the throne of his ancestors. At this juncture Asof Jah was persuaded by the new Emperor Jehandar Shah, and his crafty vizier Zulfikar Khan, to leave his retirement and take a command in the imperial army. But Jehandar Shah was betrayed to the Pretender's party by Zulfikar, and put to death—the treacherous vizier suffering the same fate—in the beginning of 1713.

Farokshir then ascended the throne of Delhi, and Asof Jah, who had again cleverly espoused the winning side, was among the number to benefit by his elevation. He was on this occasion gratified with the title of Nizam-ool-moolk, and appointed Viceroy of the Imperial dominions in the Deccan.

As already stated, the arrangement between Saho the Mahratta chief and the Emperor Bahadoor Shah, effected by the viceroy Daud Khan, had preserved the peace between them till the death of Bahadoor Shah in 1712. But the Mahrattas in this interval had

2

quarrelled among themselves, and when Asof Jah entered upon his viceroyalty, he found the country in a state of the greatest disorganization; the removal of Daud Khan had only increased the confusion, by dissolving the agreement for peace which had been made by him personally, in the interest of the Emperor; and the Mahrattas had now recommenced their attacks upon the Mogul territory.

The task of conciliation under these circumstances was difficult, but well suited to the capacity of Asof Jah, who seems to have acted on the well-known principle of "divide and conquer." By taking a side in their quarrels he encouraged dissension, and induced some of the Mahrattas to declare themselves in favour of the Imperial cause. At the close of the first year of his residence, he had been so far successful in the restoration of authority, that he had a project afoot for an expedition into the Carnatic, when he was suddenly recalled to Delhi. His successor in the viceroyalty was Houssein Ally Khan, a brother of the vizier, whom it was found convenient to remove for a time from court.

Houssein Khan not succeeding in the pacification of the country, was glad to make terms of peace with the predatory power of Saho, especially as he had formed the design of marching on Delhi in pursuance of a quarrel too intricate in its nature to be explained here. Accordingly, in 1718, when the Emperor's conduct had alienated his most powerful nobles, Houssein appeared before Delhi with a following of 10,000 Mahratta troops. The King was murdered, and furious contests broke out on every hand between the Hindoos and Mohammedans, in the midst of which Mohammed Shah was raised to the throne.

Asof Jah had been disappointed of the viziership at the time when he was recalled to Delhi by the late king, and he was now disappointed by the successful rebels in what we may call his just expectation of being restored to the viceroyalty of the Deccan. He was offered in succession the government of Malwa and other provinces, and seeing that the intention was to set him aside, he in 1720 set up the standard of revolt, and crossed the Nerbudda to rally his friends. The new Emperor himself took the field with Houssein Ally, and marched to the Deccan, where in the meantime a battle had been fought and lost by the Imperialists. On the march, Houssein Ally was assassinated by an emissary of conspirators at Delhi, who set up a rival Emperor, and made it necessary for Mohammed Shah to fight his way back to the capital. The latter succeeded in re-establishing his authority, and then offered the post of vizier to Asof Jah, who prudently delayed his return to court until he had established his authority firmly in the Deccan.

It was in 1722 that Asof Jah returned to Delhi with the hope of administering the government; but the atmosphere of the corrupt court of Mohammed Shah was far from being congenial to the disposition of a man whose character had been formed under the vigorous administration of Aurungzebe. After events which would occupy considerable space in a detailed history, he resigned the office of vizier, having first placed himself at a safe distance from the capital, and forthwith marched for the Deccan. Although this act was equivalent to a declaration of independence, it is amusing to discover what pains were taken on both sides to save appearances. The Emperor, not choosing to march in person against his late vizier, ordered the local governor of Hyderabad to oppose his assumption of power; but Asof Jah defeated and slew his antagonist, and, affecting not to recognize the Emperor's hand in the affair, sent his head to Delhi. Thus by temporizing or fighting, as circumstances demanded, he found himself, in 1724, in secure possession of the government of the Deccan at Hyderabad.

While these events were in progress, the Mahrattas had also found a master worthy of continuing the work commenced by Sevaji. The career of Balaji may be compared in some respects to that of Lord Clive. He began life as an accountant, in a village of the Concan—the narrow strip of country described in the previous chapter as forming the western boundary of Maharashtra, between the mountains and the sea. In this humble position his opportunities for intercourse with the mauraudins chiefs of the "castled crags" enabled him to display unusual capacity, and having entered the service of one of the Yadu family, he became known to the Raja, and was with the Mahratta troops which accompanied Houssein Ally to the capital before the deposition and murder of Bahadoor Shah. In course of time he succeeded in reorganizing the wild Mahratta power, and became the founder of the dynasty of Peishwas, who, until the commencement of the present century, ruled a large portion of the territory now comprised within the Bombay presidency of the British Empire. Confronted with this successful leader, Asof Jah, instead of competing with him for the sovereignty of the Deccan—in which case the two chiefs could only have torn each other in pieces, to the delight of the great Mogul at Delhi—wisely compromised his claims, and following the example of the Mahratta chief, devoted himself to securing the establishment of his own dynasty.

About two years after these events, Balaji died and was succeeded as Peishwa by his son Baji Rao, a man abler than himself, who was not slow to perceive the declining condition of the Mogul power. Taking advantage of the restless ambition of this chief, Asof

Jah played off the rapidly increasing Mahratta power against his enemies at Delhi; but also involved himself in hostilities with Baji, who so harassed his territory that he was fain to make peace. Thus for thirteen years, or from 1724 to 1737, the first Nizam's time appears to have been fully occupied in striking the balance of chances and events in the Deccan, with a view to the preservation of his independence and the extension of his authority. Nominally, however, he was still the Viceroy of the Emperor; and when the latter was threatened in his very capital by Baji Rao, at the head of an enormous force, it would have been the extremest folly had he allowed the rule of Delhi to pass under the Mahratta chief. When, therefore, in 1737, he was summoned by several letters of entreaty to aid the Emperor, he hastened to Delhi, leaving his second son, Nazir Jung, as lieutenant in the Deccan. The Peishwa for the moment beat a retreat, and Asof Jah was invested with full power to use every resource of the state. This, however, availed him little. When he took the field, Baji Rao marched against him at the head of an army said to be 80,000 strong, and Asof Jah, not daring to risk an engagement, was so thoroughly harassed by the Mahratta mode of warfare, that he was compelled to conclude a peace that could only be regarded as disgraceful to the Mogul power.

At this juncture, India was invaded by the Persians under Nadir Shah, an event of such magnitude that it at once reduced these intestine conflicts to a condition of secondary importance. Passing over this eventful period to 1741, we find that Asof Jah was recalled in that year from Delhi, by the disorders into which his government had fallen, under the administration of his son, Nazir Jung, who even rebelled against his authority. From this period, Asof Jah's life was occupied in visits to the more distant parts of his government. In 1742, he resided for a considerable period at Hyderabad, and from thence proceeded to Arcot and Trichinopoly, where his presence was necessary to calm the dissensions existing among his subordinate officers in that quarter. These events bring us to the first appearance of the French and English in connection with the Government whose history I have undertaken to relate.

The managers of the English factories on the coast had for some time past carried on intrigues with the subordinate officers of the Viceroy's government, in furtherance of their views against the French. It does not appear, however, that they had ever succeeded in gaining direct access to the Soobadar till 1747, when Asof Jah returned to Aurungabad, leaving Enuwar-ood-deen his deputy in the Carnatic. Madras had then fallen into the hands of the French, whose successes threatened the total extinction of British interests on the coast, their ally Enuwar-ood-deen turning a deaf ear to their entreaties for assistance.

In this emergency Commodore Griffin, commanding our naval forces on the station, and the Governor of Fort St. David, despatched two letters, dated March the 7th, 1747, to Asof Jah himself. They entreated him in the name of their Sovereign to call the Nawab to an account for his past transactions, and to interpose his power to restore, as nearly as possible in its original state, what had been so unjustly taken from them.

The application was favourably received by Asof Jah. Peremptory orders were issued to Enuwar-ood-deen to chastise the French, to recover his Majesty's sea-port town, and restore the English to their rights. To enforce the execution of these orders a body of horse, under the personal command of one of his sons, was detached by Enuwar-ood-deen to retake Madras, though, failing in their attempt, owing to the intrepidity of the French garrison, they were obliged to return precipitately to Arcot.

These events were taking place in the Carnatic, when Asof Jah expired in his camp near Boorhaunpore, to which place he was proceeding from Aurungabad in the summer of 1748. He had reached the advanced age of seventy-seven years, and was actively engaged in affairs of state till almost the last hour of his eventful life.

His remains were conveyed to Aurungabad and interred in the neighbourhood of that city. In the next chapter it will be seen that his death led to contentions about the succession, in which the French and English took an active part, with results which have been of the highest importance to ourselves, as well as to the rulers of the Deccan and other parts of India.

CHAPTER III.

ASOF JAH'S IMMEDIATE SUCCESSORS.

Sons and Grandsons of the Nizam—Nazir Jung usurps the Soubadaree of the Deccan—He is opposed by Mozuffur Jung, who forms an Alliance with the French—Death of both the Competitors—Salabat Jung, with the aid of the French Forces, assumes the Viceroyalty—Influence of M. Bussy—Ghazeer-oo-deen forms an Alliance with the Mahrattas, and takes the field against Salabat—Sudden Death of Ghazeer-oo-deen—Struggle between the French and English at Pondicherry—Masulipatam and the surrounding Territory ceded to the English by Salabat—Usurpation of Nizam Ally—Ghazeer-oo-deen the younger.

The descendants of Asof Jah, of whom it will be necessary to make some mention in this chapter, were Ghazeer-oo-deen, his eldest son, who, at the time of Asof Jah's death, seems to have been at Delhi; Nazir Jung, his second son, who was on the spot when his father died, and had, therefore, the best opportunity to usurp the throne; Salabat Jung, the third son, who became a competitor for the family inheritance; Nizam Ally, the youngest, in whom the dynasty was finally established; and lastly,

Mozuffer Jung, a grandson of Asof Jah's favourite daughter.

On the death of Asof Jah, Nazir Jung lost no time in seizing on his father's treasures, and being supported by the army, he proclaimed himself Soobadar of the Deccan; at the same time causing it to be believed that Ghazeer-oo-deen, his elder brother, had renounced his right. His pretensions were immediately opposed by Moozuffur Jung, who then held the Soobadaree of Beejapore, and who pretended that a testamentary arrangement had been made in his favour by Asof Jah, and in support of his claims formed a coalition with Chunda Sahib and the French Government of Pondicherry.

To remove this competitor Nazir Jung marched at once to the Carnatic, where he was joined by Mohammed Ally and a small body of English troops under Major Lawrence. Thus each force had the advantage of an alliance with one of the two great Powers who were destined to contend for supremacy in the East.

On the near approach of the two armies, and on the eve of a battle which was to decide the fate of the competitors for the Soobadaree of the Deccan, Mozuffur Jung was suddenly deserted by his French allies, owing to dissensions between the commander and his officers. Mozuffur Jung then became the prisoner of his rival, but the latter in his turn lost the support of the English, and was killed in a conflict with the French. Mozuffur Jung then assumed the viceroyalty, and was soon after killed in a quarrel with some of the native chiefs.

The first two competitors being thus disposed of, Salabat Jung, Asof Jung's third son, assumed the vacant dignity, and was supported by the French, whose influence was wielded by M. Bussy. This distinguished officer held a high command in Salabat's army, and so improved his position at Hyderabad that he ruled in a great measure the councils of the Soobabar, who, without his aid, would hardly have been able to maintain himself in power amidst the intrigues continually set on foot by the members of his family. Salabat's military force was greatly strengthened by the addition of a large body of native troops under French officers, for whose equipment and payment he assigned over to M. Bussy several districts in the Northern Circars.

As already stated, the eldest son of the Nizam, Ghazeer-oo-deen, had remained at Delhi during the contention between the first two competitors; but having formed an alliance with the Mahrattas, he now took the field in support of his claims, and Balaji was actually marching against the forces of Salabat, when he was recalled to Sattara by the insurrection of Tara Bai, aided by an invasion from the Nizam's territory under M. Bussy. The latter was already within a few miles of Poonah, when the discontent of his troops, owing to their arrears of pay and other causes, involved them in such disorder that Salabat, in the beginning of 1752, was glad to conclude an armistice, and retire into his own territory. A little subsequently the contest was renewed, Ghazeer-oo-deen and Balaji joined their forces at Aurungabad, and it is very doubtful if Salabat would have been able to make a successful resistance. At this juncture, however, Ghazeer-oo-deen suddenly died; it has been supposed that he was poisoned.

Thus ended the second contest between the descendants of Asof Jah for the family inheritance; but the struggle between the French and English, allies of these princes, was not to be so soon terminated. In a few years the former were so hard pressed, that Salabat Jung could no longer depend on their support, and began to draw towards an alliance with the English, with whom he was at war. At the very time when the French were compelled to withdraw their support, it being as much as they could do to defend their own possessions, Salabat had too much reason to fear the intrigues of his younger brother, Nizam Ally, while he was absent from the capital. He hastened, therefore, to bring the war to a close by concluding a treaty with the commander of the English force, by which he ceded to the Company the fort of Masulipatam, with a considerable tract of country round it; and bound himself for the future not to admit of any French settlement within his dominions.

In 1761 the fears of Salabat were fully justified. His younger brother, Nizam Ally, having succeeded in engrossing the power of the state, at length openly deposed him and usurped the government. Nizam Ally, in 1765, came into collision with the British power by a ferocious invasion of the Carnatic. The particulars of this event, and its important results, will be related in the following chapters, as they belong to a reign which extended into the present century, and which included, in its memorable events, the war with Tippoo Sultan, and the firm establishment of English power in the Deccan.

It will be proper to add in this place, that when Ghazeer-oo-deen marched against Salabat, he left a son at Delhi, who was afterwards honoured with his father's title and the office of commander-in-chief. This Ghazeer-oo-deen the younger turned his arms against the Emperor, and was one of the chief agents in the overthrow of the Mogul dynasty.

CHAPTER IV.

NIZAM ALLY AND THE NORTHERN CIRCARS.

The French and English in the Carnatic—The Northern Circars seized by Clive—The Nizam invades the Carnatic—Peace Negotiated by the Government of Madras—Treaty of 1766—Bazalut Jung and the Circar of Guntoor—Alliance of the Nizam with Hyder Naik—Successes of the British Troops—Renewal of the Nizam's Alliance—Treaty of Madras, 1768—Arrangement of the Madras Government with Bazalut Jung—Death of Bazalut Jung, and Retention of the Guntoor Circar by the Nizam—Mr. Johnson succeeds Mr. Grant as Resident—Instructions to press the Durbar for a Restitution of the Circar—Proposals made by the Nizam for the Surrender of the Circars and of the Carnatic—Censure and Recall of Mr. Johnson—Captain Kennaway deputed to Press the British Claims—Military Preparations of the Governor-General—Final Surrender of the Circars to the Company—Terms of the Settlement.

The theatre of war between the French and English in India, first as auxiliaries of the native princes, and afterwards as principals, may be described as the coast country known by the general name of the Carnatic and the Northern Circars. At the time when Nazir Jung and Mozuffur Jung were contending for the Sobadaree of the Deccan, the Nawab of the Carnatic was also opposed by a rival claimant, who made common cause with Mozuffur Jung. Both pretenders were supported by the French Governor of Pondicherry, and a great battle was fought, in which the Nawab of the Carnatic was killed. His son, Mohammed Ally, then threw himself upon the protection of the English.

In the ensuing warlike operations Colonel Clive took part with a force from Bengal, and in 1759 he seized the Northern Circars, which had been held by the French during the preceding six years. The Company's possession of this territory was confirmed in 1765 by the King of Delhi, when an expedition under General Cailliaud took possession of the country.

In the beginning of the same year, Nizam Ally Khan, now firmly established in the Deccan, invaded the Carnatic at the head of a large force, laying waste the country with unparalleled ferocity; but was compelled to fall back upon his own territory before a British division, commanded by Colonel Campbell. The Carnatic and the Northern Circars, though under the immediate government of Nawabs,* were subordinate in the rule of the Empire to the Viceroy of the Deccan, and Nizam Ally, though checked for the

* These Nawabs received their appointments from the Viceroy of the Deccan.

moment, showed no disposition to relinquish his hold upon these possessions without a struggle. He was making preparations for a renewed attack on the Carnatic, when the Presidency of Fort St. George, desirous of gaining the goodwill of a prince so powerful, deputed General Cailliaud to Hyderabad, with full power to negotiate for peace. On the 12th November, 1766, a treaty was accordingly concluded, by which the company agreed to pay an annual tribute of five lacs of rupees for the Circars of Rajahmundry, Ellore, and Mustaphanuggur, and for those of Chicacole and Mortizzanuggur (commonly called Guntoor), two lacs each, as soon as these territories were definitely placed in their hands. The last-mentioned district having been assigned by the Nizam to his brother, Bazalut Jung (whom I have not hitherto had occasion to mention among the sons of Asof Jah), as a personal Jaghire, it was agreed that it should be held by that prince during his lifetime, or as long as the Nizam should be satisfied with his conduct; and on his death the Company were to be placed in full possession of the district, as of the other circars. It was further stipulated by the treaty that the two powers should mutually assist each other with troops when required to do so.

At this period, Hyder Naik, father of the celebrated Tippoo Sultan, and sovereign of Mysore, was rising to distinction in his career of conquest, and in virtue of the treaty recently concluded, a British force of two battalions joined the army of Nizam Ally, and was employed by him to reduce the fort of Bangalore, and to collect the tribute due to the Nizam by the refractory poligars (petty chiefs) of the Carnatic. But Hyder Naik had the address to detach Nizam Ally from the British connection for a time, and in August, 1767, the British troops were recalled to the defence of their own territories, which were attacked by the new allies in pursuance of their project for the total expulsion of the British from the Deccan. Our previous good understanding with the Nizam, however, was soon restored by the successes of the British troops, which convinced the Nizam of the necessity of separating from Hyder Naik, and suing for peace. A new treaty was accordingly concluded at Madras on the 23rd of February, 1768.

In virtue of this treaty the Nizam, after revoking whatever distinctions had been conferred on Hyder Naik, either by himself or any of his family, bound himself to aid the Company to gain possession of the Carnatic Balaghaut—the higher lands of the Carnatic which had been conquered by Hyder Naik. The Company on their part agreed to pay the Nizam an annual tribute of seven lacs of rupees; and by another article the Northern Circars were confirmed in their possession, on condition of paying to the Nizam two lacs of rupees annually for a period of six years, commencing from the 1st of January, 1768. For several years subsequent to the conclusion of this treaty no events of importance occurred at Hyderabad, nor do any changes of moment appear to have taken place in our political relations with that court.

In 1779 Bazalut Jung, alarmed at the hostile designs of Hyder Naik, and anxious to secure the assistance of the English, in the event of his being attacked by that chief, agreed to rent the district of Guntoor to the Company, who undertook to maintain a force in the country sufficient for its defence. The presidency of Fort St. George then sent Mr. Holland to Hyderabad with instructions to communicate the terms of this agreement to the Nizam. Mr. Holland arrived at the Nizam's Court in April, 1779, and having explained his mission, was told by the Nizam that, in treating with his brother, who was his subject, the English had violated the treaty of 1768. To remove this misconception of their intentions, a letter was addressed to the Prince by the Supreme Government, in which they assured him of their friendly disposition, and expressed their regret that the unauthorized conduct of the Madras Government should have given him any cause to doubt their sincerity. An order was at the same time despatched to Madras directing the immediate restitution of the Guntoor Circar to the Nizam's officers, and this appears to have been carried into effect at the end of the year 1780.

In November, 1782, Bazalut Jung died, and the Circar, which on that event ought to have lapsed to the Company, was taken possession of by the Nizam's officers. Against this infraction of the treaty the then resident, Mr. Grant, did not consider himself warranted by his instructions to offer any remonstrance; but that gentleman resigning in 1784, a Mr. Johnson was despatched to Hyderabad with instructions to press the Durbar for the restitution of the Circar, and to arrange for the settlement of the arrears of Peshcush, due by the Company.

During the negotiations which ensued the Nizam proposed to Mr. Johnson that the Company should make over to him their right to the Circar, acquired by the treaty of 1768, on condition of receiving from him an acquittal in full for the arrears of tribute, and a present in money of one crore of rupees. This proposal, together with a subsequent one for the surrender of the Carnatic to the Nizam, was strongly recommended by the Resident to the favourable notice of the Supreme Government, and referred by them to the Court of Directors. The latter severely censured Mr. Johnson for listening to these overtures, and having deprived him of his office as Resident, Mr. Johnson left Hyderabad in 1785.

The negotiation concerning the Circars was now suspended for some time, and the relations between the two Governments remained in a very unsettled state. In 1788 Lord Cornwallis deputed Captain Kennaway to Hyderabad, with instructions to the same effect as had been previously given to Mr. Johnson. The demand, however, was now enforced by military preparations on the part of the Governor-General, and as the Nizam could offer no resistance, the Guntoor Circar was finally made over to the Company, in accordance with the original treaty, in September, 1788. The financial settlement was as follows :—

	Rs.	a.
Amount of the Nizam's claims on the Company for Peshcush for the Nizam's Circars	67,49,333	0
Amount of the Company's claims on the Nizam for the rent of the Guntoor Circar from the time of Bazalut Jung's death, Sept. 25, 1782, until the Circar was delivered over to the Company, Sept., 1788	58,32,667	5
Due to the Nizam	Rs. 9,16,665	11

Thus ended this troublesome matter, and it is but just to remark that Captain Kennaway's exertions were fully acknowledged both by the Governor General and the Court of Directors. The settlement was followed by a letter addressed to the Nizam by the Governor General, in which his lordship explained the treaty of 1768, and more especially the sense in which the sixth article was to be understood, viz., that the force stipulated for was not to be employed against any power in alliance with the Company. By a subsequent resolution of the House of Commons, this letter acquired the force of a treaty executed in due form.

CHAPTER V.

WAR WITH TIPPOO SULTAN.

Tippoo Sultan invades Travancore—Treaty offensive and defensive with the Nizam—Inefficiency of the Company's Troops—Procrastination of the Nizam—Mismanagement at Pangul—Advantage obtained by Tippoo—Despatch of the Nizam's Cavalry under Rajah Tegewunt—Encampment of the Rajah and delay of Operations—Object of the Nizam in preferring the Company's Alliance—Delicacy of Captain Kennaway's Mission—His anxiety for the advance of the British Troops—Capture of Bangalore by Lord Cornwallis—Junction of the Nizam's Troops, and Advance upon Seringapatam—Battle, and Defeat of Tippoo Sultan—Behaviour of the Nizam's Cavalry—Lord Cornwallis retires towards Bangalore, and is joined by the Mahratta Troops—Overtures of Peace from Tippoo—Meer Allum and Hurry Punt Tantia deputed to confer with Lord Cornwallis—Continuation of the War, and arrival of Reinforcements from the Nizam under Secunder Jah—Investment of Seringapatam—Tippoo Sultan sues for Peace—Terms of Pacification—Guarantee Treaty proposed by the Confederates—Affairs of Kurnool intervene.

IN 1789, Tippoo Sultan marched to invade Travancore, in defiance of the sacred engagements into which he had entered by the peace of Mangalore five years previously; and though he was repulsed in his attack on the military lines of the Rajah, the event was regarded as a declaration of war against the British power. A treaty of offensive and defensive alliance was then concluded with the Nizam (July, 1790) in which it was provided that a strong detachment of the Hyderabad army was to co-operate with the Company's troops against Tippoo. The Company were to send two battalions of infantry, with the usual number of guns, to form a part of the Nizam's army.

On this auxiliary force arriving within his highness's territory, it was inspected by Captain Kennaway, who reported that it was deficient of all the requirements necessary for a campaign. Lord Cornwallis himself was annoyed that troops so little fitted for service should have been sent to join the Nizam's army, thereby, exclusive of all other considerations, reflecting discredit upon our military establishments. He expressed his warm approval of Captain Kennaway's appeal to the Madras authorities, requiring them to take proper means to render the detachment efficient; and, considering it unreasonable to demand from the Nizam the full sum which he had stipulated to pay, for the aid of two complete and efficient battalions, he instructed Captain Kennaway to reduce the charge to a sum that should be fairly proportionate to the efficiency and number of the detachment.

The Nizam, on his part, left Hyderabad at the head of a large force of cavalry, artillery, and infantry, the Resident (Captain Kennaway,) accompanying him. After halting at several places, the Nizam encamped with his army at Pangul. In the meantime, Tippoo Sultan had obtained a slight advantage over a small detachment of British troops under the command of Lieutenant-Colonel Floyd.

Though worsted in the action, our men exhibited such a determined front to the preponderating force of the enemy, that Tippoo at once discovered the bull-dog courage of the troops against whom he was in arms. Still there was reason to fear that this victory, so to call it, might be related to the Nizam with the grossest exaggerations. To guard against the effect of any such report, Lord Cornwallis instructed the Resident to inform his highness in a guarded manner of the advantages gained by Tippoo, and to point out, that if his troops had marched sooner into Tippoo Sultan's territories, the enemy would not have dared to move far from his capital, and therefore the disadvantage we had sustained was really attributable to the slowness of the Nizam's movements. Lord Cornwallis, however, still trusted that his highness would avail himself of the favourable season that was approaching, to make amends for the slowness of his movements hitherto; and at the same time expressed his conviction that Captain Kennaway had neglected no argument that might stimulate the Nizam to exertion.

Supported by this letter, the Resident again urged the Nizam to a more hearty co-operation with the British troops in accordance with the treaty. The result was, that his highness despatched from his camp at Pangul, a large force of cavalry under an officer of rank, named Rajah Tegewunt, with orders to make a demonstration in Tippoo's country, and eventually to form a junction with the Company's troops.

Time passed on, and the Rajah, who had gone into camp, showed no disposition to move forward in accordance with the Nizam's orders. Lord Cornwallis, who commanded in person the army of the south, was exceedingly indignant at the conduct of the Rajah, who resorted to every species of subterfuge to excuse his remaining in camp. In a letter to Captain Kennaway, designed as a remonstrance to the Nizam, the Governor-General expressed his conviction, either that Tegewunt was unfit for command or that he was in the pay of Tippoo. There is reason to believe, from the Rajah's subsequent conduct, that he was deficient in the vigour, ability, and qualities of resource necessary for the important command with which he was entrusted; and that he on all occasions, when opposed to the enemy in co-operation with Lord Cornwallis's army, magnified as much as possible imaginary difficulties, in his report of occurrences to his own government, in order to enhance the merit of his services.

The ultimate object of the Nizam in joining the Company, it is supposed, was to relieve himself from the restraint under which he was held by the Mahratta power. This the Mahrattas clearly perceived, and our own government was not blind to the fact; hence the repeated injunctions conveyed to Captain Kennaway that in conducting his negotiations with the Nizam, he was "to take care to prevent the jealousy of the Mahrattas being aroused." I mention this, on account of occurrences which may hereafter demand our notice, and also to point out that Captain Kennaway's mission at the court of his highness, at the commencement of the war with Tippoo Sultan, was one requiring considerable tact, as, indeed, was fully acknowledged by the head of the Indian government. In no instance was the prudence and foresight of our Resident more clearly demonstrated than in his anxiety for the speedy march of the Company's troops from Trichinopoly, in order to divert Tippoo's attention from the advance of the Nizam. Had this not been done, there could be no doubt, that the Nizam's troops unsupported would have been met by the whole strength of Tippoo's army, and the confederates would have run the risk of being attacked—and if attacked they would most likely have been beaten — in detail.

Lord Cornwallis, by his skilful and vigorous movements, was soon able to invest Bangalore, which was taken by storm after a fortnight's siege, on the 21st of March, 1791. He then once more requested Rajah Tegewunt to move forward, but the latter adhered to his determination, and refused to march until Lord Cornwallis had advanced to Seringapatam, and thus placed Bangalore between the British army and the Nizam's auxiliaries. At length Rajah Tegewunt, after a deal of pressure, formed the much desired junction, and Lord Cornwallis, with the combined forces, advanced against the citadel of Mysore.

The Rajah's cavalry disappointed the expectations of Lord Cornwallis on the march. Instead of relieving the Company's troops from many of the harassing duties of a campaign, by marching on the flanks of the army and affording timely notice of the approach of the enemy, this unwieldy mass, accompanied by an innumerable crowd of camp followers, and beasts of burden, crowded upon the column in its line of march, and exposed it to great danger. So similar in appearance were the Nizam's cavalry to those of the enemy, that some few of the latter were able to mix with our troops, and watching for a favourable opportunity, cut off stragglers. On arriving near Seringapatam an attack was made by the forces of Tippoo in which the British were victorious, and, contrary to what had been expected from their antecedents, the Nizam's cavalry conducted themselves so much to the satisfaction of Lord Cornwallis that he congratulated the rajah on their share in the victory over the common enemy. This spurt of vigour, however, was but an expiring effort. Immediately after the action, Rajah Tegewunt represented the condition of his army, on account of their recent exertions, and their exposure to cold winds, to be so critical, that Lord Cornwallis consented to their departure for a more congenial clime. He could the more easily dispense with their services, as he had resolved to destroy his battering train, and march back in the direction of Bangalore, satisfied with having reconnoitered the fortress of Tippoo. A Mahratta force was also marching to join him, and Lord Cornwallis himself was anxious to rest and recruit his troops, after the fatigues of their recent campaign.

At this juncture Tippoo made overtures for peace to Lord Cornwallis, and requested permission to send a vakeel with a view to the settlement of terms. Lord Cornwallis, loyal to the general interests of the confederacy, declined to treat with him without the concurrence of his allies, and at the same time expressed his indignation at the "wanton and savage barbarities" which the Sultan had inflicted on the inoffensive ryots of the Carnatic.[1] He also addressed a letter to the Nizam on this subject, in which he stated explicitly his views of the proposals made by Tippoo Sultan, and declared his determination to do nothing that would tend to separate the interests of the English Company from those of the allied princes.[2] In reply to this communication, Meer Allum, great grandfather of the present minister, Salar Jung Bahadoor, was deputed by his highness the Nizam to negotiate the matters in question, and arrived in Lord Cornwallis's camp, about the middle of August, 1791. In reply to the letter of which he was the bearer, Lord Cornwallis addressed a rejoinder to the Nizam, expressing the extreme pleasure he felt in the appointment, and his conviction of the perfect unanimity with which their joint counsels would be animated.[3] About the same time Hurry Punt Tantia arrived from the Peishwa with powers similar to those conferred on Meer Allum by the Nizam.

But Tippoo Sultan was not yet reduced to the necessity of purchasing peace on terms that would prove satisfactory to the allies, and in view of the continuation of hostilities, his highness the Nizam had

---

[1] Appendix A. [2] Appendix B. [3] Appendix C.

signified his determination to despatch his second son, the Prince Secunder Jah, and his minister, Azim-ool-oomrah, with reinforcements to join Lord Cornwallis. His lordship, in reply, courteously acknowledged the confidence which the Nizam thus showed in the English alliance, but at the same time expressed his dissatisfaction with the delay which his highness had stated to be necessary on account of the reinforcements not being able to join the prince until after the Dewahe festival, when also large quantities of grain could be collected and forwarded to the seat of war. His lordship further pointed out to Sir John Kennaway,[1] the impolicy of employing the force en route, in the reduction of the fortress of Gooruncoonda, as the garrison of that fortress consisted only of 700 men, who could not be expected to hold out after the arrival of the siege guns, which had been despatched from Bangalore; whereas, if the forces of the prince were hindered from prosecuting their march by so inconsiderable a garrison, the circumstance would probably give rise to reports, far from favourable to the efficiency of the Nizam's army. The advantage of waiting until grain could be collected was also questioned, as since the fall of Nundydroog a large tract of country had

[1] Captain Kennaway, Resident at the court of the Nizam, had received letters patent constituting him a baronet of the United Kingdom.

been thrown open, and some 50,000 bullocks were employed by the Brinjarries of the country in supplying the army. Finally his lordship decided that it would be advisable for Sir J. Kennaway to accompany the prince, while Lieutenant Stewart, the Assistant at the court of the Nizam, remained near his highness.

In a subsequent communication addressed to Lieutenant Stewart, the Governor General made it almost a personal request that neither Rajah Tegewunt or Assad Ally Khan, both of whom were known to have been corrupted with Tippoo's money at the commencement of the campaign, should join the army again. At the same time, his lordship stated that in the event of his highness finding it necessary to re-employ those officers, that he would receive them in a manner suitable to their rank as officers serving a prince of the confederacy.

On the fall of the lower fort of Goorumcoondah the Nizam's son and minister, accompanied by the Resident, commenced their march to join the main army under Lord Cornwallis; while Lieutenant Stewart pressed the Nizam to send forward the necessary supplies. The prince had no sooner departed from Goorumcoondah, than a party of the enemy's horse made a dash at that fortress, and cut up many of the troops to whom had been entrusted the task of reducing the upper fort. This unfortunate mishap caused the prince to make a retrograde march in order to watch the movements of the enemy; and, as a necessary consequence, his junction with Lord Cornwallis was delayed. When at length effected, his lordship put the entire force in motion, and Tippoo's capital was invested.

Thus closely pressed, and some advantages having been gained by the allied army, Tippoo negotiated for a cessation of hostilities, and on the 9th of February 1792, signed the articles of pacification, by which he agreed to give up one half of his territories, or an equivalent in money, to be divided between the allies, and to deliver up two of his sons as hostages for the fulfilment of the treaty. This event makes one of the most interesting episodes in all the histories of the period, but a more detailed notice of it would be foreign to the purpose of this narrative, neither is it necessary to give a particular account of the distribution of territory made at the time.

After the articles of peace had been arranged with Tippoo, the minister of the Nizam, and Hurry Punt, the representative of the Peishwa, expressed an anxious desire to arrange terms with Lord Cornwallis for a future alliance, in case the Sultan of Mysore should recommence hostilities. Lord Cornwallis, therefore, addressed a letter to Sir J. Kennaway, in which he expressed his views generally on the subject, and laid down the principles which should guide them in framing a treaty of guarantee.[1] Azim-ool-oomrah thought he might now bring the government round to his own views regarding the Kurnool succession (of which we shall speak more particularly in the next chapter), and in the course of his conversation with the Resident on the proposed treaty, he stated that the Nizam would not accede to the guarantee, unless his claims against Kurnool were supported by the government. On this being reported to the Governor General, the minister was reminded that the proposition for a guarantee treaty had not originated with the English government, but having been proposed to Lord Cornwallis in camp, by the two ministers, had been simply postponed at his request. His lordship, therefore, anxious for the continuance of the good understanding between the confederates, had sketched the draft of a treaty, such as he considered would be satisfactory to all parties; and he believed that in so doing he was complying with the wishes of the allies, and particularly with those of his highness the Nizam, and his minister.

Such being the fact, Sir J. Kennaway was requested to inform the minister that if he expected the Company to support him in projects which he would not have

---

[1] Appendix D.

dared to think of before the successful event of the war, Lord Cornwallis had no wish to press the guarantee treaty upon him; and further, that his lordship, under these circumstances, did not hold himself bound to defend any part of his highness's territories, if an attack should be occasioned by the prosecution of his claim upon Kurnool.

After this, nothing requiring particular notice occurred until the affairs of Kurnool were brought forward by the Jagheerdar of that place, a narrative of which will occupy our next chapter.

CHAPTER VI.

THE AFFAIRS OF KURNOOL.

Peshcush payable by the Nawab of Kurnool to Tippoo Sultan—The Nawab of Kurnool appeals to his highness the Nizam—Correspondence with Sir J. Kennaway and Lord Cornwallis—Claims of the Nizam as Lord-paramount of Kurnool—Death of the Nawab—Interference of the Nizam in the Succession—Adherence of Lord Cornwallis and the Resident to the Policy of Non-intervention—Failing Health of the Nizam—Apprehensions respecting the Succession.

KURNOOL is now an administrative district, lying south of the Nizam's dominions, from which it is separated by the rivers Toongabudra and Kistna. It comprises an area somewhat exceeding 100 miles in length, by eighty in breadth, and has a population of about 300,000 souls. The chief town, of the same name as the province, numbers about 20,000 inhabitants. The relation of this province to the dominions of the Nizam will appear from the following narrative of events.

In July, 1792, the Nawab of Kurnool, Runmust Khan, requested instructions from the Nizam in regard to Peshcush which he had stipulated to pay to Tippoo Sultan, when his power was supreme. During the negotiations related in the preceding chapter, Tippoo was anxious to include the Peshcush receivable from Kurnool as part of the amount which it was agreed by the treaty he should pay to the Nizam, but to this arrangement the contracting powers could not agree. Tippoo then addressed himself to Runmust Khan, calling upon him to pay up arrears to the amount of twenty lacs.

Under the altered circumstances of the case the Nawab felt no disposition to comply with this request, but considering the relative powers of the Nizam, and the sovereign of Mysore, he forwarded a copy of Tippoo's letter to the former, requesting that his highness would prepare a draft of a letter in reply. His highness solicited the opinion of Sir John Kennaway, who, after perusing the sunnuds granted by the Nizam's ancestors to the Nawabs of Kurnool, conferring upon them that Jagheer, submitted the whole correspondence to Lord Cornwallis. Here it is necessary to explain that the Nawab's conduct in the late war had been far from satisfactory to the allies, he having merely sent two of his sons with a weak escort to accompany Secunder Jah in the field. His lordship, therefore, answered this appeal by stating that the Nawab had no right to expect the

English to give themselves any trouble about him at the present time, especially as any such interference in his favour might involve us in difficulties with the Mahrattas.

The Nizam then proposed to cut the knot of this difficulty, and at the same time gratify his own ambition, by taking possession of the Kurnool Jagheer and giving Runmust Khan other territories in lieu of it. Having signified this to Sir John Kennaway, the latter replied that "Tippoo would transfer his claims from the old Jagheer to the new one;" to which his highness's minister rejoined, "that Tippoo, merely from superior force, had compelled the Jagheerdar to comply with his demands for Peshcush." The Resident, however, was of opinion that such had been the practice of the native powers; and further, that there could be no doubt but that Tippoo's sway had been established over the Kurnool Jagheer, and that he had actually taken possession of two districts belonging to the Nawab. For some twenty-five or thirty years, he said, the Nizam's rights over the Jagheer had been dormant, and Tippoo's claim unopposed; therefore, according to the usage of the country, the tributary state should be held to be dependent on the power to which tribute was paid. "It could not be denied, that previous to the breaking out of the war, Tippoo had been in actual possession of the supremacy of Kurnool, and as that supremacy had not been surrendered by him at the peace, his right to it could not in justice be disputed.

This affair was still unsettled at the latter end of 1792, when Runmust Khan died, and a host of relatives aspired to succeed him in the Jagheer. His eldest son, Azeem Khan, was nominated his successor by the Nizam, who requested the Resident at his court to order the contingent force, consisting of two battalions, to the Kurnool frontier, for the purpose of assisting Azeem Khan in the event of any of his relatives opposing him in arms. Sir J. Kennaway's arguments, showing the inexpediency of the Nizam's interference, were deemed of so much importance by the government, that he was requested to repeat them to his highness. He was also directed to add, that Lord Cornwallis observed with concern the Nizam's inclination to embark in an enterprise which would be attended with much hazard, and in which assistance could not be rendered him even by the employment of the contingent serving in his army.

Subsequently, Lord Cornwallis was compelled to admit the Nizam's right to employ the two battalions in this objectionable service, as being conformable to the treaty of 1768; but he repeated his absolute disapproval of the enterprise as an infraction of the treaty of Seringapatam. "Whenever," he said in his letter to Sir John Kennaway, "the minister was capable of hearing reason, either from the resident direct, or through the medium of Meer Allum, he might be told that by quarrelling with Tippoo in matters in which the Company could not feel justified in supporting him, he would run the utmost risk of sacrificing to pride and passion those substantial and glorious advantages which had been obtained by the late treaty of peace, and which must ever reflect so much honour on his master's reign and on his own administration." The minister was further warned of the failing health of the Nizam, and of what might befall himself in the event of his highness's death while this ill-judged enterprise was in hand.

The minister then changed his tactics so far as to induce the Nizam to recognize a younger son of the Nawab, of the age of ten or twelve years, on the ground that the deceased Jagheerdar shortly before his death, had disinherited the elder, and declared his last will in favour of the boy, Alif Khan. A declaration to that effect was attested by the seal of the Kazy and by the brothers of Alif and his followers. On Sir John Kennaway still remonstrating, the former arguments were repeated on both sides; and a report having been made to Lord Cornwallis of the Nizam's intentions, he addressed the most positive instructions to Sir John Kennaway of the same tenor as before,[1] accompanied with a letter of remonstrance to the Nizam himself[2] in which he admitted that the claim of Peshcush might have been settled in the Nizam's favour had it been fairly considered when the treaty of peace was signed; but that the opportunity having been lost, it could not now in justice be enforced. In the letter to Sir John Kennaway, his lordship had expressed his opinion very strongly on the impolicy of further discussing the matter.

Notwithstanding this, it is recorded that an agreement was concluded with Alif Khan, by one article of which he was to make an immediate payment of fifteen lacs of rupees as Peshcush to his highness; in consideration, it may be inferred, of the investiture of Kurnool, recently granted to his brother, being annulled and conferred on him, exclusive of a Jagheer to be given by Alif Khan to his elder brother of 60,000 rupees. When this was brought to the notice of the resident, he denounced the arrangement to Meer Allum, and the latter addressed a long letter of remonstrance to the minister, declaring in conclusion that unless he turned his attention particularly to the state of the alliance with us, he might soon find himself isolated in a war with Tippoo. This letter resulted in an interview between Meer Allum and the minister, and

[1] Appendix E. [2] Appendix F.

to further conferences with the Resident, who adhered closely to the instructions of Lord Cornwallis, though other plausible overtures were made on the subject.

About this time the Nizam, whose health was sufficiently restored, took the field and encamped at Bidur, his ostensible object being to enforce the due execution of the treaty of Eadgheer. In reality, the demonstration was against the Poonah government, in favour of Scindiah; and we shall see by and by that the service thus rendered was expected to result in some advantage to the Nizam.

During the encampment at Bidur, Sir John Kennaway proceeded to the coast for the purpose of recruiting his health, and the minister requested Lieutenant Stewart, then officiating as Resident, to be present at court, when the Vakeel of the Kurnool Nawab should receive his dismissal. Lieutenant Stewart declined the invitation, remarking that he had nothing to do with such arrangements; and though he was assured that his highness had no intention of taking any money from Alif Khan, and plausible arguments were used to throw him off his guard, nothing could induce him to alter his determination. At length, on the 12th of October, 1793, Lieutenant Stewart reported the departure of the Vakeel, Bundallah Khan, for Kurnool, without obtaining sunnuds or paying money to the Durbar.

About this time, the failing health of the Nizam caused some anxiety,[1] as it became absolutely necessary to consider what policy we ought to pursue, if, as appeared most probable, the succession should be disputed after his demise. It was generally expected that his highness would nominate his eldest son to succeed to the Musnud, and Sir J. Kennaway, considering the character borne by that prince and his natural right, felt assured that his claim would be more likely to secure the acquiescence of all parties than any other. Eventually the government directed that a strict neutrality should be observed.

Here it becomes necessary to advert to certain events which were transpiring at the court of the Peishwah. Otherwise the reader will be surprised by suddenly finding the states of Hyderabad and Poonah opposed to each other, and actually fighting a battle, before he is aware that any circumstances existed by which a result of this nature was likely to be produced.

---

[1] It will be seen that, contrary to expectation, Nizam Ali Khan survived till 1803.

CHAPTER VII.

COMPLICATION WITH THE MAHRATTAS.

Scindiah at the Court of Poonah—His intimacy with the Chief Minister of the Nizam, Azim-ool-oomrah — Intrigues against Balaji Pundit—Statement of Azim-ool-oomrah—Grievances of long standing—Choute due for Bidur, &c.—The Nizam proposes going to Poonah—His desire to be accompanied by the detachment of the Company's troops—The request refused—Balaji's suspicion of Azim-ool-oomrah's enmity—Desire of Lord Cornwallis to prevent any rupture between the courts of Poonah and Hyderabad—Demand on the Nizam supported by Scindiah —Azim-ool-oomrah proposes to move the Nizam's Troops towards Berar—Conversation of Sir J. Kennaway with Meer Allum—Scindiah supposed to be the bearer of Demands from the King of Delhi — the Nizam contemplates Resistance — Our Government decline to interfere—Retirement of Sir J. Kennaway—His Report on the State of our Relations with the Nizam.

It would be tedious to explain in full detail all the circumstances which led to the fatal complication of affairs between the Nizam and the Mahrattas, but the following brief summary will render them, in the main, intelligible.

A short time after the departure of the Nizam from Hyderabad (*ante* Chap. V. p. 41), Scindiah, who was minister to the King of Delhi, had arrived at Poonah, and thence kept up a close intimacy with Azim-ool-oomrah, to the prejudice of Balaji Pundit, the minister of the Peishwa. This intimacy had commenced previous to the departure of Azim-ool-oomrah to join Lord Cornwallis, and of course prior to the treaty of Seringapatam, which was the result of the war with Tippoo. It could not be agreeable to Balaji, or consistent with his duty to the Peishwa, to permit, without remonstrance, the establishment of a focus of intrigue at the court of Poonah, with a power of which the Mahratta chiefs had always been more or less jealous. This intimacy, therefore, whatever might be its ultimate object, was calculated to promote distrust; and we shall presently see that there were matters in dispute between the two courts, which added very materially to the provocation it caused. Neither could an intrigue against Balaji be viewed with indifference by the representatives of British interests. His continuance in power at the court of Poonah was essential to the success of the just and pacific intentions of the government. Lieutenant Stewart, therefore, who at this time acted as officiating resident at Hyderabad, took every opportunity to impress upon Meer Allum and Azim-ool-oomrah the importance of cultivating a good understanding with the Peishwa's minister, and to show by every possible argument how destructive a rupture with him might prove to his highness's affairs. Unfortunately these representations had no effect in weakening the intimacy between Azim-ool-oomrah and Scindiah, the former explaining to Lieutenant Stewart that there were causes, connected with the dependence which the Nizam still owed the royal authority, which would ever render it necessary to keep on good terms with the minister of Delhi for the time being. He said further that the causes of dissension between the two courts originated in a period prior to his administration, and that they were now kept alive out of personal animosity to himself; which animosity he accounted for by reciting the instances in which he had upheld the dignity of the Nizam's government, and cultivated the English alliance, without reference to the opinion of Balaji, who had therefore endeavoured to procure his removal from office. Finally, he declared that he had always laboured to preserve peace, and had kept from his highness's ear many causes of complaint against the Mahrattas.[1]

The long-standing causes of disagreement alluded to in the remarks of Azim-ool-oomrah were these:— 1st. The choute due to the Peishwa for the country held by Darab-Jah; the amount of which the Mahrattas insisted should be the same as in the time of Bazalut

[1] Appendix G.

Jung, although, since the death of that prince, the country had been considerably reduced. 2nd. The choute due for Bidur; and 3rd, on the part of the Nizam, the irregularities committed by the rajahs of Nagpore on the possessions of his highness in Berar.

These points being in dispute, and the personal animosity between Azim-ool-oomrah and Balaji, threatening unpleasant consequences, the Nizam himself proposed going to Poonah, to discuss the differences between the two courts at that Durbar, and he requested that Sir J. Kennaway and the detachment of Company's troops paid by his highness might accompany him. Lord Cornwallis, however, declined compliance with this request, except in the event of the Peishwa inviting his highness, a condition which the dignity of the latter would not permit him to contemplate. It was evident that he had conceived the idea of going to Poonah to dictate a settlement under cover of the apparent support of the English government, and, failing in this, he allowed the matter to drop.

Balaji Pundit openly avowed his belief that there were enemies of his about his highness the Nizam, who were plotting against him. "But," he said, using a Mahratta proverb, "the milk would soon be separated from the water," when those enemies would meet with their desert. This threat evidently alluded to Azim-ool-oomrah, who after giving his own account of the causes of dissension, as recited above, was particularly anxious to ascertain which of the contending parties at Poonah Lord Cornwallis would favour. The cautious reply of Lieutenant Stewart at the moment, and the subsequent despatch of Lord Cornwallis, when the subject of the conversation had been reported to him, amounted to an assurance of friendship towards both the contending powers, and a determination not to interfere in the domestic concerns of the Mahratta state; it being his lordship's conviction that the alliance of the three powers was well calculated to secure the peace of India, and was equally advantageous and honourable to all.

In this dubious state of affairs our officiating Resident at Hyderabad received information (October 15th, 1793) that Scindiah had settled his business at Poonah—the terms of which settlement were also reported to his highness's minister [1]—and that no ostensible business now hindered his return to Hindostan. Still there were well-informed persons who believed that he would remain to trouble the Nizam in concert with Balaji Pundit. There was some show of reason for this suspicion, as the Poonah minister had recently made certain claims on the

[1] Appendix H.

Nizam, including a demand for an outstanding balance of Choute due for Bidur, which would not have been made if Scindiah had been disposed to prevent its transmission. There was reason to believe that he approved of its despatch, but of this more hereafter.

On the 6th of November Sir J. Kennaway returned from the sea-coast and joined the deputation at Bidur. The same evening he waited on his highness, and was concerned to find him much emaciated. He concluded that his highness might live another year, but, as we have before remarked, he lived nearly ten years from this date.

On this occasion Azim-ool-oomrah asked the Resident's opinion of the policy of despatching a body of 5,000 or 6,000 troops towards the frontier of Berar. He stated that the Rajah of Berar had stationed 10,000 or 12,000 horse under Etal-rao-Pundit at Rajoora, on his highness's frontier, which he affected to regard as sufficient cause for alarm. The fact was that the Rajah of Berar was acting by way of precaution against the minister's threat that his highness would move *viâ* Bidur and Berar with a view to the adjustment of certain differences between the Berar and Hyderabad governments; the chief cause of complaint on the part of the Nizam against the Rajah of Berar being for depredations on his

Talooks when he left Hyderabad at the commencement of hostilities against Tippoo; for which depredations no satisfaction had yet been given. Sir. J. Kennaway, in reply to the minister, cautioned him against despatching any unusual number of troops towards the frontier, as likely to add to the provocations which already existed between him and the rajah. Our Resident's advice was afterwards stamped with the approbation of Sir John Shore, who had succeeded Lord Cornwallis as Governor General.

Returning to the suspicion of Scindiah's complicity with Balaji Pundit, we find Sir J. Kennaway, in an interview with Meer Allum, inquiring into the grounds on which Scindiah and the minister (Azim-ool-oomrah) stood with respect to each other. Meer Allum related some parts of a conversation between himself and the minister, in which the latter stated that the demands of the Poonah durbar, in eight requisitions, had been addressed to him by Scindiah himself, without either publicly or privately suggesting, as the minister had a right to expect he would have done, in what manner they were to be answered, or, in other words, evaded. Meer Allum observed that a long time had elapsed, and much had been done by him (Azim-ool-oomrah) in Scindiah's behalf,[1]

---

[1] *Ante*, p. 61.

without any of the expected advantages having accrued in return. The minister exclaimed, "Advantages, indeed! it will be extremely well if we can keep our own." Considering the decided influence he had obtained at Poonah, Meer Allum thought it doubtful whether Scindiah would depart.

Our Resident was again sounded by the minister, on the occasion of an entertainment given by him at Bidur on the 19th of November. Pretending to have heard that Scindiah had brought with him from Hindostan a tunkha or order on his highness's government, from Shah Allum, for two crores of rupees, and that such an order was equally unjust and vexatious, he said that it was the Nizam's determination to resist it to the utmost. He requested to be informed if his highness might depend on the Company's mediation in the event of its being brought forward, as in that case hostilities might be avoided, or, if force were resorted to, whether he might calculate on their support. Sir J. Kennaway replied that it was impossible he could be acquainted with the sentiments of the government on this question, but he knew it to be a fact that our government wished the Nizam to be unmolested himself and to refrain from molesting others. On this being reported to the government, Sir J. Kennaway's caution was entirely approved, and he was instructed to reply to any future inquiry of the same kind, that the friendly relations subsisting between Scindiah and the Company's government would necessarily prevent them from interfering in the event of hostilities. It was equally impossible to make an offer of our mediation, and an application from both parties requesting our intercession would preclude any deliberation on the propriety of granting it. Should it be necessary to communicate these resolutions to the durbar, Sir J. Kennaway was instructed to adopt the most conciliatory language, and to express the concern of the government that the embarrassment of the Nizam's affairs should have made any reference to them necessary.

Such was the situation of affairs, when (in January 1794) Sir J. Kennaway resigned his appointment as Resident at the court of his highness. His report, in full, relative to the state of our relations with the Hyderabad durbar will be found in the Appendix;[1] but the principal points may be briefly stated in this place. It appears, then, that the Nizam in common with the other princes of the Deccan was impressed with a deep sense of respect for the Company's government, and that the Mahratta connection was proportionately disliked. The weakness of the Nizam's

---

[1] Appendix I.

government, and the character of his chief minister (Azim-ool-oomrah), were not such as to invite to a closer alliance on the part of the British government; but, on the other hand, the extent of his dominions, the great resources they would yield if properly managed, and their local importance as commanding an entrance into the territories of Tippoo, and the Peishwa, of Scindiah and the Berar rajah, were considerations of importance; and even as matters stood, the Nizam would hardly be induced to engage in any enterprise of which the Company's government had expressed its marked disapprobation. Any danger to be apprehended by the Hyderabad durbar from the Mahrattas, during the present Nizam's life, Sir J. Kennaway attributed to the cunning and ambition of Scindiah, who, however, was held in check by the enmity between him and Balaji Pundit, the Poonah minister. The character and aims of Azim-ool-oomrah make an interesting page in the report, and the question that would probably arise concerning the succession is clearly stated. As for the detachment of our troops in the pay of the Nizam — which we shall see, by-and-by, his highness talked of dismissing—Sir John Kennaway expressed his opinion that it conferred too much importance on the Nizam's government to be lightly dispensed with, while its use to ourselves was considerable in the salutary influence which it would always have on the conduct of Tippoo Sultan. This report, in short, may be referred to as an interesting general outline of our relations with the Deccan ruler, previous to the war between him and the Mahrattas, from which, as a leading cause, sprung his alliance with the French. But the preliminary skirmishing between the several ministers will yet occupy one or more tedious chapters of my unpretending narrative.

CHAPTER VIII.

COMPLICATION WITH THE MAHRATTAS—(*Continued*).

Captain Kirkpatrick succeeds Sir J. Kennaway at Hyderabad—Question renewed concerning the Employment of the Company's Troops—The Nizam threatens to dismiss them—Project to use them in Kurnool opposed by the Resident—The Governor-General's view of the use to be made of the Detachment—Question renewed as to the probable action of our Government in the event of a War with the Mahrattas—An Explicit Answer demanded to Three Propositions—The real Difficulty one of Personal Animosity between the Ministers—Artfulness of Azim-ool-oomrah—Reply of the Resident—His Report to Sir John Shore—Detailed Reply of Sir John Shore—Interview of the Resident with Meer Allum—The Correspondence between the Courts of Poonah and Hyderabad—The contemplated Mission of Meer Allum to Poonah—Invitation from Balaji Pundit—Bombast of the Nizam's Minister—Character of the two Governments contrasted—Little Hope of a Reconciliation.

Sir J. Kennaway was succeeded in the office of Resident at Hyderabad by Captain Kirkpatrick, and one of the first subjects brought under his notice by the minister, was the old question regarding the employment of the Company's troops serving in the Nizam's army.

It appeared that some delay had occurred in the making over of a district ceded to the Nizam by the treaty of Seringapatam, the cession of which was disputed by the Mahratta governor as including certain villages on his frontier. It was the wish of Azim-ool-oomrah to employ the Company's troops in securing possession of this district to the Nizam's officers, but as in the case of former overtures already related, our Resident could hold out no hope of the English government acceding to the request.

More impetuous than heretofore, the minister now began to talk of dismissing the battalion, on the pretence that it contributed in no degree to the interests of his highness's government. Conceiving the threat to be purely the effect of momentary chagrin, the Resident instructed his Vakeel, as often as it might be repeated, either to observe complete silence, or to remark shortly, "that as he (the minister) must necessarily understand best whether or not his highness derived any advantage from the services of the detachment, so he doubted not but that his ultimate determination would be the result of due consideration, and as such would in no degree derogate from his established reputation for prudence." The Resident judged this qualified kind of reply to be more advisable than such an answer as might invite the Nizam to execute his unmeaning menace, his opinion as to the utility of the force, both to the state of Hyderabad and to the Company, being similar to that of his predecessor.

Very soon another occasion for agitating the question of the employment of these troops arose in connection with the Kurnool territory. Alif Khan having, in March 1794, succeeded to his father's Jagheer, as related in Chapter VI., treated all whom he suspected of disaffection with a high hand, not excepting his uncle Bundallah Khan, whom he had formerly deputed to Hyderabad to induce the Nizam to recognize his title. His conduct clearly demonstrated that he had virtually renounced all allegiance to the Nizam, and had put himself definitively under the protection of Tippoo Sultan. For security under these circumstances he had removed part of his property to Gooty, and Tippoo, on his part, had advanced as far as Bangalore to support Alif Khan in his contumacy.

The minister of the Nizam had earnestly sought to advance the Company's troops to Gunjcootah, his motive for which, in the light of the above facts, appeared sufficiently obvious, as the detachment could not move from the station it then occupied to Gunjcootah without passing close by Kurnool. Our Resident, therefore, in this as in the former instances, could not respond in favourable terms to the Nizam's inclination, especially as there were boundary questions on the point of settlement with Tippoo, which such a demonstration would tend to delay, and two of Tippoo's sons were still held as hostages for the due execution of the Treaty of Seringapatam by which the territories in question were transferred to the Nizam. The minister was apparently persuaded by the arguments of Captain Kirkpatrick, and relinquished his project of removing the detachment to Gunjcootah.

In signifying his entire approval of the Resident's action in this matter, Sir J. Shore took occasion to make some general remarks relative to the employment of the Company's troops in the service of the Nizam, whose duties, he pointed out, consisted principally in the reduction of refractory Zemindars. Every favourable opportunity, he added, ought to be taken by the Resident to impress upon the Nizam the propriety of considering the attendance of the detachment as evidence of the friendship subsisting between him and the Company, rather than an instrument for enforcing the payment of collections from his disobedient subjects. The detachment was sent to the Nizam upon a requisition made by him in terms of the same treaty by which we claimed the Guntoor Circar, and the only restrictive provision relative to its employment was, that it should not act against any state in friendly alliance with the English. The Governor General expressed his wish that the Resident should represent this with delicacy, and avoid the formality of an official communication.

The standing question between the Resident and the Hyderabad durbar was still as to the line which our government would be likely to pursue in the event of an open rupture between the Nizam and the Mahratta power. This question was re-opened by Meer Allum on the occasion of a visit which he paid to Captain Kirkpatrick on the 23rd of March, and it was evident that the usual reply did not satisfy him. Before quitting the Resident's tents, he signified to the Moonshee that he had started the subject by the express command of the minister who would expect a more explicit answer. The next day he again waited on the Resident, and after, in the course of conversation, asserting the undoubted right of his highness to the villages on the Mahratta frontier, in virtue of the treaty of Seringapatam, he proceeded to disclose the main object of his visit, in the following questions:—

1. Whether our government would interpose its good offices for the friendly purpose of bringing about a more amicable adjustment of the differences subsisting between the Mahratta and Hyderabad states?

2. How would the Company act, if, in the event

of our agreeing to mediate, his highness should afterwards refuse to conform to our advice and opinion?

3. The Resident's private sentiments were also demanded, with regard to the tone which it was proper for the minister to assume in discussing what he considered to be unreasonable demands on the part of Balaji Pundit; in short, whether an air of defiance or of moderation would be the best suited to the occasion?

The reader who has followed the narrative thus far with a moderate degree of attention will not be misled by the apparent sincerity of these questions. The ostensible cause of disagreement lay in the disputed claim for Choute on the part of the Mahrattas, but there was no such intricacy in this subject as to render its amicable adjustment either difficult or tedious. The crisis between the two states was really produced by the personal animosity between the ministers, rather than by any substantial difference of a political nature; and in this fact lay the difficulty felt by Meer Allum in undertaking the mission to Poonah. Even exorbitant pretensions founded upon supposed treaty rights might be fairly met, but how to deal with requirements dictated by private resentment and distrust was a problem infinitely more difficult of solution. Yet the Resident was aware that the time had arrived when the minister would be compelled to take some decisive course with respect to the Mahratta claims; and having been some time in possession of the Governor General's sentiments, he thought it right to communicate his determination so far as should have the effect of discouraging any hope of interference on our part.

Some little artfulness will be observed in the second of the above questions, for although the minister affects to put the case in the name of the Nizam, it really points to the probable refusal of the Peishwa. It was not likely that the Hyderabad Court would disregard our formal decision (under the supposed circumstances) on its disputes with that of Poonah, and as little likely that it would have started a doubt so prejudicial to itself. On the other hand, it was not at all surprising that the minister should suppose the Court of Poonah likely to prove less scrupulous. Be this as it may, the Resident deemed it quite a sufficient reply to inquire in his turn, "what right our government would have to expect the acquiescence of either state in its decision, unless it had been formally requested and nominated by both parties to judge between them;" and he observed further, that "it would be time enough for the Governor General to consider what was fit to be done when he should have received an invitation to that effect." To the third query the Resident replied that he saw not how any possible advantage could result from an intemperate or irritating negotiation of the points in dispute; on the contrary, he thought it by no means improbable that a candid and conciliatory discussion of these difficulties might be productive of the happiest effect.

In reporting these circumstances to Sir John Shore, Captain Kirkpatrick recognized the importance of preserving the independence of the Nizam on the one hand, and the difficulties with which we should have to contend if we engaged ourselves in his support on the other. He pointed out that a war with the Mahrattas would have the effect of disturbing the judicious arrangements which had been made for preserving the political balance of the Deccan, and restraining the ambition of the Sultan of Mysore. In his view, the true policy of the government would be to prevent hostilities by acting as moderator between the parties, and he was of opinion that the Court of Hyderabad would more readily listen to reason than that of Poonah. He added, however, that in Meer Allum's opinion, neither party would be disposed to a policy of conciliation until they had first come to blows, and felt the smart of war.

As the object of this part of our narrative is to enable the reader to understand the circumstances under which the governments of Hyderabad and

Poonah eventually had recourse to arms, without finding an active ally, on the one side or the other, in the British power; the reply of Sir J. Shore is not without interest, as showing the sincerity of the course adopted. Captain Kirkpatrick was requested to exert himself to the utmost to penetrate through the imperfect and obscure statements of the minister, and ascertain, with all possible accuracy, the real or pretended grounds of dissension. Reasoning on the supposition that encroachments were meditated by the Poonah government, Sir John Shore thought it equally necessary to keep in view the possibility of provocation on the part of Azim-ool-oomrah, who he was desirous should receive no encouragement in measures calculated to prove offensive to the Mahrattas. To the questions put by Meer Allum he replied categorically as follows:—

1. That the Company's government as well-wishers to the Nizam and the Peishwa, and as parties to the triple confederacy, was willing to interpose its good offices for the friendly purpose of bringing about an amicable adjustment of the differences subsisting between the two states; but that, to do this with propriety and judgment, it was necessary to have a candid and particular exposition of the grounds of the differences without colour or concealment.

2. That if either the Peishwa or his highness the

Nizam should decline our mediation, or refuse to conform to our advice and opinion, we should content ourselves with pointing out the consequences of their ill-advised dissensions, and leave the termination of the quarrel to themselves.

3. With regard to the tone and temper which was proper for the minister to assume in discussing what he considered to be unreasonable demands on the part of Balaji Pundit, Captain Kirkpatrick was considered to have given a very proper reply, and Sir John Shore further observed "that it was incumbent on the minister to be assured that the demands of the Peishwa were unreasonable before they were refused, and upon this conviction dispassionately formed, that they were better opposed by firmness and moderation than by intemperate defiance."

In the course of a visit which Meer Allum paid to the Resident on the 17th of April, 1794, he assured him that the minister Azim-ool-oomrah had regulated his correspondence with the Court of Poonah in strict accordance with the opinions expressed by the Resident and the Governor General, and had declared that even the advance of Mahratta troops to the pass of Dharoor should not provoke him to use other language, or to relax his endeavours to arrive at a pacific solution of all differences. In proof of the former part of this assertion, Meer Allum sent for Captain Kirkpatrick's perusal, copies of the letters which had been written to Poonah, and which the reader himself may refer to in our Appendix.[1] The Resident, however much he may have distrusted the sincerity of the courteous language used by the minister, could not but express his satisfaction with the style adopted.

On the 23rd of April, Captain Kirkpatrick went to Hyderabad to inspect the detachment of Company's troops, which, at the request of the minister, had been directed to march on Elgundel, on the northern frontier, where disturbances had been occasioned by the refusal of certain Zemindars to pay the just dues of the government. Captain Kirkpatrick judged it proper to put the officer commanding the detachment on his guard against any attempt that might be made to embroil him with the Mahrattas and the Berar frontier.

I have remarked that Meer Allum was indisposed to undertake the mission to Poonah, in which, however, rested the best hope of preserving peace. Captain Kirkpatrick, therefore, addressed a letter to Sir W. Malet, our Resident at that court, expressing his opinion that the object of the several instructions received from the Governor General could hardly be better promoted than by his (Sir W. Malet's) encourage-

---

[1] Appendix J.

ment of the projected mission, and by his afterwards sanctioning the endeavours of the commissioner to accommodate matters. He thought it almost certain that the assurance of their joint support, the one at Hyderabad, the other at Poonah, would not only induce Meer Allum to undertake the negotiation, but to enter upon it with considerable confidence of success. It appeared to Captain Kirkpatrick that this circuitous mode of mediation would indeed be preferable to any direct offer of interference; would be more likely to attain its object, and would prevent the possibility of Azim-ool-oomrah reckoning wildly on our support, and, perhaps, of acting with dangerous extravagance in that expectation.

Before Meer Allum could be despatched on his mission, it was requisite for the Nizam's dignity that the Hyderabad court should be invited by the court of Poonah to send a confidential agent with power to adjust the differences between the two states. Shortly after Captain Kirkpatrick's return to Bidur from his visit to Hyderabad, the minister learnt from his agents at Poonah that Balaji Pundit had come to the resolution to send such an invitation; and it is almost incredible what extravagant vauntings and intemperate declarations were indulged in by Azim-ool-oomrah when this vague manifestation of a conciliatory disposition on the part of the Poonah Government became known to him. Attributing the moderation of the Peishwa to fear, he solicited an immediate audience of the Nizam, to whom he expatiated on the strong proof afforded by the present disposition of the Mahratta government of the benefit which had resulted from his highness having kept the field, and boasted of still greater advantages that were likely to be obtained by a firm adherence to the same system of intimidation. Thus, alternately, the versatile minister allowed himself to be influenced by a kind of Dutch courage to provoke the Mahrattas to a trial of strength in the field; and then again when a crisis threatened him, by a feeble desire for accommodation. At present he was so inflated with the success of the first step towards an accommodation that, mere vapouring aside, there was reason to fear that he would actually reject the proposition for deputing an agent to Poonah. It was evident that no reliance could be placed on a man whose character was marked by such levity and inconsistency. On the other hand, the conduct of the Peishwa was moderate and firm, and the Government saw little reason to doubt that he would ultimately compel the Nizam to a fair adjustment of his demands.

The superior *morale* of the Peishwa's government, and the substantial justice of its claim upon the Nizam, were tacitly recognized by Sir John Shore, who, nevertheless, expressed his conviction that no attack would be made on the Nizam without a previous communication with the Resident at Poonah, Sir C. W. Malet, who was instructed to use all his influence to prevent such an intention being carried into effect. With this understanding the Residents at either court were left to act according to the exigency of circumstances, the government having no wish to interfere directly in the quarrel so long as they could prudently keep aloof.[1]

[1] Appendix K.

CHAPTER IX.

COMPLICATION WITH THE MAHRATTAS—(*Continued.*)

Importance of Deciding upon the Journey of Meer Allum to Poonah—Interview between Captain Kirkpatrick and the Minister, Azim-ool-oomrah—Despatch of Sir J. Shore communicated to the latter—His Statements and Complaints against the Mahrattas in Reply—His Proposal for the Conditional Support of the Company in the event of War—Rejoinder of Captain Kirkpatrick—Letters from Poonah read by the Minister—Opinion of the Resident—Faithfulness of the Nizam to his Minister—The Departure of Meer Allum becomes more probable—Observations on some of the Points in dispute—the proposed Cession of Raichore—The Ministers' Criticism of the Letters from Poonah—Report of the Resident, and Reply of Sir J. Shore—Departure of Meer Allum for Poonah, with full Powers to negotiate.

As remarked in the previous chapter, Captain Kirkpatrick had been for some time in possession of a despatch from Sir J. Shore, the purport of which he was instructed to communicate to the minister, but the time for doing so was left to his own discretion. Finding that Azim-ool-oomrah was still undetermined whether or not to entrust the settlement of affairs to Meer Allum in the character of plenipotentiary at

Poonah, it appeared to our Resident that the moment had arrived when it behoved him to make some exertion to avert the evil consequences which might result from a single false step at this juncture. He therefore requested an interview with the minister, and the evening of the 24th of May was fixed for his visit. In the interim, Meer Allum was directed to apprise the Resident of the purport generally, of recent despatches from Poonah.

The conference was opened by Captain Kirkpatrick, who delivered the following message to Azim-ool-oomrah in the name of the Governor General. Though framed for the occasion, it amounts to little more than a formal communication of the sentiments conveyed to Captain Kirkpatrick in his instructions: "That it had afforded his lordship the sincerest satisfaction to learn that, after consulting with the Resident, the minister had replied to letters which had been received from Poonah in a moderate and conciliatory strain.[1] His lordship, in fact, had expected no less from the minister's wisdom, foresight, and attachment to the true interests of his highness; since it was plain that while the Mahrattas professed themselves willing to treat amicably in order to a fair adjustment of all differences, there could be no reason

[1] See the letters already adverted to in Appendix J.

on his part for any intemperate discussion, which, indeed, could hardly fail, in such a case, of producing mischievous consequences. That as now both States appeared to be actuated by a hearty disposition to accommodate their disputes, his lordship no longer doubted that this most necessary and desirable object would be speedily accomplished to the sincere satisfaction of every real well-wisher to his highness's government; and that as in particular the permanency of the immense advantages enjoyed by the parties to the triple alliance, evidently depended on the harmony and common interest which constituted the basis of that union, his lordship felt assured that the minister's most earnest endeavours would never be wanting to the preservation and improvement of a friendship involving such important objects."

Having listened with grave attention to the above address, the minister replied that he would proceed, in his turn, to show how sincerely he was disposed to conform to the principles inculcated in Sir J. Shore's message. He began by stating, that although the most perfect understanding subsisted between his highness and the Poonah government, and although the reciprocal claims of the two States were inconsiderable in themselves, and perhaps nearly balanced each other, yet those of the Peishwa had been for some time past urged with a vigour without example in former transactions between the two courts. This unprecedented conduct, he said, was caused by personal hatred to himself, arising, in the first place, from his having—contrary to the practice of his predecessors in office—asserted the honour and interest of his master's government, by negotiating independently of the Peishwa's minister, and more recently by his connection with Scindiah. He declared that the nature of this connection had been entirely misunderstood, its sole object having been the maintenance of a necessary intercourse with the person who immediately directed the affairs of the court of Delhi. Such being the case, he proceeded to remark that only two practicable modes presented themselves for a fair settlement of the points in dispute, unless actual war were entered upon, an issue which he affected to think the experience of former times gave his highness no reason to dread. It was first necessary to remove from the mind of Balaji Pundit the unjust prejudice which he had conceived against him (the minister), and, secondly, it was essential for the government to assume the office of umpire between the parties. Supposing the premises true, Azim-ool-oomrah reasoned upon them fairly enough; but he offered no suggestion as to the means by which the unfortunate prepossession of the Mahratta minister might be overcome. Perhaps he broached the idea with no other intention than to insinuate that the evil he complained of had, in a great measure, proceeded from his persistency in cultivating the friendship of the English, which he knew to be obnoxious to the Poonah government, and on which he might found a reasonable claim to the support of the Company. At any rate, he went on to say that upon condition the Company determined to defend him in the maintenance of his just rights, he should have no hesitation in pledging himself to conform precisely to whatever we might require of him, notwithstanding he was aware that our solicitude to preserve the peace of the Deccan would be but too likely to warp our judgment, and even cause us to decide against him contrary to our internal conviction. He added, that the support he requested was no more than what the vizier and nabob of Arcot would be sure to obtain in case a neighbouring Power were to form any hostile design, or set up any unfounded claim against them; as, on the other hand, they would be certain that we should discountenance and condemn any aggression on their part.

Considering it impossible that Azim-ool-oomrah should be really ignorant of the wide difference between the engagements which the Company were under to the Nizam and those which they had contracted with Arcot, Captain Kirkpatrick did not consider it necessary to expose the futility of this last argument in a formal manner, but satisfied himself with barely hinting that the parallel did not by any means hold. It is probable, indeed, that the minister threw out the remark rather for the purpose of pointing to the sort of connection he was desirous of forming with us, than for any weight he really attributed to it in the argument.

With respect to the disadvantage which the minister pretended he would labour under from our regard for peace, Captain Kirkpatrick thought it sufficient to reply that a mutual readiness on the part of the disputants to recede in a reasonable degree from their respective claims seemed to be an essential condition of any accommodation whatever. He assured the minister, that whatever concessions our government might advise on the score of political prudence, it would never pronounce that to be a just demand which it did not think to be so.

The letters recently received from Poonah were then called for and read to Captain Kirkpatrick. The minister complained both of their style and substance, observing that they neither manifested a sincere desire for accommodation, nor reciprocated the conciliatory spirit which the letters from Hyderabad had been so well calculated to inspire.

From the tenor of these letters,[1] Captain Kirk-

[1] Appendix L.

patrick inferred that Balaji Pundit had no other view in claiming interest on the arrears of Choute due for Raichore, than that of checking the presumption of Azim-ool-oomrah. If, however, it were really the design of the Poonah minister to establish the Mahratta ascendancy at the court of the Nizam, on the ruin of the minister (and the genius of his nation rendered this highly probable), Captain Kirkpatrick thought there was too much reason to fear he would succeed, unless baffled by our interposition at Poonah on the principles laid down in Sir J. Shore's instructions. It is only surprising that the Nizam was not induced by the pressure of the Mahrattas on the one hand, and the enemies of Azim-ool-oomrah on the other, to purchase tranquillity by the sacrifice of the minister; but on this point it cannot be denied that his steadfastness was admirable. In answer to a direct proposal once made to him by Balaji Pundit he is said to have replied, "that being thoroughly satisfied with the zeal and fidelity of his servant, he saw no reason for transferring the management of his affairs to other hands."

Some further conversation took place between the Resident and his highness's minister consequent on the reading of the Poonah letters, and at length, owing to the judicious firmness of Captain Kirkpatrick, and the unanswerable arguments used by him, the minister discontinued his opposition, and requested Meer Allum to prepare for the journey to the Mahratta court. Still, he would not consent that he should proceed, until a formal invitation had been received from Poonah, though he promised that the necessary notice of the determination he had taken should be transmitted thither without delay.

He then inquired whether Lieutenant Stewart might accompany Meer Allum to Poonah, which he observed would be necessary in order that Captain Kirkpatrick might have regular and accurate accounts of the progress of the negotiation forwarded to him. Captain Kirkpatrick replied that Sir W. C. Malet (who was extremely desirous of forming a personal acquaintance with Meer Allum) being on the spot, would render the presence of Mr. Stewart no less improper than useless, and with this the conference ended.

The substance of this interview having been reported to the Nizam by his minister, his highness expressed his surprise that the resident should hesitate to promise him the support of the Company under the conditions proposed, and he directed Meer Allum to communicate his sentiments to Capt. Kirkpatrick, and to require of him an explicit answer to the proposition which had been made by the minister in the late interview. On the other hand, his highness did not consider it necessary to postpone the deputation until a formal requisition should be received from the Peishwa, but determined to announce at once to the Poonah durbar that confidential agents would shortly be despatched in accordance with the proposal made to the court of Hyderabad in a letter received from one of the Poonah ministers.

Although the Nizam had not yet publicly directed Meer Allum to prepare for his journey, the Resident was sanguine in his belief that he would now be sent. Here, therefore, I may briefly advert to some of the points he would be required to discuss and decide upon.

With regard to the proposition of the Poonah government for the cession of Raichore, Azim-ool-oomrah was disposed to consider this sacrifice the best course under the circumstances; but Captain Kirkpatrick expressed an opinion that he ought not to commit himself hastily in that particular, but leave the question to be decided by the envoy. The temporary transfer of the Raichore-doab to the Mahrattas in part satisfaction of the enormous arrears of tribute due to them on account of that territory, might appear the easiest mode of settling that account; but he submitted to Azim-ool-oomrah that this cession of territory would in all probability prove highly offensive to Tippoo Sultan, and that serious consequences might arise from his dissatisfaction.

On the letters received from Poonah[1] Azim-ool-oomrah remarked substantially as follows:— On No. 1, he observed that if Captain Kirkpatrick recalled the tenour of the letter to which it formed the reply, he would perceive how very little to the purpose it was. The reference to former periods of hostility between his highness and the Mahratta state he regarded as particularly offensive. The share of merit claimed by Govind Row on the score of the great address with which the points in dispute had been postponed from time to time during a period of five years he stigmatized as mere pretension, because nothing but the war with Tippoo, which broke out at the time, had prevented an immediate settlement, and the same obstacle had continued to operate till the peace. Since then, he had waited anxiously for the season when the discussion of these matters could be commenced with a probability of success; and the arrival of which, whenever it should occur, Hurry Punt had (at Seringapatam) promised duly to announce. Up to this moment, however, Hurry Punt had not sent the promised intimation, which was to have satisfied the Hyderabad durbar, that the Poonah government was seriously inclined to an adjustment of all differences between the two states.

---

[1] Appendix L.

On No. 2, the minister offered no observation, yet Captain Kirkpatrick was of opinion that this letter considered by itself pointed strongly, through its whole tenour, to the desire of the Poonah government for the renewal of that species of connection between the two states which had subsisted under the ministry of a former dewan, who was notoriously devoted to the interests of the Mahrattas.

On No. 3, Azim-ool-oomrah remarked that nothing could be more unfair than to garble a treaty, and refer only to the single article that suited a particular purpose. This remark had reference to a certain claim upon the grass produce of all that part of Berar in the possession of the Nizam, which had been commuted in concert with the confidential officers of Nagpore, though the arrangement was now disavowed. Captain Kirkpatrick thought it would be unreasonable just at this period to offer any strictures either upon this or the other remarks of the minister; but it was sufficiently obvious that the merits of the question could only be determined by reference to the powers under which the agents who formed the settlement had acted, or otherwise, by ascertaining whether that settlement was ever acquiesced in by their principal (the Bhonsla).

On No. 4, it was observed by Azim-ool-oomrah that though Balaji Pundit affected to represent the choute, &c. of the late Darab Jah's country as having been fixed at five mehals, the fact was it had been settled for eight, three of which had been seized on by Hyder Ally Khan: so that whether or not a deduction ought reasonably to be allowed on account of this dismemberment, the statement, at least, was uncandid. The minister added that, although his highness had often had scores of this sort to clear with the Mahrattas, it had never before happened that interest was claimed on the arrears of choute; and finally, touching Balaji's proposal for transferring the management of the whole Talook to the Peishwa's Sircar, he observed that though the project was so worded as to convey the idea that it originated with the Nizam, it would be found on reference to his highness's letter[1] that no arrangement of the sort had been even distantly suggested.

For a more particular summary of the critical circumstances between the two governments, and for an explicit statement of the view taken by the Resident, I must refer the reader to his report[2] addressed to the Governor General in June, 1794, at the time when Meer Allum was preparing for his journey to Poonah. The despatch in reply from Sir J. Shore may also be consulted for a full exposition of the corresponding sentiments on the part of the Government.

[1] Letter of the Nizam in Appendix J. [2] Appendix M.

Some difficulties had been started respecting the departure of Meer Allum by the Mahratta Vakeel, who seemed to think that some plan of adjustment ought first to be determined upon by the two courts; but these objections, by the advice of Captain Kirkpatrick, were overruled, and towards the end of June Meer Allum received his dismissal from the Nizam. On the 1st of July he commenced his march for Poonah, bearing with him the following letter addressed by his highness to the Peishwa:—

"Prior to this," it ran, "I informed you that I would shortly depute Meer Allum to your court. Accordingly, by the aid of God, the said Meer obtained dismission. God willing, he will reach Poonah, and will employ himself in obtaining a knowledge, and will ascertain beyond doubt, in a true and fair manner, whatever is equitable with respect to the affairs pending between us. The said Meer is entrusted with absolute powers on my part in this business; he will accordingly do what is equitable and fair, and settle the affairs of both sides."

CHAPTER X.

THE HYDERABAD AND MAHRATTA ARMIES IN THE FIELD.

Retrospective Notice of the Restoration of Tippoo's Sons—Also of the Settlement of the Boundaries of the Ceded Territories—And of Border Disputes—Ulterior Motives of the British Government suspected—Death of Scindiah—Arrival of Meer Allum at Poonah—Declaration of his plenary Powers to Negotiate required by the Peishwa—Affairs of *Jusviat* and *Kulliat* Distinguished—Reservation of the Hyderabad Durbar—Personal Feeling of the two Ministers—Advice of Sir J. Shore—Instructions to the Resident—Domestic Embarrassments of the Peishwa—Scindiah and Northern Hindostan—Commander of the Forces of Scindiah and Meer Allum—M. De Boigne—Policy of Appa Sahib and Dowlut Rao—The Nizam misses his Opportunity—Concentration of Troops at Bidur—The Nawab of Kurnool sends his Quota—Advance of the Mahratta Army—Counter Demonstration by a Detachment of the Nizam's Army—Application for the Company's Troops refused—Application for the Loan of French Prisoners and for Leave to Recruit refused—Composition of the Nizam's Advance—The two Armies draw near each other—Their respective Strength.

THE state of suspense which followed the departure of Meer Allum for Poonah, may be properly marked by a pause in the narrative, taking advantage of which, we may glance at a few subjects of minor importance, which have necessarily escaped notice while considering the important negotiations in progress with the Mahratta State.

Our review of events has reached to the date of midsummer, 1794. In March previous, the two sons of Tippoo Sultan, who had up to this time been held as hostages, were restored to their father. This act, although it announced to the public the complete fulfilment of that prince's engagements to the Company and their allies, was not, perhaps, completed with the best grace by the Hyderabad durbar, some of whose territorial claims under the treaty of Seringapatam, were still unadjusted. The principle upon which Lord Cornwallis had agreed to settle the Company's remaining claims of the same nature was, in fact, much too liberal to be readily adopted by the Hyderabad court, and though Azim-ool-oomrah was eventually prevailed upon to address Tippoo Sultan, concerning the points in dispute, in the prudent and conciliatory spirit of Sir John Shore's letters to the Nizam on the same occasion, he was not so easily induced to act in a spirit conformable to his professions.

Perhaps there was little love lost on either side. Upon the marriage of the Nizam's son, Secunder Jah, to the minister's granddaughter, a complimentary letter of invitation was forwarded by the Resident, and transmitted through the Madras government to Tippoo. This act of courtesy was contemptuously disregarded by the Sultan, who shortly afterwards placed his neglect in the most unequivocal light, by inviting the Peishwa to assist at the wedding of his younger son, and making no communication whatever on the subject to the court of Hyderabad. This hostile temper of mind may have been considerably aggravated by the unaccommodating spirit which the minister had evinced in the restoration of the princes; but the original animus may be referred to the undisguised alacrity with which the Nizam had engaged in the successful confederacy against him. More than once he is said to have remarked, that whatever grounds the English and the Mahrattas might have had for conspiring his ruin, Nizam Ally Khan had none, and that in uniting with those powers he had manifested no less indifference to political considerations than to the interests of the religion which he professed.

After much fruitless discussion by letter on the limits of the ceded districts, it was agreed by both parties to resort to local investigation in order to find the basis of a final adjustment, and the inquiry was commenced some time about the month of March this year. Little progress had been made, however, by the Ameers or supervisors employed on the occasion, when the one deputed by Tippoo Sultan departed for Seringapatam, in order, as he affirmed, to obtain fresh instructions. The business then remained at a stand-still, until, in the month of August, a new agent presented himself on the part of Tippoo, and the Hyderabad court immediately directed its original commissioner to give him the meeting he solicited.

The tranquillity of the border states had been well preserved since the peace of Seringapatam. In one instance only had the refractory Zemindar of Kupputhal (a dependency of the Hyderabad State), made some predatory excursions into the Sera district belonging to Tippoo. The Resident at once called Azim-ool-oomrah's attention to the expediency of taking seasonable precautions against an evil which, if it had not a tendency to embroil the two states, was, at least, ill calculated to promote a good understanding between them. The minister earnestly exerted himself, and the Zemindar was speedily reduced to obedience, and compelled to enter into engagements with the Hyderabad government, in which the interests of Tippoo Sultan appear to have been as much considered as the nature of the case would allow. On the other hand, the Hyderabad State was not without its little grievance, real or pretended; the allegation being, that the officers on the Mysore border were but too ready to protect the fugitive renters and tributaries from his highness's territory. Complaints so trivial could only grow to any importance between the two States, owing to the want of a direct channel of communication by which mutual explanations might be offered.

Returning to the main stream of events recorded in this narrative, the probability of a rupture between the Hyderabad and Mahratta States excited but little surprise at this time; it being generally known that the respective ministers were on bad terms with each other. Ostensibly the claims of the Poonah durbar were confined to the liquidation of the heavy arrears of choute due by the Nizam; but there were some who discerned ulterior motives of a political nature, as I have before intimated, in the persistency of Balaji.[1] In either case, it was our interest to avert a rupture which would not only endanger the political equipoise of the Deccan, but expose to imminent hazard the immense advantages to all concerned which had been secured by the triple alliance. I reserve for the next chapter a review of our own treaty obligations, and a general survey of the alliances and ulterior combinations which naturally presented themselves in view of such an event; only remarking here, that the Government saw with regret the two states actively preparing for war, at the very time when every honest

[1] Appendix N.

effort was made on their own part to preserve peace, and when a decided step had been taken in that direction by the despatch of Meer Allum to the court of Poonah.

While the result of this mission was in suspense, and the ulterior objects of the court of Poonah suspected, Captain Kirkpatrick could not, in fairness, expostulate further on the score of these preparations with Azim-ool-oomrah, unless that minister had manifested some fresh symptom of extravagance or unsteadiness—such, for example, as making overtures for support to Tippoo Sultan, whereby the crisis would have been much aggravated. The error in policy would have resembled that of the shepherd in the fable, who called in the wolf to drive away the fox, but history supplies many examples of such a mistake ; nor is it very extraordinary that, under the pressure of distress, a distant danger should be overlooked by a weak government, in its solicitude for present relief. To this extremity of rashness, however, the Nizam's government did not resort, and thus, at the present juncture of affairs, no fresh occasion was given for the interference of our Resident.

In March of this year, Madajee Scindiah died, and was succeeded by Dowlut Row, whose minister, Appa Chitnavees, appears to have sold himself and his master to the Peishwa. Had this not been the case, much advantage might have been reasonably hoped for by the Hyderabad durbar from the good offices of the Scindian branch of the Mahratta State; the original purpose of the Nizam's advance to Bidur having been to support Scindiah in his claims on the Peishwa, though the ostensible object of the demonstration was to enforce the due fulfilment of the treaty of Eadgheer.[1]

On his arrival at Poonah, Meer Allum was requested, before opening the negotiation, to address a letter to the Peishwa in his own handwriting, signifying that he was entrusted with full powers to adjust the matters in dispute between the two states. Having courteously expressed his own readiness to comply with this request, as a matter of form, he first reported to Hyderabad, and was then instructed by the minister that he might deliver such a note, couched in the same terms as the Nizam's letter, by which he had been accredited to the Peishwa.[2] Some qualifying expressions, however, used by Azim-ool-oomrah served to intimate that only matters of *jusviat*, or financial details, were to be entered upon by him, and that affairs of *kulliat*, or political differences, were to stand over for future development. Thus Meer Allum was not really entrusted with plenipotentiary

---

[1] *Ante*, p. 58. [2] *Ante*, p. 97.

powers, and the Mahratta court was not disposed, after all, to refer the more important questions at issue to the decision of Azim-ool-oomrah. On the other hand, it could hardly be hoped that the Hyderabad durbar would be dissuaded by any considerations whatever from securing to itself the privilege of deciding ultimately on the propriety of the adjustment that might be concerted at Poonah between its agent and the minister of the Peishwa. So soon, therefore, as the Poonah government began to inquire into the exact limits of the powers conferred on Meer Allum, the hopes of a satisfactory adjustment began once more to fade away.

Azim-ool-oomrah explained to Meer Allum that as a point of honour only, he had cautioned him against making any advance towards a personal reconciliation with Balaji; but he added, "should you observe any symptoms of such inclination in the other party, I would not have you show any backwardness in making a suitable return on my behalf." In his reply to this letter, Meer Allum informed Azim-ool-oomrah that such matters were never even remotely alluded to by the minister or his agents: "they neither reproach nor accuse; neither manifest a desire for friendship nor for peace with you." In fact, they would not so much as take a hint from Sir C. Malet, and in all their conduct showed a determination to set the Nizam's minister absolutely aside. On this issue the negotiation came to a stand-still, and the whole correspondence having been transmitted to Sir J. Shore, he made a judicial summary of the circumstances in a despatch to the Resident, which is inserted in the Appendix as expressing fully the views of the English government at this point of the dispute.[1]

It will be seen that the question, at the stage it had now reached, was viewed by Sir John Shore as one of relative superiority between the two powers; and he had no doubt that the Mahratta government would be successful if the dispute came to a warlike issue.[2] Though he was of opinion that ample powers to proceed with the negotiation had been granted to Meer Allum, if no personal animosity had existed between the ministers, he advised that the powers of a plenipotentiary should be conferred on him, inasmuch as the possession of such power would not oblige him to agree to anything unreasonable. Besides, the Peishwa, whether he entertained any secret project or not, would then be compelled to show his hand; and if it were deemed advisable to

---

[1] Appendix O.

[2] See a statement of the respective strength of the two armies, in Appendix P.

yield certain points against which the minister had hitherto protested, his personal feeling of dignity would be spared. It is evident from other parts of this letter that the Government felt itself placed in difficult circumstances. On the one hand, both the Mahrattas and the Sultan of Mysore appeared to be looking forward to the division of the Nizam's spoils in the event of his dissolution; on the other, appeared a want of candour on the part of the Hyderabad government which involved its affairs in the most disastrous obscurity. The only practical advice that could now be given to our Resident was that he should remain with the Nizam so long as his highness kept within his own dominions, but by no means accompany him in an attack on the Peishwa's territory. A personal meeting between the two rulers was suggested in the despatch, but with little hope that it could be brought to pass.

In estimating the chances of still avoiding a conflict, we must not forget the domestic embarrassments of the Peishwa, of which some interesting particulars may here be given.

When the late Mahadajee Scindiah came to Poonah in 1792, he had committed the administration of affairs in Hindostan to Gopaul Ram Bhow, the brother of Appa Chitnavees, his principal minister. He did not, however, rely for the security of his immense acquisitions in the north during his absence solely on the attachment or talents of Gopaul, but left several other chieftains behind him in charge of considerable armies, and in possession of extensive authority; all of them in a certain degree immediately responsible to himself, and some of them, as he well knew, the political rivals of his Lieutenant. Chief among the latter were Jaragee Bakshie, Ambajee, Appa Pellaulah Rao, and Luckwah Dadda. The first of these was placed at the head of a strong force, and held a kind of independent command. The second likewise exercised a separate jurisdiction, in which was included the care of the important fortress of Gwalior; the third had charge of the fort of Delhi, and, along with it, of the person of the unfortunate Shah Allum; while the last-mentioned, Luckwa Dadda, was entrusted with the government of Agra, the walls of which confined a person of still greater account than the successor of Timour. This was the Mogul chieftain, Emaun Ismail Bey, who had so often by his persevering valour shaken the Mahratta power in Hindostan to its very foundation, and who, in all probability, would still have proved its most formidable enemy, had he through any caprice of fortune recovered his liberty.

In addition to the above leaders may be mentioned a M. de Boigne, commander of a brigade of regular troops officered by Frenchmen, which was employed under Jarajee Bakshie, though this body in general was considered as peculiarly attached to Gopaul Rao. The influence of M. de Boigne must have been considerable, as Gopaul Rao seems always to have been impressed with the importance of conciliating him, and Mahadajee Scindiah had relied more upon M. de Boigne and his regular corps, than upon the whole of his Mahratta forces.

Such were the forces of whose action in any complication that might arise, the Peishwa could not be absolutely assured, seeing that Appa Chitnavees, in concert with his brother Gopaul, had intrigued to subvert the power of Scindiah,[1] and granting that such elements of discord existed they might explode at any time. For the present, Appa Sahib was able to promise the strenuous co-operation of Dowlut Rao in the prosecution of the Peishwa's designs against the Nizam, because however inimical to the true interests of his master (Scindiah), the service was not ill-calculated to promote his own, by furnishing him with a plausible reason for summoning Jarajee Bakshie, the first of the above-named commanders, to the Deccan. Nor was the removal of this chieftain from Hindostan of importance

---

[1] As before alluded to, *ante*, p. 103.

merely because it would completely rid Gopaul Rao of an odious and troublesome rival, but because by materially weakening the Sunnovi party in the North (who were the ancient antagonists of Appa Sahib), it would facilitate his projects for their utter overthrow.

Accordingly Jarajee Bakshie, with a brigade of M. de Boigne's command, and a body of cavalry were ordered to proceed to Poonah by the route of Oojein with all possible expedition. The Sunnovi faction was at once aroused by the danger which threatened them, and so bestirred themselves that Appa Sahib was disgraced and a new ministry formed from the party of his enemies; of whose co-operation in the designs of the Peishwa the latter would have no certain assurance; besides which, it was impossible to say what turn matters might take in the North. The opportunity, perhaps, would have been favorable for the Hyderabad government, had it been seized with the necessary address, and it was believed at the time that some negotiation had been commenced, but no results are on record.

Up to this time Azim-ool-oomrah had been culpably negligent in the duty of concentrating troops at Bidur; but he now considered it necessary to call on the several Jagheerdars to join the Nizam's standard with their quotas of troops. Among those who obeyed the call was Allif Khan, the Nawab of Kurnool, whose adhesion it was feared would be a fresh cause of annoyance to Tippoo Sultan, for reasons which have been already explained. The folly of the minister in having extended the invitation to him was fully discussed at this time by our Resident, and the court of Hyderabad was again assured that if any quarrel with Tippoo should be the consequence of its pretensions to the lordship of Kurnool, it was the positive determination of our Government to consider itself released from the defensive engagement which had been contracted with his highness by the treaty of Seringapatam.

About the middle of November, some portion of the Mahratta arms was moved towards Bidur, and his highness, considering this movement the preliminary of hostilities, began to think of sending forward a division of his army, by way of counter demonstration. Having asked the Resident's opinion whether such a measure of precaution could be adopted without incurring the imputation of aggression, the latter, with his usual judgment, replied that his highness's ministers were alone competent to decide whether the meditated movement were expedient or not. The advanced body was to consist of Assud Ally Khan's ressalah, amounting to 5,000 horse, and part of M. Raymond's corps, of whom more hereafter. In addition to which Azim-ool-oomrah signified his wish to have the Company's detachment ordered to Bidur, for the purpose of attending the person of his highness, who, he took occasion to mention, had no intention at present to proceed beyond Kurstanch, whither he had marched, ostensibly with a view to hunting. The Resident resisted this application with every argument in his power; and eventually the Company's troops took post near Hyderabad for the purpose of restraining any of the neighbouring Zemindars, whom the absence of the Nizam, and existing circumstances, might tempt to disturb the tranquillity of the city and its environs.

This result was by no means what the minister desired, and, as on former occasions, when his wish to use the troops contrary to treaty had been thwarted, he threatened to dispense with them altogether. On this point, however, he again changed his mind, but being determined to have some Europeans attached to the Nizam's army, and subject to no orders but his own, he commissioned M. Raymond, a Frenchman, to recruit both Europeans and natives. He even requested Captain Kirkpatrick to apply to the Company for *the loan* of French prisoners taken at Pondicherry, and for a general permission to levy recruits in the Company's district.

Our Resident, with all his anxiety to be of service

to his highness, was grieved that requests should be made with which he knew that it was utterly impossible the Company could comply; and he signified to the minister that such must be the case with regard to any application involving the aid of troops; and as for borrowing prisoners, the possibility of such a proceeding had never been thought of by the English.

The detached force under Assud Ally Khan, which had been sent forward by the Nizam, to watch the Mahrattas, was composed of the flower of his army. The cavalry was only second in efficiency to the command of Shumsh-ool-oomrah, which constituted his highness's body-guard; and the infantry, numbering twenty-three battalions of Raymond's corps, were supported by a very respectable body of artillery. At first, it was in contemplation to place Secunder Jah at the head of this detachment, but the idea was relinquished, and the Nizam's own movements were determined by those of the Peishwa. In the meantime, considering the Peishwa's intentions sufficiently proved by the advance of a large detachment of his army to Bidur as already mentioned, the Hyderabad durbar had signified its intention to recall Meer Allum, whose further continuance at Poonah did not seem to promise any advantage.

Yet, threatening as these appearances were, the

domestic embarrassments of the Peishwa had by no means diminished. An overture made by Scindiah's minister to the Hyderabad durbar, proved that he was extremely anxious to return to Hindostan, nor could the court of Poonah itself, whose political stake in that quarter was scarcely less than Scindiah's, have been insensible to the necessity of his presence there. Overruling this, for the moment, however, Scindiah was commanded by the Peishwa to move his forces in the direction of the Nizam's frontier; and this demonstration was followed by the immediate march of his highness, who entered his tents at Kurstanch, on the 17th of November. At the same time he detached a considerable part of his army for the purpose of resisting any attempt that might be made to levy contributions on the Hyderabad territory.

The two armies having thus taken the field, a detailed account of their respective strength will possess considerable interest. It will be seen from the tables in the Appendix,[1] that the Mahratta force greatly outnumbered the Nizam's; the former having consisted of some 84,000 cavalry, 38,000 infantry, and 192 guns; the latter of 45,000 cavalry, 44,000 infantry, and 108 guns. Both armies had some very efficient troops officered by Europeans under the respective

---

[1] Appendix P.

commands of M. de Boigne and M. Raymond. Such were the armies between which hostilities became every day more imminent, and which eventually came to blows with results that will rather surprise the reader not already acquainted with them.

CHAPTER XI.

THE ARBITRAMENT OF WAR.

The real Causes of the Hostilities now impending not known to the English Government—Peculiar Character of Indian Diplomacy generally—Character of the Mahrattas—Strict Neutrality preserved by the English Government—Minute of Sir John Shore on our Relations with the Nizam—Retrospective Summary of Events preceding the Treaty—Circumstances subsequent to it—The Nizam's Claim to our Assistance on the ground of Treaty Obligations, considered—The Nizam's Arguments stated, and the Reply to them—The Question argued on the ground of Expediency—Sir J. Shore's Reflections on the Situation generally—The Alliances that presented themselves, viewed with regard to British Interests—Meer Allum fears for his Safety at Poonah—Movements of the Nizam's Army—Troops under the Command of M. Raymond—The Nizam and his Minister appeal to the Resident for Advice—The Nizam reviews his Troops in the Presence of the Mahratta Vakeel—Singular Proposal—Further Attempts to compromise — Sudden Advance of the Nizam's Army—The Battle of Kurdlah—Retreat of the Nizam, and his Army—Compelled to treat for Peace, and accept the Conditions imposed by the Mahrattas—Azim-ool-oomrah sent to Poonah as a Hostage—Return of the Nizam to Hyderabad.

Although the armies of the Peishwa and the Nizam almost faced each other in the field, the real eause of dissension was still a mystery, at least to the English Government. It is true that certain claims of inferior importance had been brought forward for discussion; but it is equally obvious that the more important points of difference known to the native princes by the term of *kulliat*, had been industriously concealed from our knowledge. There could be no mistake in concluding on the present occasion that the Mahrattas had objects in view which they were determined at all hazards to accomplish. Why they proceeded with so little vigour, and continued to grope in the dark, as it were, can hardly be explained. Something, however, must be allowed for their usual habits of procrastination, and perhaps for the unavoidable retardment of their preparations for war, in addition to the imminent danger of intestine disaffection to which I have already alluded. Finally, they may have been influenced by the expectation that the Nizam would submit to their demands rather than suffer the quarrel to proceed to extremities.

The reader who has followed my narrative thus far, and especially if he has also read with attention the accompanying documents in the Appendix, will not require to be told that the English Government had adhered strictly to the policy of neutrality. It must not be supposed, however, that in refusing to support the Nizam against the Mahrattas, the Government were insensible to the probability of events occurring which might result in a fundamental change of the political situation of affairs in India. In a minute dated March the 2nd, 1795, Sir John Shore placed on record, for the information of the Board of Directors, his views in connection with the probability of an attack being made on the Hyderabad territory by Tippoo, either as a confederate of the Mahrattas, or independently, during the threatened hostilities between the Peishwa and the Nizam; which minute commences with the remark that "the only treaties which have reference to this question are those concluded at Paungul and Poonah, with the Nizam and Mahrattas, under the title of offensive and defensive alliance, in June and July 1790."

The preamble to the treaty with the Nizam specifies three parties to it, and explains that the alliance is against Tippoo Sultan. The first article confirms the friendship subsisting between the three states in virtue of former treaties. The second declares that in consequence of Tippoo having violated his engagements with the contracting powers, they have united in a league to punish him to the utmost of their ability, and to deprive him of the means of disturbing the general tranquillity in future. The third and subsequent articles, to the 9th inclusive, relate to the prosecution of the war, and to objects connected with it—to the distribution of the conquered territories, and to the mode of making peace. The 10th article in the Treaty of Paungul, which is the 13th in that of Poonah, reads as follows:—"*If after the conclusion of peace with Tippoo, he should attack or molest either of the contracting parties, the others shall join to punish him, the mode and conditions of effecting which shall be hereafter settled by the contracting parties.*"

From this summary of its contents, there can be no doubt of the meaning of the treaty as the record of an alliance between three states for a declared object, with a prospective clause for the future security of all the contending parties against a common enemy. But to ascertain, with all possible accuracy, the nature of the obligations thus entered into, I will now advert to the negotiations by which it was preceded, and to the discussions of the quoted article at periods subsequent to the war.

When Tippoo Sultan invaded Travancore,[1] it was notified to our Residents at Hyderabad and Poonah, that the Government intended to support its ally, and they were instructed to invite the co-operation of the Nizam and the Peishwa against Tippoo. Before the arrival of these instructions at Poonah, the Mahratta Government had volunteered a declaration of its

[1] *Ante*, Chap. V.

readiness to aid the Company in the expected war, and thus had made the first advance to confidence without solicitation or sacrifice on our part. The Nizam, equally ready after receiving the communication of our Resident, declared that the Governor General's resolve happily coincided with his own intention to oppose Tippoo after concerting a plan of attack with the Peishwa; but without waiting to ascertain the disposition of the latter, he now promised his hearty co-operation with the English Government. He therefore claimed the merit of a ready compliance with the Governor General's wish, and of an earlier commencement of hostilities than he had before contemplated.

The promise of the Nizam's co-operation was followed up by a somewhat astute question addressed to the Resident. If, he said, during the absence of his army, the Peishwa should form an alliance with Tippoo Sultan, and invade his (the Nizam's) dominions, what would be the course of action adopted by the Company? The reply of the Resident, which he acknowledged to be an unguarded one, was to the effect that *the Company ought to sacrifice their all in his highness's defence.* Not unnaturally, therefore, the minister requested that Lord Cornwallis would signify in general terms that any attempt to disturb the peace of his highness's dominions, whilst engaged with us in the war against Tippoo, would be regarded in the same light as an attempt to disturb those of the Company. Indeed, he had previously expressed his wish that the defensive alliance should be made general, and both the Nizam and his minister had evinced a disposition to connect themselves by the closest ties with our Government.

This request having been communicated to the Governor General, his lordship pointed out that as the Mahrattas had so heartily acceded to the confederacy, it would be highly improper in him to entertain the supposition that they were inclined to treat one of their own allies with injustice. He expressed his willingness, however, provided the Mahrattas did not positively object, to insert an additional article in the proposed treaty, stipulating that in case of differences arising between any two of the confederates, the third party to the treaty should be bound to interpose his good offices, with a view to an amicable adjustment. His lordship added, that *should an article to that effect be assented to by the Poonah Government*, and his interference be called for in consequence of it, the Nizam might always rest assured of his disposition to save his highness from the necessity of submitting to injury.[1] Thus far the circumstances which preceded the treaty.

[1] See letter embodied in Sir J. Shore's Minute, Appendix Q.

With respect to circumstances bearing on this subject which occurred subsequent to the treaty, it will be remembered that at the period of general pacification at Seringapatam, a guarantee treaty was talked of.[1] The proposal was made to Lord Cornwallis by Hurry Punt on the part of the Mahrattas, and by Azim-ool-oomrah on the part of the Nizam, by each of whom it was thought desirable to explain in full the 13th article of the Treaty of Poonah, and the 10th of that of Paungul, with a view to a more precise rendering of their terms, and to a specification of the course to be pursued by the three contracting parties in the event of the further molestation of any one of them by Tippoo Sultan. Without referring in detail to the negotiations which followed this proposal, it will suffice, in the first place, to quote the written declaration which the Residents were directed to deliver to their respective courts in case of any evasion or backwardness in entering into the proposed explanation being manifested, viz. :—"That we considered the three parties to be bound to each other, to act with their whole force against Tippoo in the event of his attacking either of them without clear and just provocation, but in no other case whatever." Secondly, to remind the reader that the

---

[1] *Ante*, Chap. V., end.

draft of an explanatory treaty was prepared by Lord Cornwallis, and transmitted to our Residents at Hyderabad and Poonah, by whom it was explained to the ministers of their respective courts. Thirdly, that the Mahrattas demanded time for consideration, but that Azim-ool-oomrah positively declared his resolution not to agree to it until his master's request concerning Kurnool had been complied with. Fourthly, that he afterwards withdrew this declaration, and expressed his assent to the propositions of Lord Cornwallis, without waiting for the adhesion of the Mahrattas. Fifthly, that the Mahrattas themselves had prepared the draft of an explanatory treaty; and, finally, that the discussion had long since been brought to a close, without arriving at any specific result. The Mahrattas, however, had made a satisfactory declaration of their readiness to act agreeably to existing treaties, and the Nizam had expressed his acquiescence in the draft which had been prepared by Lord Cornwallis.

Such were the facts; from which it is evident that the obligation incurred by our Government was one to which the Nizam and the Peishwa were both parties, and that a concurrent responsibility had been assumed by the three Governments to unite in defence of any one of them who should be attacked by Tippoo Sultan. The Nizam, however, reasoned that we were imperatively bound to assist him, if in a war between himself and the Peishwa, the latter should form an alliance with Tippoo. He argued, with some plausibility, that the defection of one party to a treaty could not exonerate the other from the obligations that had been incurred; that his reliance in making the treaty had been upon our good faith, as he well knew the treachery of which the Mahrattas were capable, and had even intimated his suspicions of them during the preliminary negotiations; that our own interests had dictated the necessity of an alliance with him, whether the Mahrattas had become a party to the confederacy or not; and that an aggression by Tippoo Sultan in concert with the Mahrattas was only a more insulting violation of the treaty, which we were obliged in good faith to resent.

The answer to these plausible arguments is obvious. We were bound by different treaties with the Nizam and the Peishwa not to assist their enemies, and we participated with both in a guarantee for reciprocal security against Tippoo. By the first obligation we were compelled to be neutral between the Nizam and the Mahrattas; by the second, we united with them, and they with us, in mutual support against Tippoo. This very stipulation involved the continuance of amity between the three contracting parties, and the treaty was subverted in principle by the occurrence of hostilities between any two of them.

The question, in fact, reduced to its simplest form, was this :—Were we to regard the treaty of Paungul as a separate and independent agreement between us and the Nizam, or was it contracted with him and the Mahrattas conjointly? All the terms in which it was expressed proved it to be a tripartite alliance against a presumed enemy, who was to be opposed by the joint efforts of all. To the argument that the secession of one party from his treaty obligations cannot be held to release the other, it is sufficient to reply that the necessity of action in the supposed eventualities involves the risk of a war with one of the parties to the treaty,—a case which certainly had never been supposed, and which was utterly opposed to all the stipulations upon which the treaty was framed. As to the remaining arguments, they are all answered by the fact that the Nizam and the Peishwa were disposed to make war upon Tippoo previous to the alliance, and the only merit that either could claim in these transactions was, that they were induced to commence their operations at an earlier period than they had at first proposed.

With respect to the clause which had been proposed conditionally by Lord Cornwallis,[1] it formed no part of the treaty, and it is evident that it would not have been consented to by the Mahrattas.

---

[1] *Ante*, p. 121.

In discussing the nature and force of the obligations imposed on us by the treaty, we were not to be biassed by any considerations of the weakness of the Nizam, and the probability of an attack upon him only. Such considerations properly belonged to the question when argued on the ground of *expediency*, and we shall find immediately, that Sir J. Shore did not fail to present the whole matter in that light in the minute from which I have derived the preceding arguments.

It is important to observe here, however, that although the occurrence of hostilities between the Nizam and the Mahrattas would have the effect of dissolving all existing treaties between them, yet they each remained bound by the conditions of the joint treaties with us. It is true they could not have assisted us while at war with each other, in case of an attack by Tippoo Sultan on the possessions of the Company; but in case of peace being restored between them, the power of fulfilling the stipulations of the treaties would return. Accordingly, Sir John Shore was careful to point out that if Tippoo were to attack either the Nizam or the Mahrattas while they were at war with each other, our proper course would be to call upon the third party to comply with the stipulations of the treaty by which he was bound in common with ourselves. If this did not induce the two parties at war to resume peaceful relations with each other, it would show, at any rate, that Tippoo's attack was made by concert with one of them, who would thus be convicted of a direct breach of the treaty. We should then be at liberty to act as we judged right under the circumstances.

It clearly appears from this argument that our government was not bound to assist either the Nizam or the Peishwa against Tippoo, unless peace was first established between the former. The question of our treaty obligations being thus disposed of, that of political expediency comes under consideration.

Sir John Shore was aware that the Nizam, after all that could be said on the question of obligation, would consider we had deserted his cause if we refused our co-operation against Tippoo; and would thus think himself ill repaid for his co-operation with us, and the anxiety he had always expressed to enter into the closest relationship of amity. Obviously, he had always been friendly or inimical to us according as it suited his immediate views. If, then, with or without reason, he should feel it no longer served his purpose to cultivate our friendship—if we refused him our support against the joint invasion of his territories by Tippoo Sultan and the Mahrattas—would not our own friendly alliance with him be endangered?

Not only so, but on the supposition of nothing occurring to break the supposed alliance between

Tippoo and the Mahrattas, the Nizam's power would certainly be destroyed, and that of his enemies aggrandized. Both the Sultan and the Mahrattas in that case would become proportionately dangerous to us, and this would be the natural consequence of leaving the Nizam without support.

On the other hand, the impossibility of directing his politics without usurping his government, and the danger of perpetual war, in case of our interference, claimed consideration. The inducement to support the Nizam at the hazard of such consequences, ought surely to be much stronger than the apprehension of future evils from the subversion of his power. And after all, perhaps, nay most probably, that event would take place before we could render him any effectual assistance, and it could not but be exceedingly doubtful if any efforts of ours would procure his re-establishment.

Considering this question still further, in the light of expediency, the situation of affairs in Europe could not be overlooked; for it was such as to preclude all hope of receiving reinforcements of troops from home. It was therefore imperative on us by every possible effort to preserve peace with all the powers in India.

Still another consideration presented itself. Should the power of the Nizam be destroyed by the combination of Tippoo Sultan and the Peishwa, it was just as probable that the latter would afterwards attack each other, as that they would unite to invade the territories of the Company. If it proved otherwise, the careful husbanding and accumulation of our resources would enable us to offer a more successful resistance to the confederacy; and though our political consequence might lose something of its importance in the estimation of the native powers by leaving the Nizam to his fate, this consideration could not be allowed to outweigh the evils attending a war with Tippoo and the Mahrattas, which we should certainly provoke by assisting the Nizam in the way he demanded.

Sir J. Shore added to these arguments (which, it will be observed, are all based on the supposition of the Nizam, that he was about to be attacked by the Mahrattas and Tippoo Sultan, acting in concert,) his own reflections on the situation generally. He was of opinion that there was no likelihood of such an alliance unless we ourselves provoked it by lending our support to the Nizam; and in reviewing the probable alliances that would be formed under such circumstances, he pointed out that the Rajah of Berar and other northern feudatories would naturally fall over to the Mahrattas; and would be assisted by the forces under the French general, De Boigne, which were alone equal to two English brigades. Then, briefly reviewing the powers which held all India, he expressed his opinion that an alliance, offensive and defensive, with the Nizam would never enable us to hold the balance between them. He reminded the Board that the British territories on the Ganges were open to invasion by Cuttack on the west, and, including the Vizier's dominions, on the north likewise; and finally concluded his very masterly document by a coup d'œil of our position in India, and of the policy which we ought to pursue. This important State document, which embraces many more points of interest than I have here indicated, is given at length in the Appendix.[1]

To resume the narrative of events, it must be obvious to the reader who has had the patience to follow me thus far, that hostilities between the states of Hyderabad and Poonah could not long be averted. Meer Allum, who was still at Poonah, was not without fears for his personal safety in the event of war being declared; and accordingly was anxious to receive his dismissal from the Peishwa's court. The Nizam's advanced army, under the command of Rajah Tegewunt, was already ordered to the pass of Dharoor, under the conviction, perhaps, that some attempt was intended by the Mahrattas on the Dowlatabad side of the Deccan. This movement, however, was subsequently countermanded; the Nizam being averse to

---

[1] Appendix Q.

the division of his forces, and having little confidence in the military talents of the chieftains stationed with the advanced army.

The most efficient part of the Nizam's forces were the troops commanded by M. Raymond, a Frenchman. Of these, I shall have to speak more particularly in that part of my narrative which relates to the progress made by the French in the Deccan.

The aversion felt by the Mahrattas to the interposition of the Company's government between them and the Nizam was shown unequivocally at this time. Captain Kirkpatrick having inquired, through Sir W. C. Malet, whether any objection would be made to his presence in the field with the Nizam's forces, was told that the Peishwa did most decidedly object to such a proceeding; and this, although the Nizam had previously expressed his acquiescence in the proposal of Sir W. C. Malet to accompany the Peishwa. His highness the Nizam retaliated by withdrawing the permission he had already granted. Subsequently, as we shall see, the resolution on both sides was again revoked.

After this, his highness the Nizam made several attempts to elicit from Captain Kirkpatrick his opinion in regard to the disposition he had made of his forces; the Resident always replying that his inexperience in tactics totally disqualified him for judging of such matters. As an illustration of the adroitness with which these questions were put, and the prudence required in answering them, Captain Kirkpatrick was one day invited by his highness to one of his tents, on the pretence of viewing the river Manjeerah from a remarkably favourable point. Here he found the minister, Azim-ool-oomrah, who led on the discourse until, in the most natural manner, he commenced describing the several passes by which the army might descend from the Balaghaut. So talking, he by-and-by asked the opinion of Captain Kirkpatrick as to which of these routes he thought the most eligible. Instead of directly replying to this question, the Resident, addressing himself to the Nizam, appealed to his candour whether he could, with the smallest propriety, considering the friendship subsisting between the Company and the Peishwa, offer any opinion on so delicate a subject. The minister then demanded what was to prevent Captain Kirkpatrick; and observed that the privacy of his present audience had been purposely arranged to guard against the disclosure of his advice. Captain Kirkpatrick, still addressing himself to the Nizam personally, demanded, in his turn, what his highness would expect from Sir W. C. Malet, were the Peishwa to consult with him respecting the best mode of attacking the army of Hyderabad. "I know," interrupted Azim-ool-oomrah, "that the answer of Sir Charles Malet would be the same that you have so often given me; he would advise a speedy adjustment of all subsisting differences, as absolutely necessary to the welfare of both sides." "And this," said Captain Kirkpatrick, "is the only reply it is now possible for me to give to the question which has been put to me." With this the interview terminated.

I have already enumerated the forces which either side at this time had marshalled in the field ready for battle.[1] On the 14th of February, 1795, the Nizam arrived at Paijory, and on the 16th he reviewed the advanced army. M. Raymond's corps, consisting of twenty-eight battalions, was then encamped within about two coss of the rear of Moorighaut. It thus constituted the most advanced wing.

The review was witnessed, at his highness's request, by Govind Row Kishen, the Mahratta Vakeel resident at the Nizam's court; who was so impressed by the display of force, that his reports to his own

---

[1] See detailed statement of the Mahratta army, and of the forces with which the Nizam descended the Moorighaut on the 4th of March, 1795, at the end of the previous chapter.

court are said to have occasioned considerable anxiety. However this may have been, the Vakeel was so desirous of preventing the Nizam from descending the Moorighaut, as he contemplated—in other words, from taking the Parinda route—that he made one of the most singular proposals ever heard of, with a view to the resumption of negotiations. He truly stated that nothing could avert immediate hostilities if his highness should persevere in his intention to descend the Moorighaut; yet he acknowledged that the Nizam could not possibly remain where he was, on account of the scarcity of forage. In order to keep the field without inconvenience, and without the risk of immediate hostilities, it occurred to him that both armies might be moved from the positions they now occupied to the banks of the Godavery, and he actually suggested certain stations which he thought would suit both the Peishwa and the Nizam; the former fifteen coss, the latter twenty-six coss, from Aurungabad, and distant from each other about fourteen coss. Strange to say, this proposal was assented to by the Nizam, at the instance of his minister, and Govind Row Kishen engaged to obtain the determination of his own court upon it in five days.

It is difficult to conceive by what argument the Nizam had been induced to accept a proposal so fraught with mischief to his affairs, It was with good reason supposed that the original intention of the Peishwa was to advance upon Aurungabad, and the advance of the Nizam's troops in the direction of Parinda had been calculated to act as a check, by threatening the safety of Poonah, and exposing the rear of the Mahratta force to attack. The proposed transfer of the operations of the war to the banks of the Godavery, on the other hand, seemed to give every advantage to the Mahrattas. Yet the latter finally determined not to move their forces, but await the proposed negotiations in the situation then occupied by the two armies. These singular circumstances would seem to indicate some ground of mistrust on either side, of which no explanation can now be given.

In this situation a letter was received by Amjud-ool-Moolk, the guardian of Shums-ool-oomrah, representing that the Peishwa was desirous of nothing so much as an accommodation of the differences between him and the Nizam, but that it was necessary some other agency than that of Azim-ool-oomrah should be employed to effect it. Thus the old stumbling-block of personal animosity again stood in the way of an arrangement, for although Amjud-ool-Moolk put this letter into the hands of the Nizam, it soon found its way into those of the minister, whom, I need not say, it failed to convince of the necessity of self-sacrifice.

At first, this letter was supposed to have been written by Roy Royan, Meer Allum's colleague, but it afterwards came out that it was from Balaji Pundit himself.

All idea of compromise was now abandoned, and on the 4th of March the Nizam's army suddenly broke ground, and marched to the banks of a stream called the Khyree, which stretches in a westerly direction from the bottom of the Moorighaut, having the town of Wakigung about two miles distant in its rear. In this position the advance of the Nizam's army was not more than nine or ten miles distant from the force under Dowlat Row Scindiah. The movement was occasioned by authentic intelligence that the Peishwa intended to occupy the banks of the Khyree, which would have had the effect of closing the Moorighaut pass, had not his highness assumed the initiative.

On the 11th of March the Nizam began to move his army from Wakigung in the direction of Parinda; and in so doing subjected his rear to a distant cannonade from the heights occupied by the Mahrattas to the right of the line of march. In consequence of this, the troops were halted until M. Raymond's corps and several bodies of cavalry were brought from the left, in order to keep the enemy in check. The march was then resumed, but the troops and the baggage were mingled together in disorder, and as a halt was made as often as the Mahrattas fired again, it was sunset before they reached the river on which it was proposed to encamp. On account of the proximity of the two armies some skirmishing now took place; two or three chiefs of distinction were slain, and Assud Ally, with one or two more, wounded. The casualties, it must be admitted, were very slight.

But the Mahratta cannonade became warmer than before, and Raymond's corps, supported by the cavalry, fell back upon the ground where the Nizam's troops were about to encamp for the night. This they might still have done in safety, and resumed the march towards Parinda the next morning; but some time after dark, when the action was supposed to be over, a body of Mahratta infantry was pushed forward against Raymond, and saluted his line with a volley of musketry, the cannonade at the same time being smartly renewed, and a little rocket practice indulged in. There is nothing to show that any great impression was made on Raymond's line by this attack, yet soon after 11 o'clock the Nizam commanded an instant retreat to Kurdlah, and he himself led the way accompanied by the ladies of his palace. The immediate consequences were not so fatal as they might have been, if the Mahratta chieftains had conceived it possible that his highness could be so causelessly dismayed. Yet the event was serious enough. The greater part of the Nizam's army, without fighting a battle, and even without suffering anything worthy of being called a discomfiture, fled.

On the morning of the 12th, the light troops of the enemy discovered this unlooked-for movement, and took advantage of it accordingly. The reports of the loss of baggage, guns, brinjarries, &c., are too vague to be mentioned, but the confusion must have been great, and the captures very considerable. The small fort of Kurdlah, in which the Nizam had shut himself up with his family, was immediately invested by the Mahrattas, and after a strict blockade of several weeks, his highness was compelled to sue for mercy, and to conclude a treaty under the enemy's dictation, to the particulars of which we shall presently advert.

It is but just to observe of men who were never deficient in personal courage, that the officers of the Nizam's durbar were anxious to try the fortune of war with the Mahrattas, but no argument would tempt the Nizam to hazard a battle. Doubtless, there were many serious imperfections in the constitution of his military force, but (speaking with reference to the enemy they had to oppose) there were no defects of so radical a nature that a single campaign would not have remedied, and such as they were, the disaster of the 11th of March could not in reason be attributed to them; the sole cause being the apparent pusillanimity of the Nizam himself. Even this admits of some explanation, for neither had his highness ever showed himself wanting in firmness. It is probable that the weakness manifested on this occasion arose entirely from his solicitude for the safety of the ladies of his palace. In all probability, his intention had been to place them in safety, and at the same time secure all his heavy baggage in the fort of Parinda, in which case he would have taken the field with his accustomed vigour.

From a newsletter, written soon after the battle of Kurdlah, and inserted at length in the Appendix,[1] we learn with what resolution the Peishwa and his minister still insisted on the dismissal of Azim-ool-oomrah, as one of the conditions of peace.

It was finally stipulated that he should remain in office two months, in order to afford time for the settlement of his accounts with the Nizam, and that, at the expiration of that time, he was to be sent to Poonah as a hostage for the due fulfilment of every part of the engagement now entered into. It will be seen on reference to the letter that the Nizam did not consent to sacrifice his minister without a struggle; indeed, there are many passages in the letter which reflect honour upon both. I may add here, that when, in the course of these final negotiations, the Peishwa demanded, not only that Azim-ool-oomrah should be

---

[1] Appendix R.

dismissed, but that he should be delivered to *him*, the Nizam was so exasperated that he ordered his equipage, and would have headed his army in an attack, if the minister had not persuaded him to act with prudence and continue the negotiations.

On the 1st of April, the terms of peace were definitively settled, and his highness reascended the ghaut on his return to Hyderabad. The treaty was based on that of Eadgheer. The Nizam agreed to relinquish territory, including Dowlatabad, yielding about thirty-five lacs of rupees per annum,[1] and besides this, to pay three crores and ten lacs of rupees to the Peishwa at the present time. Out of the latter sum the Rajah of Berar's claim against the Nizam was satisfied.[2] His highness now caused it to be officially signified to Captain Kirkpatrick that he had no further occasion for the detachment of Company's troops serving in his country, and requested that they might be ordered at once to return to the Company's territories, which was accordingly done.

Meer Allum returned from his mission to the Peishwa, about the 5th April, 1795. On the 7th May, his highness the Nizam re-entered his capital under a salute of all the ordnance mounted on its walls!

---

[1] For details of the ceded territory, see Appendix S.

[2] For details of the division of the three crores and ten lacs of rupees with the Rajah of Berar, see Appendix T.

CHAPTER XII.

PROGRESS OF THE FRENCH.

Efficiency of the Troops under French Officers—Prospect of the French becoming Arbitrators of the Deccan—The Nizam induced to employ them by our Refusal to co-operate against the Mahrattas.—Plausibility of the French Commander-in-chief, M. Raymond—His Projects are mistrusted by the Resident—Designs upon Kurpah, and probable Co-operation of the French on the Coromandel Coast—The Resident objects to the Employment of his Corps in Kurpah—Modified Plans of the Nizam, and continued Remonstrances of the Resident—Indications of M. Raymond's ulterior Designs—French Officers from Pondicherry arrive at Hyderabad—Submission of the Talookdar of Kurpah—Renewed Remonstrances of the Resident—Proposal to employ English Troops in Kurpah—Compromise of the Points in Dispute—The Residents appoint a Newswriter in the French Camp.

In this and the four following chapters, I propose to give such details as may be interesting to the reader, relative to the progress made by the French in establishing themselves at Hyderabad, until, as the result of our policy, they were finally dismissed from the service of the Nizam. An eye-witness of some of the events I am about to relate, referred to the circumstances at a subsequent period in the following words, which I quote as a suitable introduction to the subject.

He begins with the emphatic declaration, "that the progress the French had made, and were still making, would soon have made them arbitrators of the Deccan," and then observes, "their discipline and appointments, though inferior to our own, were far above those of any troops commanded by natives, and the regularity with which they had been paid since their first formation, not only enabled them to recruit with facility, and to fill their ranks with the best men of our Northern Circars, but to entice deserters by bodies from our service. The more their power is contemplated, the more cause have we to congratulate ourselves on the complete success which has crowned the sound policy which dictated the reduction of a corps so formidable. The happy manner in which that has been accomplished is calculated in the greatest degree to establish our influence on the firmest basis, and cannot fail to impress both the court and others with the highest idea of our wisdom and power."

The reader who has had patience enough to follow my historical sketch thus far, is aware of the manner in which we refused to co-operate with the Nizam against the Mahrattas. This refusal, there can be no doubt, caused the Nizam to entertain with eagerness the tender of their services made by French officers; and when, after the battle of Kurdlah, our auxiliary force was dismissed from Hyderabad,[1] his highness determined to substitute for them efficient French auxiliaries. On his return to the capital, M. Raymond visited the Nizam, and took considerable pains to impress him with an idea of the irresistible power of the French. Our Resident, on his part, could but oppose to the false and exaggerated statements thus insidiously made, a general and candid statement of facts, adding such comments as were calculated to show the probability of an early peace in Europe, which it was reasonable to suppose was not less necessary to the French than to the powers confederated against them.

Captain Kirkpatrick felt no confidence in M. Raymond personally, knowing well that he and, with one or two exceptions, all the officers of his corps were imbued with the democratic principles of the revolution; yet he felt less solicitude on this account, so long as these well-disciplined troops seemed necessary to the Nizam as a means of resisting the

---

[1] *Ante*, p. 140.

encroachments of the Mahrattas, and enabling him to maintain his independence. Since the conclusion of peace, the case was altogether different, for, as little prospect existed of M. Raymond being called into immediate action either against exterior or interior enemies, his activity and enterprise would naturally be directed into other channels. Accordingly it soon transpired that Raymond's corps, which had lost about 3,000 men during the war, was about to be reinstated in its full strength, and that his highness intended to provide for its maintenance by bestowing a jagheer on the commander. Not only so, but that M. Raymond himself was using all his endeavours to obtain Kurpah and other districts, which would have placed him along an extensive line of the Company's frontier in the Carnatic. In possession of these territories, M. Raymond would have been ready to co-operate with any French force that should have effected a descent upon the Coromandel coast, with or without the concurrence of the Nizam, and with abundant resources at his command. Under these circumstances, Captain Kirkpatrick felt that he could not be too vigilant; and, fully sensible of the amount of tact that would be required to counteract the systematic deceit and corruption of the French party, he determined to lose no opportunity of checking its further progress.

An occasion presented itself on the 17th of May (1795), when Meer Allum informed the Resident, that it had been resolved in Durbar, to revoke the appointment of Mohammed Ameen Khan Arab as governor of the Kurpah district, in favour of the Prince Secunder Jah, and that M. Raymond was to proceed to Kurpah for the purpose of settling the country. The Resident replied through his Moonshee in terms which expressed his surprise that so large a force should be stationed on the borders of the Company's territory, especially as he was not aware that the state of Kurpah was such as to require a demonstration so formidable. He expressed his fear that an unfavourable construction would be put on this proceeding by the world at large, and appealed to the usual wisdom and foresight of his highness to avoid giving cause for any such misapprehension.[1] This reply was courteously worded, in order that it might lead to a discussion of the subject, and accordingly, on the morning of the 19th, Meer Allum waited on the Resident, to communicate the modified resolutions at which, in the interval, his highness the Nizam had arrived. 1st. The prince Secunder Jah was to remain appointed nominal governor of Kurpah. 2nd. The infant prince, Soliman Jah, was to continue to hold Kummum in jagheer; in

---

[1] Appendix U.

explanation of which, I must observe that this district had, for some time past, been assigned for the maintenance of Azim-ool-oomrah's Ressalah of Silladar cavalry, but the charge of which the late minister had affected to relinquish in favour of this prince, on being permitted to adopt him for his son. 3rd. Mohammed Ameen Khan Arab was to manage the district ostensibly assigned to Secunder Jah; and was to be accompanied by 4,000 of M. Raymond's corps under a M. Peron, a native of Alsace, and Raymond's second in command.[1] 4th. The government of Kummum was to be administered by a Mahratta friend of the Peishwa's Vakeel, assisted by a detachment of a thousand men from Raymond's corps.

In the discussion which ensued between the Resident and Meer Allum, Captain Kirkpatrick confined his objections to the strength of the party to be detached from Raymond's corps, without alluding to the danger that might arise, at the then conjuncture, from the circumstance of the corps being officered by Frenchmen professing principles hostile to order in general, and to the British nation in particular. It is not unimportant, however, to state here that M. Raymond affected to consider his corps as *a French body of troops, employed and subsidized by the Nizam.* All his regimental returns were headed, "Corps

[1] Appendix V.

François de Raymond." The subsidy for frontier regiments, including their ordnance, and supposing them to be complete, was fixed at one lac thirty thousand rupees per mensem, though at this particular period only 80,000 rupees were drawn monthly, in which sum was included the supply of ordnance stores. The whole was regarded by M. Raymond as his private property, and considering that his corps numbered 15,000 strong, it must be admitted that he was in possession of a formidable instrument of power.

Towards the end of May (1795) Captain Kirkpatrick was informed that Raymond was in expectation of being soon joined by several of his countrymen from Pondicherry, particularly by some military officers of rank. With his customary vigilance, our Resident transmitted to the Governor of Madras (Lord Hobart) a list of these persons, together with such information as he had been able to collect, respecting M. Raymond's operations for procuring military stores. He also explained to his lordship by what means some of the French officers, then in the service of the Nizam, had contrived to reach Hyderabad after the reduction of Pondicherry; and, that no precaution might be omitted, he addressed a few words of advice to Meer Allum respecting the employment of similar fugitives in the Nizam's service.[1]

[1] Appendix W.

In answer to this representation, Meer Allum requested the Resident to furnish him with descriptive lists of the persons alluded to, which Captain Kirkpatrick promised to do when his information was sufficiently complete. He did, however, single out one individual, a Frenchman, who, he had particular reasons for believing, had found his way to Hyderabad, by abusing the indulgence of the Madras government, and upon whom, he said, there was some probability of the command of a certain nobleman's infantry and artillery being conferred. Captain Kirkpatrick, at the same time, instructed his Vakeel to intimate privately to Meer Allum how desirable it was that he should guard against the appointment of this person while the subject was under debate, as it would greatly augment the difficulty of any future discussion concerning him. On this point as well as on the subject of his remonstrance generally, our Resident received a satisfactory assurance from Meer Allum, to the extent of his personal influence with the Durbar.

The ostensible reason for the despatch of troops to the Kurpah district was the necessity of coercing Assud Ally Khan, the Talookdar, who was an intimate friend of Azim-ool-oomrah, the late minister. To the surprise of all, this individual suddenly presented himself at the Hyderabad Durbar, where he was received by the Nizam in the usual manner. Captain

Kirkpatrick had never believed that Assud Ally Khan meant to maintain himself in his government by force of arms, yet he was not prepared to believe that he would venture to appear at court, attended by only fifty horsemen, without security for his personal safety. This, however, was satisfactory enough in its bearing on the question at issue between the Resident and the Nizam, and Captain Kirkpatrick signified to Meer Allum his expectation that the intended expedition to Kurpah would be countermanded. Meer Allum in reply, earnestly requested him to let the subject rest for a few days, when, possibly, affairs might take a new turn, and he even hinted that Assud Ally Khan might have address enough to recover his government. The Resident complied with his wish, but was determined that nothing should induce him to lose sight of the subject.

Some days having expired, Captain Kirkpatrick renewed the subject officially, and after alluding to the submission of Assud Ally Khan, which rendered the presence of M. Raymond's troops in the district of Kurpah unnecessary, he expressed his conviction in the most courteous manner that his highness would seriously weigh in his mind the mischievous tendency of the proposed measure, which, he said, would no doubt excite considerable uneasiness on our border, and be the cause of heavy losses in revenue to the Company's government. The Resident's remonstrance was communicated by Meer Allum to the Nizam, who replied "that if the English thought fit to persist in their objections to the detachment ordered to Kurpah, he trusted they would consent to perform the service themselves, upon which it had been his intention to employ that force as the only one belonging to him equal to the execution of it!" In this, if it were seriously proposed, Captain Kirkpatrick saw nothing objectionable, as he had always wished to substitute, permanently, a body of our own troops in place of the division of Raymond's corps, appointed for the service of Kurpah; but he doubted whether his highness continued at liberty, since his treaty with the Mahrattas, to employ the military force for which he was still entitled to call upon us, and above all he saw little reason to hope that his highness would incur the heavy expense of such assistance, when, in reality, he did not need it.

On the first point, his doubts were satisfied by the reflection that Meer Allum was too sincere in his desire to preserve a good understanding between his master and the Peishwa, to propose anything that would prove a just cause of offence to the latter; and his doubt on the second point was unmistakably cleared up by the intimation that the assistance in question was to be afforded gratuitously. Meer Allum justified this expectation by observing that the detention of the troops would, in all probability, be for a short time only, and by reminding the Resident that his highness had not long since shown his readiness to afford similar aid to the Company on the same terms; he might have added also, because the only force which the Nizam could employ for the purpose with sufficient probability of success, was to be recalled in compliance with our own wishes. On the whole, Captain Kirkpatrick felt he might take upon himself to assure Meer Allum that a detachment of the usual strength was at his highness's command, and that as a further proof of the friendly sentiments entertained for his highness by our Government, he was sure the Governor General would approve of his consent to waive the Company's claim to the extra month's subsidy provided for by treaty. Indeed, the reasonableness of this can hardly be called in question when it is considered that but a few weeks had elapsed since the departure of Major Roberts's detachment, and therefore that the Company could be at no great expense for refitting. The Resident, however, acknowledged that it was not this idea so much as motives of temporary expediency, which induced him to relinquish so material a point.

After all, this concession had not the desired effect, Meer Allum observing, and no doubt very justly, that he could not propose subjecting his master to the heavy expense of a detachment of Company's troops, till it should have appeared that those of his highness were unequal to the service on which they were engaged. On the other hand, anxious though he was to keep Raymond's people entirely out of Kurpah, the Resident did not feel that he would be justified in purchasing this advantage at the price proposed, viz., by undertaking the duty ourselves. Under these circumstances, the result obtained was, perhaps, as favourable as could have been anticipated. Meer Allum agreed, eventually, to send only two of Raymond's regiments, undertaking at the same time that if this force should be found insufficient for the pacification of Kurpah, his highness would avail himself of the service of the Company's troops, and recall his own.

This point being settled, the Resident obtained permission to employ a news-writer in the camp of Mohammed Ameen Khan, hoping by this means to be kept well informed of the movements of the detachment.

As the Resident, throughout the correspondence on this subject, had deemed it necessary to conceal as much as possible the importance he attached to the movements of M. Raymond and his "French corps," so he could not expose his real motives for soliciting this favour. He merely stated that as the vicinity of the force under Mohammed Ameen Khan to the frontiers of the Company and of Tippoo Sultan, would be but too likely to occasion disputes between the respective borderers, he thought it desirable to appoint an intelligent person from whose reports he might be the better able to judge of the truth of any representations that might hereafter be made to him on such subjects. The truth is, besides the motive arising from his mistrust of M. Raymond, he had another reason for making this arrangement, to which it will be necessary to revert at the commencement of my next chapter.

At length Mohammed Ameen Khan, with Baptiste's division of M. Raymond's corps, departed for Kurpah, but did not advance beyond Nunidiah, a place situated about fifty miles south-east of Payton on the Kistnah, and nearly eighty miles north-west of Kurpah. The events which arrested their march will be related in due course.

CHAPTER XIII.

POLITICAL INTRIGUES AT HYDERABAD.

Special Reasons of the Resident for appointing an Agent in M. Baptiste's Camp—Suspicion of an Intrigue with Tippoo Sultan—Remarkable Expression of Meer Allum—Probable Implication of the French—Address of the Resident at the Hyderabad Durbar—Remarks of the Nizam and the Oomrahs on the French Reformers—Struggles at the Nizam's Court for Political Power—The Mahratta Party and the Roy Royan—Sincerity and Tact of Meer Allum—Prospect of other Troubles from the Payments stipulated to be made to the Peishwa—Application to the Mahratta Court for Jewels in the possession of Azim-ool-oomrah—The Peishwa's Officers retain possession of the Districts captured by them—Flight of the Nizam's Son from Hyderabad—Supposed Complicity of the Mahratta Vakeel—The Nizam requires the Services of the British Contingent in Kurpah—Question of the Occupation of this District by M. Raymond's Corps revived—Remonstrance of Sir J. Shore—News received of the Revolution in Holland—The Nizam begins to mistrust the French.

I HAVE alluded to a special reason, besides the suspicion of M. Raymond, which induced the Resident to solicit the privilege of appointing a news-writer in Mohammed Ameen Khan's camp. Captain Kirkpatrick had, in fact, reason to suspect that the Arab might have been commissioned, previous to his departure from Hyderabad, to open communications with Tippoo Sultan for the purpose of sounding the disposition of that prince, with respect to an offensive alliance against the Peishwa. His suspicions derived much strength from the undissembled dissatisfaction of the Nizam with the mortifying conditions imposed upon him after the battle of Kurdlah, and this dissatisfaction was openly fomented by the Roy Royan, and no doubt encouraged also by many who thought it the best means of paying their court to that minister, or otherwise promoting their own selfish ends.

Captain Kirkpatrick was struck by a remarkable change in the opinion which Meer Allum entertained of the Arab, almost immediately after the appointment of the latter to Kurpah; and although he could not be induced to explain himself, it was evident that he had some suspicion of its being the intention of the Roy Royan to employ that person in a secret negotiation with Tippoo. He entered with unusual warmth into the Resident's design for employing an agent in the Arab's camp, not simply concurring in it, but observing, at the same time, that the measure might eventually be productive of much greater advantage than Captain Kirkpatrick had appeared to anticipate from it.

By and by, it came to the Resident's knowledge that an intrigue with the court of Seringapatam had been actually set on foot with the knowledge of some of the principal chiefs of the Hyderabad Durbar. The prime mover was said to be a former agent of M. Lally, who owing to this circumstance was well known at Tippoo's court, and the Resident was informed that his highness the Nizam was not to be made acquainted with the business, until it had reached a certain stage of success. It was his opinion that the real object of Amjud-ool-Moolk, Shumsh-ool-oomrah's guardian, in the transaction, might after all be no other than to obtain the services of a few Europeans, out of the number of those employed by Tippoo. But whatever might be the ground of the rumours which reached him, he could not doubt the sincerity of the Nizam's declaration to the Mahratta Vakeel (Govind Kishen) how earnestly he desired an interview with the Peishwa, a reconciliation with whom would certainly be inconsistent with the rumoured negotiations for the alliance with Tippoo.

It is true there remained another supposition; the negotiations might be continued, but their alleged object changed; for example, the Nizam might be persuaded to make common cause with Tippoo against the Company, instead of the Mahrattas. But this the Resident was of opinion could only happen in one of two cases, viz., that of the contemplated interview between his highness and the Peishwa leading to a revival of the project for a triple confederacy against us (which was some time before imputed to Azim-ool-oomrah), or that of the French obtaining some very decided advantage over us in India. Of the latter event there was certainly no reasonable prospect. With regard to the former, it seemed unlikely that a minister so wary and intelligent as Balaji Pundit (to say nothing of the others) should feel the smallest inclination to exchange the long-experienced good faith, moderation, and forbearance of the Company for the systematic perfidy, the insatiate ambition, and the fraternizing principles of the French; after all, too, for this doubtful good, the fortunes of war would have had to be tried against us.

There could be no doubt, however, of the pertinacity of French intrigue at this time. About the end of June, the Nizam received information that the Government of France had made overtures to Tippoo with a view to a joint attack on the Company's possessions in the East. Showing the paper which contained this statement to Captain Kirkpatrick, he asked him whether he had received intelligence to the same effect, and what he thought of it. The reply of the Resident was verbatim as follows:—

"Considering the insidious character of the French,

and the circumstances they stood in just then with respect to the English, it could not (he thought) be deemed altogether improbable that they should have made the attempt attributed to them. But, on the other hand, however ready Tippoo might have been to listen to such an overture from a King of France, it did not appear to him likely that he would venture on any close connection with the then ruler of that country, of whose systematic detestation of, and enmity to all sovereign princes, as well as levelling and disorganizing principles, he could not but be sufficiently apprised."[1] Seeing that he was addressing a pretty full Durbar, the Resident continued to descant on the new-fangled doctrines of the French, and on the anarchy which had been produced in that wretched kingdom. He laid particular stress on the unhappy fate of the royal family, contrasting it, for obvious reasons, as strongly as he could with the almost unparalleled attachment and submission to their sovereigns for which the people of France were, only a few years before, eminently distinguished. He concluded by representing the misery and ruin in which the nobility of France had been plunged by the modern philosophy, all which he

---

[1] We now know, however, that the Sultan of Mysore allowed the French to establish a society in his dominions for the diffusion of "the rights of man," and that he himself was enrolled among its associates under the name of "Citizen Tippoo."

placed in such a light as he thought best adapted to interest the Oomrahs present.

When he had concluded, one of the Oomrahs observed that the French reformers, in assuming the title of "philosophers," had taken an appropriate name; a sarcasm in which the Nizam himself joined, and which it is necessary to explain by informing the reader that the word *philosopher* is frequently employed by the Orientals to signify a *sophist*. Besides this, several other comments were made by his highness and the members of the Durbar, all expressive of the horror with which they regarded the newly adopted principles and the conduct of the French. The Nizam himself observed that it was contrary to the nature of things that such a monstrous system as that which had been invented by the French should take root.

Other affairs were in agitation at the same time which indicated the expediency of depriving the French of their influence in Hyderabad; but these may all be summed up in the unsettled state of the country, with the principal causes of which the reader will become acquainted from what follows.

No administration had yet been formed at Hyderabad since the delivery of Azim-ool-oomrah to the Mahrattas, and, in the opinion of Meer Allum, the struggles for power were likely to assume a serious aspect. One party was headed by the Mahratta Vakeel (Govind

Kishen) and the Pagah chieftains, who were accused by the Roy Royan, the political chief to whom they were opposed, of intriguing with the Mahrattas for the purpose of usurping the government. The Nizam himself was so indiscreet (to use the words of Meer Allum) as to upbraid the Vakeel to his face with ingratitude and deceit; and even threw suspicion on the past conduct of the Pagah party. This was followed by a distant menace, on the one side, to call in a Mahratta force, and, on the other, to apply the money which would presently become due to the Peishwa, to the prosecution of a fresh war against him. Meer Allum, filled with apprehension and disgust, declared his determination to withdraw from the Durbar, and only attend when specially summoned. He expressed his belief that the speedy and complete wreck of the Hyderabad State could only be prevented by the English Company taking it under their protection; and even requested the resident Vakeel (Moonshee Azeez-oolah) to take an early opportunity of ascertaining from the Resident whether or not such a measure would be found practicable.

As the readiest means of defeating the intrigues which threatened so much danger to the State, Meer Allum was anxious that a meeting should take place between the Peishwa and the Nizam immediately after the rains, and he informed the Resident that before taking leave of Balaji Pundit, he had convinced that minister of the necessity for the measure. In the meantime he saw the importance of conciliating Govind Kishen, and having succeeded in impressing upon his highness also the importance of this, means were taken for an accommodation of the differences that had arisen. The Mahratta Vakeel made some acknowledgment of the justice of the complaints against him, and the Roy Royan, on his part, made such concessions as were deemed suitable. The credit of this reconciliation was due to Meer Allum.

Govind Kishen now desisted from his attempts to compel the Nizam to receive Mohammed Azeem Khan as his principal minister. As for Amjud-ool-Moolk (Shumsh-ool-oomrah's guardian), to whom I have alluded in connection with these intrigues,[1] so far was he from having taken any part in the offensive and disloyal projects imputed to the other Pagah chieftains, that a very serious difference was said to have existed between him and Mohammed Azeem Khan.

Of more serious importance than these intrigues was the question of the stipulated payments to the Peishwa. Although the first kist of a crore and a half of rupees was not due till April, 1796, Meer Allum was anxious that the Roy Royan should

[1] *Ante*, p. 156.

demonstrate his earnestness in discharging the obligation by commencing his operations for that purpose without delay, and this so effectually as to prevent the sincerity of his intentions being brought into question by the Mahrattas. This advice was given by Meer Allum on his discovering that the Roy Royan trusted to raising the amount entirely by fines and forfeitures.

At this time the Nizam made several applications to the Mahratta court for certain jewels which were in the possession of Azim-ool-oomrah, but on one pretext or another they always contrived to evade the demand. The dissatisfaction which his highness felt on this account was greatly aggravated by the conduct of some of the Mahratta officers, who still held possession of some of the districts which had been seized in the course of the late hostilities, but which ought to have been evacuated immediately after the conclusion of peace. Govind Kishen attributed this neglect to the looseness with which orders for evacuation are generally obeyed, and on the other hand it was affirmed that Dowlatabad had not been given up to the Mahrattas.

On the 28th of June, the prince Ally Jah, eldest son of the Nizam, escaped from the capital, accompanied by Nazim-ool-Moolk, and Saddasheo Reddy, the former Soobah of Hyderabad, and son-in-law of the Nizam; the latter, one of the most considerable Zemindars in his highness's dominions. It was suspected that the flight of the prince had been connected with and favoured by Govind Kishen, and it led to a series of events which will be recorded in the next chapter.

On the same day the Resident received a message from the Nizam, signifying his desire to be furnished, agreeably to treaty, and as expeditiously as possible, with a detachment of the Company's troops of the stipulated strength. It was further required that this detachment should proceed direct to Kurpah. Considering this a favourable opportunity for the recall of Raymond's troops under M. Baptiste (an object of which Captain Kirkpatrick had never lost sight since its march to Kurpah), the Resident replied that though the Company were ever prompt to fulfil their engagements, yet, on account of the necessity which his highness had imposed on our Government of providing suitably for the tranquillity of our frontier in the Kurpah quarter, there was reason to fear considerable difficulty and unavoidable delay in complying with the request. He concluded by suggesting that the employment of the contingent in Kurpah, while providing for the security of that district, would enable his highness to employ Baptiste's corps elsewhere, and thus remove the cause of solicitude to which he had adverted, and which the Government must have felt equally with himself.

Still the Nizam showed no disposition to concede this point, declaring that Baptiste's corps could ill be spared, even if the contingent went to Kurpah. The Resident replied that he was quite sure, in this case, that the Company's Government would grant in addition whatever assistance it conveniently could, and he was ready to advise that troops should be advanced in the direction of Kurpah in readiness to afford such aid as might be required. At this stage of the affair, the Nizam received a letter addressed to him by Sir John Shore, in which the former arguments of the Resident were summarized, and his remonstrance against the occupation of Kurpah by the French, strongly supported.[1]

As if to leave his highness without excuse for persisting in his policy, many days had not elapsed when he received intelligence of the revolution in Holland. He was much shocked at this first instance of the contagious character of the levelling and disorganizing principles of the French, and with much earnestness recommended that the news should be kept secret, lest by reaching Raymond's party, it should inspire them with a confidence in the success

[1] Appendix X.

of their nation, which might be productive of mischievous consequences. To keep such intelligence secret, it must be confessed, was manifestly impossible; but the request seemed to show that his highness, at length, was not insensible to the danger with which all established governments were menaced by the progress of French opinions.

CHAPTER XIV.

REBELLION OF THE NIZAM'S SON.

The Disgrace in which Prince Ally Jah lived at Hyderabad—His Flight probably encouraged by Govind Kishen for Political Reasons—He proceeds to Bidur, and is pursued by M. Raymond—Defeat of the latter in an Attack on the Fortress—M. Baptiste ordered to reinforce him with the Troops from Kurpah—Captain Kirkpatrick declines to see any Merit in the Necessity for this Measure—Overtures for the Prince's Submission at Bidur—His extravagant Demands—Indignation of the Nizam—The English Government refuse the Guarantee requested by the Prince—Machiavellian Policy of the Roy Royan—Application for English Troops refused—Major Roberts' Command ordered to Hyderabad—Arrival of a mysterious Personage from Seringapatam—Suspicions of a hostile Design against the Mahrattas—Application of the Mahrattas for part Payment of the Sum stipulated at Kurdlah—The Nizam resists the Demand of the Mahratta Vakeel—Probability of the Prince seeking Refuge or Assistance from the Mahrattas—Application to the English Government for a Loan—The Force under Major Roberts marches towards Bidur—The Prince retires on the Road to Nandair—Attempts to negotiate—Overtures from the King of Cabool and Tippoo Sultan—Complicity of the Roy Royan—Tippoo Sultan's Agent at Hyderabad—Death of the Peishwa—Surrender of Saddasheo Reddy, and the rest of the Prince's Followers—Surrender of Ally Jah to Meer Allum—Question of the Succession at Poonah—

Death of Lieut. Stewart, and Arrival of his Successor—M. Raymond and the Jagheer of Maiduk—Sinister Reports spread by the French—Death of Prince Ally Jah—Return of Major Roberts and Meer Allum to Golconda.

THE flight of the Nizam's son, alluded to in the preceding chapter, was not a very surprising circumstance, as he had for some time lived in disgrace at his father's court, and was not without apprehensions of something more serious befalling him. With respect to the supposed complicity of Govind Kishen, it seemed by no means unlikely that he had secretly encouraged the prince to take the step he did, since the embarrassment into which it could hardly fail to throw the Nizam, would be extremely favourable to his purpose of compelling his highness to remodel the ministry.

The prince had proceeded to Bidur, and the garrison of that Fort, on the first summons, opened the gates to him. M. Raymond, who had followed rapidly in pursuit, sent forward an advanced party against Saddasheo Reddy, which was attacked by the Zemindar and totally defeated; the commander of the party and his son falling into the hands of the insurgents. M. Raymond himself then attacked the fortress, and was so severely handled, that M. Baptiste (who had previously been directed to proceed to Raichore, in consequence of the application to our authorities at Madras for the British contingent) was ordered to reinforce his chief at Bidur.

The Hyderabad Durbar vainly imagined that our Resident would be led by this artifice to conclude that the French had been withdrawn from the south in compliance with his repeated applications for their return! Captain Kirkpatrick, however, had no difficulty in exposing the absurdity of such a pretence to Meer Allum, reminding him that the march of Baptiste to Raichore had been ordered, after he (the Resident) had been formally advised that instructions had been issued for his return to Hyderabad. It was impossible to form any other conclusion than that these troops had been ordered to Bidur at the instance of M. Raymond himself, who had discovered in Saddasheo Reddy a more formidable opponent than he or any one else had at first esteemed him.

The Nizam deputed to his son at Bidur, the prince's own Etaleeaq, or preceptor, charged with certain overtures for an accommodation; one of these conditions, it is understood, being an offer of the country of Adoni in jagheer. It was with difficulty he obtained an audience, owing to the suspicions of Saddasheo Reddy, who, perhaps, was far from desiring a settlement on any terms whatever, short of the Nizam's complete resignation of the reigns of government into the hands of Ally Jah. After all, the prince hardly exchanged a word with his preceptor on the occasion, dismissing him rather abruptly with answers which had been previously prepared, to the letters he brought with him.

The demands of the prince were of such a nature as could only excite indignation in the breast of the Nizam, and become a cause of grief and alarm throughout the palace. He declared that he would listen to no proposals that did not come through Govind Kishen, or the English Resident, and would accept no terms that were not guaranteed by them. Here it is necessary to remark that for some time previous to the flight of Ally Jah, Captain Kirkpatrick had observed an uncommon desire on his part to cultivate a connection with the Company, and concluding from this circumstance that the prince would eventually resort to our mediation, the Resident had applied for instructions. The reply of the Governor General, as might have been expected, was absolutely to decline undertaking any responsibility which might eventually impose upon us the necessity of interfering with an armed force.[1] Accordingly, even had the Nizam been weak enough to comply with the prince's demands, the guarantee he desired was totally out of the question.

---

[1] Appendix Y.

A more detailed account of the Prince Ally Jah's letter to his father was subsequently brought to light, and it purported that he (Ally Jah) having for a considerable time past contemplated with grief the disordered state and ruinous management of his highness's affairs, and having experienced in his own person the most unkind and mortifying treatment, he had at length been impelled to the resolution of quitting the world, and of passing the remainder of his days at Mecca. He had felt the less repugnance to the execution of this measure, he continued, because, having no children of his own, he was little animated by the desire of attaining either wealth or power, and that, finding himself thwarted in his humble design by the pursuit of his highness's army, he had been reduced to the necessity of repairing to Bidur, where he had peaceably taken up his residence, and that he wished for nothing more than the due maintenance of the honour of the family to which he belonged, and the prosperity of the people over which he ruled. Thus far the prince himself.

By his adherents it was proposed that the life and honour of the prince should be safe, that the lives and honour of Saddasheo Reddy and other chiefs should also be safe, and that the Reddy should be confirmed in all his possessions. That the office of Dewan should be conferred on the prince, and his highness (the Nizam) be left at liberty to study his personal ease, and pursue the pleasures of the chase. That these articles should be mutually sworn to on the Koran, and that they should be finally adjusted and guaranteed, as I have already mentioned, by the English and Mahratta representatives at his highness's court!

The Roy Royan's advice to the Nizam on the occasion was worthy of his race:—"It was not necessary to keep faith with rebels, and anything might be promised." The Nizam, for his part, declared that had Ally Jah ever shown himself to be either worthy or capable of ruling, he should have had no scruple in agreeing to his demands. All things considered, it was obvious that this affair would have to settle itself by the event of war, and in this position I leave it for a few moments.

The Madras Government had not yet sent the contingent which the reader is aware had been applied for by the Nizam for service in Kurpah. The truth is, the troops could not well be spared, the Madras Government having received instructions from England, in consequence of the war with France, to take the Dutch settlements under their protection, and the detachment of Major Roberts was one of those which had been ordered to proceed to the coast. In reply to such excuses as the Resident could make at the time, Meer Allum observed, with his usual astuteness, that he thought the Company had as great an interest in sending these troops to Kurpah as his highness had in applying for their services. He was alluding to the expediency of the Company taking precautions against the return of Raymond's corps to that quarter.

From the disturbed state of affairs at Hyderabad towards the middle of August, it became a serious question whether the troops under Major Roberts, should the Government be able to spare them, ought not in the first instance to proceed to the capital, especially as nearly the whole of M. Raymond's force had marched in pursuit of the prince. Soon after this had been determined in the affirmative, instructions arrived from Calcutta, ordering the two battalions to be sent at the Nizam's request, it being seen that a refusal of their services would lead to a re-agitation of the whole question regarding the cession of the Guntoor circar. Accordingly, Major Roberts marched direct for Hyderabad, and on the 31st of August took up a position between the town and the fort of Golcondah.

About this time a person named Kishnajee Pundit arrived at Hyderabad from Seringapatam, in the character of a Vakeel, on the part of Tippoo, and took up his residence some distance from the city, in a garden-house belonging to the Roy Royan. This led to a suspicion that his mission had been brought about by the Roy Royan, especially as Meer Allum, on being interrogated by the Resident, avowed his ignorance of the purpose for which he had come, as did the Rajah himself in public durbar; the latter, indeed, declared that he was not aware such a person had arrived, and certainly no such person was in occupation of a house belonging to him. His highness suggested that this stranger might be a traveller who, knowing the facility with which strangers pass through his dominions, had tarried there on his journey to another destination.

Meer Allum informed the Resident that he had heard some time before of messengers having been despatched to Seringapatam by the Roy Royan, while the army was on its return from Kurdlah. In his opinion, therefore, the appearance of Kishnajee might be the consequence of some foolish project which the Rajah had commenced at that time. In addition to this the reader cannot have forgotten the disposition which both the Roy Royan and the Nizam had manifested relative to the pecuniary engagements contracted at Kurdlah, and the menacing language which had been used towards the Mahrattas. All this being coupled with the extraordinary solicitude with which it was attempted to keep Kishnajee's arrival a secret, and the anxiety with which his public character was subsequently disavowed, can hardly fail to suggest the existence, at this time, of a design hostile to the Mahrattas.

The requisition of the Nizam for additional troops to occupy Kurpah, was finally rejected by the Governor of Madras, there being no regiments available. The danger that had been apprehended from the occupation of that district by the French had moreover ceased for the present, by the withdrawal of Baptiste's division to reinforce Raymond at Bidur. There was still the probability of that commander being sent to Kurpah at some future time, when, perhaps, his reputation and influence, augmented by the successful issue of his operations against the rebels, might render any opposition to the measure on the part of the Nizam more doubtful than ever in its results. Of this, it must be confessed, there was no immediate sign, several skirmishes having taken place between the followers of the prince and the troops under M. Raymond, without either force obtaining any real advantage over its opponents.

The Mahratta Durbar, at this period, addressing his highness on the subject of his son's flight, and of the recall of the two English battalions to Hyderabad, took the opportunity of demanding some portion of the sum due to the Peishwa, in accordance with the treaty of peace, alleging as a reason for this demand (the period for the payment of the first instalment not having yet arrived,) the information they had received of the change in his highness's disposition.[1] His highness replied to Govind Kishen by alluding to the drain on his resources, owing to the rebellion of his son Ally Jah; and also reminded him of the circumstances under which he had incurred the obligation at Kurdlah: "At that very time," he said, "I warned you that I only yielded to your importunity, and the pressure of the moment, since I was aware that to fulfil it would be difficult, if not totally impossible." He therefore requested the Mahratta Vakeel to intimate to his court that without some abatement of the pecuniary conditions of the convention, he never could meet the demands upon him.

Instead of suggesting to his highness an easy and creditable mode of satisfying the demands against him, Govind Kishen brought forward the most intolerable proposals, evidently influenced by his secret desire to get into his own hands the absolute management of the affairs of Hyderabad. His highness, however, with that spirit of which he was at times capable, declared he would abdicate rather than yield to such demands.

How perplexed he felt by the circumstances of his son's rebellion, and the pressure of the Poonah Durbar, appears from his sending Meer Allum to

[1] Appendix Z.

the Resident to inquire, in the event of Ally Jah's seeking refuge with the Mahrattas, what course it would be proper for him to adopt. When Captain Kirkpatrick replied that if his highness would adhere to the provisions of the convention entered into at Kurdlah, there was no fear that the Mahrattas would afford the prince either shelter or assistance, his highness stated that he could not possibly pay more than twelve lacs towards the first kist of 150. The Resident thought it unlikely that the Mahrattas would be contented with less than fifty, being induced to specify that sum by an observation of Meer Allum's, that with fifty lacs to offer the Mahratta court, he trusted that much could be done towards promoting a reconciliation. When he made this observation Meer Allum had requested that the Company might be asked for a loan of forty or fifty lacs, to be secured by an assignment on the revenues of Kurpah and other districts, to which request the Governor General had, in due course, replied that his highness should be discouraged from expecting any such assistance from them.

I have remarked that the detachment of Company's troops destined for the capital had taken up their position between the town and the fort of Golcondah. On the 22nd of September the Resident instructed Major Roberts to march his force to a station, north of Hyderabad, and await there for orders to march on Bidur, where it was proposed that he should act against the rebel force. On the morning of the 24th he started for his destination, accompanied by Meer Allum, by whose advice and instructions, at the Nizam's especial request, he was to be guided; so far was added by request of the Resident, as it might comport with his own sense of military propriety, and with the honour of the Company's arms. Major Roberts was further instructed not to join the corps commanded by M. Raymond on any service whatever; and if the Mahrattas in a body joined the rebel prince, he was not to act against them, but adventurers or soldiers of fortune of that nation were not to be regarded as Mahratta subjects.

His highness himself contemplated following the detachment to Bidur, and with that view his tents were pitched on the ground occupied by the Company's troops previous to their departure. On the 27th of September, however, information was received of the evacuation of Bidur by the rebels, whose retreat had not been interrupted by any part of the Nizam's army. The prince directed his march to Turkul, a place about nineteen coss on the direct road to Nandair, and it was supposed that his intention was to await there the result of some further proposals which he had transmitted to his father. His demands, somewhat more moderate than heretofore, were first, for himself a jagheer of twelve lacs of rupees in the Berar quarter, and secondly, for Saddasheo Reddy, the re-establishment of that chief in Maiduk and the other districts held by him previous to his revolt, but since transferred in temporary charge to M. Raymond. The answer of his highness merely promised for the prince personal safety; for the Polygar nothing but the restoration of his original jagheer.

Immediately before the departure of Meer Allum with the contingent en route for Bidur, Govind Kishen, the Mahratta Vakeel, informed the Resident that his highness had received a letter from the King of Cabool, Zuman Shah, in which he announced his intention of undertaking an expedition to Hindostan, and requested the Nizam to be prepared to co-operate with his forces against the Mahrattas. In answer to the Resident's inquiries on this subject, Meer Allum denied that any letter had been received from Zuman Shah himself, but acknowledged that a person connected with the court of Cabool, and residing at Delhi, had addressed his highness to that effect. He added, that a verbal reply had been given purporting that, by the blessing of God, there no longer existed any difference between his highness and the Peishwa.

Meer Allum at the same time informed the Resident that his highness had received overtures from

Tippoo Sultan, who proposed sending a body of troops to Hyderabad, and entering them in the service of the Nizam; but that a similar reply had been returned to him as to the King of Cabool.

As a further example of the intrigues which were rife at this period, the arrival of a second Vakeel from Tippoo may be mentioned; the object of Sukkaram Pundit's mission, as gathered from the Roy Royan himself, was to obtain a full discharge of his claims upon Kurnool for arrears of Peshcush, and to effect an arrangement for the future; but this was a negotiation upon which his highness could not enter, owing to his being entirely occupied with Ally Jah's rebellion. His real business, however, as subsequently ascertained, was of a very different nature.

It appeared that his highness had been extremely irritated and embittered against the Mahratta Vakeel during the march back from Kurdlah, on the subject of the Talooks ceded to the Peishwa, and that the Roy Royan had sent a secret intimation to Tippoo Sultan, that advantage might be taken of his highness's disposition to chastise the Mahrattas. He advised him therefore to address a letter of friendship to the Nizam in a soothing and conciliatory strain, and, if he appeared willing to negotiate for the purpose suggested, to send a Vakeel to Hyderabad. The Sultan accordingly had deputed Sukkaram Pundit, who was the bearer of two letters, one addressed to his highness, containing no more than general professions of friendship, and referring him for various particulars to the letter addressed to the Roy Royan. To the latter he wrote, "Whatever you have written has been understood; on that point I am ready, but upon the following conditions only, *that the understanding existing between your Sircar and the English shall cease.*" The Roy Royan having reported the above to the Nizam, was told by his highness, "that at present this would not suit, but that hereafter he should consider of it."

Though it somewhat anticipates the date, it will amuse the reader if I mention in this connection that the two Hurcurrahs who had been despatched to Seringapatam with the replies to the letters of Tippoo Sultan returned to Hyderabad on the 1st of November, and made the following report:—

"On their arrival at Seringapatam, they delivered the letters of which they were the bearers to Tippoo, and the Hurcurrah of Sukkaram Pundit having likewise delivered his letter to the Sultan, represented to the latter that Sukkaram Pundit was continually, night and day, drinking and pursuing his pleasures, and had not yet obtained an audience of the Nizam, but confined his visits to the Roy Royan. That the Sultan, on hearing this, expressed his displeasure against Subha Row (his principal secretary), by whose recommendation Sukkaram Pundit had been sent to Hyderabad. 'You have deputed,' said the Sultan to him, 'on the most important service, a very unfit man, by whom nothing has been done; you declared him to be a person of sagacity and prudence, but his only qualification seems to be his acquaintance with the Roy Royan.'" "Therefore," the report concluded, "the Sultan is now considering whom to send in the place of Sukkaram."

In consequence of the retreat of the rebels from Bidur, the Company's detachment was halted at Puttuncherroo, about twenty miles from Hyderabad, and Major Roberts was instructed, in the event of the prince being pursued into the Mahratta country, not to follow. But at the latter end of October, the Peishwa died, and it being thought far from improbable that the event would occasion a change in the policy which the Mahrattas had hitherto observed in relation to this contest, Major Roberts was authorized to act accordingly, first ascertaining that he was proceeding on assured grounds.

On the 28th of October Meer Allum and the Nizam's army, after a march of eight coss from Tandalwaddy, encamped at the village of Chickwun, where also Saddasheo Reddy arrived from Shahgoor, accompanied by 2,000 Rohillas, 900 cavalry, and 400 foot, and took up his ground at the distance of half a coss from M. Raymond's corps. His object was not to fight, but to offer his submission to the commander of the Nizam's army, who pledged himself for the preservation of his honour and life. In the meantime, Ally Jah himself, now almost deserted, had pitched his camp near Aurungabad, and there on the approach of the Nizam's army the greater part of his followers surrendered. The Prince Ally Jah gave himself up to Meer Allum, and threw himself upon the Nizam's protection. The circumstances of his capture are related in a letter from Meer Allum, which is inserted in the Appendix.[1]

The death of the Peishwa occasioned some natural anxiety with regard to the Mahratta succession, quite independent of any influence it might have had on the fortunes of the rebel prince. Captain Kirkpatrick therefore addressed an official despatch on the subject to Sir W. Malet, at Poonah, in which he indicated the probability of the Nizam's support being given to Balaji Pundit, in preference to Bajee Row, with the expectation perhaps that a considerable part of his highness's debt to the Mahratta Government would be remitted if the former were successful. The Resident expressed his regret that Meer Allum was absent from Hyderabad at this critical moment.[2]

Lieutenant Stewart, the Assistant Resident at the court of Hyderabad, after a long illness, expired at

---

[1] Appendix A A.

[2] Appendix B B.

that capital on the morning of the 14th of September. On the 8th of November, his successor, Lieutenant Kirkpatrick, brother of the Resident, arrived at Hyderabad, and entered upon the duties pertaining to the appointment.

Reverting to the position of the French, and the constant vigilance and tact that was necessary to keep them in check at the Nizam's court, it will be remembered that the jagheer of Maiduk had been transferred to M. Raymond in temporary charge.[1] Although up to the present time, the sunnuds may not have been actually issued, there was little doubt that the Jagheer would be confirmed to Raymond, as he had agreed to take that district on terms more advantageous to the Sircar than those upon which it had been held by Saddasheo Reddy. Manifestly it would be more to our advantage that M. Raymond should possess Maiduk than Kurpah, but besides the uneasiness which his possession of any establishment of the kind whatever would naturally cause, we could not be certain that his ambition would be satisfied with Maiduk, but rather the contrary. At this very time he was in virtual possession of Kummum; for although that district constituted the jagheer of one of the princes, yet M. Raymond had a fixed assignment upon the revenues,

---

[1] *Ante*, p. 178.

and he could always find occasion to employ one or two battalions on the pretence of realizing it.

With regard to the general policy of the French, M. Raymond's public agents at Hyderabad, and their countrymen generally, were not less industrious in depreciating, when they could not altogether conceal, the success of the allied armies in Europe, than they were active in magnifying those of their own nation. Constant watchfulness on the part of our Resident was needed in order to expose the falsehood or the insidious tendency of their reports. Guided by his own feelings, Captain Kirkpatrick would have preferred to leave these manœuvres to the refutation of time, especially as some of them were too contemptible for notice; but the Nizam's curiosity (or, as he himself termed it, "the friendly solicitude he felt for the event of a war in which we were so deeply interested,") left the Resident but little choice in the matter. When informed of the death of Louis XVII., and of the safety and freedom of his lawful successor, his highness expressed the liveliest satisfaction. He "thanked God that the intelligence he now heard was of a very different complexion from that which had been communicated to him only a short time previously by Myheputram (the chief native agent of M. Raymond), who had represented the French as carrying all before them in Europe—in a word, as absolutely irresistible.

On the 27th of November, intelligence was received at Hyderabad of the death of Prince Ally Jah, which had taken place at Khair, on the banks of the Godavery, on the 22nd of the same month: the Nizam had previously been informed of his indisposition, but he had no reason to suppose that his illness was of a serious nature. Rumours were in circulation which are thus alluded to by Captain Kirkpatrick in a letter to the Governor General:—"It would be premature at present either to detail or to affirm any opinion upon the reports occasioned by this event. The nature of them you will readily anticipate, since, all circumstances considered, it would be rather surprising if sinister constructions were not put upon the matter by popular suspicion." It is now generally believed that the Prince killed himself by swallowing pounded diamonds, in consequence of the Nizam having sent directions for his conveyance to Hyderabad under some kind of restraint.

On the 29th of November the Company's contingent under Major Roberts arrived at Golcondah. Meer Allum, also, for the present encamped there. Having returned from his expedition in very indifferent health, and suffering considerably from a flow of blood from his mouth and nostrils, he was unable to present himself before his highness.

CHAPTER XV.

ASCENDANCY OF THE FRENCH.

Reception of M. Raymond after the Suppression of Ally Jah's Rebellion—Proposed Mission of Meer Allum accompanied by Govind Kishen to Poonah—Application for Permission for M. Raymond's Troops to pass through the Company's Territory—Affected Indifference of M. Raymond about the Talook of Maiduk—The Resident remonstrates with the Nizam without effect—M. Raymond takes possession of his Jagheer—The Government approve of Captain Kirkpatrick's Measures—Troops held in readiness for Poonah—Expected Release of Azim-ool-oomrah—Friendly Intercourse with the Agent of Tippoo Sultan—The Contingent under Major Roberts sent to Raichore—Tippoo Sultan's extensive Levies—Kurnool threatened—Proposed Settlement by the joint Mediation of the Peishwa and the Nizam—Alarming Illness of the Nizam—Influential Position of M. Raymond—Question of the Succession—Doubtful Movements of the Troops—The Nizam Convalescent—Prospects of Secunder Jah—Ferridoon Jah and the Pagah party—Influence of M. Raymond—He is appointed Comptroller of the Ordnance—Arrest of Saddasheo Reddy—The Army ordered to Bidur—Success of the British Contingent in the Raichore Doab—Deputation to Poonah—The new Peishwa makes a Consignment of the Nizam's Debt to Scindiah—Expected Invasion of the Nizam's Territory by that Chieftain—Tenor of a Despatch addressed by Resident to the Governor General—Supremacy of the French.

M. Raymond was very honourably received by the Nizam at his presentation on returning from the expedition against Ally Jah, his highness having held him in his embrace much longer than usual, and thanked him for his services with unwonted earnestness. Yet he had neither deserved nor acquired any increase of military reputation during his campaign. His sole merit consisted in the steadfastness which he had manifested in the cause of the Nizam at this juncture, when his defection would most probably have been decisive of his highness's fate.

The indifferent health of Meer Allum on his return had prevented him from being sent to Poonah, accompanied by Govind Kishen, to arrange matters connected with the succession to the Peishwaship, but more especially to procure from the new Peishwa the remission of the three crores of rupees, for which the Nizam had given a written engagement, and the restoration of the district he had recently ceded. That this was really the object of his intended mission, appears from the letter he sent to the Resident, relating the purport of a conversation between him and the Mahratta Vakeel.[1] From the same letter it also appears that he endeavoured to obtain from Govind Kishen a verbal promise of compliance with the request, but to this the Vakeel gave no answer.

[1] Appendix C C.

About this time M. Raymond was desirous of despatching Baptiste with reinforcements to his Jagheer in Kummum, and Meer Allum requested permission for his troops to proceed to their destination through a part of the Company's territories. The Resident declined to grant a passport without the permission of the Governor General, and expressed his sense of the impropriety of the demand, when it was known to the court of Hyderabad that the French nation was at war with the English.

While affecting indifference on the subject of farming the Talook of Maiduk, M. Raymond was in reality earnestly bent upon obtaining the grant. Towards the end of December, Captain Kirkpatrick having satisfied himself that active measures were in progress to accomplish this end, sent his Moonshee to Meer Allum with instructions to urge his objections in the most unreserved manner, in the interest of his highness himself, independent of his connection with the Company's Government. The gist of his argument was the danger incurred by granting to Frenchmen of M. Raymond's principles so permanent an establishment in the country as that which he aimed at obtaining; and in this, as well as the other points urged upon him, Meer Allum expressed his entire concurrence. He recommended the Resident to address him briefly by letter on the subject, which would enable him to press the matter on the Nizam's attention.

In accordance with this suggestion Captain Kirkpatrick sent in a remonstrance repeating the former arguments, and concluding with the observation "that, considering the close connection subsisting between the English and his highness's Government, to put the French in such a manner in the way of increasing their power and consequence was liable to be received as contrary to the usages of friendship." To this, however, no attention seems to have been paid, as Raymond, supported by two regiments, took possession of Maiduk and the circar of Saddasheo Reddy, having agreed to pay for his acquisition a yearly rental of sixteen lacs of rupees. This sum, though exceeding the value assigned to it in the Asuphea Register, was, nevertheless, considered less than its actual produce, the district being a very fertile one, which either supplied the capital itself, or gave passage to most of the grain consumed by the inhabitants.

The government entirely approved of the terms of remonstrance in which Captain Kirkpatrick had addressed the Nizam on this subject. They considered his highness's conduct unfriendly, and ascribed it to the influence M. Raymond had obtained by the successful issue of his late campaign.

When the troops under Major Roberts returned to

Hyderabad, they were not at once dismissed to foraging quarters, in consequence of the Hyderabad Durbar being in expectation of a demand for assistance at Poonah. In fact, it was in contemplation at this time to invest the Prince Secunder Jah with the command of the Nizam's army, and to send him to Poonah to demand in person the release of Azim-ool-oomrah, whose presence at Hyderabad was absolutely necessary to the completion of his daughter's marriage ceremonies. It is most surprising, therefore, that rumours began to circulate of the probability of the late minister's early return, but they were generally discredited by Meer Allum, who affirmed that were such a measure meditated by Balaji Pundit there was nothing which his highness would so certainly resist.

Some indication of a friendly approach to Tippoo was remarked by the Resident, which reminds us that Sukkaram Pundit, the Sultan's Vakeel, was still residing at Hyderabad. The Nizam's nephew, Imtiaz-oo-dowlah, who had been for several years in disgrace, but was now gradually regaining a position in his uncle's favour, not only visited Tippoo's agent himself, but was attended on one occasion by the Mutseddee of the Treasury, and at another time by a brother of the Roy Royan. This indicated a stronger inclination on the part of the Nizam to cultivate a good understanding with the Sultan of Mysore than he had previously manifested, since according to the etiquette of the Hyderabad court, such meetings could not well have taken place without the permission of his highness.

The two regiments under Major Roberts had not yet been disposed of when the Company, requiring them to act in the south of India, applied to the Nizam to dispense with their services. His highness politely declined compliance, having urgent need for the use of the contingent in the Raichore Doab, where, accordingly, Major Roberts was ordered to march on the 14th of February (1796) for the purpose of reducing to obedience certain refractory Zemindars, and whence we shall by and by hear tidings of their success.

At the commencement of the year it transpired that Tippoo Sultan was levying troops in all directions, and had, by that time, collected an army of 80,000 men, of whom 50,000 were near his person, and 30,000 at Gooty Bellary, near the frontiers of Kurnool. The Nawab was seriously alarmed by the collection of so large a force, coincident with the pressing demands of Tippoo Sultan for his arrears of Peshcush; and in consequence of his appeal to the Nizam, the latter was strongly inclined to avert the ruin impending over him by negotiation. A proposition was also received through the Poonah Durbar to the effect that the arrears due to the Sultan should be discharged jointly by the Peishwa and the Nizam, who should make over to Tippoo in perpetuity a country yielding annually two lacs of rupees in lieu of the Peshcush which he claimed from Alif Khan the Nawab of Kurnool. "We will afterwards," said the court of Poonah, "adjust the matter with Alif Khan."

On the 25th of February, the Nizam was struck by palsy, but no alarming symptoms immediately followed. Dr. Ure, the Residency surgeon, found him lying upon a couch in the middle of the room, surrounded by a number of women and attendants. He had totally lost the use and feeling of his right side; the muscles of his face were convulsed, and on attempting to speak he could scarcely articulate. Dr. Ure was not sent for a second time and the Nizam recovered.

Had the Nizam died at this time, the position of the French would have been considerably strengthened, as the heir apparent to the throne, Secunder Jah, was in the habit of swearing "by the head of M. Raymond," whom he regarded as the first of men; his only objection to him being that he belonged to a nation who had murdered their king and queen. A few days after the Nizam's illness, he arrived from Maiduk with one of his regiments, and was received in his own cantonment under a royal salute. This fact is mentioned in a despatch addressed to the Governor General by Captain Kirkpatrick,[1] who, it will be seen relates some other interesting particulars, especially that guards were placed over the houses of the Prince Secunder Jah, his Dewan Sumba Chand, and all the princes, including Nasir-ool-Moolk. The factions began to raise their heads, and the probabilities of the succession excited general interest.

On the 7th of March the Nizam was declared convalescent, and the physicians appeared confident of his recovery, provided he would restrain his appetite within bounds. Some precipitancy had been shown by Secunder Jah, which gave deep offence to his father and a strict watch was kept over his movements.

The force which had been held in readiness to proceed to Poonah,[2] consisted of 5,000 horse and 5,000 foot. It was ostensibly sent to assist, on the part of the Nizam, in the inauguration of the new Peishwa, but more probably it was designed to strengthen the hands of Balaji Pundit, to enable him, if not absolutely to exclude the lineal descendants of the late Peishwa, at least to maintain himself in the administration against the designs of Dowlat Row Scindiah and others for overturning his authority. After all, it is not impossible that this measure was resolved upon in

[1] Appendix D D.

[2] *Ante*, page 189-90.

anticipation of the Nizam's death, with a view to the removal at that juncture of a considerable part of Raymond's force, in which light it may be regarded as an act of the Roy Royan. To explain this, I may remark, that prejudice ran high at Hyderabad against Secunder Jah, chiefly on account of his attachment to Azim-ool-oomrah, whose liberation from captivity and restoration to power would, it was supposed, be among the first acts of the prince's government.

The intrigue and cabal which had suddenly gathered head were not immediately suppressed by his highness's convalescence; but the prospects of Secunder Jah did not appear to improve as the days wore on to the middle of March. He was reported to be very impatient under the restraint in which he was held, indulging himself in extravagances little calculated to serve his cause. The mother of this prince was also in disgrace with his highness.

The Pagah party would have been well pleased to have secured the succession of their favourite prince, Feridoon Jah, without the participation of M. Raymond, and would even have preferred the assistance of the English; but having no hope of this, they seemed determined to enlist the interests of the French commander in their favour. In truth, this adventurer was courted by all parties, and on the supposition that neighbouring powers declined any interference, in the event of the Nizam's death, the vacant throne, as remarked in the Resident's despatch, would unquestionably have been at his disposal. Neither was his power much diminished—if that were the end sought—by the departure of his troops for Poonah, since he had just previously secured the appointment of Ameen Jinsi, or comptroller of the ordnance, the whole of which department was in future to be under his efficient direction. At the same time, the sum hitherto allowed for the maintenance of this branch of the service, 35,000 rupees per mensem, was increased to 50,000, in consideration of certain improvements which the new comptroller proposed to introduce into it, among which may be mentioned the appointment of twenty-five European artificers.

Feridoon Jah, in whose interest his party were desirous of gaining over M. Raymond, was only a few months younger than Secunder Jah. He was generally considered the superior of his elder brother both in understanding and temper; and his highness had been heard to declare that he was the very picture of what he himself was at the same age. It is by no means unlikely that this circumstance, trivial and accidental as it seems, may in the season of dotage have determined such a mind as the Nizam's in his favour.

On the 27th of March, Saddasheo Reddy was

seized while attending the Durbar, and conducted under a strong guard to Golcondah. It was pretended by the Roy Royan that he had been detected in fresh practices of a treasonable nature. This, however, was considered to be merely a device to propitiate the nobleman who had guaranteed to the Polygar his life and honour.

About the same date, orders were issued to move the entire army towards Bidur, on the pretence that the western provinces were menaced by a Mahratta army, which had been ostensibly appointed to levy the customary Choute, but, really, to obtain by forced sequestrations, the sum due to the Peishwa according to the convention of Kurdlah. The intention of his highness, however, was only partially and very languidly fulfilled, owing to the indecision of the Roy Royan, who wished to conciliate the Pagah chieftains, while the latter were not slow to express their opinion that proper steps should be taken to satisfy the Peishwa's just claims. We are not indeed expected to believe that these chiefs were very greatly concerned about the justice of the case. In reality their backwardness to carry out his highness's design arose from their jealous belief that the Roy Royan had no other object in view than the strengthening of his own credit, by removing to a distance those who might have disputed his will with regard to the succession in the event of the Nizam's death; or, on the other hand, of strengthening Balaji Pundit against his opponents at Poonah. But these surmises have been the subject of remark on a previous page.[1]

While these intrigues, or rumours of intrigue, were occupying the general attention at Hyderabad, the Company's detachment of troops had gained a considerable advantage over the insurgents of Raichore, who had for months previously set the Nizam's authority at defiance. After forcing the outposts of the rebels, and taking the Pettah of Raichore, preparations were made to open a battery upon the fort, when on the 8th of April, Major Roberts being absent at Madras, the assault was ordered by Captain Dalrymple, and the place captured. His highness was neither insensible to the importance of the service thus rendered, nor to the gallantry of the Company's troops and the spirited conduct of their commander on the occasion. It is even stated that many of the Oomrahs made a pointed comparison between these troops and those under the command of Raymond, to the disadvantage of the latter, and that his highness concurred in the observation.

Before concluding this chapter, I shall refer to the contents of a despatch addressed to the Governor General by the Resident on the 1st of May, chiefly

---

[1] *Ante*, page 193.

relating to the growing intimacy between the Nizam and Tippoo Sultan.[1] On the 7th of May, his highness despatched an agent to Poonah, charged with khilluts for the new Peishwa, whose good will it was desired to conciliate; and there is reason to believe that the envoy, Rugotum Row, was empowered to offer some kind of satisfaction to the court of Poonah, with respect to the pecuniary claims on the Nizam, though his conduct in this particular would of course be governed by circumstances, and especially by the state of parties on his arrival. To provide for eventualities, he was also furnished with khilluts for Dowlat Row Scindiah, and his principal minister. In connection with the latter it is observable that at the same time when the mission of Rugotum Row was finally resolved on, orders were issued to suspend the despatch of troops to Bidur. This change of policy was attributed to Balaji Pundit's want of decision. Had that minister showed a fixed determination to resist Scindiah by a vigorous and suitable application of the resources he possessed, no doubt existed but that his highness would have cordially co-operated with him.

A very few weeks served to show that the Nizam himself was destined to be the victim of this indecision or state-craft of Balaji. On the 9th of June,

[1] This despatch is inserted in full in Appendix E E.

letters arrived at Hyderabad announcing that the late Peishwa's youngest son Ragonaut Row had "in a fortunate hour" been placed on the vacant musnud. The same despatches brought letters to Govind Kishen, the Mahratta Vakeel, in which he was informed that it was absolutely necessary for the Nizam to discharge the engagements he had entered into at Kurdlah, the stipulated period for the performance of which had now elapsed. Nor was this the worst.

By other authentic advices which arrived at the same time, the Hyderabad Durbar was informed that the first instrument to which the seal of the new Peishwa had been affixed, was an assignment on the part of his highness in favour of Dowlat Row Scindiah for two crores of rupees; that this chief meant to enforce payment with his whole power, and also to compel his highness to reimburse him for whatever expenses he should incur in the prosecution of the claim. There was but too much reason to believe that Scindiah, beyond these demands, purposed insisting on further territorial cessions to the amount of thirty lacs of rupees annual revenue; in other words, the complete restitution of the country obtained at different times by his highness from the Mahratta Government.[1]

[1] The amount altogether being 62 lacs, of which 32 lacs reverted to the Peishwa by the treaty of Kurdlah.

Beyond all this, it merely depended on the fortune of war, whether he would not attempt the utter subversion of the Hyderabad state.

This change in the situation of affairs since the 1st of May, when the Resident addressed the despatch before mentioned to the Governor General, rather tended to strengthen his representations than otherwise. He pointed out that it was not until the sudden termination of Azim-ool-oomrah's administration by his captivity at the Mahratta court, that Tippoo Sultan had commenced those friendly advances which had since given rise to so much suspicion; from this fact he inferred that the apparent alienation between the courts of Seringapatam and Hyderabad was to be accounted for by causes personal to that minister, and as the chief of these causes was the known devotion of Azim-ool-oomrah to the English alliance, it was important to consider how far we might be concerned in the sudden friendship for the Nizam displayed by Tippoo Sultan.

The ultimate object of all Tippoo's intrigues with Hyderabad, was, he observed, to undermine the friendship subsisting between his highness and the English government; and the appointment of Sukkaram Pundit as Vakeel at the Nizam's court was only a roundabout way of working to that end. While Tippoo was thus cautiously feeling his way to an alliance with his highness, the latter was prevented from reciprocating his advances very cordially by the hope of a favourable settlement of the Peishwa's claims, and lately by the political prospect opened up at Poonah in consequence of the dissensions relative to the succession, caused by the Peishwa's death. This fluctuating policy may have provoked Tippoo Sultan to commence an intrigue with Ally Jah, then in arms against his father, and his clandestine encouragement of another member of his highness's family openly to resist his authority. The Nizam certainly did not calculate on a rupture with the English government as the result of these intrigues, but his alliance with Tippoo against the Mahrattas would necessarily have led to an interruption of his friendly relations with us.

The danger of this was greatly increased by collateral circumstances; for example, by the pedling character of the Roy Royan, who now had the management of his highness's affairs, and by the probability (in the opinion of a man so limited in his views) of the French co-operating in his designs by a descent on the coast of the Carnatic. The Resident, therefore, was of opinion, that we should best prevent his highness from establishing cordial relations with Tippoo by protecting him, in some efficient manner, from the encroachment of the Mahrattas, who at the present time were inclined to press him hard. Since the

Nizam's illness, indeed, the situation had been modified by the greater circumspection of Tippoo himself, who knew not what turn affairs might take if his highness were suddenly to die, and the late minister, Azim-ool-oomrah, be restored to power. All things considered, it seemed probable to the Resident that Tippoo was inclined patiently to bide his time; and his two agents, apparently independent of each other, at the Nizam's court, were there to watch the state of parties and opinions on the important question of the succession.

The despatch concludes with a reference to the exorbitant power acquired by the French in Hyderabad as being even a greater evil than the increased cordiality between that state and Seringapatam. It seemed to the Resident that their power was now placed beyond the reach of any attempts that could be made for its subversion; and he quotes the opinion of Meer Allum that he had allowed the opportunity to slip, when the Nizam proposed that the Company should send a few extra battalions to aid in the suppression of Ally Jah's rebellion; and when, on a former occasion, he proposed to raise a new levy to be officered by British subjects. It was Meer Allum's opinion that the combined effect of these measures would have been the complete annihilation of French influence.

CHAPTER XVI.

OUR OPPONENTS CHECKMATED.

The Situation of affairs dependent on the return to Power of Azim-ool-oomrah—Plans laid by that Minister to obtain his release—Disposition of the Nizam towards him—Proposals of his Highness for an Alliance against the Mahrattas—The Dismissal of the French held out as an inducement to the Company—The Nizam's Policy crossed by the Intrigues of Tippoo against the English—Imtiaz-oo-dowlah and Medina Sahib—Serious Proposals of Tippoo—Temporizing Policy of the Nizam—Growing probability of Azim-ool-oomrah's return—Proposals of Accommodation from Scindiah — Perplexed State of the Nizam — Resolves and Re-resolves—Azim-ool-oomrah's Attention to the Affairs of Hyderabad during his Captivity—He procures the Remission of the Obligations stipulated by the Convention of Kurdlah—The Nizam's Design for the Dismemberment of his Dominions—He dispenses with the Services of the English Troops—Azim-ool-oomrah remonstrates—His Return to Hyderabad and Reinstatement as Minister—Reddy's attempt at Suicide —Renewed Overtures from the King of Cabool—Tippoo Sultan recalls his Troops to Seringapatam—Death of M. Raymond—The Earl of Mornington succeeds Sir J. Shore as Governor-General—The Removal of the French and the Protection of the Nizam becomes the Policy of Government—Treaty of the 1st of September, 1798—Arrival of additional English Troops at Hyderabad—Dismissal of the French Officers and Mutiny of the Corps — Dismemberment and Dispersion of the entire body.

The situation of affairs as disclosed in the preceding chapter, though critical for all parties, was liable to be changed at any moment by the return of the late minister from his captivity; and from information given by Meer Allum, it appeared that Azim-ool-oomrah was really in treaty with Scindiah for the recovery of his liberty. It was confidently affirmed, and Meer Allum thought it might be credited, that the captive minister, on condition of being restored, had not only promised to discharge the whole of the Mahratta claims on his highness within a very short period, but to pay an additional crore of rupees on account of his own ransom, and this without taking a single rupee from his highness's treasury. This promise (however tempting to the other parties concerned,) was not calculated to make the wealthier classes in the state of Hyderabad anxious for the minister's success, as the only means of fulfilling such an engagement would have consisted, in laying the jagheerdar, as well as the husbandman and merchant, under oppressive contributions.

Azim-ool-oomrah's plan was to proceed in the first instance to Crosah[1] and thence arrange with the Nizam the manner and conditions of his return to the

[1] A fort in the vicinity of Rawapore, and comprehended in the Minister's own jagheer.

capital. "Whether or not he contemplated being escorted by a Mahratta force," writes Captain Kirkpatrick at the time, "is a point said to be as yet unsettled, though the report is that he himself professes a desire to be unattended on the occasion. The Nizam affects to make light of this intrigue and pretended arrangement."

In an interview with the Resident, Meer Allum declared that his highness would risk everything rather than yield to the unjust and exorbitant demands of Scindiah; and he desired to know whether or not the Company would make any attempt to hinder him from overrunning or seizing upon any part of his highness's dominions. He inquired further, whether the government would object to his highness forming an union with Tippoo, with a view to his defence against the Mahrattas, whose designs he regarded as being fraught with danger, not only to the state of Hyderabad, but to every power in the Deccan, and to the Company, no less than to others. He hinted that the Nizam had conceived the idea of a triple alliance between himself, the Company, and Tippoo, for the purpose of restraining that nation within the bounds necessary to the security and independence of its neighbours, and he seemed desirous to know whether we would take the lead in the negotiations necessary to that end. To this inquiry the Resident could only reply evasively at the moment, but promised a more distinct reply in the course of the same day. Accordingly he sent his Moonshee with a verbal message, purporting, in addition to such general professions of amity and good will as were deemed suitable to the occasion, "that in the events alluded to (which, however, he was very unwilling to regard as at all likely), his highness might rely, as in every other case, on the most steady adherence of the Company's government to its engagements."

On the same occasion, Meer Allum expatiated for the hundredth time on the *eminent advantages* which would accrue to *both governments* from the improvement of their present *too circumscribed connection* into an *unlimited defensive alliance* (*Sherâkut 'aam*). The Resident answered slightly, that the credit and authority acquired by the French at the Nizam's court rendered such very close and extensive ties as he spoke of, more impracticable and unadvisable than ever. Meer Allum rejoined that, "on the contrary, he knew of no other means by which that credit and authority could be so effectually subverted," adding, "*that he would engage to procure the dismissal of every Frenchman in his highness's country within a very short period after the conclusion of such a treaty as he had mentioned.*"

From the manner in which Meer Allum alluded

to this matter, and other circumstances, Captain Kirkpatrick was inclined to suspect that if his highness had not already actually opened a negotiation with Tippoo for his aid against the Mahrattas, he was, at least, on the point of making specific overtures with that object in view. As for Tippoo himself, he was still steadfast in his design against the English, as we shall see immediately, but a link in the chain of intrigue must first be supplied.

Imtiaz-oo-Dowlah, the Nizam's nephew, whom I have before mentioned, was at this time making rapid progress in regaining his highness's favour. The dangers which threatened Meer Allum from the intrigues of this insidious prince were a matter of some concern to us also; since, most probably, it was with a view to a connection between his uncle and Tippoo, that he aimed at the disgrace or removal of a person so likely to thwart his measures. His success was so considerable, that he inspired the Nizam with fears for his personal safety which caused him to adopt some very extraordinary measures against the supposed designs of the Pagah chiefs. One of these was a regulation limiting the number of attendants allowed to accompany the principal chiefs to the Durbar to two Khitmutghars, or confidential followers, each.

That Tippoo was labouring to detach the Nizam from his connection with the Company, and to engage him in his projected enterprise against the English, is manifest enough from the following particulars which were communicated by Medina Sahib, and embodied in a letter addressed to Captain Kirkpatrick.

The khillut and jewels lately sent by him to the Nizam, said this informant, were accompanied by a letter, in which after sundry citations from the word of God (*i.e.* the Koran), and dicta of the Prophet regarding the obligation of the people of the true faith to unite and make war upon the people distinguished by the appellation of *Dhurrul Hurruh* (*i.e.* those with whom it is fitting to make war), he proceeds to disclose his wishes to the following effect.

That himself and the Nizam should enter into solemn engagements according to the forms of Islamism, and which shall endure as long as their respective sovereignties; that continuing to give and take from the Mahrattas, according to ancient custom, he, the Nizam, should cultivate peace with them; that remaining himself quietly at home, he should dismiss the English Resident, and appoint his army to accompany him (Tippoo) to the field, when he would make war upon the English, and wrest back from them the countries which they possessed belonging to the people of the true faith. The letter concluded by requesting that Imtiaz-oo-dowlah (mentioned above) might always be the channel of intercourse between them, and with referring his highness to Medina Sahib for further particulars.

At the same time that Tippoo gave this letter in charge to Medina Sahib—the information continues,—he also delivered to him a *kurtaus* or scroll, with his seal affixed, the delivery of which to the Nizam after he should have agreed to make war upon the English, would be a sacred pledge between them. In accordance with this command, the sacred scroll was kept to himself by Medina Sahib, when he gave the presents and the letter to Imtiaz-oo-dowlah for presentation to the Nizam, who asked what verbal message Medina Sahib had brought. The latter replied that he had been commanded by the Sultan to deliver his message personally; whereupon, the Nizam, musing for a moment, observed, "that it was seven years since he had written a letter to Tippoo, to which he had not yet received a reply, and that the settlement of engagements rested entirely upon the answer to be given to that letter." He ended by sending a message to Medina Sahib, requesting him to make any communication with which he was charged to Imtiaz-oo-dowlah. The latter therefore pressed Medina Sahib to disclose the business with which he had been entrusted, observing that his highness would certainly take offence if he persisted in his reserve.

Thus closely pressed, Medina Sahib consented to

send the *kurtaus* by the hands of Imtiaz-oo-dowlah, but first requested to be informed into whose hands the letter of seven years date, mentioned by his highness, had been delivered. When this was reported to the Nizam, he smiled, and said, "It was delivered into the hands of Mehdi Ally Khan, whom Tippoo had deputed hither as his Vakeel, and it related to the same treaty and engagements now spoken of, and demanded for surety the Word of God. It is to this that no answer has yet been received." But Medina Sahib replied, that the verbal message with which he had been charged, referred to the very point in question, and that the sealed *kurtaus* which he had sent by the hands of Imtiaz-oo-dowlah was expressly intended as a surety and ratification of the same, It appears, however, that his highness took a different view of the matter, for after reading the *kurtaus*, he commanded that Medina Sahib should be told to go back to Seringapatam, and return with the ratification. Finally, he consented that the Naig of the Hurcurrahs (who was a Brahmin in the confidence of Tippoo) should be sent on this errand.

The Brahmin conveyed a letter to Tippoo, in which he was requested to send his Vakeel, Mehdi Ali Khan, to complete the arrangement, by which time (and there is some slyness in the suggestion) Azim-ool-oomrah would also have returned, and these projects would be settled. Well might Medina Sahib observe, on understanding the purport of the letter, that Tippoo was not well affected towards Azim-ool-oomrah! The Nizam answered "that he should take it particularly upon himself to reconcile them!" All this time, Tippoo was terribly in earnest, working night and day to prepare for the enterprise, and superintending everything himself. The Nizam was simply temporising, with a view to the more favourable arrangement of his affairs with the Mahratta Government.

From this relation it would appear that Azim-ool-oomrah's early return was really expected by the Nizam himself, and as something agreeable rather than otherwise. This indeed was consistent in the chief point with the general belief, but rumour added that the express and cordial concurrence of his highness was the one thing wanting to enable the late minister to complete his arrangements, and that his highness was still resolved against taking any step which might favour the idea that he was ready to satisfy the Mahratta demands in any degree whatever.

At length the arrangements that had been in contemplation assumed a definite form. On the 30th of July, the Nizam received letters from Dowlat Rao Scindiah and Azim-ool-oomrah, importing that an arrangement had been concluded between them to the following effect:—In consideration of the prompt payment of two crores of rupees, and of his highness heartily joining to support the new Peishwa on the musnud, (contributing, if necessary, a military force to co-operate with Scindiah's troops for that purpose,) Azim-ool-oomrah should not only be set at liberty, but the territories ceded under the convention of Kurdlah be restored to his highness, and the remaining crore of rupees due in virtue of the same obligation be remitted. Eighty lacs of rupees were to be paid down previous to Azim-ool-oomrah's departure for Poonah. This proposal decided the matter, but we shall see that the minister did not leave the Mahratta capital before he had given additional proof both of his talent for business, and of his devotion to his master's interests.

In the meantime the Nizam's perplexity became more conspicuous than ever. He was told by the members of his Durbar, who were adverse to the Company, that a French armament from the mother country was about to land on the Coromandel coast to co-operate with Tippoo; and was so impressed with the information, that Captain Kirkpatrick was obliged to counteract its effects by a plain statement of facts. Then, under the influence of Tippoo's Vakeel, he requested the Resident to order the Company's detachment to return to British territory; yet scarcely had Major Roberts commenced his march than a suspicion of Tippoo's designs in respect to Kurnool caused him to request that the detachment might be halted, and subsequently, that it might return to Hyderabad, which it accordingly did. Finally, Raymond's corps was ordered to Kurpah, with the view of co-operating with the Nawab of Kurnool against Tippoo, and the troops had actually moved from their lines when the order was countermanded. This was wisely done at the instance of Meer Allum, who, remembering the explicit answer of the Resident and the letter of Lord Cornwallis on this subject, remonstrated with his highness so effectually that he withdrew his orders.

The attention which Azim-ool-oomrah continued to bestow on the affairs of Hyderabad in his captivity is shown by a letter which he addressed to the Nizam relative to this claim of Tippoo on Kurnool, and the reader who takes the trouble to consult it[1] will find that the late minister really understood the merits of the case. Nor was this the only or the most remarkable instance of his vigilance and his capacity for business. In the course of November his highness announced to the Resident that arrangements had been made for the restoration of the district ceded to the Mahrattas by the convention of Kurdlah; the total dereliction of the claim for Choute on Bidur; the extinction of all pecuniary engagements, and the restoration of the fort of Dowlatabad. In a

[1] Appendix F F.

word, the provisions of the treaty of Kurdlah were absolutely cancelled.

Previous to the return of the clever minister, the Nizam made it known in his palace that he intended to portion out his territory before his decease among his three elder sons, Secunder Jah, Feridoon Jah, and Jehandar Jah. He intended to procure for this scheme of dismemberment the sanction—amounting to a guarantee—of the English and Mahrattas, and it was believed that the sunnuds for this purpose had for some time been actually prepared.

At the commencement of the year 1797 Captain Kirkpatrick was obliged to leave Hyderabad and proceed to the sea coast on account of his health, when the temporary charge of the residency devolved on his brother. The latter having represented to the Nizam that the services of the Madras contingent were urgently required by the Company in the south of India, his highness agreed to dispense with them on condition of other troops being sent to garrison his territory. For this purpose a detachment from Bengal was ordered to Hyderabad, but before its arrival his highness signified to the Resident his intention to dispense for some time with the services of any of the Company's troops. He was instigated to this by the faction inimical to the English, but assigned as an ostensible reason the great demand which he understood to exist at Madras for all available troops; and added a request that he might be informed when the exigency was over, that he might avail himself, if needful, of their future services.

This sudden dismissal of the English troops was, I have no doubt, regarded as a triumph by the faction who were equally inimical to British interests and to the return of the minister. But Azim-ool-oomrah was now actually on his way from Poonah, and having been informed of the permission given to withdraw the Madras battalion, addressed a letter to the Nizam, deprecating his compliance with that demand. Although, he remarked, these troops cost the Nizam 50,000 rupees monthly, they saved him in the end many crores, and the Bengal troops by which they were to be relieved were not nearly so efficient.

Since the Nizam's illness in March, 1796, he had continued to exhibit symptoms of rapidly declining health. On the 20th of July following he was reduced so low as to be hardly capable of raising his head, yet he had rallied from time to time, there being less immediate danger from his distemper than from the empirical manner in which he was treated. Now during the first half of 1797 he was fast losing his strength, speech, and appetite, and by his obstinacy, and the quackery to which he submitted, was hastening his own end. Under these circumstances, one of the first acts of Azim-ool-oomrah, upon his arrival and reinstalment in the ministry in July, 1797, was to induce the Nizam to allow Secunder Jah to sign all public documents and sunnuds. This measure was opposed by the whole of the inmates of the palace, but the minister carried his point.

About this time Saddasheo Reddy, who, the reader is aware, was conveyed to the fortress of Golcondah, with his family, attempted to put an end to his own and his wife's existence by setting fire to a pile of wood which he had gradually collected for that purpose. The smoke that issued from his apartment led to the discovery of the attempt. He was afterwards put in irons and kept under much greater restraint.

I have remarked under date of August, 1795, that a letter was said to have been received from a person connected with the court of Cabool, inviting the Nizam to co-operate with a force against the Mahrattas;[1] and that only a verbal reply was returned by his highness. This person, however, did not readily abandon his design. On the 21st of August, 1797, two letters were received by Azim-ool-oomrah —one to the address of the Nizam and one to

---

[1] *Ante*, p. 178.

himself, through Row Hurryhur Row, at Mortsuddy in Cabool, with similar proposals. I have inserted these letters[1] as illustrations of the intrigues which are continually fomented at Eastern courts. But Azim-ool-oomrah appears never to have replied to them either directly or indirectly.

Towards the end of the year 1797 Tippoo's advanced force, which had been stationed for some months past at Gooty, received orders to return to Seringapatam. It appears that the Poonah Durbar had remonstrated against Tippoo's intended attack upon the Nawab of Kurnool.

Another event of considerable importance to this history happened on the 25th of March, 1798, when M. Raymond, who had been ailing for some time, expired at Hyderabad. He was succeeded by his second in command, M. Perron.

On May 17th, 1798, the Earl of Mornington succeeded Sir John Shore as Governor General. Shortly after his arrival he directed the Resident to open a negotiation with the Nizam for a new treaty on the basis so long desired by his highness, of the British Government taking the State under its protection, provided the Nizam in return dismissed the French officers from his service, and consented that the contingent of troops supplied by the Company should be

[1] Appendix G G.

increased. In a despatch which I have inserted in the Appendix, his lordship demonstrates the necessity of removing the French from the service both of the Nizam and Scindiah, on account of the alarming influence which they had established in both governments, but especially in the councils of Hyderabad. The despatch is further valuable as a complete exposition of the state of affairs in India at the time of his lordship's arrival.[1]

A treaty was accordingly concluded on the 1st of September, 1798, by which it was stipulated that the subsidiary force should be made permanent and increased to six battalions of infantry, with a proportion of artillery, at an annual charge to the Nizam of 24,17,100 rupees. The French corps in the service of the Nizam was to be immediately disbanded, and their officers made over to the English to be transported to Europe as prisoners of war. So far, Azim-ool-oomrah was gratified by obtaining the long cherished wish of his heart; but the formidable question remained how the dismissal of the French was to be effected, and when it came to the point the minister was alarmed at the magnitude of the undertaking.

On the 9th of October the four additional battalions arrived in the vicinity of Hyderabad, and a formal

---

[1] Appendix H H.

demand was made by the Resident for the execution of that part of the treaty which referred to the dismissal of the French. For several days no steps were taken to effect this, but on the contrary, intrigues were set on foot to evade the obligation. In this emergency the Resident informed the Nizam that if he hesitated any longer he should order an attack on the French lines, and this spirited remonstrance being accompanied by a threatening movement on the part of the British troops, an order was immediately issued dismissing the French officers from the service and releasing the troops from their control.

Still the disarmament and dispersion of this body might have been expected to prove a work of time and difficulty. The promulgation of the order, however, produced a mutiny in the French lines, and furnished an opportunity for immediate action. Two detachments under Colonels Roberts and Hyndman were moved into position in front and rear of the French cantonments. This so alarmed the mutineers, that they immediately released their officers, who had been placed in confinement, and on the terms of surrender being explained to them, moved out in a body, leaving their cannon and arms behind in their lines, of which the British troops then took possession.

Thus by the firm and decided tone of the Resident, and the admirable arrangements made by him for carrying into effect his coercive measures, a force of 15,000 men was placed completely in our power without the loss of a single life.

It would exceed the limits of this narrative to give full details of the progress which the French had made and were still making at this critical period, to a position which must have soon made them arbitrators of the Deccan. Their discipline and appointments, though inferior to our own, were far above those of any troops commanded by the natives, and the regularity with which the corps had been paid since its first formation, not only enabled them to recruit with facility, and to fill their ranks with the best men of our northern circars, but to entice deserters by bodies from our service. The more we contemplate the power thus acquired, the greater cause have we to congratulate ourselves on the complete success of the policy which dictated the reduction of a body so formidable. The happy manner in which this success was finally achieved could not but tend to establish our influence on the firmest basis, impressing the court, and all who witnessed the circumstances, with a high sense both of the power to execute their purposes and of the wisdom which dictated the councils of the English Government.

CHAPTER XVII.

THE RULE OF ORDER INTRODUCED.

Change of Policy on the Arrival of the Earl of Mornington as Governor General—Subjugation and Death of Tippoo Sultan—Co-operation of the Nizam—Division of Tippoo's Territory—Hyderabad received into Alliance as a Protected State—Treaty of Commerce—Death of Nizam Ally Khan and Succession of Secunder Jah—First Mahratta War and Division of Scindiah's Territory—Death of the Minister Azim-ool-oomrah and Succession of Meer Allum—Intrigues of the Nizam's Favourites against Meer Allum—Restoration of Meer Allum to his Ministerial Office under British Protection—Death of Meer Allum and Renewed Controversy with the Nizam—Mooneer-ool-Moolk is appointed Dewan—Chundoo-lall accepts Office under British Influence as Peshcar under the Dewan—Reorganization of the Nizam's Army commenced by the English Resident — The Second Mahratta War—Reform of the Nizam's Administration commenced by Sir C. Metcalfe—Prosperity of the Hyderabad State under the New System—Reform of the Nizam's Financial System—The Nizam's Accounts with Messrs. William Palmer and Co.—Arrangement with the East India Company—Death of Secunder Jah—Change in the Style of Correspondence between the Nizam and the Governor General—Disorders consequent on the Repudiation of British Interference by the New Nizam—Another Change of System adopted with Disastrous Effects—Colonel Stewart's Report on the State of the Country—The

Mode of Collecting the Revenue, &c. in 1838—The Court of Directors recommend the Nizam to abstain from all Interference in Public Affairs.

THE succession of the Earl of Mornington led to results of vast importance in the history of British India. I have remarked in the previous chapter on the earnestness with which Tippoo Sultan endeavoured to organise a general confederacy against the English; and it may be here added that his correspondence extended as far as Arabia, and contemplated a religious war of extermination. If the reader will now turn to the despatch of the new Governor General,[1] he will see that the reality and vastness of this design was penetrated by his lordship, who had no sooner landed in India than he began the measures which rendered the conspiracy abortive.

The subversion of French influence in Hyderabad, and the settlement of our relations with the Nizam, were but preliminary to the sudden mustering of troops and the march upon Seringapatam. Yet subordinate as were the events which I have briefly related in the preceding chapter, they were essential to the success of the general plan. Instead of leaving at Hyderabad a disciplined body of 15,000 troops accustomed to war and officered by foes ready to take the field against us, and add to the impediments

[1] Appendix H H.

which were already almost insurmountable, the Governor General was able to draw large supports from the Nizam's army. The British contingent itself under the new treaty mustered 6,500 men, who were placed at his disposal, together with an equal number of the Nizam's infantry and a large body of irregulars. All these formed a junction with the army of General Harrison at Vellore, and subsequently assisted in the siege and capture of Seringapatam.

The Nizam's own troops on this occasion were placed under the orders of Meer Allum, who now, for the second time, co-operated with the Company's army.

The defeat and death of Tippoo, as every reader of history is aware, was followed by a partition treaty, concluded between the English, the Nizam, and the new Rajah of Mysore. The districts of Gooty and Goorumcundah were included in the portion of Tippoo's territories made over to the Nizam. Mysore itself was not divided with him, but the titular rajah was restored, because according to Lord Wellesley's minutes, its partition would have given the Nizam many strong fortresses which could not have been placed in his hands without imminent danger to the British frontier.

By a subsidiary treaty made with the Nizam and

bearing date October 12th, 1800, the British Government engaged that no state or power whatsoever should, with impunity, commit an act of unprovoked hostility or aggression upon the territories of the Nizam. To enable the Company to fulfil this engagement in an efficient manner two battalions of Sepoys and a regiment of native cavalry were permanently added to the subsidiary force to be maintained by the Hyderabad state; and to secure the regular payment of this augmented force the Nizam ceded in perpetuity to the Company all the territories which he had acquired by the treaty of Seringapatam in 1792, and by the treaty of Mysore in 1799. With a view, however, to the preservation of a well-defined boundary, some changes were made in this cession, the Nizam retaining Kupool, Gudjunturghurh, and adjacent territories, and giving in lieu of them Adoni and other districts situated to the south of the river Toombudra, which by this settlement was to form the boundary between the two states.

In the event of war taking place between the contracting parties and a third state, the Nizam agreed that the whole of the subsidiary force, except two battalions, which were to be kept near his person, should be employed against the enemy; and that this force should be immediately joined by six thousand infantry and nine thousand horse of his own troops.

In 1802 a treaty was concluded with a view to improve and secure the commerce carried on between the dominions of the Nizam and those of the Company. By this treaty it was provided, that the growth, produce, and manufactures of either state were to be permitted to enter the other on paying a duty of 5 per cent on the prime cost. The duties on British imports, it was agreed, were to be levied at the capital, and they were henceforth declared exempt from all "Radharry" duties levied by the Zemindars through whose districts they might have to pass. All articles of supply, necessaries, wearing apparel, etc., for the use of the subsidiary force, were exempt entirely from duty as provided for in former treaties.

In August 1803, Nizam Ali Khan died at Hyderabad, and was peaceably succeeded on the musnud by his eldest surviving son, Secunder Jah.

At this time the first Mahratta war, occasioned by the rivalry of Scindiah and Holkar, was in progress. On the 25th of October, Scindiah and his ally the Peishwa were defeated in the neighbourhood of Poonah, and the latter to avert his total ruin, concluded a treaty of defensive alliance with the British on the same basis as that which had been concluded with the court of Hyderabad. The war was closed in 1804 by the defeat of Scindiah; and by the treaty of peace further territorial advantages accrued to the Nizam. The territories conquered from Scindiah situated between the Adjunta Hills and the River Godavery, together with the country ceded by the Rajah of Nagpore (lying to the westward of the Wardah and to the south of the Gawulghur range of hills), were added to his dominions.

In May, 1804, Azim-ool-oomrah, the distinguished minister of Nizam Ali Khan, expired at Hyderabad. On the occurrence of this event, Secunder Jah was strongly urged by the Resident to nominate Meer Allum to the vacant appointment of Dewan. It is hardly necessary to remind the reader of this history of the numerous occasions on which Meer Allum had shown his fitness for the office, both by his loyalty to the state, and his enlightened appreciation of the English alliance; in addition to which the inexperience of the Nizam rendered it highly important that the resources of the Hyderabad state should be under the control of a minister who owed his elevation exclusively to our influence. The Nizam reluctantly consented to the Resident's proposal, and Meer Allum was appointed Dewan, but without the unlimited power enjoyed by his predecessor: subsequently he appears to have gained the confidence of the Nizam, and by humouring him secured his assistance and support in carrying into effect the extensive measures of reform which it was found necessary to introduce into every department of the state.

Towards the close of the following year (1805) Rajah Mahiput Ram, then governor of Berar, returned to Hyderabad and easily succeeded in establishing an influence with the Nizam, who retained a grateful recollection of the pecuniary assistance and other acts of kindness received from him previously to his accession to the throne. Always distrustful of the close connection which existed between Meer Allum and the Resident, the weak and timid mind of the Nizam was easily worked upon by the creatures about him to sanction the intrigues set on foot to effect the expulsion of the minister in order that Mahiput Ram himself might succeed to the vacant office. At this crisis the prompt and decided interference of the Resident alone saved Meer Allum from ruin. Although the Nizam was reluctantly induced to receive Meer Allum once more into favour, and to promise that he would hold no further intercourse with Mahiput Ram —who was directed to return to his government in Berar—the event soon manifested his insincerity. It was early discovered that Mahiput Ram, using the agency of Ismail-yar-Jung and other companions of the Nizam, was able to maintain his influence at court, and he even matured in concert with Scindiah and Holkar a plan to secure his return to power by the destruction of the minister and the subversion of the British alliance.

In this state of affairs two alternatives were open for adoption by the British Government, viz. either to abandon the alliance *in toto*, or by direct and authoritative interference to replace it on its original basis.

The first of these alternatives was abandoned, as it would in justice have been followed by a renunciation of the territories acquired under the treaty of 1800, and would in all probability have endangered our political ascendancy in India. The Governor General, on due deliberation, determined to enforce with the full weight and influence of government such measures as he deemed of importance to our interests.

Instructions were accordingly conveyed to the Resident to insist on the immediate dismissal of Mahiput Ram and Ismail-yar-Jung from his highness's councils, and in carrying this order into effect to exercise the utmost circumspection to prevent the minister, Meer Allum, from being exposed to any personal danger. To secure the latter object, Meer Allum, on the pretence of paying a visit of condolence to the Resident, left the city, and took up his residence in a garden-house within the Resident's compound, where he remained protected by a guard of the subsidiary force, till the negotiations with the Nizam had been brought to a close, and Mahiput Ram and his followers were dismissed from his highness's service. Meer Allum then returned to the city and resumed the functions of his office, but conscious of the strong feelings of dislike which his successful struggle with the Nizam had created in the minds of his sovereign and the principal chiefs at his court, he considered it essential for his safety, that a detachment of the subsidiary force should be stationed at his palace.

To crown the minister's triumph, the Nizam paid the first visit of ceremony to his minister on his return to the city, and as a mark of his favour, bestowed on his followers the several offices vacant by the dismissal of Mahiput Ram. Among others, the government of Berar was conferred on Goorud Buxsh, a brother of Rajah Chundoo-lall, who then held the situation of Meer Allum's Peshcar, and a body of the Company's troops was detached to place him in possession of his new government.

On the approach of this force, Mahiput Ram moved off with his followers to Shorapoor, and very shortly afterwards took the field as a rebel. A body of the Nizam's troops sent to oppose him were defeated with considerable loss, and it was eventually found necessary to move the subsidiary force against him, before which he retired without a show of opposition, and being pursued from one extremity of the

Nizam's dominions to the other, fled for protection to the Mahratta Chief, Holkar, by whom he was treacherously murdered.

But again in 1808, the death of Meer Allum gave rise to a protracted and angry discussion between the British Government and the Nizam in regard to the appointment of a successor. It was the wish of the Governor General that Shums-ool-oomrah should be appointed to the situation of minister, leaving to Rajah Chundoo-lall the conduct as before of the executive duties of the administration in his capacity of Peshcar.[1] The Nizam, on the other hand, while he expressed his willingness to continue to Chundoo lall the authority which he was permitted to exercise during the former administration, raised so many objections to the appointment of Shums-ool-oomrah, and betrayed so much anxiety to confer the office of minister on Mooneer-ool-Moolk, that the Resident

[1] Shums-ool-oomrah, the nominee of the English Government, was at this period about twenty-eight years of age, of a mild disposition and manners, and handsome in person. He was luxurious in all articles of European manufacture, and was ambitious of having his house, furniture, and equipage as nearly as possible conformable to European custom. He took great delight in mechanics, in all manner of handicraft work, and in the popular experiments of natural philosophy. He devoted nearly the whole of his time to these pursuits, leaving the management of his affairs and the command of his party to his maternal uncle, Umjid-ool-Moolk.

did not deem himself authorized to oppose his highness's wishes.

Matters remained in this unsatisfactory state till June, 1809, when the Resident waited upon the Nizam, and after a long and stormy interview, at which Mooneer-ool-Moolk and Chundoo lall were present, prevailed on him to assent to the nomination of Mooneer-ool-Moolk to the office of Dewan, and Chundoo lall to that of Peshcar.

The control we now possessed over the resources of the state, enabled the Resident to set about those measures of reorganizing the Nizam's irregular army, which had been long contemplated by the home authorities. A reform was rapidly effected among a considerable portion of these troops, and in the course of a few years a respectable force was organized, and equipped under the command of British officers, fully equal to any duty for which they might be required.

The Mahratta war of 1817 afforded the first opportunity for their employment, and during the campaign in Malwah and the Deccan, they early established their character for efficiency, and their vast superiority over the raw and ill-paid levies which the Nizam would otherwise have sent into the field, as the contingent he was bound by treaty to supply.

In the year 1822 a treaty was concluded at Hyderabad with the Nizam by Sir Charles Metcalfe.

By this treaty the British Government agreed to release the Nizam from his obligation to pay the heavy arrears of Choute to which they had become entitled as successors to the sovereignty of the Peishwa. They also granted him perpetual immunity from all further demands of this nature.

Several years had now elapsed (during which Mooneer-ool-Moolk had died), and the minister Chundoo-lall had been placed at the head of the government. At this period he implicitly acquiesced in the wishes of the Resident. For his steadfast adherence to the engagements of the defensive alliance, he had the advantage of being as steadily upheld by our powerful influence. Much, however, yet remained to be accomplished. Sir Charles Metcalfe, in the course of a few months after his arrival, discovered the total disorganization into which every department of the State, but more particularly the revenue, had fallen before his appointment. He applied a prompt and efficient remedy by placing European officers as superintendents in the different districts, who were entrusted with the general supervision of the subordinate officers employed by the minister. The Nizam's government entered into the scheme with the greatest readiness and seeming conviction of its expediency. The great object in view was to effect a general settlement of the land revenue throughout the Nizam's territories, and to afford the cultivators and other classes protection against oppression or extortion on the part of the government or its agents. For this purpose the country was divided into several districts, to each of which was assigned an European officer charged with the general supervision of the revenue assessments and police. The executive, however, was still vested in the subordináte officers of the native government.

This system during the experience of eight years produced the happiest results, and the country in general enjoyed an immunity from oppression, and a state of repose to which for centuries past it had been a stranger.

Coincident with these reforms the Resident's attention was directed to the necessity of effecting some arrangement by which the Nizam's government might be relieved from the weight of its pecuniary obligations. The most pressing of the demands by which it was now embarrassed arose out of its transactions with the house of William Palmer and Co., of whom it had long been in the habit of borrowing money, at first on its own responsibility, but latterly under the guarantee of the British Government.

The firm in question was first established at Hyderabad in 1811, and carried on its business in one of the presidency bungalows. In 1816 it obtained a licence from the Supreme Government, as required by the Act of 1797 to legalize its transactions, and subsequently continued its pecuniary dealings with the Nizam's government till the 12th of August, 1820, when the aggregate balance of its demands against the Nizam, on several separate accounts, amounted to above sixty lacs of rupees. On the 19th of May, 1820, Rajah Chundoo lall applied to Messrs. Palmer and Co., for the loan of sixty lacs of rupees, which was sanctioned by government on the 15th of July, 1820, the rate of interest on which was understood to be about sixteen per cent.

In addition to the claim of Messrs. Palmer and Co., which in November, 1823, amounted to 78,70,670 rupees, the Nizam was also indebted to the British government to the amount of 20,00,000 rupees, being the excess in the collections of the districts ceded by the Honourable Company to his highness the Nizam, above those of the district ceded by the Nizam to the Company under the treaty of 1822. The credit of the Nizam's government was at that time at its lowest ebb; it was utterly impossible it could extricate itself from the state of bankruptcy into which it had fallen. A proposition was therefore made by the British government to redeem the Peshcush of seven lacs of rupees per annum, due on the northern circars, for an equivalent in ready money. After considerable discussion an arrangement was effected by which the Nizam agreed to relinquish the Peshcush in perpetuity in exchange for the sum of 1,16,66,666 rupees.

In May, 1829, Secunder Jah died at Hyderabad, after a lingering and protracted illness, and was succeeded on the musnud by his eldest (illegitimate) son, Nasir-oo-Dowlah. Advantage was taken of this opportunity by the Governor General to revise the style in which the correspondence with the court of Hyderabad had hitherto been carried on. The imperial phrase, "mabu Dowlat," or royal self, used by the Nizam, and the term of inferiority, "Nayar Mund," used by the Governor General, were discontinued, and the correspondence of the parties has since been conducted on a footing of perfect equality.

The illegitimacy of Nasir-oo-Dowlah was never brought forward as an objection to his succession. The three preceding soubadars of the Deccan had all been illegitimate, so that his claim was sanctioned by usage, and had been acknowledged ever since 1809. The minister was questioned on the subject, and he replied that it was not customary among the members of the Asuphea family to contract marriages. The real name of Nasir-oo-Dowlah was Furkundah, but he was generally called by the former appellation, derived from a title which he bore in early life.

One of the first acts of the new prince on his succession to power, was to prefer a request to the Governor General to discontinue the system of supervision introduced by Sir Charles Metcalfe. The request was favourably received, and instructions were issued to the Resident to relieve the superintendents from the duties in which they were employed. Very soon the evil effects of the change became manifest, in the turbulent conduct of several of the influential Zemindars.

The line of policy adopted by Lord William Bentinck in regard to the court of Hyderabad, subsequent to the accession of the late Nizam, was one of strict non-interference.

The Court of Directors had in the meanwhile been placed in possession of the state into which affairs had fallen in the Nizam's country, and in a despatch dated 8th of September, 1835, directed the Government of India to intimate to the Nizam through the Resident, in distinct terms, that "they could not remain indifferent spectators to the disorder and misrule which had so long prevailed in his territories, and that if the present minister would not provide for the proper and efficient administration of the country, it would be the duty of the British Government to urge upon his highness the necessity of changing his minister, as well as of adopting such other arrangements as might appear to be advisable for the purpose of securing good government."

This communication to his highness was totally unexpected by the minister, and caused him the most lively alarm. He immediately professed the utmost readiness to accede to any proposition short of surrendering his control of the revenue, which the Resident might propose as a remedy for the evils complained of; and he spontaneously suggested that the British government should either nominate officers to superintend the judicial administration of the country, or appoint natives of rank and respectability to furnish the Resident direct with periodical reports of the conduct of the Talookdars.

Neither of the propositions, however, met with the approval of the Nizam, and it was finally determined to appoint ameens, or confidential servants of government to the different districts, as a check on the revenue officers, to administer justice, and to repress every species of oppression; these ameens (munsubdars of inferior rank, illiterate, and in straitened circumstances,) early became the creatures of the Talookdars, or the secret tools of the minister and his agents in the extortions too often practised in the district, under the pretence of mediating between individuals in the family quarrels. The system, in short, proved a complete failure, and the minister only evaded the storm of indignation raised against him at Hyderabad by his seeming anxiety to meet the wishes of the British Government.

From this period to 1838, I have nothing particular to record, either on the state of our relations with Hyderabad, or the administration of the Nizam's government. In the last-mentioned year, Colonel Stewart, the then Resident, submitted a report on the state of the country to the Government of India, in which he treated generally of the cultivation of the land, revenue, assessment, and police. Colonel Stewart's tour of inspection had extended through parts of the Nizam's territories seldom traversed by Europeans. In some of the districts visited, he found that the revenue was collected in money payments, in others the government demand consisted either of one-half or two-thirds of the produce, leaving but little indeed for the cultivator and his family, who had to pay wages and other expenses out of his remaining half or third.

After the presentation of Colonel Stewart's report, the Court of Directors expressed their opinion, that only one thing was wanting to give us the power of reforming the administration, viz., the formal assurance of his highness that he would abstain from any interference in public affairs, This abstinence he already for the most part practised, but were an assurance of this nature formally given it would be beneficial in the highest degree, by inducing the minister to look solely to the Resident for support.

CHAPTER XVIII.

POLITICAL AND ADMINISTRATIVE DIFFICULTIES.

General Fraser succeeds Colonel Stewart as Resident at Hyderabad—The Wahabee Conspiracy discovered—Trial and Conviction of Moobarzoo Dowlah—Resignation of Chundoo lall, the Nizam's Minister—Seraj-ool-Moolk and the Party of the ex-Minister—Vacillation of the Nizam—Attempt of Chundoo lall to influence the Supreme Government in his favour—The Nizam dispenses with a Minister—Increasing Embarrassment of the Nizam's Government—The Nizam's Force is paid by Advances from the Company's Treasury—Conditions of Repayment—Provisional Arrangement for Security—Sufferings of the Nizam's Subjects—Promises of the Nizam—Comments of General Fraser—Dismissal of the Rohilla Mercenaries—Remonstrances on the General Administration of the Nizam's Government—Seraj-ool-Moolk appointed Minister—Satisfaction of the People.

The report of Colonel Stewart, mentioned at the end of the preceding chapter, marks the commencement of what I may call the contemporary history of our connection with Hyderabad and with India generally. For this reason I have given a bare summary of the few leading events which took place at Hyderabad in the period which intervened between the administration of the Earl of Mornington and the above date. The details thus omitted are such as may be found in works of higher pretensions than the present, and my own narrative is relieved of much that the reader would have found tedious.

The year 1838 is memorable as the date of the proclamation against Dost Mohammed Khan, provoked by events which appeared to show that a general ferment had been excited in the North-West, as many think, by the agents of Russia. In April (1839) Kandahar was occupied; in July the battle of Ghuznee was fought; in August following Shah Soujah was restored to his sovereignty; in October, 1840, Dost Mohammed was defeated, and the war was supposed to be at an end. After a few months, however (November 2, 1841), Sir Alexander Burnes and other officers were murdered in a general rising against the British at Cabool; and this event was rapidly followed by the frightful massacre of our troops in the mountain passes, and other signal events which I need not stay to recapitulate. In alluding to these circumstances, I have only desired to fix the period at which I am about to resume the details of my narrative, as one broadly distinguished from a long succession of previous years.

The first occurrence at Hyderabad under this date, which I feel of sufficient importance to record, marks the character of the epoch. In September, 1838, it should be premised, General (then Colonel) Fraser succeeded Colonel Stewart as Resident at the Nizam's court, and in 1839 the Wahabee conspiracy was detected. The clue was first gained by Mr. Stonehouse, the magistrate of Nellore, who found reason to believe that Moobarz-oo-Dowlah, a brother of the late Nizam, was one of a confederacy of chiefs, which extended throughout India, and had our overthrow for its object. As it was thought desirable that the strictest inquiry should be instituted into the conduct of this chief, a mixed commission of British officers and natives of rank was assembled for that purpose at Hyderabad, under the authority of the Resident, General Fraser, and the Nizam's government.

The court was convened in June, 1839 (the British troops under Lord Keane were then busy in Kandahar), and after a protracted and careful investigation, closed its proceedings in April, 1840. It recorded its opinion that Moobarz-oo-Dowlah, and several of his personal adherents, had been engaged in a treasonable correspondence with the Nawab of Wondgherry, and had likewise taken an active part in organizing a confederacy among the fanatic Wahabees throughout India, with views hostile to the British and the Nizam's government. The opinion of the court met with the approval of those by whom it was convened, and in compliance with its suggestion, Moobarz-oo-Dowlah and ten of his principal adherents—most of them Wahabee moollahs—were ordered to be retained in custody until the government should decide that their release would be attended with no inconvenience. Moobarz-oo-Dowlah was, in consequence, sent to the fortress of Golcondah, and remained a prisoner till his death, which occurred in 1854.

The narrative of events which took place at Hyderabad in 1841 and 1842, would consist of little else than a detail of the minister's struggles with his financial embarrassments. At length, finding it impossible to carry on the government, he tendered his resignation to the Nizam, and withdrew from office on the 6th of September, 1843. After this, Ram Buxsh, a nephew of the minister, was appointed Peshcar, but he possessed neither ability nor energy. Seraj-ool-Moolk, the uncle of Salar Jung, the present minister, was appointed Vakeel.

Before accepting Chundoo lall's resignation, the Nizam had assured General Fraser that he would take an early opportunity of nominating a successor to the office; and from the circumstance of his having appointed Seraj-ool-Moolk his Vakeel, it was thought probable that his choice would have fallen upon this nobleman. Of his fitness for the office, General Fraser was himself thoroughly assured, as he testifies to his possession of clear views, and of that decision and vigour of mind so necessary for the correction of the abuses of the State, and the substitution of a better government hereafter. Even the Nizam was desirous of appointing him to the office, but his timidity prevented him from adopting the decided measures which the case required. He was fearful, on the one hand, of the ex-minister's influence at Calcutta; and, on the other, he was impressed by that personage himself with doubts of the integrity of Seraj-ool-Moolk. In this state of uncertainty, his highness endeavoured to transact the business of the State himself. As I have already indicated, he was not likely to derive assistance in the experiment from the recently appointed peshcar.

In this state of affairs, the ex-minister, Chundoo lall, addressed a letter to the Governor General, sending it, in the first instance, to the Resident, but sealed for transmission. General Fraser declined to forward it, on the grounds of not having received a copy for his own information, but he was still more influenced by the consideration that his compliance would favour the idea that there was a probability of Chundoo lall's return to office, and would prolong the Nizam's irresolution. Chundoo lall then forwarded his letter direct to the Governor General.

In this letter the ex-minister pretended to explain the cause of his resignation, and, with the cunning natural to him, threw the blame on the Resident, who, he alleged, was "bent on his ruin." The facts of the case are, however, clearly stated in General Fraser's report to Government. "In tendering his resignation the ex-minister, no doubt, thought that he would continue to be supported in pursuance of the system hitherto observed, and obtain, either from the British government, or by intimidating the Nizam, those advances which would be necessary to enable him to carry on the administration of the country." His cunning, however, missed its object, and his disappointment would appear to have rendered him totally indifferent to the obligations of truth.

In October, 1843, the Resident again pressed upon the Nizam's attention the expediency of speedily appointing a Dewan, in order that immediate effect might be given to the arrangements necessary for the better government of his highness's dominions. In addressing the Government on the subject at this period, General Fraser expatiated at some length on the state of the Hyderabad durbar, and submitted the draft of a note to be addressed to the Nizam. Its tone was that of decided remonstrance against further delay in the appointment of a minister, and the Resident added:—"I doubt whether any communication of a less decided nature will be sufficient to lead him (the Nizam) to the adoption of those measures which are now so obviously desirable." On another occasion, General Fraser had expressed his decided opinion that no improvement was to be expected until the retirement of Chundoo lall was regarded by the English government as definitive.

The Supreme Government, in reply to the Resident's representations, expressed their opinion that the time would come when his highness, seeing the failure of his project for undertaking the executive duties of government himself, would be willing enough to adopt the course best suited to his character, and either defer to our advice, or admit of our more direct intervention in the management of his affairs. In the expectation of this ultimate result, the Governor-General in council decided against any active interference at present in the affairs of the Nizam's government, beyond insisting on the punctual payment of the contingent.

The decided instructions of Government prevented General Fraser from adopting those remedial measures which, in his opinion, were imperatively called for by circumstances at this period. Accordingly, if we except occasional demands for the restitution of property plundered from the Company's districts or other adjoining territories, satisfaction for minor offences committed on the frontier, and remonstrances regarding the frequent robberies of the Company's mails, nothing transpired that could be deemed of public importance until about the end of the year, when the Nizam's government failed to pay the sum due for the contingent.

In reporting this circumstance, General Fraser stated that he had made the necessary advances, but without demanding any territorial security. He deemed this advisable, not only because he had reason to believe the amount would very soon be repaid, but also to avoid a discussion which might have elicited feelings on the part of his highness which it were better should not be expressed.

Having, at the same time, requested the instructions of Government for his guidance in the event of a further emergency of the same kind, he was authorized to advance from the Company's treasury what might be needed for paying the troops of the contingent, and to allow a reasonable time for the repayment of such advanced sums; provided, also, that if the stipulated time should elapse, and the amount remain unpaid, the Nizam should be bound to transfer to our management such extent of territory as should gradually liquidate the debt incurred. General Fraser was instructed that the Government would expect this condition to be strictly enforced. The Governor General also addressed a letter to the Nizam himself, informing him of the instructions which had been given to the Resident, and recommending him to adopt measures for the better administration of the country. His lordship added that the British Government would not consent to put down by force troubles which were manifestly caused by the oppression under which the people suffered.

In reference to the latter observation his highness observed in his reply: "I am sending six lacs of rupees by the hands of trustworthy munsubdars to different parts of my dominions, to be distributed among my subjects; doubtless this measure will be productive of comfort to my people." With respect to the payment of the troops, he observed, "The illustrious and trustworthy Rajah Ram Buxsh Bahadoor, who has been appointed for the transaction of business, will pay the contingent without allowing it to fall more than the usual four months in arrears." And, finally, with regard to the general mismanagement of the country, his highness said, "Please God, in the course of three years, the happiness of the people, and by degrees good order in general, will be apparent."

Between October, 1845, and 1846, General Fraser addressed several despatches to Government, relative to the measures taken by him for removing the Rohilla mercenaries from the Nizam's dominions, and for coercing several of the Zemindars who had grown refractory. These measures met with the approval of the Supreme Government. The just dues of these adventurers were in some instances paid after a proper inquiry into the validity of their claims, and they were conveyed under a military escort to the frontier, from whence they were ordered to make their way home. In cases of real poverty, a sufficient sum was given them to cover the expenses of the journey. Many of these returned to Hyderabad, to the great annoyance of General Fraser, owing to the defective measures of the authorities in the British territory.

While expressing his approval of the conditions on which the Resident had arranged to co-operate with the Nizam's government for the attainment of the above object, the Governor General also concurred with General Fraser in thinking that advantage should be taken of the present disposition of his highness, to impress upon him the absolute necessity of adopting a better system of government. The first step to this would be the appointment of a Dewan responsible to his highness for the conduct of the executive administration, as much of the embarrassment into which his affairs had fallen was attributable to the delay that had taken place in appointing a successor to the late Rajah Chundoo lall.[1] The time, in fact, had now arrived, when the Nizam found no

[1] The ex-minister died in April, 1845, eighteen months after his resignation of office.

other course possible than that which the Supreme Government concurred with the Resident in advising him to adopt. The investiture of Seraj-ool-Moolk took place on the 7th of November, 1846, and the change of government was hailed as a blessing by all classes of persons in Hyderabad.

In acknowledging General Fraser's despatches, relating generally to the affairs of the Nizam's country, including the appointment of the minister, the Governor General expressed his satisfaction that the Nizam had at length complied with the advice of the Supreme Government in this respect, and also that his choice had fallen upon Seraj-ool-Moolk. The Governor General further expressed his entire satisfaction with General Fraser's conduct throughout these proceedings, and was gratified to learn that the change of administration was apparently both satisfactory to the Nizam, and acceptable to his highness's subjects.

CHAPTER XIX.

THE SUCCESS ACHIEVED BY FACTION.

Opposition to the Ministry of Seraj-ool-Moolk — The Minister threatened by the Mutinous Troops of the Line—Demonstration of the British Contingent by order of General Fraser—Remarks of the Governor General with reference to his Recommendations generally—Change of Policy on the part of the Government indicated—Project for the Disbandment and Expulsion of all Mercenary Troops—The Number of such Troops in the Nizam's Service—Importance of expelling the Rohillas in particular—Increased Opposition to the Ministry of Seraj-ool-Moolk—The Nizam expresses a wish to remove him from Office — Correspondence with the Government — Dismissal of Seraj-ool-Moolk and Appointment of Amjud-ool-Moolk—The Resident is invited to the Investiture of the new Minister, and solicits Instructions from the Supreme Government — Amjud-ool-Moolk takes Office under protest from General Fraser and the Supreme Government.

THE succession of Seraj-ool-Moolk to the office of Dewan encouraged a hope that the misgovernment of the country would, at length, in some measure, be ameliorated. It will be seen, however, that he was eventually compelled to relinquish office.

The influence of the class opposed to good government made itself felt through a variety of channels, and was not less active in its remonstrances against the policy of the Resident than it was virulent in its hatred against the minister.

Here it is necessary to state that the life of the minister had been threatened by an assemblage of the half-disciplined troops of the line; in consequence of which General Fraser had acceded to the request of Seraj-ool-Moolk, and moved a portion of the subsidiary force to a position in some open gardens adjacent to the city walls. General Fraser, it is true, had no absolute or infallible assurance that his highness the Nizam had solicited his aid; yet he had all the assurance of which the circumstances admitted, all that his utmost efforts could obtain, and enough, as it appeared to him, not only to justify, but imperatively to demand, a prompt and decided line of action, when a body of men, numbering 10,000, were reported to be in a state of mutiny, and there was obvious danger in allowing the seditious spirit to gain head by remaining unchecked. In the course of a day or two, under the judicious arrangements made by General Fraser, the mutineers returned to their duty without the employment of additional coercive measures.

About this time the Governor General felt it necessary to observe that the financial embarrassments of the Nizam might, in spite of the warnings given to his highness, and the liberal aid afforded by the British Government to extricate his highness from his difficulties, bring about a crisis which might render our interposition necessary in order to save him from ruin, in which event, as already mentioned, General Fraser would receive his instructions from the Government.

In September, 1847, the Supreme Government called for a full report of the proceedings adopted with respect to the Rohillas and other mercenaries in the Nizam's service, or in the employ of other persons in his dominions. General Fraser submitted in the first instance a summary of what had been previously written on the subject,[1] wherein he had suggested that he should be authorized to urge upon the Circar the expediency of discharging at the earliest practicable period the whole of the foreign mercenaries, Arabs, Rohillas, Sikhs, natives of Egypt or Turkey, and all others, whatsoever their denomination. At the same time he forwarded a memorandum, supplied to him by the minister, of the number of these hire-

[1] *Ante*, p. 247.

lings, and of the native troops in the service of the Government, to the following effect :—

Sowars	7,763
Bushurs or Munsubdars	965
Arabs	5,747
Line	18,326
Government Rohillas	1,647
Sikhs	1,228
Ali Gole	4,374
Turks	69
Beloochees	100
	40,219
Half-castes	10,000
	50,219

General Fraser had previously represented to Government that the employment of mercenaries was one of the most fertile sources of disorder in all native states, and he again stated his conviction that so long as any of these men remained in the Deccan they would prove a constant source of disturbance and bloodshed. It will be seen from the above memorandum that the Arabs greatly exceeded the other troops of their class in number. Indeed, the Nizam's Government was, in a great measure, in their hands, and General Fraser had frequently observed that if the executive management of affairs rested with himself, he would not have hesitated to dissolve the Arab connection, and entrust the defence of the capital to the natural subjects of his highness. There was one difficulty, but not, as he thought, an altogether insurmountable one. Many of the Arab jemadars were creditors of the Nizam's Government to a considerable amount. The Resident, therefore, proposed that in case of disbanding the troops the British Government should guarantee a loan of twenty-five lacs in order that the just dues of these gentlemen might be paid previous to their deportation.

But the Supreme Government did not contemplate the entire and immediate expulsion of the mercenary troops, being of opinion that if we compelled them to disband and leave the capital, they would find ready employment with the turbulent Zemindars, and would thus only augment the existing disorder. Admitting that the discharge of all such troops, wherever employed in his highness's dominions, must be the ultimate object of the British Government if internal peace was to be preserved, General Fraser was informed that it would be necessary to temporize for a time with an evil of which the Governor General comprehended the full magnitude.

The estrangement between the Nizam and his minister was more openly manifested when, in 1848, General Fraser having proceeded to the coast on leave, the Residency was left in charge of Colonel Low. In an interview between the latter and the

Nizam, his highness expressed a wish to remove Seraj-ool-Moolk from the office of Dewan, remarking that he had now had a trial of seventeen months, and the affairs of the Sircar were not at all in a better state than formerly. In a second and private interview this desire was again expressed, and Colonel Low was requested to communicate his highness's wish to the Governor General. In doing so, the officiating Resident expressed his conviction of the eminent fitness of Seraj-ool-Moolk for the office, but owing to the determination of the Nizam and the opposed faction to thwart his measures, he saw little prospect of any good resulting from the minister's retention of office. Things had arrived at such a pass, that the minister's ordinary official orders were treated with contempt by men under the authority of the Nizam's favourites.

As for the pecuniary affairs of the Nizam's government at this period, they were in a worse condition, as Colonel Low also stated in his letter, than they had been since 1800; with the addition that his highness's private treasures were now almost entirely exhausted. The particulars may be seen in the conclusion of the letter which I have thought of sufficient interest to quote.[1]

On General Fraser's return from the coast, he was

[1] Appendix I I.

requested to inform the Nizam that the Governor General in Council had perused with deep regret the declaration of his highness's sentiments towards his minister Seraj-ool-Moolk, and of his desire to remove him from the office of Dewan; the Governor General having no reason to suppose that the Dewan had shown himself unfit for, or unworthy of, the distinguished position in which his highness had placed him. His integrity was called in question by no man; he attended to the duties of his high office; and he had shown every desire to labour for the accomplishment of those great measures of improvement which had been so frequently urged upon his highness's attention, as indispensably necessary, in order to set his kingdom free from the serious financial embarrassments under which it laboured, and promote the welfare of his subjects. If the affairs of the Hyderabad government were in a condition unsatisfactory to his highness, if the finances of the country were exhausted, and the credit of the government gone, difficulties must not be attributable to Seraj-ool-Moolk, but to the obstructions which had prevented his effecting reductions in expenditure and in public establishments, which were daily dragging the country down towards poverty and disorder.

In a despatch addressed to the Resident at this period, the Governor General again stated that "he was unable to perceive any grounds for those manifestations of his highness's displeasure which he had displayed towards the Dewan, nor any good reason for the wish expressed by his highness to dismiss Seraj-ool-Moolk from his employment. His lordship did not know by whom that individual could be advantageously succeeded in his office, for his highness ought by his intelligence to have perceived that to adopt his own proposal of appointing Rajah Ram Buxsh Peshcar, while Seraj-ool-Moolk was nominally continued as Dewan, was really to remove authority from the latter, and place all actual power in the hands of Rajah Ram Buxsh. The Rajah's incompetency for such an office had already been proved in past years, and if any further proof were required of his ineligibility for that post, it would be found in his offer of a nuzzer amounting to fifty lacs of rupees on his appointment. This his highness stated to the Resident the Rajah had actually proffered, intending to signalize his entrance into office by the observance of a mischievous custom, which would lead directly to practices of oppression and corruption on the part of the officers who sanctioned it. The Government never could have viewed with approbation the selection of such a person to be the first minister of the ruler of the kingdom of Hyderabad. At the same time the Governor General did not wish to dictate to his highness the person whom he should employ in his service as Dewan. His highness the Nizam was an independent sovereign, the British Government desired that he should continue to be so, and would rejoice to see his country made prosperous, and his people happy. His highness was free to choose for himself the man he would have to be his minister, but the Government was desirous of impressing upon the mind of his highness the grave importance of the circumstances under which he was acting, and the fatal consequences to his highness's dignity and realm that might result from his acting unwisely at so critical a time.

"If then" (the despatch continued) "his highness, unmoved by the warnings he received, should by his own act throw the country into disorder, the British Government would have to act in defence of its own interests, and would probably feel itself compelled to exercise a peremptory interference in the internal administration of his highness's dominions, in order to avert from the people the inconveniences and injuries which the disordered condition of the neighbouring state must needs inflict upon them."

On the 11th of November (1848) General Fraser had an interview with the Nizam, who made a long and desultory statement relative to the condition of the country, and attributed the embarrassment under which it was suffering, as he always did, principally to the civil interference introduced by Sir Charles Metcalfe. He complained that Seraj-ool-Moolk had done nothing effectual to regulate the affairs of the state, and, repeating the complaint he had preferred at a former interview, again observed that he acted in the conduct of affairs without giving him previous information.

General Fraser did not fail to observe that Seraj-ool-Moolk attributed the inefficiency of his management to the opposition he met with from his highness himself. The Nizam, however, made a number of remarks tending to disprove the fact, and when the minister (who was permitted to offer an explanation in his highness's presence) touched upon certain circumstances in which he had been forbidden to act by the Nizam, the latter concluded the discussion by flatly denying the truth of his assertions. The interview ended by his highness remarking to General Fraser that he was dissatisfied with Seraj-ool-Moolk, and as this sentiment appeared to be mutual he would remove him from his office, and appoint another Dewan.

Accordingly, a few days afterwards, his highness appointed Amjud-ool-Moolk his Dewan, and invited General Fraser to attend his investiture in a manner that would have implied the formal recognition of the appointment by the Government of India. Some correspondence on this subject passed between Seraj-ool-Moolk and the Resident, who transmitted copies to Government on the 23rd of November (1848), soliciting instructions for his guidance. General Fraser observed that he entered upon this subject with much reluctance, and the most profound deference to the judgment of the Supreme Government, being anxious to avoid even the appearance of creating obstacles to the full exercise of that authority which the Governor General had conceded to the Nizam with regard to the unbiassed and uncontrolled selection of his own minister. The Resident repeated the opinions which he had always expressed regarding the public character of Seraj-ool-Moolk, with the observation that he (General Fraser) could not take upon himself the responsibility of assuring the ultimate success either of the late minister, or of any other native who should be selected for the office of Dewan, throughout the whole of the Nizam's dominions. Seraj-ool-Moolk, however, was still the man, on whom rested the Resident's only hope. He was the only man in the Nizam's country whose mind had been a little enlarged by intercourse with European gentlemen, and who, by the possession of the state records connected with his family, had obtained some acquaintance with the manner in which the business of the country had been administered.[1] He alone seemed to be sensible of the necessity of reform with a view to the prosperity of the country, and the maintenance of his sovereign's independence. Above all, he was the only subject of the Nizam who, professing a sincere and cordial concurrence in the Resident's views, had expressed his full determination to give them effect if vested with power to do so.

With respect to Amjud-ool-Moolk, the newly appointed minister, he was regarded, in the opinion of the whole city of Hyderabad, as utterly deficient in understanding, and could be but a tool in the hands of others. He was not known to possess any one qualification for the office, and if his manner of life were worth consideration, he had been residing for some years past within the precincts of the Nizam's palace to escape from the pursuit of his numerous creditors. Finally, General Fraser observed that the appointment of the man, whoever he might be, who honestly and sincerely undertakes, with the assent and under the guarantee of his highness himself, to act in concurrence with the expressed views of the Supreme Government, and to carry them out with full effect, may safely be confirmed; but

[1] His father, Mooneer-ool-Moolk, and his grandfather, Meer Allum, with whom the reader has become well acquainted, had both held the office of Dewan.

failing the conditions named, the formal recognition of the Supreme Government of either Amjud-ool-Moolk or any other person as Dewan, if that recognition be understood to imply approval, would be an act which he (General Fraser) could not recommend, because he should regard it as being directly injurious to the interests of the Nizam, and but little consonant with the reality of those friendly sentiments which the British government professes to entertain for him.

With respect to General Fraser's remarks and suggestions pointing to the non-recognition of Amjud-ool-Moolk, his lordship observed "that undoubtedly the Supreme Government, as a faithful ally of his highness, might legitimately exercise, as it had ever exercised, the privilege of recommending a minister for his highness's selection; but the correspondence on the subject had previously shown that no person could be named to the Supreme Government by its officers at Hyderabad, whom they could advise the Government to recommend as qualified to serve his highness as his minister, and Seraj-ool-Moolk was declared to be 'the man on whom rested the Resident's only hope.' Under these circumstances the Governor General was unable to perceive that any practicable benefit whatever could result either to his highness the Nizam, or to the British Government, from disallowing the appointment of Amjud-ool-Moolk to the vacant office of Dewan, and declined to disallow the appointment of a Dewan by his highness in the person of Amjud-ool-Moolk, or to repeat the advice so lately tendered to him by the Resident on the part of the Government of India. "But," the despatch continued, "while the Governor General saw no advantage in disallowing the appointment of Amjud-ool-Moolk, he would by no means accord to it his approval, or allow his highness to suppose that he could disregard the advice and support of Government without inconvenience and danger to his own interests. The Resident, therefore, was instructed to abstain from attending the ceremony of investiture, and to request an audience of the Nizam, for the purpose of informing his highness that the Governor General had learnt with surprise and regret that notwithstanding the opinions expressed by his lordship relative to the Dewan Seraj-ool-Moolk, and contrary to the advice which was tendered to his highness, he had dismissed that minister from his high office, and had appointed to it an individual altogether without the qualifications necessary to fit him for occupying so important a position. Thus, Seraj-ool-Moolk retired from office in defiance of every exertion made by the Resident for his support, and under the strongest protest from the Supreme Government.

CHAPTER XX.

CESSION OF BERAR.

The Ministry of Amjud-ool-Moolk — Renewed Application of the Supreme Government for Payment of the Debt due by the Nizam—Shumsh-ool-oomrah appointed Dewan—His Proposals for paying the Debt rejected—He pays the Contingent with Punctuality—His Resignation of the Office of Minister—A Period is definitively fixed by the Government for the Payment of the Debt—Rajah Ram Buxsh appointed Peshcar—General Fraser reports on the Hopelessness of any better Administration of the Nizam's Government — Dissatisfaction of the Nizam with Ram Buxsh — Expiration of the Period fixed by the Supreme Government for the Payment of the Debt—Proposal for the Cession of some Portion of the Nizam's Territory renewed—Gunerish Rao is appointed Dewan—General Fraser reports the utter Inability of the Nizam's Government to fulfil its Engagements—Letter of Lord Dalhousie to the Nizam — Cession of Berar Payenghat and other Border Districts proposed—General Fraser's Suggestions as to the Management of the Assigned Districts — Seraj-ool-Moolk is appointed Minister—The Nizam pays a Portion of the Debt—Postponement of the Government Demands — Failure of the Nizam to pay the remaining Portion of the Debt—Attack on the Minister — Resignation of General Fraser — Colonel Low appointed Resident at Hyderabad—Continued Evasion of the Nizam—Treaty for the Cession of Berar and other Territories concluded—General Conditions of the Treaty—Death of Seraj-ool-Moolk—Salar Jung Bahadoor is appointed Minister—Mr. Bushby succeeds Colonel Low as Resident—Misconduct of a Chief of the Arab Mercenaries—Instances of Insubordination in the Capital—Salar Jung institutes an Industrial Exhibition—Death of Mr. Bushby—Major Davidson appointed Resident—Death and Character of the Nizam—Afzul-oo-Dowlah succeeds to the Musnud.

THE prospects created for the Nizam's government by the change of ministry were not so brilliant as to throw into the shade all anxiety about the debt to the Supreme Government, which now amounted to more than half a million sterling. General Fraser, therefore, was directed to intimate to his highness the expectation of Government that the interest of this debt would be paid regularly; and that the payment of the contingent in the service of his highness could no longer be allowed to fall into arrears. Further, his highness was requested to provide, without any prolonged delay, for the liquidation of the principal of the debt. In the event of these demands not being attended to and punctually satisfied, it was added, the Government would feel itself called upon to take effectual measures, both for its own security, and for protecting the interests of those to whom its faith was virtually pledged. General Fraser was instructed to report from time to time the effect which this communication might have on the Nizam's proceedings.

Accordingly, in December, 1848, the Governor General was informed that the new Dewan Amjud-ool-Moolk Bahadoor had as yet only corresponded with the Resident on the current business of his office; and, in fact, did not appear to be trusted with the transaction of the general business of the country, which his highness had taken principally into his own hands. It soon after appeared that the appointment of the minister was only temporary, and either Igtidar-ool-Moolk (a natural son of Shumsh-ool-oomrah), or Ghoolan Hyder Khan (known also under the designation of Igtidar Jung and Joomdred-ood-Dowlah), was expected to succeed to the office. Finally, General Fraser was able to report that Shumsh-ool-oomrah was the choice of his highness, and the Supreme Government expressed its unwillingness to offer any objection. This nobleman, therefore, was appointed minister in the place of Amjud-ool-Moolk, with the distinct understanding that the Governor General expressed no opinion with regard to his fitness for the office, and that the responsibility of ulterior consequences would rest entirely with his highness.

Shumsh-ool-oomrah continued in office five months only, and failed to make any provision for the payment of the debt. General Fraser reported that he had his promise to pay the interest as it fell due every month, and to reimburse the principal in instalments of five lacs annually.[1] To this arrangement the Supreme Government would not consent, the sums having been advanced as an act of friendship to the Nizam's government, and not on the footing of an ordinary loan. The Governor General, therefore, still requested that arrangements might be made for repaying the whole at an early period.

It is but just to remark, that during Shumsh-ool-oomrah's short period of office, the contingent was paid with punctuality. In May, 1849, however, he resigned office, complaining of the uncontrolled extravagance of the Nizam, and of the baneful influence of female and other favourites about the palace. His highness, on the other hand, complained bitterly of Shumsh-ool-oomrah's conduct, and, treating the debt as a matter of no moment, declared that he would settle it without difficulty.

On resigning office, Shumsh-ool-oomrah received an acknowledgment of the Governor General's satisfaction with the manner in which he had discharged his duties in circumstances of great difficulty. As for the Nizam, the Governor General was of opinion that a fitting opportunity had arrived for fixing a definitive period

---

[1] Say 50,000*l*. annually, the debt being nearly 600,000*l*. The repayment of this sum, even if the promise could be relied on, and the instalments never failed, would take about twelve years.

within which the debt due by his highness must be liquidated in full. The Resident was directed to require "that the whole amount should be discharged by the 31st of December, 1850. If on the arrival of that period, the Governor General's present expectations were disappointed, his lordship, it was remarked, would feel it to be his duty to take such decided steps as the interests of the British Government demanded."

In September, 1849, Rajah Ram Buxsh received the khillat of investiture as Peshcar from the Nizam, and in a short month afterwards the Resident's communications turned upon the total unfitness of this individual to conduct the administration, and his inability to provide for the payment of the contingent. In acknowledging a despatch to this effect, the Governor General observed, that "as his views and intentions had been frequently and clearly declared to his highness, and the date fixed, a repetition of them would be attended with no possible advantage. But," he added, "if the payment of the contingent was withheld, action by the Supreme Government may become necessary before the 31st of December, 1850."

So the time wore on, until in February, 1850, General Fraser expressed it as his deliberate opinion, formed after considerable experience of the character of the Nizam, that nothing less than a decided British administration, conducted by the Resident, in communication with the Nizam's minister, would save the country. A month later, he submitted to Government copy of a correspondence relative to the state of affairs in Berar at that time, and suggested that it seemed a fit occasion to address the Nizam in support of the advice which the Resident had so repeatedly given, viz. that "whatever minister may be appointed to carry on the executive duties of government, he should be invested with full powers to administer the affairs of the country." General Fraser received authority to make such a representation to the Nizam, though the Governor General did not anticipate much success from the step.

As the year drew towards its close the Nizam manifested some signs of uneasiness, and in conversation with General Fraser complained that he had been deceived in Rajah Ram Buxsh, who had utterly failed in the promises which he made on his first appointment. His highness inquired during one of these interviews whether Mr. Martin (the then Resident at Hyderabad) had not stated soon after his accession to the Musnud, that the Supreme Government had conceded to him (the Nizam) the right of appointing and changing his Dewan and Peshcar. General Fraser replied that this right had been conceded, and he retired from the interview with an impression that his highness entertained the idea, either of changing his then minister, or if he retained him in the office of Peshcar, of appointing another officer with the powers of Dewan. At a subsequent interview, on the 8th of October, the Nizam again complained of his Peshcar in the severest terms, and expressed his determination to dismiss him from office.

On the 4th of January, 1851, the time having elapsed within which the Nizam was required to pay the large debt due by him to the Government of India, the Resident was directed to request an audience of his highness, and remind him of this circumstance, preparatory to further instruction respecting the course to be pursued if it were found that his highness had taken no efficient measures for the fulfilment of his own assurances in this respect. General Fraser was further directed to express the surprise and dissatisfaction with which the Governor General had learned that his highness still neglected to appoint a minister for the management of his affairs; and to express the very deep regret with which the Government had observed the prevailing disorders of the state, and the still greater perplexity in which they threatened to involve him, if he did not at once exercise the authority which belonged to him. On this occasion the Governor General agreed with General Fraser that he saw no prospect of the payment of the debt except by taking possession of some portion of his highness's territories, from the revenues of which repayment could be made.

In April, General Fraser reported to Government the nomination of Guneish Rao as Dewan, whom truth compelled him to describe as a man totally unaccustomed to the management of public affairs, and therefore unfit for the office. A little later, therefore, it is not surprising to find that General Fraser reported finally the inability of the Nizam to meet the demands of the British Government, and submitted his views of the policy which he deemed it would be expedient to pursue. The Nizam, he suggested, should be immediately and urgently pressed in terms which it was not necessary should be otherwise than friendly in their tone, but which should admit of no denial. In a word, the time had now arrived when it was necessary to enforce the only practicable solution of the difficulty, viz. that which had previously been the subject of General Fraser's correspondence with the Supreme Government.

Lord Dalhousie therefore addressed a letter to his highness in which he intimated the determination which he considered it his duty to form. He called on the Nizam to make over to the Resident for the British Government those portions of his territory which would be specified, together with all the authority necessary for their management. His lordship concurred with General Fraser in considering Berar Payenghat, the border districts from thence down to Sholapore, and the Doab between the Kistna and Toombudhra (Raichore), as the districts most eligible. The Resident was directed, should his highness not comply with the requirements of the British Government within a specific time, to request a final audience for the purpose of receiving a definite reply; and if his highness should either refuse compliance on that occasion, or should fail to complete the necessary arrangements, to report the result.

General Fraser's suggestion that in the event of his highness making the districts over to our management,[1] Captain Meadows Taylor, who had for many years been Political Agent at the court of the Rajah of Shorapore, was the proper person for undertaking the direction of that portion of the territory which lay towards Shorapoor, met with approval at head-quarters. It was also remarked in the Government despatch that British interests would be greatly promoted by entrusting another portion of the territory to the management of Mr. Dighton; the objection of the

[1] It is here proper to remind the reader that whatever might be the ultimate destination of the districts mentioned in the text, their proposed assignment, as suggested by General Fraser, was for a temporary purpose only; whether or not the Nizam would hereafter be asked to set them aside for the special maintenance of the contingent, only time could reveal.

Honourable Court to the employment of that gentleman in the state of Hyderabad on a former occasion having been founded on reasons not at all applicable to the present proposal. It was added that the high testimony borne by General Fraser to the character and capacity of Mr. Dighton satisfied his lordship that in selecting him for the duties now contemplated he would have the approval of the Honourable Court. The third officer nominated was Captain Bullock, of the Nizam's contingent,—an officer of great ability and experience, and who subsequently for a considerable period officiated as commissioner of the Assigned Districts.

The Nizam, however, still hoped to avoid the unpleasant alternative placed before him, and in June (1851) appointed Seraj-ool-Moolk once more his minister. In the following month he gave the Resident his personal assurance that the debt would forthwith be liquidated, one-half immediately, and the remainder on the 31st of October ensuing. He also declared his intention of setting aside certain specified talooks in order to ensure the regular and full pay of the contingent troops. The Resident, on the faith of these promises, consented to suspend the demand which had been made for a temporary assignment of territory, and had the satisfaction of being informed by the Government that he had acted with judgment, and in full accordance with their wishes.

The appointment of Seraj-ool-Moolk was also regarded as a source of congratulation.

These promises were so far kept that on the 15th of August his highness completed the payment of the first instalment of his debt, leaving a balance due of 82,97,702 rupees. The stipulated period for the payment of this sum having passed, and only a part having been paid on account up to the 1st of December, General Fraser reported the circumstance, and the promises made by the Nizam for the gradual liquidation of the remainder. The Governor General having expressed his belief, judging from appearances, that the Nizam was now really in earnest and would fulfil his pledges, approved of the discretion which the Resident had shown in not proceeding with the extreme measures which he was authorized to enforce. He also approved of the determined language in which the Resident addressed the Nizam, for the purpose of disabusing his mind from the impression that a part of the debt having been discharged, the payment of the remainder would not be insisted on.

The virulence of the faction which had previously driven Seraj-ool-Moolk from office was exhibited at the present time in a manner still more unpleasant to that minister personally. In March, 1852, he was attacked by a party of men, and wounded in the cheek by a slug.

I find nothing of public importance to record during the remainder of this year, until in November General Fraser tendered his resignation, and was succeeded as Resident at Hyderabad by Colonel J. Low, C.B., who took office in the January following. The General does not appear to have assigned any particular reasons for resigning his appointment beyond stating that "private affairs required his presence in England."[1]

The new Resident, Colonel Low, found it necessary to advance large sums from the Company's Treasury to pay the contingent, so that in three months (March, 1853) the Nizam's debt had again risen to upwards of forty-five lacs of rupees, while the constant and pressing applications of the Resident were only met by evasions of the most vexatious nature. It was simply impossible that a system of perpetual remonstrance on the one hand, and of undignified evasions and breaches of promise on the other, should be continued. In April, the Resident

[1] General Fraser's services in India extended over a period of fifty-two years, during which time he held the following appointments:—Aide-de-camp to the Governor of Madras; Private Secretary to the Governor of Madras; Military Secretary to the Governor of Madras; Town Major of Fort St. George; Special Agent for the Affairs of the Netherlands Government; Commandant of Pondicherry; Special Agent for Foreign Affairs; Agent with the column operating against Coorg; Commissioner for Coorg; Resident for Travancore and Cochin; Resident at Mysore, and Commissioner for Coorg; Resident at Hyderabad.

was directed to submit to the Nizam a proposal for a new treaty on the basis of ceding in perpetuity to the British Government, territory to the value of about thirty-six lacs per annum, in return for which he would be relieved from his present debt, and from all future payments to the contingent.

The Nizam's objection to cede territory in perpetuity was so great that this point was conceded to him, and after much correspondence a treaty was concluded by Colonel Low in the following terms:—In lieu of the present contingent, the Honourable Company agreed to maintain an auxiliary force, to be paid from the Nizam's revenues, and entitled the "Hyderabad Contingent." It was to consist of not less than 5,000 infantry, 2,000 cavalry, and four field batteries of artillery. To provide for the regular payment of this force, of Appa Dessaji's choute, of Mahiput Ram's family, and certain Mahratta Salianadars, and also to cover interest on the debt due to the Company at the rate of six per cent., the Nizam, on his part, agreed to assign districts yielding an annual gross revenue of fifty lacs of rupees to the exclusive management of the British Resident; faithful accounts of the receipts and disbursements of the said districts to be rendered to the Nizam every year, and any surplus revenue, after the above charges were satisfied, to be made over to his highness. The treaty, at the same time, renewed the obligation of protection, and secured to the Nizam the full use of the auxiliary troops; it also released him from the liability of being called upon to supply a larger military force in time of war, and from the immediate payment of fifty lacs of rupees. To the Government of India it secured a less restricted use of the auxiliary force, a formal recognition of its existence, and security for its future regular payment, as well as for the liquidation of the principal and interest of the unfortunate debt due by the Nizam.

This treaty, concluded on the 21st of May, 1853, by Colonel Low, C.B., was considered by the Governor General in Council as singularly advantageous to the state of Hyderabad. Having been duly ratified, it was signed and sealed by his highness in open durbar on the 18th June following, and owing to the great increase of official labour consequent on the acquisition of the ceded districts, the Resident at Hyderabad was authorized to employ a second assistant.

Seraj-ool-Moolk, whose valuable services during the negotiation of the treaty had been acknowledged by the Governor General, had for some time been in bad health, and died on the 27th of May, six days after the conclusion of this business. The Nizam at once appointed his nephew, Salar Jung, to the office of Dewan, and the selection was considered by Colonel Low on the whole a happy one. Rajah Narrindhur, grandson of the late Maharajah Chundoo lall, was at the same time nominated to the office of Peshcar.

In August, 1853, Colonel Low, C.B., was appointed a member of the Supreme Council, and was succeeded as Resident at Hyderabad by G. A. Bushby, Esq.

In the preceding chapter I had occasion to remark on the correspondence which took place between General Fraser and the Supreme Government on the subject of the Arab and other mercenaries in the employment of the Nizam. The danger of tolerating these lawless bands (I allude to those who were not in the Government service) was illustrated by an event at Dewulgaun on the 22nd of September, 1853, when they fired on the British troops then in action. The despatch of the officiating Resident, Major Davidson, on this subject, was followed by a remonstrance from the Government, in which the Nizam was reminded of his responsibility for the conduct of these troops, and warned of the dangers in which he was likely to be involved by their acts of violence. It was intimated, also, that if the Government of India had desired a pretext for breaking off its friendly relations with his highness, just ground had been furnished for doing so by this outrage; and he was assured that any repetition of such an act would compel the Government to resort to the most decided measures with regard to the Arabs in his highness's service.

Another striking example of their turbulent and dangerous character occurred in the city of Hyderabad in August, 1855, and the event is further deserving of notice as showing the local power they had acquired in the face of the Nizam's government. It appears that an Arab named Biluswad, having some real or pretended claims on the treasury, and encouraged by recent examples of insubordination, increased the number of his followers, which at first was only fifty or sixty, to seven or eight hundred men, and commenced raising parapets and making loopholes in the walls of the houses in his occupation at the chowk. On receiving intelligence of this movement, the minister, Salar Jung, sent word by the jemadars that the claims of Biluswad would be settled, but in the meantime he was ordered to retire from the city on pain of punishment if he delayed. This order not having been attended to, the party at the chowk[1] was summoned, and some shots were fired, which killed one or two of Biluswad's men, and wounded two or three spectators. The next morning more troops and a couple of guns having been brought to the spot, Biluswad was compelled to evacuate his

[1] A space generally in the centre of a native town.

position, and took up his quarters with his followers at Chinchalgooda, a suburb of the city and on the same side of the river.

The minister having satisfied himself that Biluswad had no pecuniary claims of his own preferred against the government, but had undertaken the disturbance in the cause of Oomrowghur Gosein, as a hired ruffian, with no plea or provocation or excuse whatever, in the interest of the aforesaid Oomrowghur, called on the Arab chiefs to assist him in bringing Biluswad to condign punishment. It was accordingly agreed that he should be surrounded at Chinchalgooda by the servants of the Arabs, and be secured by the troops of the government, as arranged at a conference to which the chiefs and others were summoned at the minister's residence; where they were apprised by Salar Jung, that there being no longer any doubt of Biluswad's guilt, he must be punished by the laws of the country as he deserved. Biluswad and his chaoos [1] presented themselves quite unattended at the minister's house, exhibiting by the disordered state of their apparel great alarm, and surrendered themselves. His highness the Nizam directed that they should be banished beyond seas.

In 1856, the minister, Salar Jung, having observed the repeated notice taken in Europe of the elegant and much-prized fabrics of India, displayed at the great

[1] An Arab chief.

exhibitions of London and Paris, and realizing the ultimate advantage to be anticipated from those enlightened measures, resolved to encourage and extend, if possible, the manufactures of the Deccan, by giving an immediate and practical impulse to its several industries. He accordingly proposed to hold an exhibition of the raw products and manufactures of his highness the Nizam's dominions at Chudder Ghaut, which took place in November, 1856.

On the 30th of December, 1856, Mr. Bushby died at Bolarum, and Major C. Davidson, formerly first assistant at the Nizam's court, was appointed Resident at Hyderabad, but did not arrive there until April, 1857, having been for some time previously Resident at Baroda. Shortly after his arrival, the Nizam, Nasir-oo-Dowlah died, and was succeeded by his eldest son, Afzul-oo-Dowlah, the present Nizam.

The late Nizam had latterly indulged in the pleasures of the table, and, neglecting the regimen in regard to diet prescribed by the hakeems, violent diarrhœa came on, which resulted in his death. Prior to his decease, a durbar, proposed for the reception of the Resident, was postponed. Major Davidson, however, informed Salar Jung that all etiquette ought to be set aside during the existing crisis, and if the minister was unable to leave his highness, and visit the Resident according to the usual formalities attending the advent of a new Resident, Major Davidson would waive his doing so, and come and see him whenever convenient, and that if the Nizam wished it, he would attend at his council to learn his wishes. On the 6th of May, Major Davidson attended durbar at the request of his highness, when the Nizam received him in a small chamber, in a part of the palace where he had only once before been. He was surrounded chiefly by his women, and required to be supported with pillows in order to sit up. His highness endeavoured to ask the usual question in regard to the Governor General's health, but his utterance entirely failed him. While the khurreeta was being read, he lapsed into a state of somnolent insensibility: reviving for a little, he drank some water. Seeing that he signed for Pau Sooparee, the Resident took his leave.

In person, Nasir-oo-Dowlah, the late Nizam, was tall and corpulent; his features, which were very pleasing, especially when he smiled, indicated his Tartar origin, and impressed one with the belief that his disposition was humane and benevolent in the extreme. He was never known to have been guilty of any act of cruelty or oppression except once,[1] and, on

[1] When Kullunder Beg Jemadar, who preferred a false claim for pay, and proceeded to the Nizam's palace to demand what he asserted was due to him, his highness gave orders for his forcible removal, which led to the unfortunate man's being cut down by the Nizam's attendants.

the whole, bore the character of a just and humane prince, without possessing the energy and ability requisite for the high station he occupied ; but his thorough knowledge of the character of every one belonging to his durbar enabled him to regulate it in a successful manner.

Afzul-oo-Dowlah, when he ascended the musnud, was thirty-two years of age. He is six feet two or three in height; and stout and strong in proportion. He rides well, and is fond of outdoor amusements, such as shooting, &c. He also amuses himself with driving, and possesses some forty or fifty carriages, and as many pairs of Australian and other descriptions of harness horses.

CHAPTER XXI.

THE NIZAM AND THE GREAT REBELLION.

Trying Period of the Mutiny—Incitements to Sedition at Hyderabad—Apprehension of a Street Orator—Loyalty of the Nizam—Measures taken to protect the Residency—Attack repulsed—Apprehension and Conviction of the Ringleaders — Judicious Measures of Colonel Davidson—Loyalty of Shumsh-ool-oomrah—Critical State of the Capital owing to the Number of Mercenary Troops—Effect of Rumours concerning our Progress in Hindustan—Difficulty of the Nizam's Position—He resists every Overture made by Rebel Emissaries—Measures adopted by Colonel Davidson to assist the Queen's Government with the Use of the Hyderabad Force—The Hyderabad Cavalry and other Troops join the Column acting against the Rebels in Central India—The Cavalry not required at Dhar, make a forced March to the Scene of active Operations at Mahidpore—Rescue of Mrs. Timmins, and Pursuit of the Dhara Mahidpore Rebels—Attack on the Rebel Position at Rawul—Desperate Fighting and Defeat of the Enemy—Capture of Battery and Stores destined to reinforce the Rebel Army at Mundesore and Neemuch—The Garrison of Neemuch are preserved from the Fate of Cawnpore by the active Exertions and Bravery of the Nizam's Cavalry—Junction with the Column under Sir H. Rose—The Muddenpore Pass is forced—The Second Brigade and the Hyderabad Force before Jhansi—Fall of Jhansi, and general

Engagement at Koonch—March against Gwalior—Reduction of the Zemindar of Bilowah—Return of the Nizam's Troops to the Deccan—Appearance of Tantia Topee on the Border—The Hyderabad Cavalry march against him—General Efficiency of Colonel Davidson's Policy.

AFZUL-OO-DOWLAH, the present Nizam, ascended the throne at a momentous period, both in the history of his country and of Great Britain. In one sense, the death of a reigning prince is always a critical period in the East, but against all ordinary danger the fact of so sagacious a minister as Salar Jung Bahadoor being at the head of affairs was an ample guarantee. The crisis was one without a parallel, for it was the period when the wide-spread mutiny of the Bengal army leaped like fire from station to station, and from town to town, throughout the entire presidency. At Hyderabad, as elsewhere in India, incessant watchfulness was necessary. It is true that the prince inherited with his throne a friendship which had endured for several generations, but he was surrounded by a mercenary and seditious crowd, who openly manifested their pleasure when intelligence was received of reverses experienced by our troops in Hindustan. Rumours to this effect were frequently circulated and eagerly believed. It was not until the troops of the Hyderabad contingent, which had been sent to Central India by Colonel Davidson, commenced writing to their relations and friends at the Nizam's capital, that the better inclined towards us could feel satisfied that these reports were false.

On the 13th of June, in this memorable year, two inflammatory placards were posted on the walls of one of the mosques, in the city of Hyderabad, tending to excite sedition, and fixing a day for a general rising. The city and bazaars continued from time to time to be agitated by rumours.

A faqueer was apprehended by an Arab jemadar, and handed over to the minister, in the act of addressing the populace in seditious language, in the course of which he told them they would be joined by a regiment from Secunderabad. This corps did right good service afterwards against the mutiniers in the Shorapore country. At this time a great seditious gathering took place at the Mecca mosque, in the city of Hyderabad, when a green flag—the emblematic colour of Mohammedanism—was hoisted. The crowd was dispersed by Arabs sent by the minister; and again, on some mutineers taking refuge in the city, Salar Jung at once ordered their apprehension, proving in this manner that he was determined to support the British government to the utmost of his ability and power.

On the other hand, the Nizam himself showed by words and deeds that he was determined to suppress, with a high hand, any attempt at revolt. He posted his troops (*i. e.* those under command of the minister) at the several thoroughfares leading to the Residency.

At six o'clock in the morning of July 17th, in accordance with intelligence of a conspiracy previously received, an attack was made on the Residency by a band of Rohilla and other insurgents.

The troops at the Residency under the command of Major, now Colonel Briggs, military secretary, received them so warmly, that after fruitless attempts to force the several posts occupied by the defenders, they were compelled to retire. The two ringleaders in this attack, Jemadar Toorabaz Khan and Moulvie Alla-oo-deen, were afterwards taken prisoners, and the former, in attempting to escape, was shot dead, owing to the active and resolute measures taken by the minister. The latter, Moulvie Alla-oo-deen, was tried, and sentenced to transportation, which he is now undergoing in the Andaman Islands. The Residency house (including the Government Treasury) was put in a state of defence by Colonel Davidson, at the trifling cost of 18,000 rupees, and the imposing effect of the bastions commanding the several approaches prevented any second attack being attempted throughout the rebellion.

The fact of the insurgents having been permitted to march against the Residency unmolested, and the escape of most of them afterwards with their wounded, are sufficient proof that the Nizam's own troops were not very warm in our cause. At the same time, the loyalty of the Nizam was abundantly proved. Towards the end of the month, he sent his minister with expressions of regret for what had occurred on the 17th, for the purpose of removing any feeling of anger which the Resident might naturally have entertained on the subject of the attack.

The loyalty of Shumsh-ool-oomrah, a near relation of the Nizam's, also deserves mention. This nobleman was uncle to the late Nizam; he has a son married to a sister of the present king, and a grandson to a daughter of his highness. He was highly respected by all classes at Hyderabad, and never once during the rebellion did the populace receive any countenance from him.

After the termination of the mutinies several thousands of Poorbeahs flocked to the Nizam's capital, and their bearing showed that they were men who had been subject to military discipline. The turbulent population of the city already consisted of every class of military adventurers. I cannot term the Arabs so any longer; but Rohillas, Sikhs, Scindians, Africans, Toorks and Moghuls, and the worst of all, the half-caste progeny of all these enumerated, added to the recent accessions, probably numbered 26,000 men in a total population of some

300,000, nearly every man of whom carried weapons, while many thousands of the dangerous class of adventurers were armed to the teeth. With such a population, it is not surprising that attempts were made to tamper with the sepoys at Secunderabad, the head-quarters of the subsidiary force, situated about five miles from the capital. The circumstances were reported by Colonel Davidson, who impressed upon the Government the necessity of adopting effectual means of counteracting the evil, and of securing the fidelity of our native troops. Towards the end of the year (1857) he renewed his representations with especial reference to the location of a larger European force, in future, at Secunderabad. In consequence of these representations, the force was increased by a regiment of dragoons, a corps of European infantry, and some artillery.

The faithfulness of the Nizam through all the occurrences of 1857 and 1858 was not so much a matter of course, as some may be inclined to believe, but was subject to severe trials. I have already alluded to the swarming thousands of armed and turbulent men who form so large a proportion of the population of Hyderabad, and though nothing particular had occurred beyond the incidents I have related, there was at times much uneasiness and excitement. Rumours of disaster befalling our troops in the North-

West were frequently spread, and as frequently believed. The prevalent feeling seemed to be one of disappointment, if not of shame, that whilst their brethren in the field had dared the chances of an open conflict with us, the city of Hyderabad was at peace. Thus, followers in abundance were ready at the call of any man of influence who was willing to commit himself to the movement, and this being the case, the city required constant and careful watching. As I have remarked at the beginning of this chapter, the feeling of uneasiness continued until the troops of the Hyderabad contingent, which had been despatched to Central India by Colonel Davidson, achieved a succession of brilliant victories under the distinguished general who appreciated their soldier-like qualities. The intelligence communicated by these troops to their friends at Hyderabad respecting the progress of events in the north, obtained credence as coming from "the faithful," and of course had a quieting influence.

The services of the Nizam's troops may fairly claim a distinguished place in the history of our connection with Hyderabad, but the reader must be contented, for the present, with a brief recapitulation. First, however, I deem it an act of bare justice to his highness the Nizam, to place on record the absolute proof of his personal fidelity to our alliance.

In May, 1858, the Supreme Government forwarded to Colonel Davidson an extract from a deposition made before the Judicial Commissioner of Mysore by a prisoner who was suspected of being implicated in the rebellion; desiring that inquiries might be instituted, in order to test the truth of the statement that the Nizam was not entirely innocent of rebellious intentions. Colonel Davidson replied that he was inclined to think the deponent had made use of the Nizam's name merely to give consequence to his statement, adding that "*he had caused the Nizam to be narrowly watched from quarters and in ways he little suspected, and although emissaries had come to him, he had, after listening to their stories, refused complicity in any movement against the British Government.*"

In recording the general measures adopted by Colonel Davidson for the preservation of order throughout the Nizam's country, it will be necessary to revert to the services performed by the troops of the Hyderabad state, alluded to above. The extensive territory ruled by his highness was suffering from large bands of foreign mercenaries in the employ of the numerous Zemindars, and the disaffected were not without hope that the rebellion would be joined by that splendid body of troops, around whom as a nucleus the Rohillas, half-caste Arabs, and other roving bands were ready to gather.

They reckoned, however, without their host, for instead of joining in any conspiracy against the British Government, or opposing the wishes and inclination of the Nizam, these gallant soldiers of the contingent marched for fifteen months, and after the termination of a glorious campaign returned to the Nizam's country. A brief review of their movements will not be uninteresting.

A very large force, consisting of cavalry, artillery, and infantry, from the Hyderabad contingent, was assembled at Edlabad, one of the chief outlets of the Deccan, on the high road to Central India. Here they remained during the rains of 1857, but on the roads drying up, they struck tents, and hastened to join the column already in the field, among the opium plains of Malwah. After coercing en route the refractory Zemindars of Peepliah and Raghooghur, they joined the first Central India brigade (as the force was subsequently named) before the fortress of Dhar, and at Colonel Durand's request they proceeded *at once* in pursuit of the rebels who had made good their escape from that place, and to obtain intelligence generally of the movements of the enemy in advance.

For their services on this occasion, the contingent have been in expectation of being allowed to share in the Dhar booty. They were certainly not present when the garrison escaped,—I mean that portion of the force which was commanded by Major W. Orr; but to their credit, I will add that they arrived after continuous forced marches, and fighting their way to the assistance of their countrymen, soon enough to be in time to pursue the enemy. The organization of these troops was in those days, and to a certain extent still is, of a nature to admit of their turning out at a moment's notice for field service. To arrive in camp before Dhar, therefore, and to be informed that the garrison had escaped, was simply to make every man and soldier feel that the time had again arrived for them to maintain their long-established reputation as light horsemen. As my narrative will now proceed to show, the far-famed "Nizam's horse" gave the first blow to the rebellion in Central India, by the capture of the stores, guns, ammunition, etc., carried away from Mahidpore by the contingent at that station after they had been joined by the garrison which escaped from Dhar. Under these circumstances doubtless a liberal Government will recommend her Majesty to satisfy the expectations of the contingent, and setting aside the question of co-operation in this service, direct the prize to be divided among all the forces who so gallantly made a stand, and kept the field through two hot seasons, and ultimately carried all before them.

The escaped garrison, as remarked above, had been joined by the Mahidpore contingent, who had killed several of their officers, and the whole body had marched to Rawul, when the Hyderabad cavalry came up with them. The following particulars of the fight are quoted from a letter which appeared in the *Englishman* newspaper :—

"On the second morning after leaving camp, the cavalry, who had marched some sixty miles, arrived before Mahidpore, and ascertained that the mutineers had left the same morning; carrying with them all the guns, stores, and ammunition from that place. For the last two days they had made the most diligent search for Mrs. Timmins, the wife of the officer who commanded the Mahidpore contingent, that lady having been unable to effect her escape, owing to her horse having been shot, or some such reason; but their endeavours to find her place of concealment had been frustrated by the exertions of a faithful tailor. On the arrival of our troops, and after the tailor had satisfied himself, from the appearance of several European officers, that the Nizam's troops were really friendly, he pointed out his mistress's place of concealment, and she was immediately escorted to camp, from whence, under a sufficient guard, she started to join her husband.

"The Hyderabad contingent having watered and fed

their horses, followed the Mahidpore mutineers, and the Dhar garrison who had joined them, and after a pursuit of twelve miles, the cavalry came on the rebels at four o'clock in the afternoon, at the village of Rawul, where the insurgents had taken up a position, with their right resting on the village, and their front covered by a muddy nullah, or stream. It is impossible to conceive a more difficult position for the approach of cavalry, and in selecting it, the enemy proved that they were not wanting in a knowledge of military tactics. The famous Nizam's horse, however, numbering on this occasion only 350 sabres, led by their several officers, all eager to imbrue their swords in the blood of the rebels—and though stoutly opposed by such preponderating odds, and received with round shot and canister—overcame all obstacles opposed to their advance, charged home, and cut down the rebels at their guns. When the enemy were put to flight the cavalry followed, cutting up many in the pursuit, and but for the standing crops, consisting of fields of jowarry and hemp, a greater number of the insurgents would have been killed; however, 175 bodies were counted on the field the day following, and buried in pits. Eight guns of different calibre, three of which were siege, with large quantities of stores, were retaken at Rawul.

"The material consequences of recapturing, at

this stage of the mutiny, this efficient battery from a disciplined force several thousands strong, who the next day would have joined their comrades at Mundesore, requires no comment from me," adds the writer I am quoting; and he continues, "but I have not the least hesitation in declaring that but for the success attending the fight at Rawul, these siege-guns would have been placed in position before Neemuch (it being proved by intercepted letters with what anxiety the rebel army at Mundesore and Neemuch were looking for the arrival of the Mahidpore battery and stores), when, of course, the walls of Neemuch would have been battered down. At Neemuch 4,000 mutineers were in full force round the small fort in which some of our countrymen were holding out. Had the enemy been reinforced by the Mahidpore contingent with the siege-guns, I believe that in three or four hours the wall of the fort must have been battered down, and a repetition of what occurred at Cawnpore enacted there. The charge of the Irregular Horse at Rawul, however, saved the Neemuch garrison from such a fate, and most effectually relieved that place from the besieging army. Again, when the rebel force, raising the siege of Neemuch, retraced its steps towards Mundesore, had they been accompanied by the Mahidpore battery, in addition to the guns they brought to bear on us, what execution might they not have done on the ranks of the Malwah column, possessing as they would the same terrible engines of destruction as those we opposed to them? for the stores of the Mahidpore contingent captured at Rawul consisted of shot, shell, and canister, and all that was required to convert a battle fought with their aid into a contest of the most sanguinary description.

"So satisfied was Colonel Durand with the work performed by the Hyderabad cavalry, and with the successful result of the action at Rawul, that he took upon himself the responsibility of authorizing the payment of an extra five rupees per month to each horseman of the Nizam's cavalry during the time they remained in the field. This had the good result of proving to all in the corps that their labours had been appreciated."

The writer in the *Englishman* dwells at some length on the successful results which had attended the opening of the campaign in Malwah. This he attributes to the efficiency of the Hyderabad troops, who, on the return of the 1st brigade Central India column to Indore, after the battle of Mundesore, remained encamped at that town until the 26th of December, when they commenced their march *viâ* Goonah to meet Sir H. Rose at Saugor, who had proceeded with the 2nd brigade Central India field force to that station. This column, after the relief of Saugor, and capture of Ratghur and Ghurrahcottah, met the Nizam's field force two marches beyond Saugor, on the Jhansi road. At Muddenpore the two columns forced the pass, and the 2nd brigade halted until Sir H. Rose was in receipt of intelligence regarding the movements of the 1st brigade, the latter having remained encamped at Indore until further reinforcements arrived at Mhow, when they started to join Sir Hugh Rose, *viâ* Chanderee. This place being in the possession of some rebel troops, the brigade diverged from the direct road to Jhansi in order to chastise them.

The Hyderabad contingent, after the battle at the Muddenpore pass, proceeded in advance, and after taking the fortress of Talbeit, thirty miles south of Jhansi, remained encamped there until the arrival of Sir H. Rose, who, on receiving information of the fall of Chanderee, continued his march, accompanied by the 2nd brigade, and followed by the 1st, which had received instructions to march direct on Jhansi.

In March, the 2nd brigade Central India column and the Hyderabad troops arrived before Jhansi, and the greater part of the cavalry surrounded the town and fortress at once. In the course of a few days the 1st brigade arrived, and operations commenced. On the fall of Jhansi, the Hyderabad force proceeded in advance of the general column, and encamped on the banks of the river Betwah; and when the two Central India columns marched, the Hyderabad column again advanced to the vicinity of Koonch, where, on the arrival of the whole force, a general action took place glorious to the British arms, fought at a season of the year when Europeans are usually sheltered in houses or barracks under the influence of a cool atmosphere, procured through artificial means for making the climate endurable; but here, in the scorching heat, did we combat with the foe, and our most destructive enemy was found to be the sun.

After this action the entire column proceeded to Calpee, which succumbed in the course of a week; on which event the Hyderabad contingent received instructions to return to the Deccan, and en route to coerce the refractory Zemindars of Bilowah. This was most effectually done, the enemy losing in the attack about 150 men; and now all hands viewed with pleasure the prospect of a speedy meeting with their friends in the Deccan.

This, however, was not yet to be; the ubiquitous Tantia Topee suddenly appeared at Gwalior, and against that fortress the Hyderabad contingent received orders to march. On the fall of Gwalior, "we commenced our march in earnest for the Nizam's country, where we arrived in August 1858, after thirteen months under canvas. Three months afterwards, when Tantia

Topee appeared on the north side of the range of mountains which separates the Deccan from the valley of the Nerbudda, Colonel Davidson sent 1,200 sabres to meet the enemy, but they had no wish to feel again the keen swords of the Hyderabad cavalry, which had so frequently, in the plains of Central India, dealt death among their ranks, and the demonstration sufficed to put them to flight. Great commotion had been produced throughout the Hyderabad territory by the near approach of this leader, but it rapidly subsided when the Hyderabad contingent marched against them."

As an officer of the Hyderabad contingent field force, of whose action in Central India the above is a meagre though accurate summary, I may remark that no sounder policy could have been pursued than that adopted by Colonel Davidson. By his skilful management, the excitement which it was only natural for the native troops to feel under the circumstances, was never allowed to gain head: the men were protected from themselves, and instead of remaining in quarters to hatch sedition and eventually bring destruction on their own heads, they were guided to the plains of Central India to win the renown deserved by their gallantry, and at the same time render efficient service to those who would not fail to serve them well in return.

CHAPTER XXII.

RECOGNITION OF THE NIZAM'S SERVICES.

Complimentary Visit to his Highness after the Return of the Hyderabad Troops from the North-West—Attack on the Resident and Minister—Satisfactory Conduct of the Nizam—Despatch from the Governor General—Instance of Party Influence opposed to the English Government—Alteration of the Coinage—Alteration of the Seal—The Queen's Supremacy not to be questioned—Instance of Lawlessness in the City—Presents to his Highness and the Members of his Court—Territory ceded to his Highness in further Acknowledgment of his Services—Remission of the Debt—Presents designed by his Highness for the Resident and the European Officers—Opinions of the Resident and the Governor General—Institution of the "Star of India"—The Nizam is created one of the Knights—State Ceremonials on the Receipt of the Letters Patent—Persian Placards posted up in Hyderabad attributing a Political Significance to the Investiture—Investiture of the Nizam in full Durbar.

THE sequel of the critical occurrences adverted to in the preceding chapter supplies me, on the whole, with an agreeable task, though I have to commence by recording an event which fell little short of becoming a tragedy. In January, 1859, I was appointed second assistant Resident at the Court of his highness the Nizam, and in February, 1859, Colonel Davidson proceeded to Calcutta, and on his return paid a visit to the Nizam, with a view to the presentation of a khurreeta (despatch) from his Excellency the Governor General. On returning from durbar, close to the room in which this interview had taken place, a native, said to be from Hindustan, discharged a carbine and wounded one of the minister's attendants, and then, drawing his sword, rushed upon Colonel Davidson and the minister, who at this moment were walking arm-in-arm in conversation with each other. I drew my sword and threw myself before Colonel Davidson, but fortunately the assassin was intercepted by the minister's dependants, and cut down. Had the man attempted to pass me, I should there and then have cut him down, but seeing that several of the minister's attendants were cutting at him, I refrained from joining them, and Colonel Davidson observed to me afterwards, that it was fortunate I had done so, as most probably the crowd, who were all armed to the teeth, would have become excited at seeing the Feringhee killing a Mohammedan, and would have fallen on the whole of the staff, and thus all our lives might have been sacrificed. There can be little doubt, Colonel Davidson reported, that he shared in the fanatical feeling of the period against all Europeans throughout the country, and that he had expected, by the destruction of the Resident or the minister, to gain for himself the envied title of Ghazi (champion of the faith)!

The Nizam recalled the party to durbar, and though he appeared agitated, displayed no want of presence of mind. Addressing himself to the minister, he observed: "I desire that you will institute the most searching inquiry into this affair." He then invited the Resident and staff to retire for a short time into a private garden adjoining the hall of audience, where they remained for above half an hour. The Nizam's whole retinue was then called out to accompany the Resident and staff to the Residency, where they arrived in safety. The minister and Shumsh-ool-oomrah's sons kept near them to the last; and it is almost unnecessary to add, that the Hyderabad government felt considerable anxiety as to the manner in which the occurrence might be viewed by the Government of India.

In due course a despatch was received from the Governor General, in which he warmly congratulated the Resident on his escape. He was satisfied to observe the anxious concern with which the crime had been regarded, not only by his highness the Nizam and his minister, but by the whole of the Hyderabad court. The conduct of his highness had been dignified and calm, and the measures taken by the minister prompt and judicious. At the same time Lord Canning warned the Nizam that the event could not be regarded as one of slight moment. The British Government, he said, held the person of its representative sacred from all insult and violence, and to no court which could not give protection to the representative of the Governor General, would his Excellency trust the life and honour of a British officer. Accordingly, the Nizam was requested to take the most vigorous measures to prevent the recurrence of so lamentable an act as that which had been perpetrated, and the durbar was clearly informed that they were held responsible for the safety of the British Resident within the Nizam's dominions. The Resident's measures in countermanding the troops which had turned out at Secunderabad on the first alarm reaching that station was approved, and the thanks of the Government of India conveyed to the officers and gentlemen who formed the Resident's suite.

The opposing influences at work at the court of Hyderabad, and the necessity of asserting the Queen's supremacy, appeared in certain circumstances connected with the coinage. In 1858, attention had been called to the inscription of the King of Delhi on the currency in the Nizam's dominions, and the minister having agreed with our Government that no object could be served by retaining an inscription which referred to a sovereign who no longer existed, the coin was altered.[1] A new seal was also prepared, from which all allusion to the Nizam's former allegiance to the King of Delhi was omitted. It appears that no question arose out of these changes until October, 1859, when the Nizam proposed a change in the inscription on his coinage, which could have no other object, in the Resident's opinion, than to show that he considered himself an independent prince. As there could be no doubt that he was influenced in the matter by the host of vagabond and seditious faqueers by whom he is always surrounded, and who are ever ready to say or do anything hostile to our Government, the Nizam was officially informed, that any act of his designed to call in question the supremacy of her Majesty would certainly be regarded as a breach of friendship. The minister explained that some of the Nizam's dependants had presented him with nuzzurs, which included several of the new coins, and the Nizam inquired why "92," and not "Mohammed," had been inscribed on them, and then sent an order to the minister to make the change. Salar Jung himself considered the change unnecessary, remarking that the question had been fully discussed the previous year when the inscription of the King of Delhi had been removed from the

[1] The new coinage was inscribed "Sicca Nizam-ool-Moolk Bahadoor Asuf Jah, 1275," and on the obverse, "Zurb Fur Koondlah, Boonyad Hyderabad Jhooloos Mymuth Manoos."

coinage. After the communication from the Government of India on this subject, the Nizam requested the minister to stay further proceedings, and no change was made.[1]

The latent anarchy of the Nizam's capital, owing to the general practice of carrying arms and the presence of many thousands of idle adventurers in the city, has been more than once alluded to in these pages; and that educated persons opposed to English influence were always ready to avail themselves of the inflammable materials thus kept ready to their hand, is proved by an instance to which I shall have occasion to allude at the close of this chapter. The same spirit of lawlessness appeared in domestic matters of the most ordinary kind, the following example of which will here fall into its proper chronological place.

A sowcar or native banker inhabiting the Residency bazaar, appears to have possessed a garden which was coveted by the Nizam's uncle, Mozuffur-oo-Dowlah. The latter insisted on its being made over to him, even after it was sold to some other person,

---

[1] The 92 referred to signifies the value in figures of the name "Mahomed." The letters comprising the name are—Meem, 40; Hey, 8; Meem, 40; Dal, 4: totalling 92. The Nizam wished to substitute Mahomed for 92; but Colonel Davidson informed him that as the figure 92 already on the rupee signified the name, a change was not to be desired.

and at last endeavoured to obtain his wish by seizing the banker and placing him in confinement. The Resident demanded the banker's release; whereupon Mozuffur-oo-Dowlah placed himself in open defiance to the Nizam's government, and surrounded himself with armed Rohillas. For twenty-four hours the main-street leading to the chowk and other parts of the city were completely closed, as well as the approaches to the minister's house, which were fired upon, and several persons lost their lives in attempting to traverse them.

Colonel Davidson intimated to the Nizam, through the minister, that his highness would be entirely wanting in what was due to himself and his government if he did not visit with condign punishment both his uncle and his rebellious followers. The Nizam, however, had advisers who persuaded him that the act of defiance should not be heavily visited on a prince of the royal house, and he acquiesced in the suggestion. The uncle was persuaded to come to terms, and his followers were called on to lay down their arms.

In March, 1858, Colonel Davidson had recommended that rewards should be bestowed on his highness the Nizam and certain members of his court, in recognition of the services rendered by his highness personally, and by the government of

Hyderabad, during the disturbances of 1857–58. In pursuance of this recommendation the Governor General had the satisfaction of addressing a letter to the Nizam (February, 1859), in which he thanked him for the zeal and constancy with which he had adhered to the long-established friendship between the two governments, and pointed to a future time at which it might be in his Excellency's power to offer his highness a public mark of the acknowledgments of the British Government.

In July, 1860, the Governor General requested the Nizam's acceptance of presents of English manufacture, valued at one lac of rupees, as an earnest of the desire of the British Government for a lasting concord between the two states, whose interests, it was observed, were in all respects the same. In addition to these gifts, our Government made over to his highness in full sovereignty the lapsed Sumesthan of Shorapore, which by the rebellion of the late Rajah had reverted to the British Government. A few remarks respecting the rebellion of the chief of this state will not be out of place here.

The "principality" of Shorapore originally formed part of the kingdom of Beejapore; but about the period of Aurungzebe's invasion of the Deccan, "Chup Naik," an ancestor of Rajah Venkutuppah Naik Bulwunt Bhyree Bahadoor of Shorapore, availed himself of the confusion of the times to revolt. He purchased a nominal independence by the payment of a tribute to the Nizam.

Disputes about succession and other disorders which the rulers of the principality were too feeble in themselves to suppress, induced the family to throw themselves upon the protection of the British Resident at the court of the Nizam, which was cordially given.

On the death of his father in 1842, Rajah Venkutuppah Naik was placed for education under the guardianship of Captain M. Taylor, an officer of the Nizam's infantry. On attaining his majority he was left to the independent management of the principality, and his character and disposition were at that time represented by Captain Taylor in very favourable terms.

During the seditions and outrages of 1857, however, rumours reached the Resident at Hyderabad that the Rajah was engaged in treasonable practices, and Captain Rose Campbell, second Assistant Resident, was sent to Shorapore to institute inquiries. The Rajah at first utterly denied the truth of the accusations against him; but after continued remonstrance and advice, he confessed that he had ordered the enlistment of a band of mercenaries, and directed them to assemble at Shorapore. A detachment of the Hyderabad contingent was at that time engaged in preserving the peace of the country, and on the 7th of February, 1858, was encamped before Shorapore. About 5½ P.M. this detachment was attacked by the Rajah's troops, who continued to harass it by firing at intervals until midnight. One of the Rajah's jemadars, Bulwunt Rao, had that day been on an amicable visit to Captain Campbell, and the attack by the Rajah's troops was alike unprovoked and treacherous. The following morning the detachment of the contingent having been reinforced by a portion of the Lingasagoor field force, the Rajah's troops were easily routed; but Captain P. K. Newberry, having got in advance of his men, was killed by a musket-shot. The Rajah fled to Hyderabad, and surrendered himself. He was tried by a general court-martial, and sentenced to transportation for life; but while *en route* he contrived to secure a pistol, and died by his own hand.

Besides the territory made over to his highness, a debt of fifty lacs of rupees, with interest, was also cancelled for reasons assigned, and the districts of Raichore and Dharaseo restored to him; but regarding this arrangement I shall say more hereafter.

In a similar manner, to the Nizam's uncle, Shumsh-ool-oomrah, to whose good influence on the Mohammedans of the city the preservation of quiet at Hyderabad was largely due, the Governor General desired to present a khillut of the value of 30,000 rupees.

To the minister, Mookhtar-ool-Moolk Salar Jung Bahadoor, a khillut of the value of 30,000 rupees. The Governor General in Council at the same time informed Salar Jung, that the ability, courage, and firmness with which he had discharged his duty to the Nizam and British Government, and opposed the counsels of those who would have brought disgrace and ruin upon his highness, were highly appreciated, and entitled him to the most cordial thanks of the Government of India.

To Yakoob Ally Khan, the Jagheerdar of Tickapilly, and his son Mohammed Ghous, the Governor General desired to present a pair of shawls and sword each, the latter bearing a suitable inscription in Persian, accompanied with a letter under the Resident's signature, expressing the thanks of the Governor General of India.

To Rajah Ramesur Rao, of Woonpurty, an English double-barrelled rifle, a sword and embroidered belt with suitable inscription, and a Colt's revolver pistol. This gentleman dresses in the English costume, and commands a considerable body of troops in the Nizam's service. Presents were also given to several other native chiefs, including the Arab Jewadem.

On the 5th of October, 1861, the above-named presents to the Nizam and the officers of his court were delivered in full Durbar. On this occasion, after the usual ceremonial inquiries, his highness put the diamond ring, which was among the articles presented, on his little finger, and requested the minister to get it enlarged, in order that he might wear it. He also took the jewelled sword in his hand, and placed it alongside of the weapon usually worn by him at Durbar.

The brigadiers commanding the Hyderabad subsidiary force, and the Hyderabad contingent, the officers of their respective staffs, together with several other officers belonging to the cantonments at Bolarum and Secunderabad, making, with the Resident's own staff, thirty in all, attended at the Durbar, and his highness directed each to be presented with a "Sirpesh" (ornament for the head) and other jewels, proportioned to the rank and position of each.[1] The Nizam expressed his anxious desire that the officers might be allowed to accept these presents as a remembrance of having attended his Durbar; but the Resident deemed it proper to retain them in the custody of the Residency treasurer until he received instructions from the

[1] The value of the Nizam's presents was estimated as follows:—The Resident, 22,000 rs.: brigadier commanding Hyderabad subsidiary force, Hyderabad contingent, 1st Assistant Resident, military secretary, and four other officers, each 8,000 rs.; in all, 24,000 rs.: twenty-two other officers, each 2,000 rs.; in all, 44,000 rs.: total value, 90,000 rs.

Government as to their disposal. On the part of himself and the officers of his staff, Colonel Davidson recommended that the rules in force with regard to political officers receiving presents should be adhered to; but with regard to the other officers who attended the Durbar, perhaps the Governor General might be inclined to pursue the course adopted by the Marquis of Dalhousie in regard to the gifts presented to the officers who accompanied the mission to the court of the King of Ava.

The Governor General, however, would not listen to any relaxation of the rule with regard to presents intended for European officers; the distinction drawn by Colonel Davidson between himself and his staff on the one side, and the officers of Government on the other, was considered quite inadmissible.

In this year (1861) the new order of knighthood called "The Star of India" was instituted. Besides the Sovereign and Grand-master, it consists of twenty-five knights, Europeans and native princes of India, and a limited number of honorary members, of whom the late Prince Consort and the Prince of Wales are examples. The order was gazetted on the 25th of June, and in July the Nizam received a khurreeta from the Governor General, enclosing a grant under her Majesty's sign-manual, constituting his highness a knight of this "Most Exalted Order." The honour thus paid to the Nizam was formally conferred upon him at a Durbar held on the 31st of August, when the Resident delivered the Queen's grant, the purport of which and of the letters patent had been previously explained to his highness with all necessary care.

The Nizam showed his appreciation of this honour by every means in his power. All the high officers of state who have the entrée at the Durbar were in attendance. His highness's large retinue waited in state at its various posts, and his line and other troops were drawn up in full dress, headed by their respective bands. They presented arms, and a royal salute was fired after the khurreeta had been read and the grant produced. A similar salute was fired at the neighbouring stations of Secunderabad and Bolarum.

The Nizam, in reply to the letter from the Governor General, expressed himself highly gratified to receive the happy announcement that her Majesty the Empress of India and Queen of Great Britain had been graciously pleased to confer on his Excellency the high dignity of Grand-master, and to appoint and nominate him (the Nizam), of her most gracious favour, to be a Knight of the Most Exalted Order of the Star of India. It was not until the 25th of November, however, that Colonel Davidson finally attended the Nizam's Durbar, and, assisted by the minister, invested his highness with the insignia. The Resident was accompanied as before by the brigadiers commanding the Hyderabad subsidiary force and the Hyderabad contingent, with his (the Resident's) and their respective staffs, and several officers from Bolarum and the Hyderabad subsidiary force.

The Nizam was most friendly and cordial; he spoke much more openly, and in a more affable manner than he was in the habit of doing, asking the Resident twice to sit nearer to his musnud, and catching him by the arm to induce him to do so. He assured Colonel Davidson that he considered the presentation of the Star as a great honour, and alluded to certain placards[1] which had been stuck up in the city, which he characterized as being all lies, and without a shadow of foundation; all the endeavours, however, of the city police to trace the authors of the placards had failed.

The Resident assured his highness that he had judged most correctly, and that the dignity was conferred, not for any political purpose whatever, but simply to increase his honour and the respect of his subjects, and was forwarded to him by her Majesty the Queen as an acknowledgment of his eminent services.

---

[1] A translation of the seditious placard is inserted in the Appendix J J.

The Nizam expressed himself much delighted, and said that the Governor General had always been most kind and friendly to him, and that Colonel Davidson had ever shown himself to be the well-wisher of the two Governments.

Her Majesty's warrant dispensing with the personal investiture of his highness with the insignia of the Most Exalted Order of the Star of India, was delivered to the Nizam, and the covenant making provision for the due restitution of the insignia was duly signed by his highness in Durbar.

After the Durbar a royal salute was fired by the order of the Nizam, which was returned from Secunderabad and Bolarum.

His highness, with a view to show how highly he appreciated the honour conferred on him, directed the minister to give an entertainment in the public rooms at Secunderabad to the whole of the European community of Hyderabad.

CHAPTER XXIII.

THE CEDED DISTRICTS AND PUBLIC WORKS.

General Improvement of the Districts assigned to Government by the Treaty of 1853—Negotiation for the Abolition of Transit Dues on the River Godavery—Cession of Territory on the Banks of the River—Restoration to the Nizam of a Part of the Assigned Districts—Supplementary Treaty of 1860—Completion of the Channel between the River Moosey and the Houssain Saugor Tank—Construction of the Sholapore Road—Plan and Details of the Road—Bazaar and Bridge over the Moosey completed by the Nizam—Improved Administration of the Assigned Districts—Steady Advance of the Revenues derived from them—Purposes to which the Revenue has been applied—Improved Administration of Justice in Civil Cases—Criminal Justice and Decrease in Crime—Organization of a Police System—Erection of Gaols—Education—Village Schools opened—Public Buildings and Village Roads—Revenue subsequent to the Conclusion of the Supplementary Treaty of 1860.

It will be my object in this chapter to show the general improvement under British management of the districts assigned to Government by the treaty of 1853,[1] reserving such remarks as I have to make on the value of Berar as a cotton-producing district for

[1] *Ante*, p. 277.

distinct treatment. The subject is so intimately connected with that of the water-supply for purposes of irrigation, with the formation of public roads and bridges, with fiscal and other improvements tending to facilitate commercial intercourse, and with the social condition of the people, that all these subjects may fairly claim some preliminary notice.

In the year 1860 the authorities at Madras urged upon the Government of India the necessity of entering into some arrangements with the Nizam relative to the transit dues on the river Godavery. By the treaty of 1802 the Nizam had the right to levy five per cent. on all goods in transit by that river; the abolition of this duty was regarded as an indispensable preliminary to any expenditure being incurred in the improvement of the navigation, according to a scheme which had been proposed with that object in view. I ought to remark, that the levy of five per cent. was charged upon all goods except salt, upon which the Nizam's government levied whatever duty they pleased, as an offset to our own similar practice with opium.

The British Government also required the cession of a strip of land on the left bank of the Godavery, from below the junction of the Saveri to about thirty miles above the mouth of the Wyne Gunga. This tract was of little real value. It yielded a revenue of only 20,000 rupees, but its acquisition was desirable as a means for checking the vexatious exactions of certain petty Zemindars, who levied a sort of black mail on goods in transit, in defiance of the Nizam's authority and the treaty arrangements with his highness.

The Government of India, on their part, as stated in an earlier part of this narrative, cancelled the debt of fifty lacs due by his highness, and gave up so much of the Assigned Districts as would leave in its possession thirty-two lacs of revenue required for the regular payment of the contingent and other engagements entered into by the treaty of 1853, stipulating that the surplus revenue should be paid to the Nizam. The territory which it was thus proposed to return (Raichore and Dharaseo) yielded a revenue of twenty-one lacs of rupees.

The Nizam, in agreeing to abolish the levy of five per cent. on the Godavery, stipulated that the arrangement for the abolition of duty was not to apply to merchandise brought by the Godavery route, when it was landed and sent into the interior of the country; nor would he consent to make over the territory retained in Berar to the unreserved management of the British Government, and to be administered through any agency they pleased, as had been proposed. His highness held this point to be of such cardinal importance, that he refused to proceed further with the negotiations until it was settled. Colonel Davidson was then requested to negotiate, as a kind of compromise, for the non-rendering of accounts in future, and the widest latitude in the requisite ministerial expenditure. All this the Nizam agreed to, with the understanding that so much of the treaty of 1853 as provided for the payment of any surplus revenue into his treasury, and for the administration of the ceded districts being vested in the Resident at his court, should remain unchanged. The result was the supplementary treaty of 1860, concluded in the above sense.

The vast improvement of the Assigned Districts under British administration will be the subject of remark further on in this chapter. First in order of time, I have to record that in October of this year Colonel Davidson submitted to government a sketch-map of the Moosey channel, which had been commenced in 1856 while Mr. Bushby was Resident, and reported that the important work of connecting this river with the large Houssain Saugor Tank, near the cantonment of Secunderabad, by a channel thirty-six miles long, had been completed, owing to the exertions of a native engineer, Condasamy Moodellie, more familiarly known as the son of the Sir Christopher Wren of Hyderabad.

This important channel is mentioned by the writer

in the *Englishman* newspaper, a portion of whose letter has been quoted in a previous part of this narrative; but neither by him, nor by the other authorities referred to, is any account given of the tank itself. I am in possession, however, of an extract from the records of the family of the person who constructed the tank, and as the document is in many respects a very curious and characteristic one, a translation of it is inserted in the Appendix.[1]

One of the results arising from the better management of the Assigned Districts, was the construction of the Hyderabad and Sholapore road, running between Hyderabad and Bombay, and meeting the railway at Sholapore.

This road is 172 miles in length, and the whole of the works were completed in the three previous years (1857—1860), at a total cost of 4,15,937 rs. 8 a. The traffic is calculated at 400 carts per diem, but no regular return has as yet been taken.[2]

In June, 1861, a bazaar in the vicinity and bridge over the Moosey river were completed at Hyderabad under the orders of the Nizam's government, at a cost of 1,30,814 rs. The present Nizam inaugurated his reign by ordering the above works to be executed.

The circumstances under which the Assigned Dis-

[1] See Appendix K K.

[2] For other details and plans of the roads, see Appendix L L.

tricts were relinquished to our management by his highness the Nizam have been related in previous chapters; but I may recall to mind that for many years previous to 1853 the several Residents at the court of Hyderabad had endeavoured to obtain from the minister in office the necessary funds for paying the contingent, and that money was frequently advanced by the Company for that purpose. In 1852 the Nizam's debt amounted to 41,32,231 rs., and no prospect existed of its liquidation. The treaty of 1853 was the result, as we have already seen, and our officers, on taking charge of the talooks assigned to our management, at once commenced that course of improvement which has proved so advantageous to the country.

Having related the circumstances under which a portion of these Assigned Districts was restored to the Nizam (by the supplementary treaty of 1860), this will be a suitable place for showing the receipts during the intervening period. The steady rise of the revenue places the fact of a substantial improvement having taken place in the administration of the districts beyond all manner of doubt.

LAND AND OTHER MISCELLANEOUS REVENUE.

	RS.	A.	P.
1853—1854	39,71,678	3	0
1854—1855	41,00,092	0	6
1855—1856	39,90,968	15	7

	RS.	A.	P.
1856—1857	41,85,542	8	2
1857—1858	43,71,975	8	6
1858—1859	44,02,446	13	10
1859—1860	45,02,749	6	5
1860—1861[1]	52,23,218	11	4

This statement is conclusive as to the progress made in the Assigned Districts during eight years of our administration. Those who are interested in the details will find a complete schedule for the above years in the Appendix,[2] together with a distinct statement of receipts and disbursements, showing in separate columns the charges for administration, the military payment under treaty, expenditure on public works, interest for debt, &c.[3]

But it is equally important to remark, that good use has also been made of this prosperity. Sixteen lacs of arrears of pay to the contingent have been liquidated; the transit or Sayer duties have been remitted, amounting to 2,95,355 rs. 0a. 6p. yearly. Several public buildings have been erected in the districts (such as the Deputy-Commissioners' cutcherries, Tehsildars' cutcherries, penitentiaries, central gaol, &c.); and the

[1] The actual collections in 1860-61 amounted only to 42,18,256 rs., owing to the transfer of the Dharaseo and Raichore districts having been completed in February, 1861. The collections for two months (March and April) were, therefore, made by the Nizam's Government, and raised the revenue for the year to the above total.

Appendix M M. [3] Appendix N N.

Bombay road *viâ* Sholapore, passing through a portion of the Dharaseo division, has been constructed, as previously mentioned, at a cost of 4,15,937 rs. 8 a. It should be remembered that there are no sea customs or port dues in these Assigned Districts, as in our own provinces, to augment the revenue, which is solely derived from the usual resources of an inland province. Income-tax is only levied on the salaries of revenue officers under British jurisdiction.

The revenue of Raichore and Dharaseo, restored to the Nizam, amounted to 21,36,762 rs. We retained, in Berar, old districts amounting to 23,86,391 Company's rupees, to which has been added additional territory, the revenue of which is estimated at eight lacs. In all, our demand, to meet every engagement, amounts to thirty-two lacs of net revenue. But there is every prospect of a considerable increase from the growing prosperity of the province, more especially when the country is opened up by the railway, which it is expected will be completed during the present year (1865). The Nizam very wisely insisted that so much of the old treaty as provided for all surplus revenue being paid to him should be adhered to, and doubtless the British Government, honourably performing what they have undertaken, will pay yearly to the Nizam a large amount of cash.

The improvement in the condition of the people

generally will appear, from the observations I have to make under the heads of civil and criminal justice, police, education, &c.

Civil Justice.

In 1853, when the administration of the Assigned Districts fell into our hands, no uniform system of judicature was in operation. The districts were for the most part destitute of courts of justice; little or no attempt was made to better this state of things during the first year. In the following year the facts were reported to Government, and in 1856-1857 we find a record of 7,096 civil causes instituted, of which 3,448 were decided. In 1857-1858 the number of suits, including appeals, were 6,040; or, adding those which had been pending from the previous year, 7,539; of these 6,201 were decided, and 1,338 left over for the following year. In 1858-1859 the total number of cases was 6,678, of which 5,648 were decided. In 1859-1860, out of 5,952 suits pending or instituted, 5,445 were decided, and eleven small-cause courts introduced. Finally, in 1860-1861, of 2,517 suits pending and filed, 1,764 were disposed of, leaving 253 only undecided; but in the meantime Raichore and Dharaseo had been restored to the Nizam, which would of course have some effect in the reduction of the figures. On the other hand, the facilities of judicature were improved. An additional assistant-commissioner's court was sanctioned for West Berar, and all assistants and extra assistants who had passed the higher standard of examination were empowered to try civil suits to the extent of 5,000 rs. instead of 1,000 rs. as formerly.

Criminal Justice.

For the first and second years of our administration nothing is reported, but in the third year, 1855-1856, we find that Thuggee had disappeared, and gang robbery decreased; though violent crime was still very prevalent. In 1856-1857 the rates of crime to population was ascertained to be 0·280 per cent., against 0·167 per cent. for the previous year, and the number of persons tried 8,769, of whom 7,350 were convicted and 1,419 acquitted. The amount of plundered property recovered was estimated at 26 per cent. against 22 per cent. in 1855.

In 1857-1858 the number of persons arraigned before the magistracy and police was 4,196, and the number of cases in which they were concerned, 2,765. Of these 127 cases were committed to the sessions court, by which tribunal three persons were condemned to death and thirty-nine to transportation.

In 1858-1859 the number of persons arraigned was 10,544 in 6,767 cases. The estimated value of stolen property was 1,06,820 rs., of which only 12½ per cent. was recovered.

In 1859-1860 crime had sensibly decreased. The value of property plundered was 2,10,941 rs., of which 33,723 rs. were recovered.

In 1860-1861 the decrease of crime in general is still apparent, but offences of a heinous nature were more in number. Property was plundered to the value of 75,957 rs., of which 11,817 rs. was recovered. No change had been made in the courts of criminal jurisdiction.

POLICE.

No time was lost by our officers in providing the district with this essential element of civilization. During the first year, 1853-54, the most troublesome classes of the population were enlisted in the cause of order, and the responsibility of the Goand Rajahs was defined and insisted upon; the general district and town police was embodied; and a body of village watchmen, subsisting by their usual hugs, or rights, aided by small pieces of waste land, was instituted. The system of management generally was the same as that practised in the North-West.

In 1860-61 the operations of the police were deemed not altogether satisfactory, owing, it was believed, to the intermixture of the Surf-i-khas estates, the additional district assigned to British management, on the restoration of Raichore and Dharaseo to the

Nizam. Reorganization on the most approved principle was in contemplation.

Gaols.

No regular gaols existed in the districts when they came under our management, and consequently no discipline could be enforced among the prisoners. Under date of 1856 we find that they were confined in 14 separate buildings at a cost of 43,371 rs. 4 a., including gaol guards and other contingent expenses. In the year following the Government ordered a central gaol to be erected at Dharaseo, and materials were collected for the purpose. District gaols at the Sudder stations were also determined upon, but not definitively provided for. The central gaol at Dharaseo was handed over to the Nizam's government with the district.

Education.

There were no funds of any kind available for education in the districts, and nothing was done until 1856-57, when three Canarese teachers were employed to instruct a class of village schoolmasters. In the following year 41 new schools were started in Raichore, and 12 qualified teachers sent out from Singsoogoor. Since then an expenditure of 1,000 rs. per month has been sanctioned for each district, or 24,000 rs. per annum. This will be supplemented by a grant from the local funds, and the number of schools will be increased.

PUBLIC WORKS.

Some remarks have already been made under this head. During the first year of our administration a few public buildings on a small scale were erected in West Berar, and in the western district 4 tanks or reservoirs were commenced at a sanctioned cost of 12,654 rs. 11 a. In Western Raichore tank repairs and works of irrigation were in progress at a cost of 5,599 rs. 4 a. 5 p.; and in Eastern Raichore the construction of a metalled road thirty miles long was commenced. This was sanctioned, in an emergency, at a cost of 13,208 rs. It is an extension across the Doab of the road towards Hyderabad constructed in the Bellary district as far as the Tongabudra river.

In February, 1856, a department of public works was established, and a chief engineer appointed. Arrangements were made for district establishments early in the following year, and 221 miles of village roads opened.

Between the latter period and 1860, the construction of roads was continued, especially of such as were necessary to feed the railway from Oomrowtee to Nagpore. The Oomrowtee cutcherry was completed, and that at Akolah considerably advanced.

REVENUE.

In the first year of our administration, after deducting the charges of administration from the gross revenue, it was found that a sum of 34,06,136 rs. remained for treaty purposes; but in the third year, 1855-6, the receipts were adequate to meet all the demands created by the treaty. From that period the balance continued to increase in favour of Government, as shown in a previous page.[1]

An abstract of the general budget of receipts and disbursements since the supplementary treaty and the surrender of a portion of the Assigned Districts to the Nizam, will be found in the Appendix.[2]

---

[1] *Ante*, p. 322. [2] See Appendix O O.

CHAPTER XXIV.

THE NIZAM, THE MINISTER, AND THE RESIDENT.

Retrospect—Succession of Salar Jung to the Office of Dewan—Succession of his Highness Afzul-oo-Dowlah—Opposition of the Anti-English Faction to the Minister—The Nizam signifies his Intention of dismissing Salar Jung from Office—Court Intrigue against the Minister detected—His Popularity among all Classes at Hyderabad—He is supported by the Resident and the English Government—Despatch from the Viceroy—Reconciliation with the Nizam—The Minister's Occupations—Court Etiquette—The Shoe and Chair Questions—The late Resident, Colonel Davidson—His judicious Management of Affairs at Hyderabad—Summary Account of his Administration—Concluding Remarks on the Nizam's Government—Troops—Adawluts—Police—Land Revenue, &c.

It will be remembered that Salar Jung was appointed to the office of minister on the death of his uncle Seraj-ool-Moolk, which took place on the 27th of May, 1853. The selection at the time was considered a happy one by the Resident, and it has proved to be so. The succession of the present Nizam, on the death of Nasir-oo-Dowlah in 1857, found him still in office. Owing to his tact and sagacity, the disaffected were kept under restraint during the mutinies, as I have already related. The training of an Eastern prince in the seclusion of the harem sufficiently accounts for the ignorance he usually displays when first ascending the musnud, and therefore the present Nizam may be congratulated in possessing a minister so experienced and loyal as Salar Jung. Occasionally a master spirit arises superior to circumstances, and shapes his own policy. Such, it is to be hoped, the Nizam will prove to be under the guidance of so faithful a servant to his government as Mookhtar-ool-Moolk, the title conferred on Salar Jung by his master.

While at the present moment the most perfect cordiality exists between the Nizam and his minister, I have to relate a circumstance which occurred in 1861 which proves how necessary it is for a political officer at an Eastern court to be cautious in the selection of his native friends, more especially when he intends to employ them as confidential agents.

A native gentleman named Yakoob Ally Khan had always borne a high character at the Residency, and during the mutinies had rendered such good service to the British Government, that he was numbered with those entitled to the distinction of a present, when a similar honour was conferred on the Nizam, the minister, and other noblemen of the court, as recorded in the preceding chapter. It is not surprising, therefore, that this gentleman was intimate at the Residency, and that he became the frequent medium of Colonel Davidson's communications with the Nizam through some noblemen of the city.

When the districts of Raichore and Dharaseo were restored to his highness, and should have been made over to the minister as a part of his resources for the service of the state, an unaccountable delay took place which astonished everybody at Hyderabad. The messages sent by the Resident to his highness produced no effect, but were always met by pretexts, which afterwards proved to be the pure invention of the good Yakoob, who so falsified his messages as to make it appear that the Resident was himself anxious for the minister's dismissal. To carry out his plan, he first communicated the supposed wish of the Resident to an officer in the confidence of Shumsh-ool-oomrah's eldest son, Oomdut-ool-Moolk. This nobleman was really persuaded that the Resident was desirous of raising him (Oomdut-ool-Moolk) to the dignity of minister, and that the mere expression of his highness's wish to Colonel Davidson would secure the dismissal of Salar Jung.

Colonel Davidson had no suspicion of this intrigue, and was much annoyed by the Nizam's inattention to his advice respecting the restored districts, and the consequent embarrassments of the minister. At length, in May, 1861, the Nizam requested an interview with the Resident, and signified his intention of removing Salar Jung from office. His astonishment may be conceived when, instead of finding the Resident prepared to acquiesce in his design, the most determined opposition was made to it. He concluded that Colonel Davidson was dissembling, in order that he might not be thought too eager in seizing the proffered opportunity, and in that conviction turned to the officers of the staff, and requested them to bear witness to the expression of his decided intention to dismiss Salar Jung. Colonel Davidson, equally in the dark, and consistent with his conviction of the minister's superior fitness for the office, positively refused to carry on business with any other than Salar Jung until he reported the circumstances to his own Government, and was in possession of their instructions.

On his return to the Residency, Colonel Davidson addressed an official note to the Nizam, repeating his resolve, and his highness was so alarmed, that he entered into an explanation of the circumstances under which he had been led to propose Salar Jung's dismissal, stating that in doing so he was under the impression that the Resident himself was anxious to nominate some other person to office. In the meantime Colonel Davidson had forwarded his communication to the Governor General, who replied that he was considered to have acted with judgment, and that his proceedings were approved. Further, his excellency expressed his surprise and regret at the announcement of his highness's intention, to which he could give no countenance. While acknowledging the Nizam's claims to the consideration of the British Government for the fidelity and friendly attachment he had evinced since his accession to power, he reminded his highness of the heavy burden and responsibility which had fallen on the minister, and of the admirable manner in which he had borne it. Finally, he exhorted the Nizam to remember that no ruler, whatever his power or capacity, can afford to dispense with a faithful and able minister who will do his duty honestly and speak the truth without fear, and that for a sovereign to divest himself of such a minister for reasons vague and unsubstantial, would, wherever it became known, be viewed as anything rather than a proof of wisdom and justice.

The facts I have related relative to the conspiracy had, however, been already discovered as the natural result of the Resident's unqualified support of the minister, and the endeavours of the guilty persons to exonerate themselves when the causes of the misapprehension came to be investigated. Instead of their machinations having the desired effect, the eyes of the Nizam were opened to the conduct of Yakoob Ally Khan, and his confidence in Salar Jung being fully established, he now occasionally honours the minister by taking up his abode for a few days in his palace. Among the sowcars and traders of Hyderabad Salar Jung is most popular, and even the higher classes of the nobility feel confidence in his ministry.

I must not dismiss this episode without informing my readers that Yakoob Ally Khan, in reward of his ingenious industry, was ordered to reside upon his jagheer (estate). A punishment so light must be attributed to the forgiving disposition of the minister whose downfall he had endeavoured to work.

It will not be out of place if I here offer a few details relative to the minister's daily occupations, which may be introduced by a citation from Mr. Elphinstone's history relative to the general manners of the natives of India. "Great attention," he says, "is paid to ceremony. A person of distinction is met a mile or two before he enters the city; and a visitor is received (according to his rank) at the outer gate of the house, at the door of the room, or by merely rising from the seat. Friends embrace if they have not met for some time; Brahmins are saluted by joining the palms and raising them twice or thrice to the forehead; with others the salute with one hand is used, so well known by the Mohammedan name of sálám. Brahmins have a peculiar phrase of salutation for each other. Other Hindus on meeting repeat twice the name of the god Rámá. Visitors are seated with strict attention to their rank, which, on public occasions, it often takes much previous negotiation to settle. Hindus of rank are remarkable for their politeness to inferiors, generally addressing them by some familiar or civil term, and scarcely ever being provoked to abusive or harsh language.

"At formal meetings nobody speaks but the principal persons, but in other companies there is a great deal of unrestrained conversation. The manner of the Hindus is polite, and their language obsequious; they abound in compliments and expressions of humility even to their equals, and when they have an object to gain. They seldom show much desire of knowledge or disposition to extend their thoughts beyond their ordinary habits. Within that sphere, however, their conversation is shrewd and intelligent, often mixed with lively and satirical observations.

"Entertainments, besides occasions of rare occurrence, as marriages, &c., are given on particular festivals, and sometimes to show attention to particular friends; among themselves they commence with a dinner; but the essential part of the entertainments is dancing and singing, sometimes diversified with jugglers and buffoons, during which time perfumes are burnt, and the guests are dressed with garlands of sweet-smelling flowers. Presents, as before described, are no less essential.

"At courts there are certain days in which all the great and all public officers wait on the prince to pay their duty, and on those occasions the crowd in attendance is equal to that of a birthday levée in Europe.

"All go up to the prince in succession, and present him with a nuzzer, which is one or more pieces of money laid on a napkin, and which it is usual to offer to superiors on all formal meetings. The amount depends on the rank of the officer; the lowest in general is a rupee, yet poor people sometimes present a flower, and shopkeepers often some article of their traffic or manufacture. A dress of some sort is on most occasions given in return; the price of one dress is equal to many nuzzers. The highest regular nuzzer is 100 ashrefis, equal to 150 or 170 guineas; but people have been known to present jewels of high value; and it is by no means uncommon, when a prince visits a person of inferior rank, to construct a low base for his musnud of bags containing in all 100,000 rupees, or 10,000*l.*, which are all considered parts of the nuzzer. So much is that a form, that it has been done when the Nizam visited the Resident at Hyderabad, though that prince was little more than a dependant on our Government.

"The rich rise at the same hour as the common people, or perhaps not quite so early; perform their devotions in their own chapels; despatch private and other business with their immediate officers and dependants; bathe, dine, and sleep. At two or three they dress, and appear in their public appointments, where they receive visits and transact business until very late at night. Some also listen to music till late; but these occupations are confined to the rich, and in general a Hindu town is all quiet soon after dark."

As for the Nizam's minister, Salar Jung, he rises about 6 a.m., and after a bath and a cup of tea, proceeds to business. The darogahs of the feel-khana, &c.,[1] first wait upon him, and make their reports. A public durbar is then held, to which the poorest of the people have free access and opportunity given them of making their representations. The various jemadars (officers) of the troops attend this durbar, and make their reports.

The minister then proceeds to his private sitting-room, when he inspects the accounts of the treasury receipts and disbursements, and the moonshee of the darool-in-sha (office of correspondence) waits upon him

[1] Superintendent of the elephants.

with official letters for his approval and signature, and to receive communications respecting unanswered letters. The Nazim (dispenser of justice) of the Adawlut is then granted an audience.

By the time the above business is gone through, it is half-past ten o'clock, when the minister goes to breakfast, which does not detain him above a quarter of an hour. He is now waited upon by the moonshee in charge of the uruzkhana (office where petitions are given), who submits summaries of all petitions received the previous day, and receives orders thereon. The rest of the time till half-past twelve is occupied in attending to business of a miscellaneous nature, in receiving visitors, &c. At half-past twelve o'clock, the noblemen and other courtiers from his highness the Nizam's palace, with the kotwal (magistrate's deputy) of the city, attend to pay their respects. They are received in durbar, and the representations listened to which any of them may have to make. They are usually dismissed in about ten minutes, but to such of them as desire it, private interviews are granted by the minister in his sitting-room; afterwards, his highness's hurkurrahs (messengers) attend and make their reports, and the correspondence from the Residency is attended to. The minister then takes his siesta for about half an hour, if there be no other pressing calls on his attention.

It is now about two o'clock, p.m.; after the afternoon prayers, the undermentioned officers of government are received, and their business is gone through in succession, namely, the dufterdars (record keepers) and their mutseddies (clerks), the jemadars (officers) and serishtadars (accountants) of the different corps, and the talookdars (local governors), and others. The sowcars (bankers) also attend at this time of the day, and have audiences granted them. Afterwards various accounts are looked into and orders given; the Resident's letters are received, the Nizam's Vakeels (confidential agents) also generally attend, &c. The minister is thus occupied till half-past five or six o'clock, when he goes into his garden, and either rides, drives, or walks for half an hour. The Nizam's horses as well as the minister's are brought out for inspection at this hour.

The minister returns to his private sitting-room, and after evening prayer goes to dinner for about half an hour. After dinner the letters received from talookdars are perused, and answers to them endorsed. He signs letters prepared; examines and signs abstracts of pay; examines also talooka (district) accounts, or drafts letters of importance to the Resident; all this occupies until about half-past ten or eleven o'clock, when he retires to rest.

The peculiar customs of the East have occasionally given rise to embarrassment, as in what I may call "the shoe and chair questions," regarding which the late Resident, Colonel Davidson, writes:[1]—"In ceremonial visits to the houses of the rich, it is customary for equals to sit in opposite rows down the room; the floor being entirely covered with a thin mattress, over which is spread a clean white cloth. For a prince or any great chief, an additional mattress is placed at the head of the room, between the rows, and covered with a small carpet of embroidered silk.[2] The musnud," of which mention has often been made in these pages, "is nothing more than this raised mattress, with the addition of an embroidered bolster behind, and it serves as a throne for sovereigns under the rank of king. Visitors, before entering *any* person's house, take off their shoes, and the sovereign also sits on the musnud without his shoes.

"Out of respect to the Nizam our successive Residents at Hyderabad for more than half a century have followed this custom, but recently some desire has been expressed to make a change. There can be no doubt that it would be extremely painful to his highness if this subject were pressed on him; as he would have to depart from his established custom, either by arranging a separate reception-room for the

---

[1] Colonel Davidson died, 2nd August, 1862, at Hyderabad.

[2] Silks are used only on occasions of marriages and other rejoicings; ordinarily, a white quilted cloth is spread on a cushion.

Resident, on a principle to which he is an entire stranger, or to wear his shoes on the musnud. The noblemen of the court, who always attend the Durbars held for the Resident, would also be inconvenienced. Accustomed to pay the utmost deference and respect to their sovereign, it would be no less distressing to them than humiliating to his highness, if they sat on chairs, and the only alternatives would be, either to stand during all the time of the conference, or not attend the Durbar at all."

I propose to conclude this chapter with a few statistics relative to the Nizam's government, beginning with a statement of the troops under the Dewan.

CAVALRY.		
Troopers of Foreign Tribes.		
Moghuls	75	
Candaharees	85	
Seiks	100	
		210
Men of the country		4,440
INFANTRY.		
Men of Foreign Tribes.		
Arabs	5,958	
Rohillas	1,000	
Scindians	1,121	
Seiks	1,090	
Rūmy (Turks)	74	
Beloochees	50	
Rahtoors	310	
		9,603
Carried forward		14,253

INFANTRY—*continued.*

Brought forward		14,253
Men of the Country.		
Line	12,300	
Aligole	2,350	
Carnatic.....	438	
Bargheer	600	
		15,688
Statement of Troops under Ameers to whom Villages are given to keep up.		
Cavalry	200	
Infantry	1,600	
		1,800
Grand total of troops under the Dewan		31,741

The above statement is exclusive of the Surf-i-khas and Pagah troops. The former, about 8,000 in number, were originally a small body maintained under the name of the "Umur Pagah." After the accession of the late Nizam Nasir-oo-Dowlah, his highness intimated his desire to Rajah Chundoo lall to raise a new body of men. Chundoo lall gladly seized the opportunity, having political motives of his own, and set apart revenue to the amount of 4½ lacs of rupees for the maintenance of troops, which he named Surf-i-khas, which numbered 750 horse and 1,000 foot. Though ostensibly the Surf-i-khas were troops attached personally to his highness the Nizam, yet in reality they were completely under the immediate orders and control of Rajah Chundoo lall himself, who appointed Rajah Balmokund, his own Vakeel with the Nizam, as Serishtadar of these troops, and in charge of the Surf-i-khas districts. After the removal and death of Chundoo lall, the succeeding Dewans were allowed no control over these troops and districts. Subsequently, additional funds having become available by the lapse of allowances to members of the Nizam's family, the late Nizam increased the Surf-i-khas troops by about 1,500 men, and his present highness has added 5,000 more to their numbers.

The Pagah troops, according to the records of Chundoo lall's time, number 1,339 horse, and 2,870 foot. They amounted to this number after the transfer by Chundoo lall of a certain number of their body to the contingent.

ADAWLUTS.

The *Fowjdarry and Dewanee* Adawluts.—These courts were in existence when the present minister came into office.

The Padshaee Adawlut.—Established by the present minister, in consequence of the infirmity of temper of the Nazim of the "Fowjdaree," which occasioned great dissatisfaction and irritation among the clients of that court, especially when they happened to be Arab soldiers. The Nazim in question was notwithstanding a man of great learning and talents, and *the* luminary of the law in Hyderabad. In the "Padshaee Adawlut," both criminal and civil suits are entertained in the case of Arabs as well as others.

The *Cazy's Court*, for the trial of cases of murder, marriage, and inheritance, in the city and suburbs.

Two minor Courts, for the trial of cases of minor importance.

Provincial Courts.

In the provinces, each large town has a court presided over by a judge called a "Meer Adil," and in smaller towns sometimes "Moonsiff's" courts exist. From all the provincial courts, appeals in matters criminal and civil are allowed to the Fowjdarry Adawlut at the capital. All the courts of justice in the country are guided in their proceedings by rules prepared by a collection of English and Mohammedan laws and rules, during the administration of the present minister's uncle, the late Seraj-ool-Moolk, with the approval of the British Resident, General I. S. Fraser.

Police.

The chief magistrate of police in the city is the Kotwal, who, with his subordinate officers, takes cognizance of all police matters in the city and its environs, and has charge of the principal gaols of the city. The police in the city is inefficient, in consequence of its possessing no power over the servants and dependants of the princes and some of the chief nobles of the country, who all claim a prescriptive right to exclusive jurisdiction over their retainers.

In the provinces, a body of police under the name of "Nizamut" are employed under their officers, all of whom are under the immediate control and direction of the Talookdars of the respective districts. In cases of emergency, the police are assisted by the troops of the line, &c. stationed in the districts, and by zilladars recently appointed to put down the ravages of the Rohillas. Each zilladar has from three to four hundred men under him, according to the extent of country under his charge.

The *Munawaree* system obtains in the Hyderabad territory.

In the Telingana districts, to the north-east and south of the capital, the munawar has charge of the village police. His duty is to appoint watchmen to every village, trace out robbers, and apprehend them, &c. If unsuccessful in capturing the perpetrators of a robbery, he is obliged to make good the property plundered in any of the villages under his charge. A munawar's charge extends sometimes over a pergunnah of some one or two hundred villages, and sometimes over a circar of several pergunnahs. There are, however, some villages over which there is no munawar, the watch being maintained by the village authorities, such as the potail, &c.

The munawar is paid by jagheers or mukhtahs, &c.

In the Mahratta districts, to the west of the capital, there are no munawars so called, but the duty is discharged by the zemindars, and the responsibility is incurred by them.

Land Revenue.

In *Tehingana*, in some districts, there are generally four crops raised.

The *khureef:* the produce being yellow jowar, maize, green gram, rala, castor-oil seed, til (sesamum), sanwa (panicum frumentaceum), and other small grains.

The *abee:* paddy, fine and coarse.

The *rubbee:* chenna and white jowar.

The *tabee:* paddy of inferior kind.

Land Tax.

For the *khureef*, the tax is imposed on the land by the beegah, and it does not exceed eight annas per rupee on the value of the produce.

For the *abee:* in some places it is in kind, and in others in money. On land under tanks, the rate on produce is twelve measures of twenty to the government, and eight maas to the ryot. Under wells, according to kowls, the general rate being half to the government, and half to the ryot.

For the *rubbee:* the same as for the khureef.

For the *tabec:* on lands well irrigated by tanks, twelve maas to the government and eight to the ryot. On lands where irrigation cannot be carried on without manual labour, half to the government, and half to the ryot, or according to kowls (agreements); on lands watered by wells, according to kowls, generally ten or twelve maas to the ryot, and remainder to the government.

Bhagat, or Garden Lands.

Lands cultivated for sugar-cane, wheat, tobacco, barley, chillies, and vegetables of other kinds. From 100 to 150 rupees per beezah annually on sugar-cane; on other produce according to the means of irrigation afforded by wells, the average being less than half to the government.

Mahratta Districts.

In the Mahratta districts there are only two crops.

The *khureef*—in which is produced cotton, jowar, til, bajree, grain and black gram, &c.

The *rubbee*—chenna, white jowar, linseed, mussoor, peas, lak (a kind of pulse), wheat, tobacco, kurrur, &c.

For Bhagat, or garden lands—poppy, sugar-cane, paddy, plantains, &c. The same rates of land-tax as in telingana.

CHAPTER XXV.

BERAR AND RAICHORE AS COTTON-FIELDS.

The Valley of Berar—Quality of the Soil—Species of Cotton grown—Foreign and Indigenous Plants—Season of sowing Cotton—Proportion of Cotton Seed to an Acre—Government Demand on the Crop—Cost of Cultivation—Time occupied in the Growth of the Plants—Number of Gatherings and Cost—Mode of separating the Seed—Proportions of Cotton and Seed—Local Price of Cotton Seed—Process of Cleaning and Spinning—Value of the Yarn—Time of sowing Cotton and its Maturity—Rotation of Crops—Various Estimates of Cost—Prospects of Sale and Transport—Introduction of the Railway—Roads generally—Similar Particulars of the Raichore Doab—Question of European Colonization—Conclusion.

The Raichore Doab and the Dharaseo district having been restored to the Nizam, in virtue of the treaty of December 31st, 1860, the valley of Berar is now the only portion of his highness's territories which we hold in trust. In this chapter, however, I propose to offer some details relative to cotton cultivation in Raichore as well as Berar.[1]

[1] I have derived some encouragement in the preparation of these details from the recognition of my remarks on the subject by a distinguished commercial body in England. When hostilities broke

The valley of Berar (between latitude 20° 15′ and 21° 40′, longitude 76° and 78° 2′) is about fifty miles broad, and comprises an area of nearly 9,000 square miles. It is drained by the Poornah, a branch of the Taptee, and its numerous tributary streams, which afford an ample supply of water to the cotton lands. Irrigation is not resorted to either in the Berars or the Raichore Doab, and Captain Meadows Taylor—an officer who for many years was employed in this district, and whose opinion, from his long local experience, is worth recording—states that it is not advisable. In Raichore, he observes, it would certainly not improve the quality, though it would very greatly increase the quantity of the cotton.

The soil in West Berar is of a rich black loam, and the extremes of heat and cold are not so great as in many other parts of India. In East Berar the soil is of all descriptions; from the deepest black loam to the lightest red soil in the undulatory talooks to the south of the district. In the Raichore Doab, if sixteen be assumed as representing the different qualities of soil in the district, ten may be taken as

---

out between North and South America, I endeavoured to convince the Bombay merchants that it was quite in their power to compete with the native purchasers of cotton in the interior of the country, and for these observations the Manchester Cotton Supply Association awarded me their medal.

black soil, or fitted for the cultivation of cotton, being of the same nature as the black soil of Berar, but inferior in richness and productiveness.[1] Mr. Mann is of opinion that Berar presents a larger scope for action as a cotton-field than any other part of India, and were it but put on the same footing as the sea-board district in respect to means of transport, there is little doubt but that a breadth of land would then become available adequate to supply the full demands of Great Britain.[2]

The cultivation of the soil in Berar is of the most primitive character—hardly more than scratching the surface. The plough may be used once in five years, or even ten. Two indigenous varieties of cotton are cultivated, viz. the "Jherry" and "Bunnee," which derive their names from the localities in which they are grown. American seed had not been fairly tried in the Berars at the date of Colonel Davidson's letter; but writers of more recent date speak with confidence of the success of exotic cotton, if the seed supplied be good, and ready for sowing immediately after the first rainfall about June. The introduction of a new tillage might be expected to accomplish wonders.

---

[1] Letter addressed to G. R. Hayward, Esq., by Colonel Davidson, our late Resident at Hyderabad, dated March 6th, 1861.

[2] *The Cotton Trade of Great Britain; its Rise, Progress, and Present Extent*, by James A. Mann, F.S.S., p. 66.

The following particulars relative to the cultivation of cotton and of food grains in Berar may be relied upon for their accuracy.

The ground is prepared, and the seed sown after the first fall of rains, say between the 15th and 30th of June; the plants having grown till September, commence budding and blooming in rapid succession. To the blossoms succeed capsules which burst, and the cotton shows itself in November, from which month till March the cotton fully matures, and the crop is gathered.

Three pucker seers (say 6 lb., 84 tolahs each) of cotton-seed are sown in each beegah[1] of first-rate land, which would produce 10 maunds or 120 seers of cotton with seed; when cleaned the result is 30 seers of cotton, 88 seers of seed, and the remainder refuse.

The same quantity of seed is required for second-rate soil as for the first, but the yield is less, being only 50 seers to a beegah of cotton with seed, which on being separated gives 12 seers of cotton, and 28 seers of seed, inclusive of refuse or rubbish. This proves how very necessary it is to sow cotton in only first-rate land, and the cultivators should be encouraged by rewards to manure the fields previous to planting.

Three seers of seed sown in third-rate soil will

[1] Equal to 2,256¼ square yards.

give only 25 seers of cotton and seed, which on being ginned yields 8½ seers of clear cotton, and the remainder seed and rubbish.

The cost of separating the seed is 1 anna (Company's) per maund. The maund is usually 12 seers, but when the cotton is thoroughly cleaned it would only contain 9 seers. Every maund of cotton with seed when separated will therefore leave 9 seers of seed and 3 of cotton. In preparing cotton for the spinning wheel, every maund or 12 seers will lose 2 seers in refuse, leaving 10 seers of spun wool. Two seers of ginned cotton when further cleaned loses 4½ tolahs in the process, and when spun the result is 4 skeins, valued at 4 annas each. The time occupied by a woman in spinning 1 skein is 7 days; thus 4 skeins would entail full 1 month's daily labour to finish. This spinning is generally performed by the old dames of the establishment, who like sitting either in the sun or shade according to the season, and while watching the younger children of the family entrusted to their care, while the father is occupied in his fields, and the mother is preparing the daily meals, earn sufficient to clothe themselves, and perhaps have a bit of cloth occasionally for a favourite grandchild. When the fibre is of a good quality, and the yarn is finely spun, the spinner receives something additional in the way of remuneration.

With 3 of these skeins 1 khadie or piece of coarse

cloth can be prepared in 4 days, measuring 1 yard broad and 9 yards long, and sold for 1 rupee (Company's). The same piece of a fine texture would fetch as much as 2 rupees (Company's).

From inquiries made of the cultivators, it appears that by growing cotton on good and suitable soil, which is called naguttee, some considerable profit is realized. It is, however, to be observed that the above remarks are only applicable in cases where the cultivation is carried on by the ryots' own means and appliances; when they have recourse to the usurer little or no profit accrues to themselves.

The following estimates will afford the means of some useful comparisons.

I.

Statement showing the Expense of cultivating One Beegah of new Land with Cotton, and its Yield in Berar.

DETAIL OF EXPENSE.

	RS.	A.
Government Land-tax	2	0
Four Ploughings at 2 rs. each	8	0
Digging up Stumps	5	0
Clod-crushing	1	8
Levelling the Ground	1	0
One Maund of ten seers Cotton-seed	0	8
Sowing the Seed with the Drill-plough.....	2	0
Seven times Weeding, at 1 r.	7	0
Hoeing	2	0
Wages for gathering Cotton	4	0
Carriage to Local Market	1	0
Total	34	0

YIELD.

1½ Candy, or 30 Maunds Cotton at 30 rs.	45	0

REMARKS.

The seed is sown between the 15th of June and the third of July, and the cotton gathered in six months from the time of sowing. It is to be observed that if the cattle and labour employed are the ryot's own, he is benefited by the cultivation; if they are paid for, or the cultivation carried on by borrowed means, he derives little or no advantage whatever.

II.

Estimate of Cost and Yield of Three Beegahs of cultivated Land sown with Joar.

	RS.	A.
Government Land-tax at 2 rs. per Beegah	6	0
Levelling the Ground	2	0
Cutting Bushes	0	4
Sixteen Seers Seed	0	11
Four times Weeding, at 1 r.	4	0
Sweeping off Worms from Plants	1	12
Six Coolies for Cutting the Crop.....	1	2
Carriage to the Barn	2	0
Husking	1	4
Winnowing	1	8
Total	20	9

YIELD.

	RS.	A.
Two Candies of Joar, price 14 rs., or	15	0
Stalks, Husks, &c.	9	11
Total	24	11

III.

Estimate of Cost and Yield of Three Beegahs of cultivated Land sown with Jowaree.

Detail of Expense.

	RS.	A.
Government Land-tax, at 2 rs. per Beegah	6	0
Levelling the Ground	2	0
Cutting Bushes	0	4
Fourteen Seers Seed	0	8
Drilling the Seed	2	0
Five times Weeding, at 1 r.	5	0
Hoeing	2	0
Pruning	0	8
Cutting the Crop	1	2
Carriage to the Barn	2	0
Treading the Grain	0	12
Winnowing	1	8
Total	24	10

Yield.

2 Candies of Jowaree, price 16 rs., or.....	17	0
400 Bundles of Stalks, at 3 rs. per 100	12	0
Total	29	0

Note.—Estimate of moong, or green gram, same as Jowaree, with this exception, that it produces no kurbee or stalks, but husks to the value of 1 r.

IV.

Estimate of Cost and Yield of Three Beegahs of cultivated Land sown with Wheat and Linseed respectively.

	RS.	A.
Government Land-tax	6	0
Levelling, &c., seven times	7	0
Cutting Bushes	0	6
80 Seers Seed Wheat	3	8
Carried forward	16	14

	RS.	A.
Brought forward	16	14
16 Seers Linseed, 1r. 4a.		
Drilling the Seed	2	0
Reaping paid in kind	–	–
Carriage to Barn	8	0
Threshing paid in kind	–	–
Carriage to Market	1	0
Total	22	14

YIELD.

2½ Candies Wheat or Linseed, 25 rs., or	26	0
Husks, &c.	2	0
Total	28	0

NOTE.—Sown during Dewalee and Dusserah, or in November, and comes to maturity in six months.

V.

Estimate of Cost and Yield of Three Beegahs of cultivated Land sown with Chenna and Lak.

DETAIL OF EXPENSE.

	RS.	A.
Government Land-tax	6	0
Clearing Bushes	0	6
Levelling the Ground five times	5	0
112 Seers Seed	5	0
Drilling the Seed.....	2	0
Reaping paid in kind	–	–
Carriage to Barn	8	0
Threshing paid in kind	–	–
Carriage to Market	1	0
Total	22	6

YIELD.

2½ Candies of Chenna or Lak, price 22 rs. 8 a., or	23	12
Husks, &c.	2	0
Total	25	12

From these statements it could hardly be inferred that farming is a profitable employment when hired labour is engaged. But the native cultivators are generally in possession of their own bullocks and implements, and many of them have large families; as a rule, therefore, the price set down as hire under the several heads enumerated in the above statement of cost must be counted as the farmers' profits. Their cattle also cost them little or nothing, as after the cotton has been cleaned, the seed is available for food, and where jowaree and other grains are sown, they invariably retain sufficient forage for the consumption of their cattle for the year. The remainder is sometimes sold, and very profitably so, when any high-road passes near the villages. What remains at the end of the year is burnt and made use of for manure.

The disinclination hitherto evinced by the farmers to grow a greater quantity of cotton is to be attributed, I think, to first, that the profits from this article were not sufficiently remunerative. My remarks, it must be remembered, apply to a time when cotton was selling at a price not exceeding 60 rupees a kandy, while now 550 is about the average. It is quite impossible now that these prices can last. Immediately the war in America ceases, cotton will be a drug in the Indian market. And, secondly, that in almost all descriptions of grain sown, the husk in some instances, and in others the stalk, is available as forage for the cattle, and where there are no extensive grazing grounds this must be a paramount consideration.

That the introduction of the railway will materially develop the latent resources of the Berars in particular, I entertain the most sanguine hopes, and in the facilities afforded for travelling the farmer will himself proceed to the great marts and learn the real market value of cotton; and when the village bunniahs and district sowcars are no longer the only rivals for the purchase of the poor man's stock, we may expect an extensive increase in the cultivation of cotton, as the farmer, no longer confined within local limits for the disposal of his produce, will obtain a fair value, the profits having gone hitherto into the pockets of the local capitalist.

With regard to roads, although they are not traversable in the rains, at which season there is not much traffic, during eight months of the year nothing can be better than the tracks throughout the cotton soil. Almost every well-to-do villager in Berar possesses his cart and pair of bullocks, and it is customary with them to attend all the weekly fairs held in their neighbourhood; hence, well-worn tracks exist throughout the country, and the only thing necessary is for the district authorities to issue stringent instructions in view to the cultivator not encroaching upon the road, the breadth of which should invariably be marked out, and clearly defined, and any infringement of the order severely dealt with. It is in contemplation, however, to construct several lines of road to meet the railway.

Under British jurisdiction the jungles are gradually disappearing, and as the farmers discover that the demand for cotton increases, and that increased profits arise from its cultivation, they will require no pressing to bring under the plough the extensive waste lands still existing in the Berars.

In the Raichore Doab, according to Colonel Davidson's report addressed to Mr. Hayward, about a million of acres are said to be fit for the growth of cotton; but less than 43,000 acres were planted in 1861, the return being as follows:—

		Acres.
Talook	Raichore	10,576
,,	Alipore	8,377
,,	Sindnoor	9,857
,,	Manvee	7,179
,,	Deodroog	6,893
	Total	42,382

The different varieties of cotton cultivated in these districts are classed under the two heads of foreign and indigenous. The foreign includes the varieties known as "New Orleans," "Sea Island," and

"American." The indigenous comprises two varieties called in the Mahratta tongue, "Búnsee," and "Bondee." The "Bunsee," which is known in Canarese as "Deshuttee," and "Jowaree Huttee," derives its name from the staple being long, fine, and strong. The seed is large, and much relished by cattle—a most important consideration to the Indian farmer. The Bondee, in Canarese, "Myalum Deshuttee," or upper-country cotton, is so named from the circumstance of hemp, or the pulse called "Joor" being sown in the same field with it. This variety is but little cultivated in Raichore and the adjoining districts; the staple is coarse, short, and flaccid, and in colour inclining to yellow. The seed is very large.

Cotton is sown in these districts at the commencement of the Astral period of Mugha, which falls about the 25th of August. If it rains much during Mugha, the sowing is prolonged to Poorwah, say the 9th of September, or even to Ootara, about the 25th of the same month, the duration of these stars being fifteen days each. The last-mentioned period is not so much in favour with cultivators as the first two.

The seed sprouts in five days after sowing. In some instances where the soil is of the worst quality, and the moisture insufficient, it takes six or even seven days for the seed to come up.

In good and first-rate soil the plants grow high,

vigorous, and full of lateral branches. In medium and poor soil, the plants are smaller and with fewer branches. Under sufficient rains the plants arrive at maturity in two and a half to three months. They then commence blossoming, and continue to do so for about a month or a month and a quarter, if the soil has a greater degree of moisture. In lands under tanks the flowering continues a month and a half. After the buds are blown, the flowers remain for three days, at the end of which they wither and fall off, giving place to the incipient capsules containing a white fluid which, in course of time, becomes cotton. In rich and vigorous soil the flowers remain on the plants for five days.

In the course of a month after the decay of the flowers the pods arrive at maturity and commence bursting by the action of the sun. The partial or full opening of the capsules being dependent upon the low or high temperature at this stage, after the first development of the cotton it arrives at maturity in ten or twelve days: it then disengages itself and hangs pendent from the capsules, when the gathering takes place.

A crop raised on first-rate land yields four gatherings; and that grown on second-rate, or third-rate land, three gatherings.

The labour of gathering cotton is generally paid

for in kind, in the proportion of one-sixth to the gatherer of the quantity gathered by him in the whole day. When labourers are scarce the proportion is one-fifth at times when the crop is ready. Should signs of untimely rain appear, or a drizzling take place on such occasions of emergency, the gatherer gets one-third. In some places where the ryots are well-to-do, they pay for gathering in cash, at rates varying from 1½ annas to 1 anna per woman, and from 1¾ anna to 1½ anna per man a day; the quantity gathered by a woman per day being 20 seers, and that by a man from 24 to 25 seers.

In the second gathering the hired labourer gets one-fourth of what he gathers, and should labourers be scarce he obtains one-third; the rates of cash payment are the same in this as in the first gathering, and do not vary.

In the third gathering the labourer's share is one-third, but in the event of scarcity of labourers, one-half.

In the fourth gathering the collection is shared half-and-half between the owner and labourer, but in case of dearth of labourers two-thirds go to the gatherer, and one-third only to the owner.

In first-rate black soil, when the season is favourable, the produce of one khoodkee (or four and a half acres) is forty-eight maunds, or 576 seers, at twelve seers per maund, a seer weighing eighty-four tolahs. If the season is indifferent, the produce is less; but when the fall of rain is abundant, the produce increases from fifty to fifty-two maunds per four and a half acres.

In second-rate black soil the yield of the same extent of land is thirty-six maunds, or 432 seers, and in third-rate soil it is thirty-two maunds, equal to 384 seers.

The ordinary rate is ten pice per maund, or 2.8 rupees for cleansing forty-eight maunds; but when labour is scarce the cost amounts to from three to three and a half rupees.

The produce of four and a half acres of first-rate soil, namely forty-eight maunds, would yield twelve maunds of wool, and in case of abundance of rain during the growth of the crop, a maund or two maunds more would be the result, and the remainder seed.

The result of thirty-six maunds grown on second-rate soil is nine maunds of clean wool to twenty-seven maunds of seed, and that of thirty-two maunds, the yield of third-rate soil, eight maunds of wool to twenty-four maunds of seed.

In 1860 cleaned cotton was variously sold at twenty-five, thirty, thirty-two, and thirty-five rupees per bale of twelve maunds, according to prices current in different localities. Those ryots who had received advances from the sowcars only realized twenty rupees per bale. Seed was sold in some places, as Linsoogoor, &c., at fifty, forty-five, and forty seers per rupee, and in villages from fifty-five to sixty-seers per rupee.

The Bombay prices in November, 1861, were—cleaned cotton, 60 rupees per bale of 12 maunds, and seed 24 seers per rupee.

The local prices in the district, in December, 1861, were as follows:—Cleaned cotton from 46 to 48 rupees per bale of 12 maunds; seed in Talooks Kowtul, Alphore, and Raichore, 34 seers per rupee; seed in villages, Talooks Kowtul, Alphore, and Raichore, 36 seers per rupee; seed in Talooks Deodroog and Manvee, 36 seers per rupee; seed in villages, Talooks Deodroog and Manvee, 40 seers per rupee.

With reference to the above, the out-turn of 1 koodkee (or 4½ acres) may be estimated to realize 48 rupees in cleaned wool, and 12 rupees in seed, making a total income of 60 rupees per 4½ acres of cotton crop. This, however, is merely a rough approximate estimate, as the prices are subject to constant fluctuations, and the produce is dependent on the season.

The ryots declare that cultivation of cotton is more profitable than that of grain, provided they can keep out of the hands of the local bunniahs, and be not dependent on them for advances; but they are necessarily obliged to observe a rotation of crops to ensure their productiveness. In a field sown with cotton one year, jowareé, wheat, or chenna is sown the next year; for if every successive year cotton is raised in the same field, neither the plants thrive well, nor do they produce large pods; but by a judicious alternation of cotton and grain, the change contributes to the fertility of the soil and the mutual productiveness of the different crops. In a field sown with grain one year, the soil deriving manure from the decomposed husks, leaves, roots, &c., a crop of cotton becomes very productive the next year, and the same advantage is derived by a grain crop in a field sown with cotton.

In regard to the sale and means of transport of cotton, the ryots anticipate much advantage to themselves, when the railway is extended to the district. They hope that when the railway is brought from Madras to Bombay, and when the road is open up to Moodgul, each ryot will himself take his produce of cotton to the Bombay market for sale, or send some one on his part, or sell it to European merchants on the spot. As the cost of carriage by railway is by many degrees less than by the present mode of cart transport, those ryots who are well to do, are anxious to avail themselves of the facilities the railway will afford, to proceed in person to the Bombay market to dispose of their cotton;—while those who are poor and cannot afford the railway fares, anticipate a great throng of cotton purchasers in the district to be brought by the railway, and trust thereby to secure more advantageous terms than they are at present able to do. They, moreover, anticipate that the ryots nearer Moodgul will be able to carry their produce to that emporium, as it must become more frequented than other markets whose villages are situated farther off.

The following estimates of the cost of cultivating cotton and grain in the Raichore Doab may be compared with the similar tables for Berar given in a previous page.

I.

Statement of Expenses for clearing and preparing one Koodkee (equal to 4½ Acres) of Waste or Fallow Land for Cotton Culture.

Details of Expense.	RS.	A.
First clearing and ploughing the ground with a plough of 12 bullocks for six days	6	0
Second Clearing and Ploughing in the above way and time.....	6	0
First Clod-crushing in the above way and time	6	0
Second Clod-crushing in the above way and time	8	12
Removing Rubbish, &c.	2	4
Third Clod-crushing with two bullocks	2	4
Sowing of the Seed	1	8
Further passing the Clod-crusher over the ground	1	8
Cleaning the field after Sowing	1	0
Cleaning the field second time	1	0
	Rs. 31	4

NOTE.—Waste land is let free to the ryot for one year, or two or three years, according to the terms of the kowl, or engagement, entered into.

II.

Statement of Expense on one Koodkee (equal to 4½ Acres) of Lag, or Cultivated Land, sown with Cotton.

Detail of Expenses.

	RS.	A.
Hire of six bullocks and one man Clod-crushing twice	2	8
Hire of four bullocks and one man Clod-crushing third time	1	8
Hire of four bullocks and one man sowing the Seed	1	8
Purchase of Seed, 2 maunds or 24 seers, from 12 annas to	1	0
Hire of man and beast for cleaning the field of Rubbish, Grass, &c. after sowing	2	0
	Rs. 8	8

Government Demand on one Koodkee (or 4½ Acres) is as follows:—

		RS.	A.
1st sort of land	....	9	0
2nd	do.	6	12
3rd	do.	4	8
4th	do.	3	6

Note.—The above is the average nominal expense, as the ryots and their families employ their own means and labour in the cultivation. Different ryots estimate the same expense at different sums, varying from 10 rs. to 11 rs., 8 rs., and 7 rs.

Wheat.

In first-rate land the produce of one koodkee (or 4½ acres) sown with wheat, when the season is favourable, is 3 koodohs, equal to 360 seers at 120 seers per koodoh. In some places the koodoh is 128 seers.

In second-rate land, of 4½ acres the produce is 2 koodohs or 240 seers.

In third-rate soil of the same extent, the yield is from 1½ to 1¾ koodoh on 180 to 210 seers.

CHENNA.

The produce of 4½ acres of first-rate land is 4 koodohs, or 480 seers; that of second-rate, 3 koodohs, or 360 seers; that of third-rate, 2 to 2½ koodohs, or 240 to 300 seers.

JOWAREE.

Red Jowaree.—The produce of 4½ acres of first-rate land is 8 koodohs, or 960 seers; that of second-rate land, 6 koodohs, or 720 seers; that of third-rate land, 4 to 5 koodohs, or 480 to 600 seers, besides kurbee or stalks. It is to be noticed that Red Jowaree is generally sown in mussub, or red soil, and but seldom in régur, or black soil.

White Jowaree.—The produce of 4½ acres of first-rate land is 8 koodohs, or 960 seers; that of second-rate land, 6 koodohs, or 720 seers; that of third-rate land, 4 to 5 koodohs, or 480 to 600 seers, besides kurbee.

In estimating the value of the Raichore Doab as a cotton-producing district, it must not be forgotten that this territory has been restored to the Nizam, and the native farmers are not likely to make experiments except under British superintendence.

With regard to European colonization, the widest diversity of opinions exists; some advocating a system of English landlordism, and clamouring for acts of legislation favourable to its establishment; while others maintain that the landlord must be "tied to the soil, born, bred, and destined to leave his bones in it, connected with his tenants by blood and language, belief and customs." Colonel Davidson has expressed an opinion decidedly adverse to the former, in the following words: "The only way in which it appears to me that real benefit could be derived from European capitalists, would be by encouraging them to establish agencies in the districts for the purpose of purchasing produce direct from the cultivating classes instead of through middle-men," and he adds, that "every facility should be afforded them of erecting cotton-screws, gins, spinning machines, oil-mills, and similar factories."

I do not know that I can close this subject more appropriately than by repeating a recommendation which I communicated to the *Bombay Times*, when attention was called to the importance of the Assigned Districts as a cotton-field, after the commencement of the civil war in America. I would suggest to the local authorities at the several large termini on the line of railway, the necessity of establishing civil courts, disembarrassed of all irrelevant functions, and exclusively devoted to the settlement of civil suits arising between the traders in this important staple. This measure is equally necessary on the line vià Sholapore to Bellary, and on that which skirts the cotton-fields of Berar, as at Oomrowtee and Khamgaum.

APPENDICES.

APPENDIX A.—(p. 46).

Extract from the Official Correspondence of Lord Cornwallis, being his Reply to the Overtures for Peace made by Tippoo Sultan.

"Tippoo is well acquainted with the extent of the injuries and losses that the English and their allies have sustained from him, and I must acknowledge that I consider the wanton and savage barbarities which he has recently exercised on the inoffensive ryots of the Carnatic, as the highest aggravation of all the other grounds of complaint which the Company has cause to make against him; but should he now manifest a sincere disposition to put an end to the destructive war, by offering just and ample reparation for the injuries and losses which the English East India Company and its allies have sustained by his violation of former treaties, he is at liberty to transmit his propositions directly from himself to me, and after consulting with our allies, I shall inform him whether these propositions can be considered by us as reasonable preliminaries upon which negotiations might be opened, with a prospect of bringing all our differences to an accommodation."

APPENDIX B.—(p. 46).

Letter addressed by Lord Cornwallis to the Nizam on the subject of Tippoo Sultan's Overtures for Peace.

"Influenced by my determination to adhere to the engagements subsisting by virtue of the treaty ratified between your highness, the Peishwa, and the Company, I have considered it incumbent on me to transact that share of the operations of the war, depending on the forces entrusted to my management, not only in the manner most likely to ensure the end expected from the alliance formed between the three powers, but to publish to the world that the interest of the allies has the same weight in my mind as those of the Company.

"Upon this principle I have uniformly resolved to decline to receive any persons whom Tippoo Sultan might be desirous of deputing to me, lest such a measure might bear the appearance of a deviation from our engagements. Your highness will have been informed of my sentiments in this respect, by the correspondence which passed between Tippoo Sultan and me, transmitted to Captain Kennaway for that purpose.

"Having been joined by the forces of the Peishwa under the command of a person who bears so great a share in the councils of the Mahratta states as Hurry Punt Tantia, and whose disposition I have found to be equally sincere with my own, to preserve inviolate and in full force the articles of the treaty, it has afforded me a considerable degree of satisfaction that his sentiments have coincided with my own in every respect and in the reception of a vakeel on the part of Tippoo Sultan. But as Hurry Punt, on the part of the Peishwa, has advised that we should learn the extent of the concessions and compensations which Tippoo Sultan is willing to make to the allied powers, I have been induced to relax in my own resolution, and to agree to receive his vakeel, provided I be assured that his desire is to establish a friendship and to negotiate a peace with each of the allied states.

"And as Tippoo Sultan has addressed a letter to each of the confederate powers, and has expressed his desire to re-establish a friendship with them by negotiating a peace through the means of a vakeel fully authorized to treat with the three states, I have granted my consent to receive his vakeels, as well as to comply with the advice of Hurry Punt Tantia, as from a consideration that it would enable me to judge how far the proposals which the vakeel is authorized to make to the confederate states on the part of Tippoo Sultan, may render it expedient to proceed in assembling the deputies from the powers concerned in the war.

"Hurry Punt has received the letter addressed to the Peishwa, and as the person your highness may have deputed is not yet arrived, it has been agreed between Hurry Punt and myself to transmit that addressed to your highness, accompanied by a letter from each of us.

"Your highness may rest assured of my strict adherence to my resolution to consider the interests of your government with the same attention as those of the English company, and that I shall postpone making any reply to the proposals which may be made by the enemy until I shall have the pleasure of knowing your sentiments on them, or of seeing the person your highness shall think proper to depute on the part of your government to superintend the management of your interests."

APPENDIX C.—(p. 46).

Letter addressed by Lord Cornwallis to the Nizam, in reply to his Highness's Letter sent by the hand of Meer Allum, accrediting the latter as his Representative to negotiate the Peace proposed by Tippoo Sultan.

"The receipt of your highness's friendly letter by Meer Allum has afforded me very great happiness.

"Having had the pleasure of a former acquaintance with

Meer Allum, and at that time having been fully convinced of his abilities and good qualities, of his zeal for your highness's welfare, and his earnest desire to strengthen and increase the intimacy between the Company and your highness's government, I was made very happy by the choice of Meer Allum as a person of confidence and authority to join me, and to preside on your part at any congress of deputies that might assemble in order to examine and discuss the claims and pretensions of all parties concerned, and to consult on terms for an honourable and advantageous peace; and since his arrival his conduct has proved the wisdom of your highness's selection of him, and by confirming the sentiments I had before imbibed of his warm zeal for the prosperity of your highness's government, and of his earnest desire to cement the friendship between us, and to promote the success of the present alliance, has afforded me inexpressible satisfaction. Pursuant to the instructions which Meer Allum received from your highness, he proceeded on his journey with the utmost despatch and made me happy by an interview in the vicinity of Oosoor. He related to me the full particulars of your highness's confidence in my resolution to pay equal attention to the interests of the confederacy, informed me of the plans and arrangements which your highness has made for giving efficacy to the united efforts of the alliance, and represented to me the circumstances on which depend the arrival of your highness's son, Secunder Jah, and the Nawab Azeem-ool-oomrah. From the confidence which I place in Meer Allum, I have made him acquainted with my private opinions, and have informed him of every circumstance, past and present, as well as those depending on future opportunities, relative to the preparations which I am making for carrying on the war with vigour, and to the steps necessary for ensuring its success, which it is advisable your highness should pursue. The unanimity of opinion which prevails between us on the measures requisite for prosecuting the war with vigour, and on the propriety of being prepared to avail ourselves of any opportunity to procure an honourable and advantageous peace that may be offered, is a striking instance of the strong basis of our friendship, and assured as I am by the contents of your highness's letter that Meer Allum possesses full powers on your part, I shall at all times consider him authorized to express the sentiments of your highness's government, and empowered to join with myself and Hurry Punt Tantia, who is invested with the same authority on the part of the Peishwa, in the measures necessary for carrying on the war, or for finally concluding an honourable and advantageous peace. I have conversed with Meer Allum fully on these points, and availing myself of the friendship subsisting between us, I have explained my sentiments to him on the subject of your highness's intentions to send the Nawab Secunder Jah and Azim-ool-oomrah. He will have informed your highness of all these particulars."

APPENDIX D.—(p. 50.)

Letter from Lord Cornwallis to our Resident at Hyderabad, Sir J. Kennaway, relating to the proposed Treaty of Guarantee between the Three Powers, after the Defeat of Tippoo Sultan.

"Although there seems at present to be no reason to apprehend that Tippoo Sultan will for a considerable period be disposed to come to a rupture with any of the members of the late confederacy, yet as it is of great importance for preserving our reputation for good faith, as well as for the general interests of the British nation, that the grounds should be clearly explained, on which the allies can, in consequence of the 130 articles of the treaties of the alliance that was formed at the commencement of the war, demand assistance and support from each other against any hostile attempt of their late common enemy, I look upon it as proper and desirable that the treaty of guarantee which they are bound to enter into should with all convenient despatch be put into a distinct form, and I therefore wish that you should take an early opportunity to confer fully with the minister upon the subject.

"Every consideration will induce me to examine and discuss any propositions that may be made by him in the most amicable manner, but the greatest care must be taken that no vague or ambiguous expression shall be admitted into this new instrument, and that the stipulations shall in no shape go beyond the spirit of the article upon which they will be founded.

"I shall defer entering much into detail until you can inform me of the Nizam's sentiments and expectations; but it is proper that you should be acquainted with my ideas of the general principles which should form the basis of the agreement.

"The allies are bound to guarantee against Tippoo the territories that each of them might possess at the conclusion of the war; but it must always be adverted to that the stipulation is merely defensive, and cannot operate unless Tippoo should attack either of them without just provocation.

"It must therefore be clearly expressed in the treaty of guarantee, that in case any difference should arise between one of the latter and Tippoo, the other allies are to have a right to expect that the nature and circumstances of such differences shall be fully communicated to them, in order that they may give their opinion and advice, and endeavour to settle it by a temporary negotiation, and that they shall not be considered as bound to take up arms in his favour, until they are convinced that he has justice on his side, and all the means of conciliation shall have proved fruitless.

"Should a rupture become unavoidable, the interest and safety of the contracting powers will be so evidently and deeply involved in the event, that it would be highly injudicious in them to limit their exertions in endeavouring to bring it to a speedy and honourable conclusion, and it must consequently be stipulated that the whole force of each state is to be employed for that purpose. The distress and danger of the party that may be attacked, being entitled to the greatest attention from the other members of the alliance, it ought to be understood and settled, that whilst no time should be lost in preparing their whole force to take the field, every immediate assistance that may be practicable should be afforded with such troops as may be in actual readiness for service.

"The above are the fair principles for the treaty of guarantee; and to render any further treaty unnecessary, in the event that Tippoo's conduct should again force us into hostilities during the existence of the guarantee, it may be proper to insert in it that a general plan of operations for the confederate forces is to be concerted as soon as possible after a rupture becomes certain, and that conformable to the terms of the alliance that was made at the commencement of last war, no one of the parties shall enter into separate negotiations, but (under the exclusion of unreasonable objections,) all measures for concluding a peace shall be conducted with the knowledge and approbation of the whole."

APPENDIX E.—(p. 57).

Letter from Lord Cornwallis to Sir J. Kennaway relative to the Recognition of Ally Khan as Nawab of Kurnool by his Highness the Nizam.

"Agreeably to my former sentiments upon the subject, I again explicitly declare my decided opinion that his highness ought to withdraw from all interference whatever in the succession, and leave the payment of the Peshcush to be settled between Tippoo and the sons of Runmust Khan.

"Nothing appears to be more evident than that the Nizam has in fact, though not in form, suffered his title of Lord-paramount of Kurnool to be superseded, and that he must be considered to have given it up when he ceased to protect his feudatory against the usurpation of Hyder Ally; and even if it were otherwise, it would be impossible to reconcile the discordant claims of a demand for tribute by Tippoo with that of a paramount right in the Nizam.

"Considering the measures that his highness has already adopted, I suppose that it will not be without a considerable degree of repugnance that he will agree to follow my advice; but I conclude that he will ultimately adopt that resolution in consequence of the explicit declaration which I have made, that he must not expect the interference of the allies in support of his claim. This interference could only be warranted by a formal establishment of the Nizam's rights to the property of Kurnool. To this he does not pretend, and his title of Lord-paramount was certainly, as I have already said, superseded when Hyder exacted a tribute from his alleged feudatory, without resistance on the part of the Nizam.

"Although the treaty that connects the Nizam with us and the Mahrattas affords him sufficient security against all future attempts to encroachment on the part of Tippoo, yet I make great allowance for his anxiety to obtain Kurnool as a frontier on that side, and I should be sorry that Tippoo should acquire any further right or ascendancy in Kurnool than that of enforcing the payments of the established Peshcush.

"When you deliver my letters to his highness, you will of course endeavour by the most conciliatory language to reconcile him to the advice which it contains, and you will support the sentiments which I have expressed in it by such arguments as may occur to yourself, or by such of those that I have made use of in the course of the correspondence on this subject, as can with prudence be stated to himself or to the minister; and with a view of softening their disappointment, as well as of discouraging Tippoo from making any further attempts upon Kurnool, than that of realizing the Peshcush, you may recommend to them to do no more than merely to withdraw from all interference in the affairs of Kurnool, without agitating further the question of right or making any declaration of their having relinquished the intention of exercising it.

"I trust that by these means his highness and the minister will be brought to reflect with temper and coolness upon the imprudence of their own conduct, and the propriety of my advice, and as this discussion has already continued too long and the danger of protracting it is so evident, I cannot but express an anxiety that it may now be finally closed."

APPENDIX F.—(p. 57).

Letter of Remonstrance addressed to the Nizam by Lord Cornwallis, deprecating his Interference in the Affairs of Kurnool, and his Claims for Peshcush.

"In the commencement of this business, when your highness did me the honour to desire my opinion, I considered myself bound by the ties of personal friendship and political regard to weigh the circumstances of the case in all their relations, as affecting the rights of your highness and Tippoo Sultan, or as involving in their consequences the interference of the allies; and after the most mature deliberation on a subject in which so many important interests were concerned, I could not hesitate on the ground of justice and policy to recommend to your highness to desist from interfering in the affairs of that district.

"It appears to me that your interference might involve serious consequences to your highness's government alone, as no engagement existed by virtue of which the Company could unite with your highness; nor any, as far as I was informed, betweeen your highness and the Peishwa, that could warrant the assistance of the Mahratta State in support of such measures.

"The respect which I entertain for your highness's wisdom and character, as well as the sincere regard which I profess for your highness and the interests of your government, have induced me to reconsider what I before wrote, and to weigh and compare the reasons which I offered to your consideration in support of my opinion, with the arguments which you have urged in reply to them, and I should be wanting in that friendship and esteem which I profess for you, if I did not candidly and explicitly declare that the more I have deliberated on the subject, the more my opinion is confirmed that you should leave the discussion of the succession to Kurnool, and the demand for the Peshcush to be settled between the sons of Runmust Khan and Tippoo Sultan, and that it is for your highness's dignity to withdraw your interference.

"The proper time for discussing the claims of Tippoo Sultan and the Peshcush from Kurnool was before the conclusion of the peace with him. At the conferences upon this subject, your highness's ministers objected to the insertion of the Peshcush in the schedule of Tippoo Sultan's revenue, and denied the existence of any agreement under the signature of Runmust Khan to pay the Peshcush. Here the matter rested, affirmed by one party and denied by the other; and the ministers of your highness, although importuned by the sons of Runmust Khan to obtain an adjustment of the business, did not prosecute their objection, and bring the point in dispute to a final decision. Thus the opportunity of deciding the affair was lost, and the right of Tippoo Sultan to the Peshcush of Kurnool, which he and his father had exercised at different times for upwards of twenty years, was not respected by the allies when they had the power to reject or admit what they pleased. I request, therefore, your highness to consider with what justice this right can now be contested, or with what equity Tippoo Sultan can now be called upon to produce the agreement of the Nawab of Kurnool. It is my duty and determination, as well as that of the English nation, to adhere inviolably to the faith of their treaties and the terms of their agreements; when it pleased the Almighty to crown the armies of the allies with success, they demanded what they thought proper from Tippoo, and whatever they did not exact must be considered as his property, which they have no right to demand at this time. It is certainly probable that at the period of the negotiations for peace, if a proper attention had been given to the affair of Kurnool on the part of your highness's ministers, the amount of the Peshcush or a territorial equivalent would have been required by the allies; but since from haste or inadvertence, or other cause, the matter remained then undecided, and no claim was made upon this account on Tippoo Sultan, he would then have just reason to complain of an infringement of that amity which has been established by the treaty of peace if a demand were now made upon him.

"These are the reflections which have occurred to me, and which I have already communicated to your highness, who on this occasion, as on all others, will act agreeably to the dictates of wisdom and justice. Your highness, adverting to the mode by which Hyder and Tippoo acquired their present power and rendered the Nawab of Kurnool tributary to them, seems to consider it as no foundation of right on their parts; but every page of history in which your highness is so well instructed, shows that the Almighty disposer of events bestows kingdoms and victory, and raises and depresses according to the inevitable decrees of his eternal wisdom, and that most of the great monarchies now existing were founded, under the permission of his Providence, by the power of the sword; and, in fact, unfortunately for the peace of mankind and for the prosperity of states, the rights of sovereigns are too often decided by an appeal to force, instead of being settled by amicable councils and reciprocal conciliation. It was by taking advantage of the times that Hyder Ally, as your highness observes, established his power; and such is also the foundation of other great powers in Hindostan. By the blessing of God peace is now everywhere established, and my endeavours, as well as those of my successor to this Government, will be constantly exerted to render it perpetual.

"Your highness proposes to engage for the payment of the arrears of the Peshcush to Tippoo Sultan, and of the Peshcush itself in future, when the amount is ascertained by the production of the agreement of the Nabob of Kurnool. Permit me to state to your highness that on this point it has occurred to me that in fact it would be to make your highness tributary to Tippoo Sultan, and to request that you will reflect that even if you could consent to such a degradation, by making a private agreement of that nature with Tippoo, the country of Kurnool can never be considered by the allies in the same light as the other dominions of your highness, for the guarantee of which against the attacks of Tippoo Sultan the faith of the allies is mutually pledged.

"I have complied with the duties of friendship in communicating, without reserve, what has occurred to me on this subject, and I trust that your highness will be persuaded that in doing so I have been actuated by the most sincere concern for the interests of your Government. Your highness, in calling for my opinion, has imposed that task upon me, and I should have been happy if my sentiments on this occasion had coincided with those of your highness, as it is my earnest wish to act conformably to your inclinations; but the obligations of friendship indispensably require that I should write what, after the most mature consideration, appears to me to be dictated by justice and policy. The decision rests with your highness's wisdom, which will, no doubt, suggest what is proper and right."

APPENDIX G.—(p. 62).

The Reply, in full, made by Azim-ool-oomrah, the Minister of Hyderabad, to Lieut. Stewart, then Acting Resident, on the cause of the contention between the Courts of the Peishwa and the Nizam, explaining more particularly the cause of the Personal Hatred of Balaji for the Minister of the Nizam.

"The enmity formerly subsisting between the Nizam and Scindiah exceeded all bounds, but that when the latter had completely established himself in the direction of Shah Allum's affairs, he thought it advisable, in consequence of a jagheer, houses, tombs, &c., near Delhi, belonging to his highness's family, which had been attacked by former ministers, to conciliate Scindiah's good-will, in which he had succeeded so far that all his premises had been restored; that attention to the above and other points connected with the dependence the Nizam still owed the Royal authority, would ever render it his interest to keep on good terms with the minister for the time being, and that as long as Scindiah held that office, and no longer, it was incumbent on his highness to preserve his friendship. Azim-ool-oomrah professed himself very ready to live on terms of harmony with Balaji Pundit as far as was consistent with his duty to his master, and was ready to adjust the points of difference existing between them, provided Lord Cornwallis thought it worth while to bring about such a footing between them; that it was not owing to any backwardness on his part that these points, which owed their commencement to a period prior to his administration, had not been already settled, but that Balaji kept them alive as arguments to urge against his conduct that his (Balaji's) animosity to him was inveterate, and originated in three causes:—1st. Because during Rookmi-oo-dowlah's long, and Shumsh-ool-oomrah's short, administration—but particularly the former—the influence of the Poonah durbar was such, that its views and wishes operated as a law on the Hyderabad Government, but on his assuming the ministry, this influence was reduced to such bounds as he deemed consistent with his master's dignity, without encroaching on the friendship and attention which the two Governments owed respectively to each other. 2nd. For his complying with Lord Cornwallis's demand for the Guntoor Circar, and sending Meer Allum to Calcutta without consulting him (Balaji). And, 3rd. For his prompt acceptance of Lord Cornwallis's overtures for engaging in the war against Tippoo without previously demanding Balaji's opinion. In consequence of these unjust grounds of discontent, all of which originated in his having consulted solely his master's credit and interest, without favour or affection to any one, Balaji had twice attempted to take advantage of domestic occurrences in his highness's Government, to remove him from his office by making two direct applications to that effect, to both of which his highness had given firm and decided refusals, and that in return for such conduct he (the minister), instead of fomenting any coolness between the Nizam and the Mahrattas, had industriously kept back from his highness's ears many causes of complaint which they had afforded.

APPENDIX H.—(p. 64).

Scindiah's Arrangement of his own Affairs at Poonah as reported to our Resident at Hyderabad.

"On the 1st of October, 1793, the officiating Resident was informed that a letter had been received from Poonah by the minister, stating that Scindiah had settled all his business at Poonah agreeably to his wishes, that his accounts had been signed by the Peishwa, acknowledging a balance in Scindiah's favour of five crores of rupees, that Scindiah could not get any ready cash from the Poonah ministry, had accepted a transfer of the Peishwa's share of the conquests in Hindustan, empowering him to withhold the payment of it, and stipulating that no demands should be made on him by the Poonah government on account of such share, till the whole of the above balance should have been by this means liquidated; that Scindiah was to have the sole management of affairs in that quarter, and to be furnished with such troops, either with or without their chiefs, as he might require from the Poonah government to serve under his orders during his future operations."

APPENDIX I.—(p. 68).

Report of Sir John Kennaway to the Supreme Government on resigning his appointment as Resident at the Court of Hyderabad, in January, 1794.

"The inclination which his highness felt to cultivate and improve his connection with the Company by the manner in which the negotiation for the surrender of the Guntoor Circar was prosecuted, was further confirmed by the subsequent upright and conciliatory conduct of the late administration, and the brilliant successes of the late war, which impressed him, in common with the other states of the Deccan, with a deep and increased respect for the stability and puissance of our government. In proportion as that respect augmented Azim-ool-oomrah's antipathy to the Mahratta connection and his personal animosity towards Balaji Pundit increased the Nizam's bias in favour of this long standing-alliance, and should it ever be found advisable to meet his wishes of drawing close with the Company in any degree commensurate to their extent, which I conceive is to establish a connection approximating to that which subsists between us and the Nawab of Oude and the Carnatic, there would be no difficulty in weaning him from intrigues with any other Power, and guiding him entirely by our councils.

"The imbecility of the Nizam's government and the character of his present chief minister (Azim-ool-oomrah) are adverse to his being considered in all respects such an ally as we might desire, and may therefore appear to be an argument against too intimate a connection; but on the other hand, the extensiveness of his dominions, the great resources they would yield, if properly managed, and their local importance, equally commanding an entrance into the countries of Tippoo, the Peishwa, Scindiah, and the Berar Rajah, from which latter only anything is ever to be apprehended that can disturb the tranquillity of Bengal, might seem in favour of our adopting such an alliance with his highness as would confer on us a right to speak to him in that sort of mild but firm tone regarding men and measures, as in the case of the Kurnool business, must be attended to, and without trenching on the independency of his government, could not fail gradually to restore it to that rank and respectability it is naturally entitled to.

"Should, however, such an alliance, and the kind of interference above alluded to be deemed improper, and the limits to which it is at present confined be considered as sufficient, the friendship for, and confidence in us, which has been so happily established in his government, and the reliance which the Nizam must ultimately place on the Company for checking any hostile league which the Mahrattas may form against the rights and dignity of his government, will, I imagine, always prevent his engaging in any measure to our prejudice, and induce him even to be very guarded in adopting any of which our very marked and pointed disapprobation may ever be expressed.

"The chief danger during the Nizam's life that his government is exposed to from the Mahrattas, arises, I conceive, from Scindiah, to whose art, turbulence, and ambition, its riches, and the character of its minister, seem to form a mark exactly calculated. Balaji Pundit, besides being attached to the Nizam by personal obligations (if any native can be attached by such a principle), and a similarity of disposition, is of a mild and pacific nature, and from him I conceive there is little to fear, nor, I apprehend, is there even any very strong grounds of apprehension from Scindia, so long as jealousies shall exist between him and the Poonah minister, jealousies which will in all probability last as long as their lives, but should those jealousies ever yield to a sincere and cordial reconciliation, and leave Scindia at perfect liberty to pursue his project, I think the event would be extremely alarming to this state, since the causes of offence afforded by Azim-ool-oomrah are too deep and inveterate for Balaji to interpose, or indeed neglect any fair opportunity he may have of avenging them. Even though Azim-ool-oomrah's destruction should draw after it the ruin of his master, Scindia and Balaji seem equally anxious to prevent a good understanding being established, and to thwart any already subsisting between his highness and them respectively; and the Nizam on his part is not less intent to keep alive, by every means in his power, the distrust and difference that exist between the chiefs. Agriculture and the state of cultivation in the Nizam's dominions are at a low ebb; the late famine,[1] which was not meliorated by the smallest exertion or liberality on the part of the government (bating about 150 poor wretches who were fed daily by the minister), desolated many parts of the country heretofore inhabited, and the tyranny of the government many more, yet such is the power and impolicy of the minister that he endeavours, and part real and part nominal succeeds, in keeping up the collections by fines, sequestrations, and heavy imposts, to the former but forced standard instead of the natural one, which his undue

[1] The extent and severity of the famine may be conceived by two circumstances which Meer Allum represented to me as facts:—1st. That in the space of four months 90,000 dead bodies had appeared, by the Cotwal's account, to have been carried out from Hyderabad and its suburbs, in which those who perished in their houses and enclosures were not inserted; and, 2nd. That of 2,000 weavers' huts which were full of families in a district of Raichore, before the famine broke out, only six are now inhabited.

lenity to some Amils, and excessive severity to others, have reduced it; from the disorders and defalcations, however, which such measures must inevitably lead to and will shortly appear in all their native deformity, and indeed have already shown themselves in the flight of Shunker Naik Amil, of Neermul, and Azeem-ool-Moolk, Amil of Aurungabad, the former indebted to the Circar in an accumulated balance of ninety, and the latter twenty lacs of rupees; while Assud Ally Khan is caressed by the minister, although he has held the valuable district of Kurpah and other considerable Pergunnahs nearly two years, without having made any material payment from their revenues to the state, or being subjected to any muster of, or inquiry into, the military establishment in the support of which he pretends to have expended them.

"The great dexterity of the minister, and the success that attends his arts for preserving the confidence of his master, notwithstanding the ruin and mismanagement which surround him, is as surprising as the weakness, or rather infatuation, of his conduct in other respects is remarkable; whether his ambition has aspired to, but not yet attained the point that he thinks will enable him to throw off the mask and dictate to the Nizam in the soft but absolute style of Ruccan-oo-dowlah, or that he is apprehensive a similar exercise of his power may be attended with the fate of that minister (who was put to death by Nizam Ally Khan), whether it be from that distant and slavish awe which a dependant sometimes feels for his despot, Azim-ool-oomrah in the most trivial instance has never failed in his respect, or presumed to act without first consulting his highness's pleasure, which he punctiliously seeks to obtain in every act, both of his public and private life. Once only, since my residence at this court, has the slightest degree of estrangement on the part of the Nizam appeared towards him, which occurred when he attempted, on the death of his rival Shumsh-ool-oomrah while the Nizam was involved in grief for the loss of that favourite servant, to secure the sequestration of his jagheer and effects.

"It is most probable, I think, that the fate of Ruccan-oo-dowlah, who was the creature of the Mahratta government, and assassinated apparently for a failure of respect after having so far established his power as to confine the Nizam to a stated monthly allowance for his immediate expenses, may dwell upon his mind; for though of a rash, and, in many respects, of an ungovernable temper, I have no very respectable opinion either of his political firmness or personal resolution. If any other cause operates, if he thinks the Nizam not sufficiently in his power, while the strength of Shumsh-ool-oomrah's adherents (many of them the most respectable characters at this Durbar) remains unbroken, that obstruction I do not conceive will remain long in his way, for although his highness not long ago was prevailed upon, at the earnest representations of Bukshy Begum, to recall the authority he had unwarily given him, to attach Shumsh-ool-oomrah's estate and pay the Pagah and establishment of troops for whose support it is held immediately from the treasury, yet as he acquiesced in an inquiry being instituted into the real produce of those lands, which owing to the lenity and judicious management of their holder, had increased in value considerably above their original assessment, this right to interfere, I have little doubt, will ere long be turned to such an account as to enable him to annul an establishment so obnoxious to his ambition if he aspires to present uncontrolled power, or to his future views of securing the undisputed succession to Secunder Jah; if he does not, the immediate result of the inquiry instituted has been, that the lands shall stand at fifty-four, instead of thirty-eight lacs of rupees, at which they were before rated.

"Of the succession above alluded to, I am happy to think, if, as said, the Nizam's dropsical complaint has left him, the time may yet be considerably distant; considering, however, his advanced age, and the freedom with which he indulges his appetite, especially that for women, which I understand has increased upon him, I conceive it would be advisable we should be prepared what line of conduct to adopt in respect to the competitors that will start up when the event takes place. These, I think, may be confined to Ali Jah, Secunder Jah, and Darah Jah. The first his highness is conjectured to consider as his successor, but he has never declared it by any formal act or any express terms, and the servility and superstition of his women and ministers, who all think, or from interested motives pretend to do so, that his preparing for death, or being warned of his danger, would be provoking its stroke, will, in all likelihood, leave him in ignorance of his situation till it is too late to make any effectual arrangement for what is to happen after his decease.

"Of the only two chiefs who, in point of rank, pretensions, or ability, could be considered as rivals to the minister, Azim-ool-moolk, as before mentioned, has fled, and Imtiaz-oo-dowlah, his highness's nephew, is in disgrace. He is supposed to be attached to Tippoo, for intrigues with whom, whether real or pretended, the minister effected his downfall. He is slowly recovering his ground, but while Azim-ool-oomrah's influence remains, his restoration to any material degree of power is not to be expected.

"Meer Allum, bating ignorance of military affairs even as the natives understand them, and of sickly habits, is otherwise equal to important considerations, and considering his qualifications altogether, and the sincere attachment I believe he entertains for our government, were I called on to give my opinion of the proper person among the chiefs of the Durbar, I am not certain I could fix upon a better man.

"The value that is set upon the detachment of our troops is too great, and the respect it gives this government in the eyes of the neighbouring powers is, I conceive, too considerable for them ever cheerfully to part with it, nor do I imagine it to be without its use to ourselves, in the salutary influence which its situation may always be supposed to have on the conduct and designs of Tippoo. I cannot leave this subject without expressing the great satisfaction I have derived from Major

Roberts's conduct since he has been in command, and my opinion that a better officer could not be found in every point of view for this delicate and important trust."

APPENDIX J.—(p. 81).

Copies of Letters addressed by the Minister of Hyderabad to the Government of Poonah on the question in dispute between the Peishwa and his Highness the Nizam.

[The reader will observe that Letter No. 4 consists of the articles referred to in Letter No. 3. Captain Kirkpatrick, in translating them, could not render them more exact and intelligible without applying for explanations which he deemed unadvisable. In their defective form, however, these voluntary communications convey a tolerably clear idea of the nature and extent of the differences between our allies, and perhaps abundantly confirm the opinion of Meer Allum referred to in the preceding report, concerning the real importance of the subjects in dispute. At this time Captain Kirkpatrick had grounds for believing that the demands of the Peishwa were, for the most part, perfectly reasonable, whatever pretensions he might have contemplated starting hereafter in his vicarious character of Vakeel-ool-Moolk. This seems to have been Meer Allum's opinion also, though he thought some abatement of the present claims might be justly demanded, and with very little address procured, provided only that Azim-ool-oomrah were prepared to concede what the Poonah Government might fairly insist on. It was his doubt on this latter point which deterred Meer Allum from undertaking the negotiation.]

Translation of a Copy of a Letter from the Nizam to Balaji Pundit, dated the 6th April, 1794.

"Negotiations were carried on regarding the business of Adoni to the time of the late Meer Abud Khan's death. At this time the Peishwa cannot be more thoughtful than I am about the means of rendering its adjustment easy. The treasure, whether much or little, and the other effects of the deceased are ready in hand, the claims of the troops there now require adjustment, the disturbance occasioned by them is well known. In consideration of our friendship, the Peishwa should send a person on his own part to settle the business of the troops, and also his own matters, from whatever the deceased has left, and should fix upon some mode for the future, with Meer Shoolam Hussain, the son of the deceased, and, agreeably thereto, to collect the amount yearly."

Translation of Copy of a Letter from the Nizam to Govind Rao Bugwunt, dated 6th April, 1794.

"From the first our respective claims on each other have been firmly established on all states, particularly after the murder of Hyder Jung, when Ballaji Bajee Rao favoured me in preference to others, and I, after the decease of Narrain Rao Bullal attached myself to the good wishes of Row Pundit Perdham's government, neglecting the advantages of powerful allies and their intrigues, and strictly uniting, cheerfully took trouble on myself. I performed everything that friendship dictated, and praise be to God, my endeavours were successful.

"For some time past the unadjustment of detail matters between us has given occasion for talk to those who look for opportunities. The detail matters between us involve just claims on each other. The adjustment of them for the present, as well as for the future, is a thing that is to take place. Certainly it is about being accomplished, and will be effected; the gain or loss attending it can be matter of no great difficulty, considering the greatness of the two states. God is witness that I have no wish for any loss to Row Pundit Perdham, and doubtless his wish is also the same in respect to me. Kishen Rao Bullal from the first was acquainted with all matters, both general and particular. You, from having been with him, are also duly informed, and no point is unknown to Balaji Pundit: with a due regard to the rights of both parties, determine on whatever is fair for the adjustment of the detail matters between us and inform me thereof. You will learn further particulars from the letters of my illustrious son Azim-ool-oomrah and Row Govind Kishen."

Translation of Copy of a Postscript to the above Letter written in the Nizam's own hand.

"I am far from wishing any loss to Pundit Perdham, and much less that any diminution in the reputation of our friendship, which is known to the world, and become the common talk of friends and enemies, should take place, on account of the above-mentioned points; duly impressed with this, fix with Balaji Pundit upon such plan for settling the detail matters as may not be obnoxious, and send information thereof to me, who am fully impressed with confidence in your and his good wishes.

Translation of Copy of a Letter from Azim-ool-oomrah to Govind Rao Bugwunt, the Deputy of Govind Row Kishen, dated the 16*th of April*, 1794.

"You and Rajah Ragotim Rao are perfectly well acquainted with the particulars regarding the adjustment of detail matters between the two Circars. You and the said rajah, agreeably to summons, were therefore sent there; at the time of your departure, the mode of adjustment was frequently explained to you at large, notwithstanding which, eight articles[1] concerning the detail matters were sent from thence, and answer to them was sent by Baboo Rao, who explained the same to the

---

[1] *Vide* termination of letter.

minister. At this time I learn from Baboo Rao and Ragotim Rao's letter that the minister's answer was, that as the negotiation had been protracted ten years, so, in like manner also, it still bore no appearance of adjustment; that you should come here to close the negotiation by having some mode fixed upon that should be carried into effect. With respect to the mode of adjusting the detail matters, whatever was to be said was explained to you from hence, but if, notwithstanding this, a due impression be not made, there is no help for it. In consideration of the union between the two states, his highness the Nizam is never in any manner desirous of occasioning loss to Row Pundit Perdham, and this being the case, how can the latter approve of occasioning loss to his highness? You, who are an old well-wisher, and entrusted with the secrets of both states, should with the knowledge of the minister, fix upon whatever may not be hurtful to either, and write me of a mode of adjustment to take place through the medium of Govind Rao Kishen, in order that I may represent the same to his highness and prevail on him to approve of it. In all our conversations the subject of our discourse was, that whenever there should be a certainty of an inclination to adjust matters, the mode of doing it should then be fixed on, and followed up; if, therefore, you think the time of adjustment is now come, settle the mode and send me intelligence of it. As you are there, and Govind Rao Kishen here, what occasion is there for Baboo Rao and Ragotim Rao coming here? their coming is perfectly useless. Do you fix upon a mode of adjustment, and inform me of the same. When you were here the minister was at a loss how to ascertain the final wishes of his highness, which cannot be the case now you are there. Whatever you may be prompted by your good wishes to write will be strictly attended to, and answers will be sent to Baboo Rao and Ragotim Rao after the receipt of an answer from you to these matters. You will learn the remaining particulars from Govind Rao Kishen's letters."

Translation of Persian Translation from the Mahratta Language of Eight Demands of the Poonah Minister on his Highness the Nizam, and of the Replies and Rejoinders which have passed on the subject between them.

THE POONAH DEMANDS.

FIRST DEMAND.

"You have withheld the quarter of the Choute, and of the Deshmooky of the Soobah of Bidur till an investigation takes place; release and pay the same, and make an investigation."

The Nizam's Answer to the above.

"In regard to so much as has been ascertained to have been paid in the time of the late Asuf Jah, be guided according to such ascertainment. The sums he used to pay for the remaining Mehals have not been ascertained. At present, Ameens are to be appointed to investigate them; till they are known the fourth will remain in my circar. Let all the Mehals of the Soubah of Bidur be investigated by both parties; till then the present practice will be continued."

The Poonah Reply to the preceding.

"You have written that with regard to what was the standard in the late Asuf Jah's time, the payments should now be regulated thereby for such of the Mehals for which that standard has already been ascertained. As the investigation does not prove satisfactory, Govind Row was spoken to on this subject. It was formerly engaged that the investigation should be accomplished in twenty-four months, and Munnoo Sunajee was accordingly stationed for this purpose some time ago. Since then, Runput Rao and Wuntish Rao have always been there, but on your part no Ameens having been appointed, the investigation has not taken place. Though to the present year, twelve years have elapsed, yet you still bring forward the plea of defect of investigation, which is improper. Do you now settle the account of the fourth from the first to the present year, and pay the amount, and with respect to the future, instead of withholding the fourth let it be paid yearly. If you withhold the fourth, my officers will take from the Mehals."

The Nizam's Rejoinder to the above.

"In reply to your assertion that I have withheld the fourth of the Choute of Bidur: till it be ascertained what sums were paid in the late Asuf Jah's time, you say I should give it up: the above detention holds good till those sums can be made the standard of adjustment. The Zemindars have furnished accounts of them for some Mehals; for all such as they have done so, this standard should therefore take place, and with respect to the remaining Mehals, the above standard for which has not been ascertained, Ameens should be deputed to make inquiry, and having speedily ascertained whatever was paid by Asuf Jah, the same should afterwards be also paid for them. Your remark is very just that no satisfaction is derived from investigation; therefore this being the case, send me a written memorandum from the drafter of the agreement in the time of the late Asuf Jah, and engage to restore whatever shall be found on investigation to be erroneous in it. After this, let the said memorandum be the standard on both sides, till an investigation of the late Asuf Jah's payments takes place. In case the production of this memorandum from the drafter should occasion too much delay, send me a written one of the agreement in Mahderow's time, and let Ameens be deputed. Till the ascertainment of the payments by the late Asuf Jah, the arrangement for adoption is this—the accounts of the revenue in plentiful years being examined, an adjustment of them should then take place."

SECOND DEMAND.

"The Choute and Sir Deshmooky of the current year being transferred for payment to the following one, and complaints from Amils being thereby occasioned, the payment for each year from harvest to harvest at and during them should be made good from the Mehals and the Jagheers, and Amils or Jagheerdars should not plead in excuse the want of orders from you."

The Nizam's Reply to the above.

"Injunctions having been issued to the Jagheerdars and Talookdars that of the fourth of the choute and Sir Deshmooky of the Soubah of Bidur, the fourth of the former (the choute) from the year 1191 Fussley, is to be withheld by me till the amount paid by the late Asuf Jah shall be ascertained, and that with respect to the remainder to the end of the year at the Dessarah, they must adjust and pay it to your Kamasdars year after year, from harvest to harvest. If any Jagheerdar or Talookdar should owe a trifling balance, and will not liquidate it, notice thereof should be sent by your Kamasdars to me; afterwards in the space of two months from the Dessarah, the necessary deductions for what may have been paid will be made, and for the balance that remains due a voucher will be taken, and the amount paid by me to the Kamasdar. If your Kamasdars receive the amount from me, they must collect the same from the Amils and Jagheerdars, and refund it to me. If after any receipt of such refund from your Kamasdars there should be any balance due together from the Mehals on account of the following years, the same will also be paid by me in the manner above specified."

The Poonah Rejoinder to the above.

"The engagement in regard to the time for ascertaining what was the former practice in the Soubah of Bidur, was twenty-four months; these are now lapsed, yet you still plead as an excuse the want of investigation for withholding the fourth, which will not now be allowed; you say that I should take the adjusted balance of arrears, and henceforth the amount for each year at the Dessarah, but if there should happen to remain any little balance, it will be paid by you, my Kamasdars giving you a voucher for the same, agreeing to collect it from the Jagheerdars and refund it to you. As this is an innovation you should not mention it. My Kamasdars and chiefs will collect from the Mehals according to custom, yearly, at and during the harvest of Kheriff and Rubby. Should any little balance happen to remain due, they will collect it in the interim of Dessarah. The Jagheerdars and Amils should not plead as an excuse the want of orders from you; let your injunctions be given to them on this head."

The Nizam's Reply to the above.

"All men of business collect the claims of each year within that year, and on that principle also are my orders to my Talookdars and Jagheerdars grounded. If by any means the whole sum for any one Mehal should not be paid within the year, repeated orders being sent will cause it to be forthcoming. The permission to withhold a certain portion was granted till the ascertainment of the sums paid by the late Asuf Jah. After they are ascertained, the restriction of course of its own accord will fall to the ground. Nobody will then plead as an excuse the want of orders from any one, and good government will be established."

Third Demand.

"A balance amounting to 5 lacs and 30,000 rupees on account of the Mehals of the late Zuffur-oo-Dowlah remains unadjusted, let it be settled."

The Nizam's Reply to the above.

"If a letter arrives from you Balaji Pundit dictated by good wishes, and an adherence to truth, the means of settling will be adopted, and an adjustment will take place."

The Poonah Rejoinder to the above.

"I speak in my ministerial capacity, and what I speak is not without confirmation. Therefore, with a due consideration for both sides, I have mentioned the sum I have fixed on to Govind Rao Kishen. If you are firmly bent on settling on it, and Govind Rao Kishen is convinced that you are, he will then state the sum."

The Nizam's Reply to the above.

"Since a good understanding has taken place, the signature to papers expressive of being dictated by good wishes has been affixed, the letter from you has arrived, and Govind Rao Kishen has stated matters: that amount will be paid, but let the amount first be understood."

FOURTH DEMAND.

"Nineteen years' Choute and Sir Deshmooky of Adoni remain unadjusted; settle the whole from the first, and deliver it."

The Nizam's Reply to the above.

"After the war which is now on foot, injunctions for an adjustment will be given to Darah Jah."

The Poonah Rejoinder.

"In the above-mentioned Talook, great arrears of Choute and Sir Deshmooky are due, the adjustment and payment of which would have been formerly effected, but Musheer-ool-Moolk Bahadoor having become responsible for the whole, the business was protracted. The said Bahadoor has long been negotiating about Adoni, but still no adjustment has taken place; how much longer is it to be waited for? He brings forward the story of Hyder Ally Khan having taken a large sum of money, and also occasioned loss, as a large sum is due on account of this Circar's Choute and Sir Deshmooky, notwithstanding that, by way of favour, the sum of one lac and seventy-five thousand rupees, exclusive of Dowlut Row's Muckassy, was fixed Bilmookta for payment. Let the said sum be paid yearly to the Circar without trouble, but all this is done away, and objections are started. The agreement of the Circar being Bilmookta, no loss in the Mehals can affect it. Pay the money due to the Circar without trouble. You now start innovating objections about losses; if you are to give me the Ain Choute and Sir Deshmooky of my agreement for the above Talook, determine it so. In this case, after the fair ascertainment of the amount Hyder Ally Khan may have taken, and of the depredations he may have committed in the country, the deduction of a share will be allowed by this Circar in proportion to the sum which it is entitled to receive. Do you, agreeably to what I have written, settle and pay it, and for the future let the mode of Akár be observed."

The Nizam's Reply to the above.

"In what manner is the voucher of Azim-ool-oomrah from hence expressed? Produce it."

FIFTH DEMAND.

"The Choute and Sir Deshmooky of the Mehals of the Soubar of Berar are not adjusted agreeably to former custom. Some deficiencies are made. Settle for the past agreeably to the former custom, and let the same be observed in future."

The Nizam's Reply to the above.

"You are responsible for the good conduct of the Bhonsla's troops; send a detailed account of the Mehals, with respect to such of them as by it shall appear to be but in a small degree flourishing; the charges on them for sebundy, grain, grass, kanoon khurch, deshmooky, deshpandiahs, and just claims shall be deducted, and from whatever balance remains, your share shall be given proportionately to the amount of my receipt. With respect to the other Mehals, Mahde Row's settlement will be observed, provided you fulfil the terms of the above responsibility."

The Poonah Rejoinder to the above.

"You have written, but if agreeably to former engagement you will give the Bhonsla grass and grain yearly, at and during the proper season, why should he cause any trouble? If unreasonably he occasions trouble, injunctions will be sent to him; the details of the Mehals were formerly sent. With respect to the deduction of the charges of sebundy, &c. in the Mehals, which are in a small degree flourishing, and afterwards my taking from the balance my share proportionately to your receipts, also with respect to the other Mehals that I should take from them the amount of Mahde Row's settlement—these proposals are innovations: how, then, can they be agreed to? Pay the balance that may be due according to the late Asuf Jah's settlement, and for the future by enjoining the Jagheerdars and Amils to observe former usage, cause the same to be forthcoming. These Mehals have been long desolate; there is no likelihood of their becoming flourishing by endeavours on the part of your Circars. Why, therefore, need I wait longer? this being the case, pay the whole according to former settlement. If half of the Mehals were to be transferred to this side for the purpose of being cultivated, and the other half were for the same to remain with you, the profit or loss would soon appear evident. If half of the Mehals, for the purpose of being cultivated, are given to this side, then the Akerham will be adopted. Always make use of the expression of the whole of the Mehals in the Soubar of Berar, and never hint any of them being deficient in point of being in a flourishing state."

The Nizam's Reply to the above.

"Some Mehals of Ballaghaut, Berar, &c., on account of the troubles occasioned by the Saloo-wala, and the grass and grain of the Bhonsla, have been injured and are so still, besides which they have taken from the Jagheerdars of these Mehals what they liked, more than was before customary, and have also committed depredations in the country. The Jagheerdars, from being on duty at my court, have undergone great hardships, and suffered heavy losses. Notwithstanding all this, it is said there has been a deficiency in the payments on the part of my Circar. Send me a written account of any Mehals for which less has been paid than was stipulated by Mahde Row's settlement. Till the late Asuf Jah's settlement is ascertained, the means may be talked of for adopting that of Mahde Row. With respect to the second proposal about the Mehals which have been deficient, let the half of them, for the purpose of being cultivated, remain in the hands of Hurry Pundit and Govind Row Kishen, and the other half in this Circar in the way of Akarham, till they shall become flourishing; as soon as they shall have attained this state, let the late Asuf Jah's settlement be observed, and afterwards the Mehals remain with this Circar. In case it should so happen that any increase on the late Asuf Jah's settlement should take place, you will receive a proportionate share thereof."

Sixth Demand.

"The Choute and Deshmooky of the Mehal which was given in Jagheer, in the year 1185 Fussley, for that year remains unadjusted. Let the same be adjusted and paid.

The Nizam's Reply to the above.

"It was formerly written on the paper presented by Govind Row Bugwunt, that, for the purpose of investigation and examination of the accounts, Ameens should be deputed."

The Poonah Rejoinder to the above.

"What Ameen is to be appointed? Appoint one, and obtain a settlement. On the part of this side, Gunput Row and Wungteish are there. Whenever negotiations are renewed, you desire a speedy adjustment of accounts; but afterwards cause delays and procrastinate matters; therefore no adjustment takes place, as the adjustment of accounts will require some length of time, limit a period for it, and let it be commenced."

The Nizam's Reply to the above.

"With respect to the adjustment of the Sooraj of the Pergunnah of Pythum and Mehals which came into the hands of my Circar in the year 1185 Fussley, as the engagement was that the revenue of these Mehals should be paid to me from the beginning of the above year; therefore, from the latter period to the time I received possession of them, refund whatever you may have collected from them, as also whatever you have received from the late Fuxel Baighkhan on account of the Choute, or any sums which you otherwise received. After these restitutions shall have been made, let Ameems mutually give and take credit as may appear proper on an examination of accounts."

SEVENTH DEMAND.

"Notwithstanding a balance remained due to this Circar from the Talook of Halghurrah in the Pergunnah of Nullnigy, you took back that Talook. Let the above balance be settled and paid to this Circar."

The Nizam's Reply to the above.

"Formerly I wrote on the papers presented by Govind Row Bugwunt, that for the purpose of examining and comparing accounts, Ameens shall be despatched on both sides."

The Poonah Rejoinder to the above.

"It was written on the papers that if any balance on an examination of the accounts by the Mootsuddies of Rajah

Ram Chunda should appear to be due to this Circar, it would be ordered to be paid, and *vice versâ*; if I had received too much I should refund the excess. Notwithstanding this having been written by you, no Ameen was sent on your part, now you write for their being sent. A sum of money on account of the arrears of this Circar was due to Jadhoo Row, for which you having delivered the Talook of Halghurrah to us, it remained seven years in our possession, and the accounts of that period were furnished you many years ago. You seem to be very distrustful and suspicious of their accuracy; well, let them be examined and investigated; but as Gungerdur Bhut's papers were attached at Hyderabad along with Imtiaz-oo-Dowlah's property, and the said Bhut is since dead, produce the papers from amongst the said property, and examine and compare them. If on a strict investigation of them anything should appear against us, I will allow for it from the balance that is due to the Circar. Settle the balance or else send for the Zemindars' papers, and let an adjustment take place by comparing them with the receipts I gave them; in this manner it will be effected. Unreasonably bringing forward the plea of investigating the business of Halghurrah, you delay the payment of somewhat less than three lacs of rupees on account of Jadhoo Row. This conduct is not proper. Since last year the Ameens on both sides who have been deputed have needlessly incurred expense, and are still at their station. The Talookdars and Zemindars do not send to the Mokuddums and Putwarries of each village for the Ain accounts, to have them examined and compared; therefore pay the balance agreeably to the account calculated by this Circar, and afterwards investigate it. If any error in it should be discovered, let it be allowed for accordingly."

The Nizam's Reply to the above.

"Prior to this, in the lifetime of Sevaji Pundit, the Mootsuddies of Ram Chunder Mahdoo, in examining the Ain accounts, discovered an error in the sum for the liquidation of which Halghurrah was consigned. Owing to this error the excess in your receipts from Halghurrah may have been occasioned, therefore refund it. It was then said that Imtiaz-oo-Dowlah had Gunghadur Bhut's papers; on inquiry, however, it was evidently found he had not. If you will produce the papers from wherever they may be found, and have them examined and compared, let credit be given for whatever balance of the actual sum at first due as shall appear to be unpaid."

Eighth Demand.

"The Pergunnah of Nursa and Mehals were under the charge of the late Zuffur-oo-Dowlah. Settle the Choute and Sir Deshmooky of the said Mehals, and cause the same to be paid."

The Nizam's Reply to the above.

"Formerly Govind Row Bugwunt presented a paper on which I wrote a reply: agreeably thereto I will act. Send a detail of the Mehals, and for the purpose of investigation let Ameens be sent on both sides."

The Poonah Rejoinder to the above.

"Formerly on the paper it was written thus, that Ameens should be appointed to examine, and that whatever they discovered to be the usage in the Mehals should be observed; but for the accomplishment of this investigation you did not furnish an Ameen. Formerly Row Jee Sewaji and Mosum Ally Khan went to make inquiry about the Mehals, but they did not even ascertain in the usual manner a single one. Now in the seven or five articles you refer to making investigations. The state of the matter of investigation is this: the Zemindars are under the control of the Jagheerdars and Amils, therefore a fair and true investigation cannot be had, and quarrels will be occasioned. Therefore to prevent quarrels between us, let the Zemindars, &c. be made obedient to the Ameens, that a faithful and true investigation may take place. Satisfy yourself in regard to this point and appoint an Ameen; on the part of this Circar, Gunput Row and Wungteish are there. Whenever negotiations about any points are entered into you seem anxious for speedy investigations, but never accomplish any. Do not act in this manner, or think that there is any error in my statements. Notwithstanding the matters are fair and just, you always refer to inquiries about them. Why do you do so? Your detaining the whole balance till an investigation takes place is improper. It would be a better mode were you to withhold a lac or 50,000 rupees of the balance till an investigation took place, and to settle and pay the rest. Do act in this manner, determine upon investigations and despatch Ameens. When the examinations have taken place, if anything appear against me it will be deducted from the sum you withheld. You will require some time to make the investigations; fix a period for them, and appoint Ameens. In case you approve of this, the above conditions will be observed."

APPENDIX K.—(p. 84).

Letter from Sir John Shore to Captain Kirkpatrick in reply to a Despatch from the latter, containing a copy of the Peishwa's Demands on the Nizam.

"It is unnecessary to point out to you, that the supposition on which I first authorized our interposition are so far varied, that the demands of the Peishwa, so far as I can judge from the communications which have hitherto reached me, are founded on justice and upon agreements, and cannot therefore be considered as exactions; and the tenor of our interposition, if it should take place, must be accordingly modified. It is our object to prevent a rupture between the two courts of Hyderabad and Poonah, and not to support one against the other. I do not, however, imagine that the Peishwa will proceed to attack the Nizam without previous communication with our Resident, Sir C. W. Malet; but I shall at all events instruct him, in the event of appearances indicating hostilities on the part of the Peishwa, to interpose his endeavours to prevent them, by offering the friendly advice of this Government for an amicable termination of the matter in dispute between the two courts, on the grounds of our mutual connection and alliance with both. With respect to Sir C. W. Malet and yourself, this and my former letters having sufficiently explained the principles of our interposition, which you both appear thoroughly to understand, I leave you to act upon them according to the exigency of circumstances and the information you may possess, adding only that it is by no means my wish to interfere as long as it can prudently be avoided."

APPENDIX L.—(p. 90).

Letters addressed by the Poonah Government to that of Hyderabad, forming part of the Correspondence already alluded to (Appendix J.), and read by the Nizam's Minister at a formal Interview with Captain Kirkpatrick, on the 24th of May, 1794.

[See the remarks of the minister on the tenor of these letters, in the text of our narrative (pp. 94—96), to which we may here add the explanation which he gave at the same time of the claim advanced in the third of these letters. The *ganse dânah*, or "grass and grain" contribution, was, it seems, a sort of commuted claim which the Bhonsla (or Rajah of Nagpore) had upon the grass produce of that part of Berar in the possession of the Nizam; amounting, with other pecuniary items, to no less than sixty per cent., except in certain districts heretofore comprising the Jaghire of Salabut Jung, Nizam Ally Khan and Shahawar Khan, which were assessed only at forty per cent. This claim the minister declared to be contrary to the general stipulations of the treaty alluded to in the letter from Poonah, and he insisted much on the obligations under which the Rajah lay to the Nizam for the readiness with which the latter had acknowledged his succession.]

Letter No. I.

"I have been honoured and exalted by the receipt of your highness's gracious favour, stating, &c. [here follows a recapitulation of the letter No. 2, transmitted with my (viz. Meer Allum's) address of the 17th April], and have fully comprehended the contents. Nana Sahib (Mahderow) who rests in heaven, deputed the late Kishen Rao Bullal (father of the present Vakeel Govind Rao Kishen) when you were on excursion towards Medhuk, to transact business with your highness. The late Moorad Khan was then the agent through whom the affairs were transacted, and at that time the above-mentioned Row, not being much acquainted with your highness's disposition, did not on this account venture to represent and state matters freely. After the death of Nana Sahib, Betul Pundit (the minister of the Nizam at this period) forsook the path of prudence, and adopted that of folly. These matters are fully impressed on your highness's mind; since that time the fame and prosperity of the friendship and union between the two mighty states for these thirty-three years past have been daily increased; the time and manner of the excellent exertions which were made to effect this, are too well known to your highness to require being enlarged upon. After the death of Kishen Rao, the Peishwa deputed Govind Row Kishen to your presence to adjust all points both general and particular. I was along with him; since then five years have elapsed, notwithstanding the repeated injunctions of the Peishwa and his minister for the adjustment of detail matters: for, being desirous that it should be effected by the mutual consent and pleasure of both parties, we have artfully continued to let the above period elapse without settling them. All these circumstances will, no doubt, be known to you. I have been very anxious for the arrival of such a period for adjustment as would occasion no loss to either party, and for your highness being inclined to have matters adjusted. By the grace of God, I have been favoured with your highness's letter, and it has so far convinced me of the arrival of this period, that I am certain that the object of my good wishes will be fully accomplished.

"Conformably to your highness's orders, I stated every particular to the Peishwa and his minister, the former of whom declared that he had no desire to occasion you any unfair loss. This being the case, both parties are disposed to and bent on what is reasonable. But my station subjecting me to obedience and control, and the adjustment of details being a matter of account, send a confidential person of your government hither, that I may exert myself to the utmost through him towards effecting their adjustment. On the arrival of a confidential person from your highness, I shall be heartily bent and ready to perform whatever is incumbent on good wishes. I and Govind Rao Kishen have nothing great at heart but good wishes for both states, the preservation and encouragement of which wishes rest with your highness. I have written particulars to the said Rao, who will represent them to your highness."

Letter No. II.

"At this time I have been highly honoured by the receipt of your very kind and acceptable letter written in your own hand, and have derived the highest satisfaction from hearing of your health; you kindly inform me that your highness is by no means in any shape desirous of loss being occasioned to the Peishwa, or of any diminution taking place in the friendship so well known to subsist between the two states. You desire, that keeping this in remembrance, I should fix on a mode for adjustment with Balaji Pundit that may not be vexatious, and you declare that you have the most perfect confidence in the good wishes of the state, all of which contents I have fully understood. The two states have long been great and respectable; the practice of friendship and cordiality with each other has been well and firmly attended to; besides this, double rulers united and two administrations in one place, which nowhere else has ever been heard of; by the favour of God, this excellent system has, and still subsists between the two states, and has been very duly observed on both sides, particularly in the time of the late Mahderow, when the observance of it daily increased. Since then the treaty that was concluded during the march productive of peace to Eidgheer, and the confidence with which your highness inspired the minister, removed every idea of disunion completely. Afterwards Govind Rao Kishen and I, agreeably to this Circar's orders, having been stationed with your highness: we repeatedly, prompted by our good wishes, urged its being by no means proper that in the union of the two states any disturbance should be occasioned by the delay in the adjustment of the detail matters, as such delay afforded subject of talk to the evil-minded, and that the adjustment of these details should, therefore, be effected. At this time, it occurs to your highness that this is an advisable measure. The letter written in your own hand, with which I have been honoured, inspires me with great confidence on this head, and convinces me that your highness will not take in ill part any reasonable demands of this state. May God always keep your highness's kind shadow on the heads of your good friends—what shall I say of the advantages of the union and connection between the two states, and matters of foresight which occur to your highness? By the favour of God, the above-mentioned Govind Rao Kishen, with whom I have been serving, has long been a well-wisher of your highness; in whatever was proper and consistent with the obedience due to your highness and the friendship subsisting between the two states, every practicable and excellent exertion has been made, and the wish of my heart is, that as long as I live, nothing may occur inconsistent with good wishes for both states; as your highness will also be satisfied with respect to this, there can be no occasion to say anything on the subject."

Letter No. III.

"I have to acquaint you that prior to this, in the treaty that was settled between you and Lena Soubah Sahib Ragojee Bhonslah, during the march to Berar, through Lena Dhonundar Madhajee Bhonsla, there is an article concerning grass and grain, which stipulates that whatever was the usual custom theretofore should be observed by both parties, and further states that Ameens should be deputed on both sides to the Mehals to investigate and ascertain the said customs exactly on the spot, and that your Jagheerdars and Amils should pay agreeably thereto. Accordingly Noohussir Alli Khan was sent on this business on your part, and Appajee Rao Gopaul on that of the said Bhonsla. It was proper that after having ascertained what was really customary in your Pergunnahs, they should have first reported the same to their ministers in order that whatever was reasonable should have been paid. It appears that this was neglected, and in places where ten rupees should have been paid, they decided that five should, and where five were due they fixed on two. What advantage your highness could have conceived derivable to yourself from this scheme, I do not know.

"There being in states always many servants of a selfish disposition who represent matters from interested motives, the said Bhonsla, therefore, repeatedly wrote you that your respective officers, having consulted only his loss throughout their decisions, how could he abide by or approve of them? besides this, even the custom, as fixed by these officers, has not been observed. In all the Pergunnahs, some places pay too much, others too little, and some nothing at all; and in this state the matter has rested. Where cordiality and friendship subsist, difficulties about detail matters are improper. The said Bhonsla is, above all things, heartily desirous of increasing friendship, and has for a long time past been stating to this Circar his wish to have no dispute about detail matters; his agents, who are now here, have also been stating the same, and negotiating on the subject. I therefore observe to you from motives of friendship, that in the world of friendship and union, disputes about details are contrary to good counsel; and that the terms of the treaty are, that the grass and grain should be given agreeably to former custom. At this time that the said Bhonsla entertains doubts of the decision of the Ameens of both sides who went to the Mehals not being conformable to former custom, what signifies their determination? the grass and grain is not a business of lease or contract, but of account. In case, in the investigation, a mistake has been introduced, what harm can there be in complying with repeated requests for a new one? I hope that for the purpose of settling this difficulty, you, my friend, will nominate some person on your part; on the part of the said Bhousla, a respectable person will also be summoned; even an Ameen from this court will be appointed, that the matter may undergo so fair and thorough an investigation, as shall not only afford a sure guide for the conduct of both parties, but tend to remove the doubts which the said Bhonsla entertains. Considering also the friendship subsisting between the parties, this arrangement appears proper, looks well, and can occasion no loss to either side. After an ascertainment and examination shall have taken place, the amount due for past years will be calculated in one sum; the money which may have been paid being deducted therefrom: whatever balance remains, the payment and adjustment of it can be made by your Jagheerdars and Ameens possessed of penetration. This arrangement taking place will prevent disturbance in the Mehals, and may tend to the prosperity and quiet of the country."

Letter No. IV.

" I have been favoured and made happy by the receipt of your highness's gracious letter, stating, &c. [here follows a recapitulation of No. I., transmitted with my address of the 17th April], and have fully understood the contents. The state of the business has long been this, that though the Choute and Sir Deshmooky of the five Mehals of Adoni Raichore, Kowtahl, Bunoo, and Liddypoor, amounted to a large sum, yet this Circar, by way of favour and kindness to the late Bazalut Jung, exclusive of the Mukassah of the Gudjanderghur chieftain, Dowlut Rāo Grupmah, fixed and received a mukta, and this arrangement remained in force till the time of the late Nawain Rao. It was proper that ever since that time the amount of the said mukta should have been made good yearly ; but instead of this you have for many years past only talked about settling, or would cause to be given, and in consequence of a wish to please your highness, you have always said you would cause an adjustment and payment to take place, and of Azim-ool-oomrah's even going the length of making himself responsible for an adjustment, the matter has been allowed to remain as it was at first. Your highness must be acquainted with the loss that has been occasioned to the Peishwa by taking up loans payable with interest, on account of the above mukta from sowcars, and paying the troops therewith ; and that even the whole mukta is not sufficient to liquidate the interest due to the sowcars. Now that Meer Abud Khan is dead, you, as an illustrious parent, should arrange the business of the talook, the treasure, effects, &c., concerns of the family, and should send the amounts of the claims which the sowcars have on the Peishwa, the adjustment of them depending on the above mukta. It is proper that you should also arrange and settle in a dignified manner the prosperity and splendour of Meer Goolam Hoossein, the son of the deceased. Since both our states are united, and are as but one and the same in consideration of our union, you desire in your letter above recited, that the Peishwa's circar should settle these matters. If this be your highness's pleasure, it is well; let the treasure, effects, and other concerns of the deceased be made over by, and with the knowledge of, your highness to the Peishwa, and let letters be written to Meer Goolam Hoossein and this state by your highness, expressive of your having written about the administration of affairs to the Peishwa, on whose part a confidential person will be sent to him, who will be able to manage the whole talook, to settle the complaints and disturbances of the troops and the amount of Choute and Sir Deshmooky; and that he (Meer Goolam Hoossein) must accordingly, without fear or delay, act agreeably to the advice and counsel of the said confidential person. If letters from your highness to this effect are furnished, the business will be managed by this state; a person on the part of your highness should also be sent. Of these two modes, whichever meets your highness's pleasure, favour me with intelligence thereof; what more can I represent?"

APPENDIX M.—(p. 96.)

Captain Kirkpatrick's Report on the state of affairs between the Courts of Poonah and Hyderabad, at the time of Meer Allum's departure for Poonah, at the end of June, 1794.

"In the first place, however little credit there may be due, generally speaking, to the declarations of Eastern courts, yet I own I do not see that the sincerity of the Nizam's professions with regard to his wishes for a fair and amicable adjustment can at present be reasonably or justly questioned. He has determined to depute to Poonah, for the purpose of negotiating such an accommodation, one of his principal servants, and has declared his intention of vesting him with ample powers on the occasion. If the Poonah Government should meet the proposed discussion with no more than equal alacrity, the real views and inclinations of both parties will soon develop themselves. In the interim, I deem it of no consequence whether the claims of the Mahrattas have been fully and faithfully stated by this court or not. It has pledged itself to comply with all the *just* demands of the Peishwa, and I still think, with Meer Allum, that if other more powerful obstacles were not in the way, there would be no considerable difficulty in adjusting all the claims of that description, which refer entirely, I believe, to the Mahratta right of *Sherakut*, or participation, consisting principally of Choute and Sir Deshmooky. And although, under the same circumstance of Meer Allum's approaching departure for Poonah, I consider it premature to offer any opinion with respect to those particular points which Mr. Malet seems to think likely to be agitated by the Poonah court, yet I trust I shall be excused for observing that I cannot discern the advantage derivable to our Government from the dismission of the Nizam's present minister at the instance of Balaji Pundit. It is not to be denied that there are gross defects in the character of Azim-ool-oomrah; but though there should be at this court any man better qualified to conduct its affairs, yet it is by no means clear that his highness's choice would fall upon the individual, or, supposing it did, that such an one would be agreeable to the Mahrattas. As to the latter being restrained from interfering in any shape in the selection of a successor, I need only remark, that if they should be able to compel the Nizam to discard Azim-ool-oomrah, there must necessarily from that moment be an end to the independence of his highness, and though they were not openly to meddle in the nomination of a new minister, yet I humbly conceive, that whoever he might be, he would be but too apt, warned by the fate of his predecessor, to enter completely into their views. In such an event, I am so far from perceiving anything favourable to the interests of the Company, that I own I should rather expect it to lead rapidly to the deduction of the political equipoise of the Deccan, and to the dissolution of our connection with this state. On the other hand, it is far from being certain that his highness would sacrifice his minister without a struggle for the maintenance of his independence in so material a point, in the course of which it may be reasonably doubted whether an attempt would not be made by this court to strengthen itself by an alliance with Tippoo Sultan. Although, therefore, I readily admit it to be highly desirable that there should be no necessity for our taking any steps with a view to the prevention of such evils, yet whenever this necessity shall become apparent, our exertions on the occasion will, no doubt, be proportioned to the importance of the object in view; in the prosecution of which, however, I flatter myself I shall not be thought inclined to go any lengths that can possibly have any effect of involving us in a war with the Mahrattas; since however pregnant with mischief to us, I consider the subversion or enthralment of this state by that nation to be, I am far from being of opinion that the danger would be so imminent as to justify our hazarding such an extremity in the present posture of things. I shall close my observations on this subject with taking the liberty of referring you, honourable sir, to the second part of my predecessor's letter to the Resident at Poonah, under date the 18th of January, 1793, wherein he has treated the very point here under consideration with great clearness and force."

APPENDIX N.—(p. 102.)

Portion of a Letter from Captain Kirkpatrick, addressed to the Government of India, expressing his Conviction of the reality of the ambitious Designs entertained by the Poonah Government.

"I have for some time past strongly suspected that the views of Balaji Pundit instead of being limited to the pretensions which the Peishwa derives from existing treaties, actually extend to the entire subversion of Azim-ool-oomrah's ministry, if not to objects of still greater magnitude ; in the prosecution of which it may be proposed to exercise vicarious powers held by the Peishwa on the part of Shah Allum, and, in fact, should the court of Poonah, intending more than a mere menacing air, have seriously determined on drawing together the immense force which they are capable of doing, and should this force actually assemble in the Deccan, it may fairly be presumed that it will not be disbanded, till some advantage shall have been obtained through its means, at least, commensurate to so enormous and expensive an exertion."

APPENDIX O.—(p. 106.)

Despatch from Sir J. Shore, addressed to our Resident at Hyderabad, containing his View of the Controversy between the two Courts, after it was known that the Mission of Meer Allum had failed to effect a Reconciliation.

"Any suggestions for promoting the desirable object of a reconciliation between the two states can only be safely formed on general principles, under a due consideration of their relative power and resources.

"Little doubt can, I presume, be entertained of the superiority of the Mahrattas in these respects, and consequently of the inability of the Nizam to maintain a successful war against them, and if this be admitted, it follows, that it is the interest of his highness to avoid a contest which will probably confirm his dependency on the Peishwa from which he so naturally wishes to emancipate himself.

"With this view, the deputation of Meer Allum was prudent and proper, and the powers with which he was on this occasion invested, appeared to me sufficient for opening the negotiation with the Poonah minister, and would probably have been deemed so by the latter, if the disagreements between the two courts were of a public nature only, without any mixture of personal jealousy and animosity.

"Without considering in this place the probable motives of the Poonah ministry in requiring a demonstration of plenary powers from Meer Allum, for concluding the articles of discussion between his sovereign and the Peishwa without reference to the former, I shall only observe that the suggestion for demanding a similar declaration from Balaji Pundit appears to me superfluous and unnecessary; that it was not calculated to answer any useful purpose, and that the notification of the demand was very prudently suppressed by Meer Allum, as advantage might have been derived from it to protract the commencement of the negotiation, which cannot, with a view to the interests of the Nizam, be too earnestly urged. And here it may be proper to add as a general principle to be observed throughout the negotiation, that the Nizam and his minister should be very cautious in suffering any demur to intervene on articles of mere etiquette, or to show any hesitation or reluctance upon matters that are not of real importance.

"In the instructions given to Meer Allum on this occasion, the point of reference is still maintained, but subject to a further modification, which is certainly reasonable, and as such ought to satisfy the Poonah ministry. Of this determination you are at this time apprised; but as it is possible they may still adhere to their original requisition, I give you my opinion that this point, if insisted upon as an absolute preliminary, ought to be conceded; and that I see less danger in it to the Nizam than to Meer Allum, from the greatness of the responsibility which will, in consequence, devolve on him.

"This opinion, suggested by the preceding observations, may be supported by the following reasons: it does not follow from the delegation of plenipotentiary powers to Meer Allum, that he is obliged to sacrifice the true interests of his master, or to yield more than justice or sound policy requires. His highness may himself, if he judges it expedient, prescribe the limitations of his concessions, and the demands which he may think it right to insist upon in all points where the grounds of altercation are known; the term required for discussion will occasionally afford opportunity for reference and time may even be gained for the purpose. If unforeseen subjects should occur, the discretion of Meer Allum must be trusted, and the interests of the Nizam may, perhaps, be safer in this confidence than in the decisions of his minister; the Resident at Poonah, as far as prudence and propriety warrant, will afford him the advantage of his advice, and your communications will assist the former on the grounds of it.

"The advantages to be expected from this measure are these: that it will bring the sincerity of the two courts to a test, and, what is of the greatest importance to the Nizam, the real intentions of the Mahratta minister must be immediately developed; after this concession the Peishwa, without a violation of the principles of propriety and equity, cannot longer decline and refuse a discussion of his claims with the representative of his highness.

"I am not very apprehensive that the Nizam will evince great reluctance in conferring plenipotentiary powers on Meer Allum, as this minister cannot but see that his pride and vanity will thus escape the mortification of those concessions which, sooner or later, he will be compelled to make.

"It is of the last importance to the interests of the Nizam for him to ascertain the mere grounds of the reserve of the Poonah ministry in stating their claims upon his highness.

"If, as I suspect, they originate in a distrust of Azim-ool-oomrah and animosity to him, the reflections which I have detailed, derive new force from this consideration; if former jealousy and dislike of our interposition, that may be easily remedied, if it cannot be otherwise surmounted; but if the cause of this reserve should exist in motives that cannot be explained, such, for instance, as the removal of Azim-ool-oomrah from the control of his highness's administration, and the reduction of the Nizam to his former dependency on the Poonah government, or in an intention to gain time for the commencement of hostilities which have been predetermined, it behoves the Nizam to be well upon his guard, and to weigh the consequences of submitting to these claims, with his means and power to resist them. On such conjectures it is impossible to speak to the Nizam more than will be sufficient to lead him to serious reflections on the perils of his situation. If after yielding what equity requires, and any points not of very material consequence, which, in equity he might refuse, the demands of the Poonah government should remain unsatisfied, it remains with him to consider and determine how far he possesses power to resist those exactions, and whether a war with the Mahrattas would involve him in deeper embarrassments, or extricate him from the thraldom they might wish to impose upon him.

"I perfectly agree with Sir C. W. Malet, that in the event of a contest with the Mahrattas, his Highness could entertain no hopes of assistance from ——————— it is further evident to me, that if the Berar Rajah should take any part in the contest, it would be against the Nizam, and that any expectations which he might form of assistance from Tippoo would most likely prove visionary. The contempt of that prince for the Nizam is sufficiently apparent in his late neglect of paying the same compliment to him as to the court of Poonah, and it may not be improper to inform you, that I learn from Captain Doveton that it was evident in the language of Tippoo's officers, they did not hesitate to express these sentiments; adding, that they considered the period of the Nizam's death as a signal of the dissolution of his state, making use of this expression, 'that the game was prepared and would be soon begun.'

"By whom the treaty of Eadgheer was first infringed or whether Nanna or Azim-ool-oomrah first gave cause of provocation or animosity, are questions of importance only as they may become subjects of discussion, and in this view, if the charge could be clearly ascertained to rest with Nanna, the imputation might be forcibly opposed in reply to those accusations, which he has good grounds to urge on the intemperance and arrogance of Azim-ool-oomrah's language; on his connections with the Scindiah for a purpose which he disclaimed to the Poonah ministry, and on his march to Bidur, to support the objects of that connection. It is, therefore, proper that Meer Allum should be fully instructed on these points, but I would by no means recommend that they should be introduced by him, or that they should be discussed without necessity. It would be more prudent, if they should be brought forward by Nanna to reply, that although he is satisfied, he could vindicate his court and the minister to the satisfaction of Nanna, by showing that the grounds of imputation were not on one side only, that he is instructed to waive the discussions by an offer of the personal friendship of Azim-ool-oomrah, and a promise of the continuance of it in future. At the same time it may be possible that the discussion of the infraction of the original treaty of Eadgheer may be unavoidable, but this may be made on public not personal grounds.

"I entirely agree with you that your support of Meer Allum cannot be advantageously exerted, unless his communications with Azim-ool-oomrah are candid and explicit, and I trust Sir C. W. Malet has already explained the necessity of it to him.

"Great embarrassment is stated to result from the variety of emissaries employed by his highness at Poonah: whilst the conduct of Meer Allum merits his highness's confidence, I would advise that he should be made the sole channel of communications if it be practicable (of which you and Mr. Malet must judge), leaving it to him to employ such inferior agency as he may think necessary.

"If the present dissensions should proceed to hostilities, I would recommend to you to continue with his highness's person as long as he remains within his own territory, but not to accompany the Nizam into those of the Peishwa, without his consent, leaving it at the same time with you to use your discretion in retiring to any situation which you may think proper. It is scarcely necessary to add, that the Company's troops stationed with the Nizam cannot be employed offensively or defensively against the Mahrattas; under this restriction, they may be of use to his highness in suppressing or preventing internal commotion, or in the protection of his capital during his absence from it.

"In the opinions which I have detailed, you will find, I imagine, instructions for your general guidance in most cases, and in your conferences with the Nizam and his minister. But as we are absolutely precluded from assisting his highness with the troops of the Company, and as our mediation is introduced under a restriction to avoid any imputation in the consequences, if it should prove ineffectual, you will carefully attend to these principles.

"For the same reasons, it should be left to the Nizam's reflection to decline the advice which I wish to press upon him, from questions and inferences, rather than by direct communications, unless it should be required in such unreserved terms as to render a candid, explicit declaration in reply, unavoidable.

"Since writing the above, I have received your despatches of the 31st August, and Sir C. W. Malet's of the 26th, with a copy of his private letter to you of the same date, and from the tenor of them I am sorry to observe that the object of Meer Allum's negotiations seem as remote as ever, and that the disagreement between the two ministers appears to be so inveterate as scarcely to admit of reconciliation.

"These circumstances plainly suggest a conclusion that the discussions of the two courts will never be brought to an amicable termination, whilst they continue to be immediately conducted by the two ministers, and strongly point out the necessity of the measure which I have recommended for investing Meer Allum with plenipotentiary powers, or that some other plan should be adopted to remove what appeared to me insuperable obstacles to the conclusion of the negotiation as now carried on. For this purpose, no better way could be devised than a meeting of the Nizam and the Peishwa without the presence of the minister, as it would relieve us from an interposition which will probably prove inefficacious; but in giving my opinion as to the expediency of the measure, I by no means suppose it practicable; that the existing difficulties might be diminished, even by a direct correspondence between the Nizam and the Peishwa, I have no doubt. But how far his highness would be inclined to make the advances in terms calculated to promote the intended object under an assurance even that they would be accepted, is a consideration which I leave to you, with a discretion to suggest it or not, as from circumstances you may judge expedient."

APPENDIX P.—(pp. 106 and 114).

List of the Mahratta Army present with the Peishwa at the Battle of the Kurdlah.

	Cavalry.	Infantry.	Guns.
Peishwa's Pagah, or Household Troops	6,000	—	—
Pangrah	3,000	—	—
Hoojirat, or Imtiaz	5,000	—	—
New Levies	8,000	—	—
Balaji Pundit's	2,000	—	—
Baba Bhurkia and his Brothers	1,000	—	—
Rung Rao's	1,000	—	—
Sewajee Vitul's	1,500	—	—
Ram Chunder Powar's	500	—	—
Jahdo's	300	—	—
Pirtiniddy's	2,000	—	—
Rausta's	3,000	—	—
Purseram Bhow's, &c.	3,000	—	—
Dureekir's	300	—	—
Peishwa's (armed with Muskets, &c.)	—	15,000	44
Carry forward	36,600	15,000	44

	Cavalry.	Infantry.	Guns.
Brought forward	36,000	15,000	44
Perseram Bhow's, &c.	—	2,000	—
Belonging to Dowlut Rao Scindiah	20,000*	12,000†	98
„ to Tucojee Holkar	5,000	3,000	35
„ to Ragojee Bhonsla	12,000	6,000	15
Grand total	73,600	38,000	192

To the above were added about 10,000 Horse and Foot belonging to Purseram Bhow and Appa Sarlohhir.

Abstract Account of the Forces, Ordnance, and Ammunition with which the Nizam descended the Moorighaut, 4th of March, 1795.

CAVALRY AND INFANTRY.

Cavalry under the Native Chiefs :—		
Ordinary Establishment	32,550	
New Levies	12,100	
		44,650
Infantry:—		
Ordinary Establishment	23,700	
New Levies	9,000	
		32,700
Under Monsieur Raymond		10,840
		88,190

ORDNANCE AND AMMUNITION.

Guns and Mortars with the Native Chiefs	49	
Attached to the Tinsi	31	
Attached to Monsieur Raymond's Corps	28	
		108
Timbrels with the Native Chiefs	101	
Belonging to the Jinsi	459	
Attached to Monsieur Raymond's Corps	46	
		606
Round Shot, of Sizes, with the Native Chiefs	22,800	
With the Jinsi	74,700	
With Monsieur Raymond's Corps	10,000	
		107,500
Rockets with the Native Chiefs	2,575	
Belonging to the Jinsi	3,850	
With Monsieur Raymond's Corps	300	
		6,725
Flints, inclusive of those served out to different Chiefs, and exclusive of what each Chief had previously provided himself with		110,000

* Including those lately joined with Jarajee Bukhshi.

† Including six battalions of Sepoys under Monsieur Perron (of De Boigne's corps) and independent battalions under Micnace.

DRAFT AND CARRIAGE BULLOCKS.

Draft Bullocks attached to the Jinsi	11,106	
Attached to Monsieur Raymond's Corps, with the Native Chiefs not particularly known	1,200	
		12,306
Carriage Bullocks attached to the Jinsi	4,500	
Attached to Monsieur Raymond's Corps	700	
		5,200
		17,506

Grain and Kruzzauch, 73,000 Bullock-loads.

APPENDIX Q.—(p. 130).

Minute of Sir J. Shore, bearing date 2nd March, 1795, referring to the Political Situation of Affairs in India, previous to the Commencement of actual Hostilities between the States of Hyderabad and Poonah.

[This important Minute was penned by Sir J. Shore for the information of the Board, and it contains his views, generally, on the action that it would be prudent to take in the eventualities to which it refers.]

"The only treaties which have a reference to this question are those concluded at Paungul and Poonah, with the Nizam and Mahrattas, under the title of offensive and defensive alliance in June and July, 1790.

"The preamble to the treaty with the Nizam specifies three parties to it, and that the alliance is against Tippoo Sultan. The first article confirms the friendship existing between the three states by former treaties, and the second declares that Tippoo having violated his engagements with the contracting powers, they have united in a league to punish him to the utmost of their ability, and to deprive him of the means of disturbing the general tranquillity in future. The third and subsequent articles to the 9th inclusive, relate to the prosecution of the war, and to objects connected with it, to the distribution of the conquered territories, and to the mode of making peace, and the tenth article of the treaty of

Paungul, which is the 13th in that of Poonah, is in the following terms:—

"'*If, after the conclusion of peace with Tippoo, he should attack or molest either of the contracting parties, the others shall join to punish him; the mode and conditions of effecting which shall be hereafter settled by the contracting parties.*'

"The treaty therefore, from this summary recital of it, is clearly an alliance between three states for a declared specific object, with a prospective clause for the future security of all the contracting parties against a common enemy.

"To ascertain with all possible accuracy the nature of the obligations of the treaty, I now advert to the negotiations preceding the formation of it, and to the discussións of the quoted article, which have taken place subsequent to the war.

"Upon the receipt of intelligence that Tippoo had invaded the territories of the Rajah of Travancore, instructions were sent from this Government to the Residents at Hyderabad and Poonah, to notify its determination to support our ally, and to propose a co-operation with the Nizam and the Mahrattas against Tippoo.

"The Resident at Poonah, previous to the receipt of these instructions, had obtained from that court an unrequested declaration of its disposition to take part with the Company in the war against Tippoo. The first advance to the confidence was therefore made by the Mahrattas without solicitation on our part.

"To the information communicated to the Nizam by the Resident at Hyderabad of the unprovoked aggression of Tippoo against the Rajah of Travancore, and of the determination of this Government to support him, and to the expressed expectation of the Nizam's co-operation, his highness replied without qualification, that it was his intention after an interview with the Peishwa, and after concerting with him a plan of attack, to commence hostilities against Tippoo, and that the Governor General's resolution very happily coincided with his own plans; that it had long been his intention to attack Tippoo, and that he had communicated it to the Peishwa.

"The Nizam, however, claimed the merit of a ready co-operation with the English, of a decision in their favour without waiting to ascertain the disposition of the Peishwa, and of an earlier commencement of hostilities than he had intended.

"The Nizam's declaration was soon followed by a question from him to the Resident, as to the part which the Company would take, if, during the absence of his army, while assisting the Company, the Peishwa, invited by Tippoo, should invade the dominions of his highness, and the reply of the Resident, which he acknowledges to be unguarded, was, that the *Company ought to sacrifice their all* in his highness's defence.

"The minister subsequently requested that Lord Cornwallis would introduce in one of his letters an expression implying in general terms that he should consider any attempt to disturb the peace of his highness's dominions whilst engaged with us in the war against Tippoo, in the same light as an attempt to disturb those of the Company. He had previously signified his wish that the defensive alliance should be made general, and both the Nizam and his minister had evinced a disposition to connect themselves by the closest ties with this Government.

"The following extract from the Governor General's letter of the 12th April, 1790, to the Resident at Hyderabad, will furnish the most material information on this subject:—'You may likewise take that opportunity to express both to himself (the Nizam), and to Azim-ool-oomrah, how highly sensible I am of the liberal manner in which they received my propositions to join with the Company in the present war, and of the openness and fairness with which they have discussed the different articles which are to constitute the terms of our alliance, and you may give them the strongest assurance, that they shall have no reason to repent of their having treated me with so much candour, but that in return I shall have a pleasure in embracing every opportunity that offers, to give them convincing proofs of my sincerity and friendship.

"'I trust that the more that his highness reflects upon the nature of his proposition that I would engage to interfere, in case the Mahrattas should at any time make unreasonable demands upon him, he will more clearly see, that as the Mahrattas have acceded heartily and cordially to the confederacy, it would be highly improper in me to suppose that they would be inclined to treat one of their own allies with injustice, and consequently that such an assurance must appear to them in a light highly injurious and offensive; but in order to prove to his highness how anxious I am to go every justifiable length to show my regard to his interests, and to gratify him in his wishes, you may inform him that, provided the Mahrattas do not positively object to it, I will agree to its becoming an additional article in the present treaty, that should differences arise between any two of the confederates, the third party shall be bound to interpose his good offices, and to take every means in his power to bring those differences to a just and amicable settlement; and you may add to his highness, to Azim-ool-oomrah, and to Meer Allum, that should an article to that *effect be assented to by the Poonah government*, and any case should arise in which my interference should be called upon in consequence of it, they will always find me in the best disposition to endeavour to *save his highness from the necessity of submitting to injury.*'

"This is the substance of what preceded the treaty; it now remains to state what passed subsequent to it. At the period of general pacification at Seringapatam, Hurry Punt on the part of the Mahrattas, and Azim-ool-oomrah, on that of the Nizam, proposed to Lord Cornwallis to enter into a guarantee treaty, in full explanation of the 13th and 10th articles of the treaty of Poonah and Paungul, with a view to render the terms of them more precise, and to define the operations to be pursued by the three contracting parties, in the event of future molestation, or attack by Tippoo against either of them.

"It is unnecessary to detail the negotiations which followed these propositions; it is sufficient to observe the written declarations which the Residents were instructed to deliver to their respective courts, if they manifested backwardness, or evasion in entering into the proposed explanation; viz.: 'That we consider the three parties to be bound to each other, to act with their whole force against Tippoo in the event of his attacking either of them without clear and just provocation, but in no other case whatever.' That the draft of an explanatory treaty was prepared by Lord Cornwallis, and transmitted to the Residents at Hyderabad and Poonah, by whom it was explained to the ministers of their respective courts, that the Mahrattas required time for considering it, but Azim-ool-oomrah positively declared his resolution *not to agree to the guarantee treaty*, until his master's request concerning Kurnool had been complied with; that he afterwards retracted this declaration, and expressed his consent to accede to the propositions of Lord Cornwallis without waiting for the determination of the Mahrattas, that another draft of an explanatory treaty was afterwards prepared by the Mahrattas, and that the discussion had long since been brought to a close without any specific agreement, under a satisfactory declaration from the Mahratta minister, that his state was ready to act agreeably to existing treaties, and an expressed acquiescence of the Nizam to the proposed draft of Lord Cornwallis.

"I shall now consider the arguments by which the Nizam presumed to urge his claim to our assistance in the event of the premised suppositions. That he is by treaty entitled to the assistance of the Company, as well as that of the Mahrattas, if Tippoo should attack his dominions without just cause or provocation, and the defection of one party to the treaty cannot exonerate the other from the obligations which it has contracted to discharge, that so far from being justified in refusing him aid against Tippoo, it is incumbent on us to stand forth and compel the third party to perform its stipulations.

That the articles imposing the obligation of assistance is clear, and positive in its terms, and contains no expressions or condition to justify a secession on our parts; that his reliance in making the treaty was upon our good faith, as he not only well knew the treachery of the Mahrattas, but plainly intimated his suspicions of it during the preliminary negotiations; that at the period of making the treaty, our interest dictated the necessity of entering into an alliance with him, whether the Mahrattas became parties to it or not, and it cannot be doubted that if he had insisted upon an offensive and defensive engagement in general terms, it must have been acceded to; that if we are at liberty to renounce the performance of our stipulations, because the Mahrattas have violated their engagement, or for other reasons of convenience or policy, that good faith, which is the basis and cement of treaties, is subverted, as a pretence equally valid can never be wanting to authorize a departure from the most solemn obligations.

"That Tippoo's aggression must be with or without the concert of the Mahrattas, and in either case we are bound to oppose it, but more particularly should he take the field against the Nizam as the confederate of the Peishwa, as such a confederacy would be, on his part, a direct and insulting violation of the treaty, which it would be an indispensable duty to resist. To these arguments the following may be opposed.

"Nothing can be clearer than that the treaty, by the terms of it, is a tripartite engagement, binding and uniting three states for their reciprocal security against a declared common enemy, and supposing the guarantee established by it to be maintained by the joint efforts and co-operation of the three allies; upon this principle all explanations and acts originating out of the treaty were to take place by mutual communication and the concurrence of the three allied powers. That as the union of the three allies was the basis of the treaty, the continuance of that union, or friendship, is essential to the performance of the obligations imposed by it, and a war between two of the parties totally changes the relative situation of all.

"A junction between Tippoo and one of two parties to the treaty, whilst at war with each other, is to be considered with reference to the causes of hostilities between the two parties engaged in them. The treaty can never be construed with that rigour as in all cases to preclude any of the parties to it from forming such alliances as may be necessary to his safety, and upon a supposition that the justice of the war between the Nizam and the Peishwa is decidedly on one side, and that the other has been compelled into it by unprovoked aggression, self-preservation would justify an alliance between the aggrieved party and Tippoo. On the other hand, a confederacy between him and one of the parties to the triple alliance against any other party from ambitious motives, may be pronounced a gross infraction of that alliance with respect to the state confederating with Tippoo. The inference from this reasoning in point of fact bears rather against the Nizam, as his advance towards Bidur, if not an act of aggression against the Mahratta state, was indisputably with a view to take part in the dissensions between Scindiah and the minister, and so far an indication of hostilities. In an early stage of those measures which have contributed to involve the Nizam in his present embarrassments, the consequences of them were distinctly pointed out to Azim-ool-oomrah, and whilst the importance of a good understanding with Balaji Pundit, to the prosperity of the Nizam's government, was urged to him, he was at the same time apprised of the destructive tendency to his highness's affairs of a rupture with the Mahratta minister.

"To support the Nizam against Tippoo if he should seize the opportunity of actual hostility between his highness and the Mahratta, to attack the territory of the former without provocation, must necessarily involve us in a war with the Mahrattas, a predicament which the obligations of the treaty never supposed. I state this as a necessary consequence, for the operations of the field would lead to it, even if the invasion were not originally concerted or intended between Tippoo and the Peishwa. We cannot conceive it possible for us to fight against Tippoo alone in defence of the Nizam, and with the co-operation of his forces, whilst he is engaged with the Mahrattas; and to prosecute the war with effect against Tippoo, we must commence hostilities at the same time with the Mahrattas. But if a contrary supposition were admissible, the whole burden of repelling and punishing the aggression of Tippoo would exclusively fall upon us, contrary to the spirit, meaning, and terms of the triple alliance.

"We are respectively bound by different treaties with the Nizam and Mahrattas not to assist their enemies, and we are bound in a guarantee with both for the object of reciprocal security against Tippoo: the first imposes a neutrality on our parts with respect to the Nizam and the Mahrattas; and the second, the obligation of mutual support against Tippoo. The stipulations of the last imply and express the continuance of amity between the three contracting parties, as the foundation of that concert which is the very essence of the treaty, and by which the security derived from it can alone be maintained. Hostilities between any two of the parties is, in fact, as long as they last, a subversion of the principles of the treaty.

"The primary question, as far as regards the operation of the treaty, is reducible to a very narrow compass, and is resolvable into this statement, whether the treaty of Paungul is to be deemed a separate independent agreement between us and the Nizam, or contrary in all its obligations with him and the Mahrattas. The terms of it most clearly prove it to be a triple alliance, by which the parties are bound together against a presumed enemy for their reciprocal security, which is to be maintained by their joint efforts, and if necessary, with their whole powers. To the argument that the secession of one party from performing the obligations of the treaty does not release the other because it is not so expressed in it, and because such a clause would have been inserted if this had been the intention of the contracting parties, it may be replied, that this construction is inadmissible, for it requires more than was intended by the treaty itself, as it involves the necessity, or at all events the risk, of a war with one of the parties to it. This is a case which the treaty never supposed, and all the stipulations in it are formed upon a contrary presumption.

"In reply to other arguments, it may be observed, that both the Nizam and the Mahrattas were previously disposed to war with Tippoo, and that in all probability they would have carried this intention into effect if the Company had not been compelled into hostilities with that prince, that they embraced with alacrity the favourable opportunity afforded them by the determination of this government, and can claim no other merit than that they were induced by it to commence their operations at an earlier period than they had first proposed. The claim to which Lord Cornwallis signified his conditional acquiescence was not inserted in the treaty, and it is evident that it would have been objected to by the Mahrattas. The Nizam himself has afforded a proof of the latitude in which he views the article of this guarantee treaty under description by his declaration to withhold his acquiescence to the proposed explanatory engagement until our concurrence was obtained to the object which he had in view.

"In discussing the nature and force of the obligations of the treaty, we are not to be biassed by any consideration of the weakness of the Nizam, and the probability of an attack on him only. Such considerations apply to the question of *expediency*, and the point of *obligation* is to be argued in the same manner as if the supposition extended to an attack on the Mahrattas by Tippoo. If the terms of the treaty under the stated circumstances prescribe the obligation of assisting the Nizam against Tippoo, they must be construed to require our assistance in favour of the Mahrattas under similar circumstances if attacked by that prince, and the probable ruin of the one with the aggrandisement of the other would be the necessary consequence of such aid.

"Although hostilities between the Mahrattas and the Nizam are a dissolution of all existing treaties between them, yet they are both still bound to us. I am at the same time aware that if Tippoo were to attack the possessions of the Company, while the Mahrattas and Nizam are at war with each other, however they may profess an adherence to the terms of the treaty, they would not be in a situation to meet them, but with the restoration to peace, the power of fulfilling their stipulations may again ensue, and the contracting parties may again stand in the situation which the treaty supposed. Upon this principle, if Tippoo were to attack either the Nizam or Mahrattas whilst at war with each other, I should deem it necessary in the first instance to call upon the third party to perform his stipulations. It might induce the two parties at war to make peace with each other, and at all events would either show that Tippoo's attack was by concert with one of the allies, or prove a direct breach of the treaty against the ally refusing his aid in defence of the party attacked, and thus leave us at liberty to act as we might think proper; but I do not hold this Government bound to assist either party against Tippoo unless peace were previously established between the Mahrattas and the Nizam.

"Having discussed the obligations of the treaty, I shall now consider the question of assisting the Nizam on the grounds of political expediency.

"In deciding against the Nizam's claim to assistance against Tippoo without the co-operation of the Mahrattas, I am not to suppose that he will yield his conviction to these arguments which have satisfied my judgment. On the contrary, we are to conclude that he will be inclined to view our neutrality as a desertion of his cause, which ill repays his co-operation with us, and his anxiety to unite with us by the closest ties. We are, therefore, in the occurrence of the supposed event, which I am far from deeming probable, to look to the indisposition of the Nizam to the British interests in India, and to the consequences of it. In truth the whole tenour of the Nizam's conduct from the earliest period, proves that he has been friendly or inimical to the British Government as it suited his immediate views, and that his later union with us has proceeded from a motive of deriving support from our countenance and power.

"The apprehensions and dangers suggested by this consideration are remote, and at present the question, the decision of which presumes them, has not been forced upon our determination, but whilst they are possible, it is our duty seriously to weigh the probable consequences of neglecting the Nizam, or of supporting him against the joint invasion of the Mahrattas and Tippoo Sultan.

"The destruction of the Nizam's power, and the aggrandisement of that of his enemies, must be the consequence of leaving him without support, and Tippoo and the Mahrattas will of course become proportionately dangerous to us.

"On the other hand, when we reflect on the vices and imbecility of the Nizam's administration, the impossibility of directing his politics without usurping his government, and the dangers of perpetual war, the consequences of such interference—when we consider the difficulty of making any effectual impression on the Mahratta state by our forces, the comparative facility with which they might injure us, the magnitude of the resources and exertions, as well as the number of troops, both native and European, which would be required to oppose the united efforts of the Mahrattas and Tippoo, and the inevitable ruin of a long protracted war—the inducement to support the Nizam at the hazard of such impending circumstances ought to be much stronger than the apprehension of future evils from the subversion of his power.

"This event, before it could be effectually opposed by the assistance of this Government, would be the probable consequence of an invasion of his dominions by Tippoo and the Mahrattas, and it is at least dubious if any efforts on our part could procure his re-establishment.

"But, above all, it is indispensably necessary to advert to the situation of affairs in Europe, which precludes the expectation of receiving any considerable reinforcements of troops during the continuance of the war, and impresses the necessity of preserving by every effort peace with all the powers in India.

"Under the supposition of the annihilation of the power of the Nizam by the combination of Tippoo and the Mahrattas, the probability is as great that they would attack each other, as that they would unite to invade the territories of the Company, and if it were otherwise the progressive accumulation of our resources would enable us better to resist their confederacy against us.

"Our political consequence might lose something of its importance in the estimate of the native powers by leaving the Nizam to his fate, but although I am fully sensible of the value of opinion in this country, it cannot be placed in competition with the greater evils attending a war with Tippoo and the Mahrattas, which I consider the unadvoidable consequence of supporting singly the Nizam against Tippoo, if that prince should attack him while engaged in hostilities with the Peishwa.

"Independently of the reasons for affording protection to the Nizam which are suggested by a consideration of the consequences following the denial of our assistance, other motives occur. The conduct of the British government in resenting the attack upon their ally the Rajah of Travancore during the war, and in the negotiations for the termination of it, not only gained us the confidence of our allies, but established the British reputation throughout India for good faith, firmness, and moderation; but in weighing motives we must attend to self-preservation, including the permanency of the British possessions in India.

"I have now considered a question which I most sincerely hope we shall not be compelled to decide, and I shall take this opportunity of recording some reflections which I have frequently revolved.

"Whether the dissensions between the Peishwa and Nizam are terminated by war or by negotiation, there is too much reason to fear that the Nizam will fall under the subjection of the Mahrattas, and on this event, his power, under their control and direction, will become an accumulation of their strength, already exorbitant.

"This apprehension cannot have escaped the Nizam, and it seems natural to conclude that, having no expectation of our support, he would endeavour to avoid subjection to the Mahrattas by forming an union with Tippoo. Whether he has really ever had this in contemplation I am not informed, but I have already assigned reasons which I still think satisfactory for deeming it impracticable.

"Surmises have been propagated on the other hand of a meditated confederacy between Tippoo and the Mahrattas; this also I deem improbable, unless the latter should be forced into it by our avowed support of the Nizam against them. They are, I presume, satisfied on this head. Tippoo would be, I doubt not, ready to accept any overtures from the Peishwa for such a confederacy, but I think they will not be made, and I entertain little apprehension that he will at present venture to attack the dominions of the Nizam without the concert of the Mahrattas. If he should, the most probable consequence of such attempt would in my opinion be this, that the Mahrattas in the first instance would make their own terms with the Nizam, and then unite with us to defend his territories against Tippoo.

"The sovereignty of India may now be considered to be

exercised by the Mahrattas, Tippoo, the Nizam, and the English.

"The power of the house of Scindiah has become subject to the control of the Peishwa by means that were foreseen, without any immediate prospect that his successor will recover that independence which Scindiah himself possessed, and the paramount government of Poonah enjoys and exercises a most extensive influence and authority over all the constituent and dependent members of the Mahratta empire.

"If then there be assignable limitation it is with regard to the Berar Rajah, who from situation and circumstances had less interest and concern in the general politics of the Mahratta State, and carries on its administration independently of it. But his dependence is constitutional, and the present Rajah, as I am informed, received the confirmation of his succession with the insignia of his investiture from the Peishwa, and although it should be granted that he is not disposed to enter into any measures inimical to the British interests in India, we may with certainty conclude that he would take no active part with this Government against the Peishwa.

"The power of the Mahratta empire, with the co-operation of the Berar Rajah, is sufficiently formidable; and the forces under General De Boigne may perhaps be deemed equal to that of two English brigades.

"The nature of the Mahratta government is well known to be avaricious, grasping, and ambitious; that it never neglects any opportunity of extending its power, or aggrandising its wealth, with little solicitude as to the rectitude of the means employed in obtaining these objects.

"But although the accumulated power of the Mahrattas is great, it is not collected for enterprise without delay and difficulty, as we may learn even from recent events. This difficulty and delay may be imputed to the nature of the Mahratta constitution, to the separate interests and pursuits of the dependent members of it, which seldom admit of a distant or speedy diversion of their forces, and to the great extent of the empire from which the troops are to be drawn. In this diversity of interests a principle of discord exists, which, although it may disappear whenever the safety of the Mahratta State is endangered by attack, opposes an impediment to the union of the efforts of the empire for the purpose of hostile invasion. Friendship or alliance now subsists between the British Government and the Mahratta states and its feudatories the Rajah of Berar, Scindiah, and Holkar; but although some advantage may arise from a friendly connection with the feudatories, and greater perhaps from the apprehension which they may entertain of danger to their respective interest in the event of hostilities between the British and the Mahratta state, it would be unsafe to rely too much upon this consideration. On the contrary, if that event should occur whilst we employed the best means which policy could suggest to effect a disunion of interests among the different chieftains, fair exertions must be made on an expectation of the united opposition of all.

"With respect to all the powers in India, our actual security is our strength; but with regard to the Mahrattas, the alarm of danger is lessened by a consideration that a wiser and safer career is open to their ambition in the absolute subjection of numerous petty states in Hindustan, some of which are independent, whilst others are partially under their control, than by attacking our possessions or those of our allies. Our security may be deemed to be further confirmed by our avowed principles on comparison with those of Tippoo Sultan, whose ambition is as notorious as our disavowal of extending the British territories by arms. But after all, we are never to forget that a dominion exercised by foreigners must ever be viewed in a hostile light; that an union merely political is in the highest degree precarious, and that if the whole power of the Mahratta state were directed against us, we should find ourselves very vulnerable in many parts, and in some perhaps at present unsuspected. If Tippoo were at the same time to join the confederacy, or an European enemy superadd the weight of his power, the successful termination of the contest would require the utmost exertions, both here and in Europe.

"The British territories on the Ganges are open to invasion by Cuttack on the west and including the Vizier's dominions on the north. With respect to the Vizier I shall only here say, that whilst his administration continues on its present footing, we should derive no effective assistance from his troops, and that we must rather expect to find enemies than friends in his dominions, which are inhabited and surrounded by numerous hardy and needy adventurers without attachment or allegiance, and ready to take arms in any cause that would provide them spoil.

"It is unnecessary to expatiate on the character of Tippoo, the leading principle of which is ambition, and that has no friendship. We know by experience his abilities; he has confidants and advisers, but no ministers, and inspects, superintends, and regulates himself all the details of his government. He maintains dignity without ostentation, the peasantry of his dominions are protected, and their labours encouraged and rewarded. Before the late war, reports were continually propagated of his cruelty and tyranny with respect to his subjects in Malabar; they were not ill-founded, but that they were greatly exaggerated may be established by one consideration, that during the contest with him, no person of rank, character, or influence in his hereditary dominions deserted his cause. With less bigotry than is usually imputed to him, we know his zeal for his religion to be strong, and his ambition acquires new motives of action from this principle.

"Since the termination of hostilities he has faithfully discharged all the obligations of the treaty of peace, and his attention appears to have been more particularly directed to the improvement of his finances by economy, to the internal administration of his country, and to repair and strengthen Seringapatam. No part of his conduct has indicated hostility towards us, or our allies, but we have information that he entertains a particular resentment against the Nizam, and a contempt for him.

"His obvious policy is to wait until events produce a disunion among the confederates and to foment it if he can.

"The weakness of the Nizam's administration would probably prove an irresistible temptation to his resentment and ambition, if he were not protected by the triple alliance; but the subversion of the British power as opposing the firmest barrier to his ambition must naturally be the object which he has most in view.

"Of the three powers, therefore, which I have mentioned, I shall observe that the aid of the Nizam can never enable us to hold the balance of India. That the ambition of Tippoo has more and stronger motives of action than that of the Mahrattas, and that the consolidation of our alliance with the latter is an object of the first importance to us; with their aid, which we might expect, we could always oppose Tippoo and every European power. From Tippoo we could never hope for assistance, nor scarcely for neutrality.

"In the event of hostilities with the Mahrattas, I think it probable that an useful alliance might be formed with the Northern Rajahs, and perhaps even with some of the Sikh chiefs. But I should not advise offensive and defensive alliances with them as a precautionary security, on this principle, that the danger attending them would probably exceed the advantage to be derived from them in times of necessity. It is safer, in my opinion, to trust to the formation of alliances when that necessity exists, and this may certainly be promoted by the moderation and sincerity of our language and conduct at all times. The correspondence between the Government and the principal Northern Rajahs is regular; with any of the Sikh chiefs, occasional only.

"These general reflections may assist the judgment in forming a determination on the primary question which has insensibly led to the introduction of them, and if the Board concur in the result of my opinion upon it, they will further, I imagine, agree with me that there is no immediate probability that we should be involved in war in India. But with this conclusion under the uncertain consequences of hostilities between the Mahrattas and the Nizam, the precarious situation of affairs in Europe, and the desperate exertions of the French, we must admit the necessity of being prepared to meet any extremity. This in fact is an obligation of primary necessity at all times, although our preparations must be extended or abridged according to the impulse of circumstances.

"With respect to the Coast of Coromandel, I should have submitted some propositions founded on this consideration to the Board if I had not been informed by the Right Honourable President of Fort St. George, in a letter of the 18th December, that for similar reasons he had called for a list of stores and provisions on the frontier posts; that he would take care that they were amply supplied, and that the camp equipage should be in a state of preparation to admit of our taking the field upon a short notice. To these measures, I expressed my concurrence, and the Board may recollect my verbal communication of them.

"In Bengal, as far as immediate precaution may be expedient, little remains to be done.

"The Commander-in-Chief long ago noticed an evil of a very serious tendency, the dispersion of the regular troops in detachments upon civil services. Exclusively of the impossibility of enforcing a proper discipline over troops so divided, it would be difficult to collect any considerable body at a short warning in any part of the provinces, Calcutta perhaps excepted, and whatever reliance we may place on the submission, timidity, or attachment of the subjects of this Government, nothing can be more obvious than the necessity of being prepared at all times to quell insurrection.

"At the verbal or recorded suggestion of the Commander-in-Chief, some information was called for as preparatory to an arrangement for correcting the evil noticed by him, and lately further information has been required. It will be probably ready by the period of his return to the presidency, which may be very shortly expected, and we may then avail ourselves of his advice and assistance in forming the necessary arrangements.

"But after the matured reflection on our situation in this country, on the policy, the characters, the powers, and ambition of the different native powers in India, and the dislike which they must entertain to the manners, religion and dominion of Europeans, it is impossible to suppose that, with all our caution to avoid war, we shall be always at peace. Any inability on our parts to oppose the enmity of our neighbours would immediately make us sensible of its effects, and for these reasons, our consideration should extend beyond a provision for immediate exigency. We know from experience that the natives of India improve in military tactics, and that every new war with them requires augmented exertions and forces on our parts; and we are further to reflect that exclusively of the protection of these provinces, we must have it in our power to send assistance to the other possessions of the company when attacked.

"Our military establishment was formed nine years ago, and in the interval, we have been engaged in a war which requires the united efforts of the three presidencies, not to mention the co-operation of the Nizam and the Mahrattas, under the direction of superior military and political abilities, to bring it to a fortunate conclusion.

"In addition to these observations, we may assume it as an undeniable principle, that to impose peace on our neighbours by the strength of a military establishment ready at all times for active or extensive exertions, is not only the wisest but the most economical system.

"Under the influence of these reflections, I propose, therefore, that the Commander-in-Chief should be required to take into his consideration the military establishment of this government, and to communicate his sentiments, whether he deems it sufficient for the protection and security of the country which it is to defend, adverting at the same time to the reflections which I have stated, and to suggest any augmentation either of the whole, or the parts of it which he may deem expedient, or any alterations either in the disposition of the troops, or otherwise, which he may think proper.

"I have ever been disposed to adhere as literally as possible to the strictest interpretation of the restrictive clause in the Act of Parliament against entering into hostilities, but in the course of my present reflections, a question has originated from it which I think proper here to state. To pursue schemes of conquest and extension of dominion in India, are declared in the preamble to the clause to be measures repugnant to the wish, the honour, and policy of the nation, and with this preamble, the prohibition against declaring war or commencing hostilities is connected, except where hostilities have actually been commenced, or preparations actually made for the commencement of hostilities against the British nation in India, or against some of the states or princes dependent thereon, or whose territories the united Company shall be at such times engaged by any subsisting treaty to defend or guarantee.

"This clause, in literal construction, if my interpretation of the guaranteee treaty with the Nizam and the Mahrattas against Tippoo be admitted, is decisive against any interference on our parts in his favour against Tippoo without the co-operation of the Mahrattas, and the circumstances of the case are such, under all the considerations stated, as to confirm the constitution in point of expediency.

"But it is possible, that without any view to the extension of our dominions by conquest, a case might arise in which the security of the British possessions in India might be best consulted at the risk, and even certainty of hostilities, by taking part with one state against another, and the question upon this supposition is, whether we should be justified in such a determination where we are not bound by treaty to defend, or guarantee the state which it might be expedient to assist, and it should I think be referred to the Honourable the Board of Directors.

"To their particular notice also, the question which is the subject of this minute should be pointed out; repeating my opinion of the probability of its being forced on our decision, that we may obtain their instructions for our guidance at any future period in case it should hereafter occur."

APPENDIX R.—(p. 139).

Translation of a Newsletter detailing the Negotiations between the Peishwa and the Nizam after the battle of Kurdlah, in March, 1795.

"At first his highness agreed with Govind Kishen that Azim-ool-oomrah should be dismissed at the end of two months. The said Kishen, though not satisfied, said that if he (the minister) should in the meantime be prevented from entering the durbar, he would state the matter to the Peishwa, who it was probable might be satisfied, and took his leave. After this his highness sent for Govind Kishen, and informed him that the delay of two months was unsuitable, that it would require six months to settle fifteen or sixteen years' accounts with Azim-ool-oomrah, with whom accounts of crores of rupees rested. Upon hearing this, Govind Kishen, with some warmth, replied that his highness was his own master, and might do as he liked. Retiring from the durbar to his tent, he prepared to quit the camp. His highness being informed of his displeasure, sent Ghazi Meah to summon him back. On his arrival, his highness said that if six months could not be allowed, he agreed to the two months as at first proposed. His highness's real intention appears to be to procrastinate the adjustment of this point till he has a meeting with the Peishwa, in the idea that he may have influence to effect a reconciliation for Azim-ool-oomrah. Govind Kishen, aware of this, observed that he was a well-wisher and servant of both states, that whatever his highness directed he would communicate to the Peishwa; and, *vice versâ*, whatever the latter said he would state to his highness; but that the Peishwa being firmly bent on the above point being settled previous to any meeting taking place, he (Govind Kishen) thought it necessary to say so to his highness, in order that hereafter no sort of blame or reproach should fall on him. Afterwards taking leave, he retired to the gateway, where the three Rajah Chieftains were assembled, and told them that he would deliver his highness's commands to the Peishwa; that if the latter approved of them, so much the better; but if he did not, he would not return hither till the above point was finally agreed to and settled. After this he set out.

"Azim-ool-oomrah sent a letter to his highness, advising him not to hesitate complying with the Mahratta demands concerning him, as his highness's refusal on this head might occasion much disorder in the affairs of the state, and would render an adjustment afterwards more difficult. His highness wrote an answer to this letter, but summoned Azim-ool-oomrah to the sleeping apartment. When the latter came in, he requested his highness would preserve his honour, and send him to Oosah. His highness desired him to have patience, and to be at ease, for that he had other intentions at heart respecting him, and that time would show what the Almighty would bring about. The party furnished by Azim-ool-oomrah over his highness's sleeping apartment having been withdrawn, he (Azim-ool-oomrah) entertained great apprehensions of his life, and engaged Assud Ali and Rooshun Khan solemnly to prevent any mishap to his honour or life, and to exert themselves in preserving him.

"Yesterday, Govind Kishen wrote to Kunsipunt to state to his highness that the Peishwa was unalterably bent on the point concerning Azim-ool-oomrah being first settled, and a meeting taking place afterwards; that the Mahrattas had no intention to fight, but that if his highness had, he should come out. Accordingly, Kunsipunt stated this to his highness, who prepared a letter for Govind Kishen, and gave it to him, saying that if a satisfactory answer was not sent to it he would fight, and that, though the Mahrattas might not wish to fight, he would begin himself. The said Punt set out.

"In the evening orders were sent to Sheriff-ool-oomrah to attend the durbar the following morning.

"At seven p.m. Sheriff-ool-oomrah, agreeably to summons, attended the durbar, and was admitted to a private conference in the sleeping apartment, which lasted about forty minutes; his highness observed that certain things which should not have happened had occurred, and wished to know what was advisable at this time to be done, adding that as he (Sheriff-ool-oomrah) for a long time back had cultivated habits of friendship with the Mahrattas, he should employ such efforts as should preserve Azim-ool-oomrah in office, and at the same time bring about an arrangement of all matters of business. The latter replied that his services were at his highness's command, that he had certainly, agreeably to his highness's orders, kept up a channel of intercourse with the Mahrattas, that he would first write what was necessary to be written, and if they summoned him, he would proceed to their camp. After declaring that he would not fail in attending to his highness's orders, he took his leave, went to his tent, and writing four letters for Purseram Bhow, Tuckojee Holkar, Dowlut Rao Scindiah, and Baba Turkia,* he forwarded them through Govind Kishen's deputy. As yet no answers have been received. I hear that Govind Kishen agreed that two months should be allowed agreeably to his highness's desire for the dismission of Azim-ool-oomrah, but having requested security for the due performance of the same, and his highness having hesitated to grant any, he

(Govind Kishen) departed in disgust. The Mahrattas now say that his highness wants to defer Azim-ool-oomrah's removal for two months, that they will allow three months in order that his highness may settle his account at his leisure, but that both parties must remain where they now are, and that after his highness shall have settled his accounts and dismissed him (Azim-ool-oomrah), they, the Mahrattas and Nizam, will have meetings with each other, and that they will afterwards set out for Poonah, and his highness for Hyderabad."

APPENDIX S.—(p. 140.)

Detailed Statement of the Territories ceded to the Mahrattas after the Battle of Kurdlah, amounting in all to Thirty-four and a Half Lacs.

Names of the Mehals ceded to the Rao Pundit Perdham.	Rated Amount of Cession.		
	RS.	A.	P.
1 Souba of Aurungabad, Sircar Dowlatabad	4,27,047	3	0
Sircar of Parinda	3,50,644	5	9
Sircar Futtehabad commonly called Dharoor	3,05,735	9	0
Sircar Jalnehpore	1,82,206	6	0
Sircar Puttun	2,61,856	6	9
Sircar Beer	6,06,360	0	9
Souba of Bidur, Sircar Nandair	5,05,778	5	3
Souba of Bijapoor, Sircar Nuldroog	5,624	4	3
Souba of Chandaise, Sircar Assere	1,25,464	3	6
Souba of Berar Balaghaut, Sircar Bassim	33,224	10	0
Sircar Maikhur	47,993	14	6
Sircar Pathree	3,48,064	11	3
Mahals ceded to Ballajee Inmardhen Furnavese and others; Mootsuddies and Brahmins, servants of Rao Pundit Perdham—Souba of Aurungabad, Sircar Dharoor	66,087	11	5
Sircar Parinda	28,301	11	9
Sircar Ahmednugger	1,23,637	11	3
Sircar Beer	1,000	0	0
Souba of Bidur, Sircar Nandair	13,605	7	9
Souba of Bijapore, Sircar Nulldroog	17,367	5	9
Grand total, Rs.	34,50,000	0	0

APPENDIX T.—(p. 140.)

Particulars (on the authority of Meer Allum) of the Division of Three Crores and Ten Lacs of Rupees, which his Highness the Nizam agreed to pay to the Peishwa after the Battle of Kurdlah.

		Crore	lacs.
On account of	arrears of Choute	1	0
ditto	Indemnification	1	0
ditto	Dowlat Rao Scindiah	0	50
ditto	Durbar Charges, ditto	0	10
ditto	Grass and Grain to the Rajah of Berar	0	25
ditto	Balaji Pundit, Durbar Charges	0	25
	Total........ Crores	3	10

APPENDIX U.—(p. 145.)

Reply of Captain Kirkpatrick, through his Moonshee, when informed by Meer Allum of the Nizam's intention to send M. Raymond with his Forces into Kurpah.

"I have communicated your note to Captain Kirkpatrick, who, after desiring me to make his acknowledgments to you for the friendly intimation contained in it, has desired me to say that when he adverts on the one side to the firm friendship and union subsisting between the English Company and his highness, and on the other hand to the novel determination of stationing so large a force on their border, he is utterly at a loss to understand so extraordinary a measure, the more especially as he is not aware that the state of the Kurpah country is such as to require, with a mere view to its settlement, anything like the number of troops proposed to be detached thither. Under these circumstances, he cannot help entertaining a fear that very unfavourable constructions will be put by the world at large on the proceeding in question. Having the most unbounded confidence, however, in the wisdom and foresight of his highness, he instructs me to declare his thorough persuasion that no arrangements will be made on the present occasion but what will be perfectly consonant with sound policy and with the observances due, in all such cases, to the proper maintenance of appearances."

APPENDIX V.—(p. 146.)

Particulars of the Force destined for Kurpah by the Nizam.

"The force which the Nizam proposed to send to Kurpah, after receiving the remonstrance of Captain Kirkpatrick, consisted of the following troops:—5th regiment, commandant Baptiste or Talliade; 7th regiment, commandant De Boigne; 11th regiment, commandant Tardewall; 12th and 13th regiments doubled up, on account of their reduced state, forming at present one corps; 14th regiment, command vacant; each regiment had two field-pieces (from three to six pounders) attached to it. Three hundred men were, it is stated, to proceed from this party to Kummum."

APPENDIX W.—(p. 147.)

Note addressed to Meer Allum by Captain Kirkpatrick, in May, 1795, relative to the Employment of French Officers arriving in the Nizam's Capital from Pondicherry.

"It has lately been reported to me that some of the people of Pondicherry (who, since the capture of that place by the Company, are, agreeably to the laws and usages of Great Britain, to be regarded as living for the present under the authority of his Britannic Majesty,) have arrived in his highness's dominions in search of service. Now, as in such a case (the certainty of which, however, is yet to be established), it is very possible that I might find myself under the necessity of troubling his highness on the subject, I am moved equally by feelings of friendship and prudence to apprise you beforehand of the expediency of his highness's servants proceeding with great circumspection in a matter of such delicacy as that of admitting and employing persons of the description in question would doubtlessly be. Thus, by the seasonable observance of due caution in this business, all future discussion and altercation respecting it would be happily avoided."

APPENDIX X.—(p. 164.)

Letter of Remonstrance on the Occupation of Kurpah by a Detachment of Raymond's Corps, addressed to the Nizam by Sir John Shore, about the end of June or beginning of July, 1795.

"Considering the friendship and alliance subsisting between your highness and the Company, I should have hoped that the representation made to your highness, through Meer Allum, by Captain Kirkpatrick, would have induced you to revoke a measure so evidently liable to the misrepresentation of indicating an unfriendly appearance towards your allies. The principles and disposition of the French are known throughout Hindustan; your highness cannot be ignorant of them, nor unapprised that the English and French nations are at war; and under these circumstances I had a right to expect from your friendship that after the deputation of a large force to a station bordering on the frontiers of the English territories were necessary, your highness would have employed any troops in preference to those commanded by French officers. In the continuance of your highness's friendship, I have the greatest confidence, but external appearances, from which the judgment of the world is formed, should correspond with your real sentiments; and it is evident that the deputation of M. Raymond's corps to a station so near to our frontier may lead to consequences beyond the reach of your highness's immediate control, and to measures as dangerous to the interests of your highness as to those of the Company. I trust, therefore, that your highness, in conformity to the friendship which has so long subsisted between you and the Company, upon full consideration of what I have written, of the representations which Captain Kirkpatrick will communicate by my directions, will gratify me by the recall of the detachment of M. Raymond's corps."

APPENDIX Y.—(p. 169.)

Reply of the Governor General to Captain Kirkpatrick's request for Instructions in the event of the rebel Prince Ally Jah requesting the English Resident to mediate with the Nizam, and to guarantee the fulfilment of whatever Terms might be agreed upon previous to his Surrender.

"The guarantee is entirely incompatible with our situation and principles, and in the event of any application being made to you on the subject, you will state in proper terms the impossibility of our acceding to an obligation of this nature, which might eventually impose upon us the necessity of interfering with our arms for the support of it. At the same time, you should express our earnest desire to see the unfortunate disunion in his highness's family speedily and completely removed; nor do I object to your occasionally using, at a proper opportunity, any argument of a conciliatory nature for the accomplishment of the wished-for accommodation."

APPENDIX Z.—(p. 175.)

Letter addressed to his Highness the Nizam by the Mahratta Durbar, on the occasion of his Son's Rebellion.

"The late occurrences are not of a very embarrassing nature, and at all events we are ready. It is absolutely necessary, however, that the engagements entered into at Kurdlah be fulfilled, and as we understand that since his return from Kurdlah, his highness's inclinations have assumed a different complexion, it is in consequence requisite that he give us on this head some satisfactory proofs of his resolution to abide by them; but mere verbal assurances will not suffice. Let him, therefore, give some money immediately."

APPENDIX A A.—(p. 182.)

Letter from Meer Allum containing his Statement concerning the Capture of the Prince Ally Jah.

"On the 21st Rubbi-ul-sani, we reached the river near Aurungabad, where a pair of hurkurrahs brought letters from Ally Jah, intimating a wish that we should halt on the bank of the river, and set on foot a conference; but not judging it requisite to send any answer, I confined the hurkurrahs, crossed the river, and reached the neighbourhood of the city. At night Ghazi Khan (the villain) and Budda Allah Khan drew out a few thousand horse and foot, but after firing four shot, they retreated precipitately, and the same night evacuated the city. In the morning, a conference having taken place, I sent, in conjunction with other sudars, a Koran to Ally Jah, with an assurance of security to his life and honour on the part of the presence. Preparations were likewise making to bring him into camp, but it being sunset before this could be accomplished, by the advice of Aydur-oo-Dowlah (Mons. Raymond,) it has been postponed till the ensuing morning. During the night parties of horse were posted round the city, and kept continually patrolling around it. In the morning he (Ally Jah) will remove into camp, when by the blessing of God, taking him into my charge, and measuring back the distance, I shall enjoy the happiness of returning to the presence."

APPENDIX B B.—(p. 182.)

Letter addressed to Sir W. Malet, our Resident at Poonah, by Captain Kirkpatrick, on the subject of the Mahratta Succession, in consequence of the Peishwa's Death.

"The present conjuncture is, no doubt, extremely critical for the state, since not only its future relations with respect to your court, but as far as they may be supposed to operate in such a case, the future colour also of its connection with our Government, depend, in no inconsiderable degree, on the conduct of the Nizam in the affair of the succession to the Peishwaship. Whether or not he has yet taken his resolution on this head is more than I will venture to say, though if I were to judge either by the urgency of the occasion, or by certain appearances which have recently occurred, I should be inclined to conclude in the affirmative. It is to be lamented, perhaps, that Meer Allum should have been absent at so momentous a period, since he is unquestionably the wisest as well as the most disinterested of his highness's counsellors, if not, indeed, the only one among them capable of discerning the course most proper to be pursued by his master under circumstances of equal difficulty and importance. I say *perhaps*, because although he had been present, it is by no means clear that his opinions would have prevailed if they had happened rather to differ from those of the Roy Royan or to oppose the secret inclination of his highness himself. The influence of Meer Allum was far from being of a fixed or predominating nature previous to his late expedition, nor is it certain that it will be ultimately increased by this service, though its successful termination appeared to have procured him much additional credit with the Nizam. Yet it is easy to perceive that the duration of it will become very precarious, should he strenuously resist the meditated disgrace of Ally Jah, which Mustakin Dowlah declares he has no doubt of his doing.

"There are, probably, very few princes or states upon

earth who would not prefer the pursuit of self-security—when this might be deemed at stake—to the suggestions both of dignity and generosity. But however this may be, it is not difficult, I think, to conceive what the election of the Nizam is likely (not to say certain) to be on such an occasion. In the present case, indeed, his Highness's determination may be reasonably supposed to be governed, not only by the prospect of danger presented in the succession of Bajee Row, but by the hope of immediate advantage, by supporting Ballajee Pundit in his attempt to supersede the rights of that prince. Of the nature of these advantages I can form a clearer idea than of their probable extent, though it may, I imagine, be safely presumed that they embrace at least the remission of a very considerable part of his Highness's present debt to the Mahratta Government."

APPENDIX C C.—(p. 187.)

Letter from Meer Allum to the Resident, reporting his Conversation with the Mahratta Vakeel, on the subject of the proposed Mission to Poonah.

"Govind Kishen yesterday paid me a visit to inquire after my health, when he said that as now in a week's time I should recover sufficient strength, I had only to pay my respects to his highness, and be despatched to Poonah. To this I replied: 'It is evident I shall not be capable of travelling in a week, but am I a hindrance to your departure? There is no want of trustworthy, well-affected persons in this state.' 'Where is there,' he asked, 'another like yourself, able, trustworthy, and well-inclined?' 'You' (said I to Govind Kishen) 'who importune me to go to Poonah, first hear, and answer what I have now to say to you! Whether his highness sends me or any one else, his view is to obtain certain advantages. Now, if you will pledge yourself solemnly to me to send me back completely to his highness's satisfaction, I will tell you what he wants in a few words: that you will relinquish the three crores of rupees for which you took a written engagement from him, and that you restore to him the country you made him lately cede. Now, if these objects are unattainable, it is perfectly equal whether I go or not. Were I to go, his highness, relying on my abilities and attachment to him, would immediately flatter himself that I should certainly accomplish his views, so that if I were to return unsuccessful, how mortifying would it be to me to show my face in his presence.' Govind Kishen observed that it would not become his highness's dignity to give utterance to such thoughts. 'True,' replied I, 'he will not give utterance to them, but they are nevertheless his secret sentiments. I do not positively demand a written engagement on the subject from you; all I require is a strong and positive verbal promise that you will not dismiss me from Poonah without fulfilling my wishes, and upon this condition I am ready to accompany you thither.' To this Govind Kishen gave no answer, but remained rapt in silence. After this, I observed that these were merely my private sentiments which were of no avail, but that whatever was ordered from the presence would alone be of weight."

APPENDIX D D.—(p. 193.)

Despatch from the Resident at Hyderabad to the Governor General, on occasion of the Nizam's Illness, in February, 1796, showing the situation of Affairs at that time.

"The day before yesterday a guard was placed over the house of Secunder Jah, a measure that is differently accounted for; some attributing it to his mother's anxiety to provide for his personal safety against the machinations of the partisans of Feridoon Jah, while the general and more probable opinion seems to be, that it was occasioned by the discovery of some intrigues which he had set on foot with Monsieur Raymond and others, and which are pretended to have indicated too great an impatience to profit by the death of his father. The heads of the party supposed to be favourable to the pretensions of Feridoon Jah, are Mohammed Azim Khan, Ghazi Meah, Zuffur-oo-Dowlah, Salabat Khan, Kassim-oo-Dowlah (Aruzbeggie), Suzzawur-ool-Moolk, and Rajah Jade Singh, all of them among the principal Oomrahs of this state. It is even imagined by some that the Roy Royan is half inclined to connect himself to this faction.

"Imtiaz-oo-Dowlah, on the other hand, is said to be disposed in favour of Akbar Jah, the younger maternal brother of Secunder Jah, and betrothed to the daughter of Imtiaz-oo-Dowlah, whose views, however, would not seem at present likely to be seconded by any great weight of interest at this court.

"Assud Ali Khan, who proceeded some time since for his Talook, has in consequence of his highness's illness expressed a desire to be allowed to repair to court, to which his highness is said to have signified his dissent.

"Mons. Raymond arrived here this morning from Maiduk with one of his regiments that accompanied him thither, and was received in his own cantonment under a royal salute.

"It cannot be doubted that the Frenchman stands in a situation which enables him, in the event of the Nizam's death, to raise whom he pleases to the vacant musnud. It is not so certain, however, that he is of a character to act with the promptitude and decision which would be necessary to the success of such an undertaking.

"The heads of some of the inferior departments of Government having represented that, owing to his highness's sickness, the business of their offices was at a stand, and having suggested the necessity of the nomination of a delegate, ad interim, to give the usual stamp of authority to their proceedings, it is expected that his highness will name the Roy

Royan for this purpose. I am told, however, he has hitherto declined making any answer to the application.

"I am just informed that a guard has been placed by the advice of the Roy Royan over the house of Sumbah Chund, the Peshcar or Dewan of Secunder Jah. Strict orders are likewise said to be given to the usual guards of all the princes, including Nasir-ool-Moolk, to prevent the access of improper persons to them."

APPENDIX E E.—(page 198).

Despatch addressed by Captain Kirkpatrick to the Governor General, May 1st, 1796, *relative to the growing Cordiality between the Nizam and the Sultan of Mysore, the Political Objects kept in view by Tippoo, and the Supremacy acquired by the French in the State of Hyderabad.*

"I purpose to lay before you such reflections as have been suggested to me by the latest view which I have taken of the growing correspondence between the Nizam and Tippoo Sultan. I have always thought it of importance in the consideration of this matter, to bear in mind, that it was not until the removal of Azim-ool-oomrah from the direction of the affairs of this state, that Tippoo began to manifest any disposition towards an interchange of even the most ordinary civilities with his highness, and that no sooner had this event occurred, than he appeared to be abundantly ready to avail himself of the very first occasion that presented for renewing the intercourse which had heretofore subsisted between the two courts. It is true that a design hostile to our interests, and involving the appearance of some sort of secret understanding with Tippoo, was at one time imputed to Azim-ool-oomrah, and what is still more probable, is, that the latter may really, in the difficult conjuncture alluded to, have made overtures to a closer connection with that prince, for the purpose of strengthening himself, as much as possible, against the Mahrattas. But whatever reason there may be for attributing such projects to the late minister, there has never been any reason for believing that his advances in either case were favourably received by Tippoo. On the contrary, if the latter was preparing, or inclined to take any active share at all in the war kindled last year between the Peishwa and the Nizam, by their respective ministers, there is most positive, as well as deducible, ground for suspecting that he meant at a fit period to have thrown his weight into the scale of the former.

"These reflections, if just, leading to the conclusion that the shyness (for there was not probably any absolute repugnance in the case) shown by Tippoo, during the administration of Azim-ool-oomrah, to the cultivation of an amicable intercourse with this state, sprung from causes having reference to that minister exclusively, and little or perhaps none to the Nizam himself (as I always, I own, have been most inclined to think). It is in the next place of importance to determine the nature of these causes, a knowledge of which will help us considerably to discover how far we are likely to be immediately concerned in, or hereafter affected by, the change that has taken place in the deportment of the two courts towards each other since the removal of Azim-ool-oomrah.

"It seems to me, then, that there are only two motives of adequate cogency to which we can ascribe the former backwardness of Tippoo to enter into any correspondence with this court. One of these is that inveterate personal antipathy to the late minister, which it is not difficult to believe he may have conceived towards the man, who, losing sight (as he would be ready to judge) of the common interests of Islamism, had strenuously employed the influence he possessed over the mind of his master, not only in estranging him from, but in drawing him into a league against, a cause which he ought rather to have excited him to espouse. The other is his entertaining so full a persuasion of Azim-ool-oomrah's entire devotion to the connection which he has been so active in cementing between the Nizam and the Company, as amounted to a despair of ever being able, while the councils of his highness continued to be guided by that minister, to gain any ground at this court of the kind and tendency to which he would be most likely to direct his views. I scarcely need add that I allude to the undermining of the union subsisting between us and his highness, which, however slowly or indeterminately prosecuted, will always, it may be safely presumed, constitute the ultimate object of his intrigues in this state. Nor would the force of the persuasion upon which I am here reasoning have been liable to be much affected, even by Azim-ool-oomrah's supposed plan of a triple confederacy against the Company; since though such a proposal should really have been made to Tippoo, yet that prince, on duly weighing the several circumstances attending it, might well suspect its sincerity, if not its insidiousness, without incurring the imputation either of a vain refinement, or of an overstrained distrust.

"Of these two modes of explaining the conduct of Tippoo in the particular point in question, I own the latter appears to me to be the best entitled to the preference. Ambitious princes are rarely known to allow the gratification of personal dislikes to impede the pursuit of what they consider to be their interests, and there would not seem to be any trace in the character of the Sultan to warrant the assumption that he would be any exception to so very general a rule.

"The sudden extinction of Azim-ool-oomrah's ministry, combined with the early solicitude of his virtual successor in office and authority to open a correspondence with Tippoo, was doubtlessly much more favourable to the supposable views and wishes of this prince, than he could a short time before have reasonably hoped for. It must nevertheless be allowed that he did not profit by the conjuncture in the manner or to the extent which might have been expected, since he was far from availing himself of the occasion to establish at this court such an agent as was qualified to render him any material service, whether as an intriguer or a spy; while with regard to the particular conciliation of the Nizam, and the formation of new engagements between the two states, if they were not at this time altogether out of the contemplation of the Sultan, they must at least have been unconnected with the objects of his first deputation. I am, for this reason, as well as on some other grounds, inclined to believe that whatever advances he may have received from the Roy Royan, they were neither of so definite nor of so unreserved a nature as to encourage him to risk the commitment of himself in any material degree, or to preclude the necessity of his proceeding by slow and cautious steps. His appointment of Sukkaram Pundit may in this case be well enough accounted for by supposing him to have discovered that matters were not yet rife enough for his selecting an abler or more confidential instrument, or for pursuing his designs by any other than by a circuitous route, and therefore to have judged it expedient to content himself at the commencement of his operations, with the agency of a person who, if not expressly proposed to him for this purpose by the Roy Royan, would, he knew, be at least sufficiently agreeable to that minister. And in fact there is abundant reason to believe that this correspondence, originally planned by the Roy Royan, and perhaps too countenanced by the Nizam (for it is by no means certain that his highness was privy to the preliminary movements of his minister in the matter,) under the first impressions of that mortification and resentment excited by the disgraceful and disastrous issue of the Mahratta war, was not entered into even at the outset with any determinate or well-considered view—and if the object of it was vague and unsettled in the beginning, when the passions which had given birth to the project were at their height, it seems to have become more and more so, according as the heat of these was allayed by time and other intervening circumstances. Thus, at one period, the hope of obtaining a considerable abatement of its pecuniary claims from the Mahratta government (a hope which even Meer Allum did not regard as altogether visionary), at another the favourable prospect opened by the discussion following the death of the Peishwa, and sometimes a speculation on the probable advantages derivable from an union with Balaji Pundit, would, by diminishing the force of the original inducement to a connection with Tippoo, be each in its turn sufficient to render such a statesman as the Roy Royan extremely cool and remiss in the cultivation of it. On the other hand, when none of the motives to a suspension of his ardour in this pursuit happened to operate, he would naturally enough resume, as he had not yet any intention of dropping it.

"This fluctuating policy, however, cannot be supposed to have escaped the observation of Tippoo, who, though he should neither be disgusted nor incensed at it, can hardly fail to be in some measure both disappointed and discouraged by an indecision so obstructive to his desire of raising his importance, and firmly fixing his influence at this court.

"But whatever obstacles may oppose themselves to his suddenly or extensively improving the footing he has already acquired here, he will most probably be found patient enough to persevere in maintaining it. In the meanwhile, it is not to be expected that he will be content to sacrifice to the uncertain and distant fruits of his present correspondence with the Nizam, any advantages that he may perceive to be derivable either from the domestic divisions or the foreign embarrassments of this state. Rumour has wronged him, if, very soon after deputing Sukkaram Pundit hither, he did not commence an intrigue with Ally Jah, then in arms against his father, and there are still stronger grounds for believing that he has since clandestinely encouraged another member of his Highness's family openly to resist his authority. Nor is it unlikely he would have gone much farther on both occasions, if he had not been restrained by the apprehension of embroiling himself prematurely with us.

"Although there has never been the least room to imagine that either the Roy Royan or his master entertained any thoughts of an hostile nature to the Company at the period of their first embarking in the correspondence under consideration, yet it was always, I conceived, to be apprehended that whatever new engagements the Nizam, with an eye to his Mahratta neighbours, might be induced to contract with Tippoo, they would necessarily be but too likely to lead to an interruption of the friendship subsisting between his highness and us. But besides the natural tendency of such an intercourse, the danger of it was not a little aggravated by two circumstances of an extrinsic and accidental kind, to which it will be proper to revert.

"The first of these respects the character and dispositions of the new minister, in whom I have never been able to perceive the least appearance of predilection in our favour, while, in point of political wisdom, he is most deplorably deficient, displaying, even in the conduct of the most important affairs, no other than the contracted views of a peddling Mootsuddee. It is plain that such a man, besides being incapable of really estimating the value of our friendship, must be extremely liable to conceive, or to be drawn into measures, the probable result of which it will be beyond his capacity to calculate. I would not in this case be supposed to mean (having, indeed, no sufficient ground for thinking) that the Roy Royan has at any time shown a positive or direct indisposition towards us. The general tenor, however, of his conduct, as far as we have been concerned in it, has certainly indicated much indifference for our sentiments, and no solicitude at all to improve or strengthen the union of the two Governments. This coldness has been occasioned, perhaps, in some degree by his jealousy and hatred of Meer Allum, from whom it may have reflected itself, if I may so speak, upon ourselves.

"It is also possible that it may have been partly infused into him by Govind Kishen, with whom he seems to have drawn very closely ever since the death of the late Peishwa.

"The next source of the additional anxiety which has been alluded to, presented itself in the French quarter, because were Raymond to perceive any strong probability of the arrival of a powerful armament from France, it was reasonable to suppose that he would be but too ready to encourage and forward a connection which he saw the Roy Royan sufficiently disposed to establish, and by which the interests or designs of his own nation would be so likely to be promoted. Excepting, however, in this hope and with this view, there seems but little room for imputing to him any desire to see the Nizam embroiled with the Company; even his present limited and shackled intercourse with the Carnatic is on more accounts than one an object of too much importance to him to be sacrificed lightly without considerable reluctance. What I take, however, to operate as an infinitely stronger restraint upon him in this particular, is a consciousness of his utter incompetency, unsupported by an invasion of the Carnatic from Europe, to meet us in the field, without greatly hazarding the ruin of his personal fortune.

"It will be perceived that the considerations suggested in the two preceding paragraphs are as applicable to present as to past circumstances, nor will they indeed lose any part of their force, so long as the councils of this state continue to be guided by such a wretched minister as the Roy Royan, and there remains any chance of the French being able to make a serious attempt on any of our possessions on either coast. It is an encouraging reflection, however, in this case, that every day would seem to add to our security from such an event.

"I have sometimes, in revolving the subject of the present address in my mind, been ready to imagine, if possible, that one of the views of this court, in manifesting a disposition to be upon cordial terms with Tippoo, might be to inculcate the necessity of our contributing effectually to the protection of his highness from the encroachments of the Mahrattas, if we did wish to see him throw himself, for this very purpose, into the arms of that prince. Be this, however, as it may, it is not, I think, to be questioned that the Nizam would much rather desire this support from the Company than from Tippoo. On the other hand, should he be again hard pressed by the Mahrattas (of which there appears to be just now no small danger), it must be admitted to be extremely likely (whatever may be thought of the policy of the proceeding) that after some fruitless endeavours to engage us in his quarrel, he will apply himself seriously to obtain the assistance of the Sultan.

"But, although he should be driven to this extremity, I am far from thinking the compliance of Tippoo to be a matter of course; for, without insisting on the hesitation he might feel to unite with this against the Mahratta state, on account of the uncertainty he would probably be under in regard to our sense of such a proceeding, and supposing him to surmount or to disregard this difficulty, it is to be recollected that the face of things at this court is become very different, in consequence of the dangerous sickness with which the Nizam is afflicted from what it was a few months ago. This event has already produced such cabals as may well satisfy Tippoo that the death of his highness can scarcely fail to be followed by a contested succession.

"Under these circumstances, he may probably perceive the expediency of meeting any advances from hence to an offensive union against the Mahrattas, however alluring they should be, with considerable circumspection and reserve, lest the sudden demise of his new ally should, by bringing about a total change in the politics of this court, at once exclude him from all the advantages of which he was in pursuit, and leave him simply exposed to the resentment of a powerful neighbour, now aided possibly by the very state in support of which he had taken up arms. Such, indeed, are the consequences which he might reasonably enough apprehend from the succession of Secunder Jah, who, influenced by Azim-ool-oomrah and his partisans at this court, would most likely be eager to enter into any accommodation which should have the effect of restoring that minister to his freedom and former functions.

"On the other hand, by remaining entirely disengaged, by waiting patiently the death of the Nizam, and by placing himself in the interim in a suitable situation for profiting according to circumstances by that event, he would stand a still better chance of acquiring the sort of influence in this state, to which I suppose him to aspire, than by means of any connection to which the temporary embarrassments of a Prince, ready to descend to the grave, might invite him.

"On the present state of the intercourse between Tippoo and the Nizam, a few words, after what has been said of its past and general complexion, will suffice. Its object most probably is the same as ever on the side of his highness, with this difference perhaps, that he may just now, in consideration of the danger which threatens him from the Poonah quarter, be rather more bent upon the serious pursuit of it than heretofore, and it is at least certain that the Roy Royan has of late been at more than usual pains to give such an air to their correspondence as may create an universal belief of its teeming with momentous consequences on the part of Tippoo. However, it may be doubted, for the reasons I suggested above, whether he has at present any other view in maintaining two agents at this court (apparently unconnected with each other), besides that of ascertaining through their means the state of parties and opinions on the grand question of the succession. As to either of them having authority to pledge this prince to the support of any particular faction or candidate, or to negotiate any other important affair, or even to declare his sentiments or opinions on any point of magnitude, except in a very vague and general way, I confess myself strongly inclined to believe in the negative. But while I avow this notion, it is proper I should add, that I found it almost entirely upon the apparent insufficiency of both these envoys to the management of such weighty and delicate concerns.

"The prejudices of the Roy Royan oppose considerable difficulty to the free interchange of sentiments between me and the Nizam, for it is rarely that Meer Allum thinks proper to pass him by in addressing his master on English affairs. It must therefore be a very strong case that would enable me to insinuate any useless alarm or distrust in his highness's mind, with regard to the secret views of Tippoo in his present correspondence with him, since the minister would, at any rate, probably endeavour to render my motives to the communication suspected. I shall not be inattentive, however, to any favourable occasion that may offer for inspiring his highness with that degree of jealous watchfulness which is reasonably due to every operation and movement of so restless and designing a neighbour.

"I consider with you, honourable Sir, the exorbitant weight which the French have acquired in this state, as a much more serious evil than the growing intercourse between the Nizam and Tippoo, because while this last is obnoxious to many checks, the other would appear to be placed beyond the reach of any attempts that could now be made for its subversion. Meer Allum contends, indeed, that the means were at one time in our hands, alluding to the Nizam's project of officering a new levy of men with British subjects, and to the applications made to us, during the rebellion of Ally Jah, for the assistance of a few extra battalions, in addition to the detachment stipulated for by treaty; the combined effects of which measures would soon have appeared (as he pretends) in the gradual decline, and ultimately in the complete annihilation, of the French influence and force."

APPENDIX F F.—(p. 218).

Letter from Azim-ool-oomrah to the Nizam relative to Tippoo Sultan's claim on the Nawab of Kurnool, which, at the time, he was about to enforce by recourse to arms.

"What passed between Mr. Utthoff and me on the day he came to see me respecting Kurnool, was as follows:—

"I observed, on occasion of Tippoo's army and his intention of employing it to enforce payment of what he claims from Kurnool, being mentioned, that when the treaty of Seringapatam was concluded, Sir John Kennaway on the part of the Company, Govind Rao Bugwunt and Buckajie Pundit Murdla on the part of Rao Pundit Perdham, and Meer Allum on the part of his highness, were present; that on Tippoo's delivering in the statement of his country through Ali Reza Khan and Gholam Ali Khan, and on its being noticed that two lacs of rupees on account of Kurnool Peshcush were included in the same, it had been urged that if a document of the engagement made under the seal of the late Mohammed Runmust was produced, the allies would in that case, taking their own share of the same, make an arrangement for his (Tippoo's) share thereof, and that to this Ali Reza Khan had replied that there *was* such an instrument under the seal of the said deceased in the Dufter, which should be produced.

"I next observed that I fancied that these two lacs of rupees thus claimed by Tippoo had not been divided (as the rest of Tippoo's possessions) by the allies; that at this date it was incumbent on the Company and the Peishwa's ministers to state the matter as above to Tippoo Sultan, and to call upon him to produce the aforesaid document; and that if it should in consequence be produced, an arrangement would be made; but that if it was not produced, he (Tippoo) must desist from his claims.

"Mr. Utthoff replied that nothing of this was written in

the treaty of Seringapatam. I rejoined that if it was not so written, there were nevertheless credible witnesses of the matter forthcoming. I then proceeded to state that there were three ways of settling this affair; that the first of them was to call upon Tippoo to produce the document in question; that the second was, that the allies, after deducting their own share (a moiety) of the said two lacs, should provide for Tippoo's remaining share (or moiety) of one lac, by each of them assigning over to Tippoo, from their respective territories, a country of 33,300 and odd rupees, and afterwards adjusting the matter to their mutual satisfaction among themselves; that the third mode was, for some one of the three allies, according as might be agreed upon, to assign over to Tippoo a country of one lac of rupees, the three allies afterwards settling the matter among themselves, so that an end might be put to this dispute, which would otherwise, one day or other, operate to the disturbance of existing treaties. Mr. Utthoff did not give a decisive answer to this, waiting probably to hear from Sir C. Malet and the Governor of Madras on the subject. To-day being Friday, the 19th of Rubbi Sani, Fukhrad-oo-Deen Hussain Khan coming to me from Mr. Utthoff, discoursed upon certain matters which shall be communicated hereafter, when I gave such answers to the same as I thought proper, and as soon as I receive his reply, the particulars shall be imparted. On this occasion I sent word to Mr. Utthoff, that the Company and Rao Pundit Perdham did not set their hearts on an adjustment of the Kurnool business, so that if Tippoo's army passed his highness's boundary for the purpose of enforcing his claims, his highness's ministers would be obliged to take one or other of these two courses: namely, either they would send a force to repel the attempt of Tippoo, or if any circumstance existed to render this measure inconvenient, they would try to amuse Tippoo as well as they could (in the original, *Dar Mudár*). Now in either of these cases, I observed, the allies would no doubt be ready to reproach his highness, but then reproach would be of no use, because having been advertised of the matter beforehand, and having neglected to attend to it, they could afterwards have no right to expect his highness to pay regard to their reproaches on the subject. When I get Mr. Utthoff's answer to this, I shall give the same notice to Purseram Pundit."

APPENDIX G G.—(p. 217.)

Two Letters received at Hyderabad, August the 21st, 1797, through Row Hurryhur Row, a Mootsuddy at Cabool, from the Court of Zeman Shah. The First inscribed: "From Mohammed Munsoor Khan, son of Shah Wullee Khan, the Wuzeer of Ahmed Shah Doorany, to Azim-ool-oomrah.

"When you were at Poonah, his majesty (Zeman Shah) turned his arms towards Lahore for the purpose of extirpating those heretics the Sikhs, and settling the districts of Lahore and the Punjaub, &c., and a rukkum (letters from Zeman Shah are so termed) was prepared for the Nawaub Asuf Jah, and a letter from the Nawaub Sheer Mohammed Khan, my elder brother, to you, under their proper seals. But in consequence of your absence at Poonah, a *copy* of the rukkum was, with the advice of Row Hurryhur Row, transmitted to his highness the Nawaub, and an answer was waited for, when sudden intelligence reached his majesty from Cabool, that Aga Mohammed Khan Kutchen was committing disturbances; upon which his majesty immediately set out on his return, leaving the Sikhs as before in the possession of the country; but they, seeing their opportunity, slew Ahmed Khan Shahmshy Banshy, and plundered his baggage. In the meantime, his majesty having settled matters with Mohammed Khan Kutchen, intends to march again into the Punjaub, &c. countries, after the rainy season is over, which will shortly be. In consequence of your having now returned to Hyderabad, I write to you for the purpose of communicating this intention, and it has been intimated by his majesty and the Nawaub Sheer Mohammed Khan, that if it be your pleasure to establish a friendship with his majesty, on your communicating the same, a letter will be sent, and an answer required, which you will transmit. I therefore beg leave to state that, prior to this, an answer to this subject addressed to the Row above mentioned, acknowledging the receipt of the copy of his majesty's rukkum, was received here, which specified that an Aigdasht would subsequently be transmitted, and contained a request that he (Row Hurry) would arrange the business; now if it be his highness the Nawaub's pleasure to adjust his affairs, you will speak to him and present the letter which I now send to his highness's address, and do me the favour to transmit a reply, when I will send the original rukkum, which is yet with me. But I have to request that the answer to that also may be sent through me, as it will improve my consequence with his majesty and the Nawaub Sheer Mohammed Khan. You will reflect well on the answer to these points, and intimate it to me, as I am anxious for its arrival.

"In consequence of the length of time required for an answer to arrive from that quarter, and to be transmitted from hence through Lahore to Cabool, I have given you this early intimation. I hope for a favourable reply."

The Second Letter, delivered at the same time as the foregoing, was addressed to the Nizam.

"Prior to this, when his majesty was at Lahore, I transmitted the copy of a rukkum from his majesty, the original of which is with me, together with a letter from myself through Row Hurryhur Row, and I learned in answer verbally from the said Row, that your highness is disposed to adjust this system (of alliance). I, on my part, was from the bottom of my heart solicitous to bring it about. In the meantime, however, his majesty, after humbling the Sikhs and exterminating the obstinate, on hearing of the disturbances in Cabool, Mohammed Khan Kutchen having excited commotions, returned, and no answer was sent from that quarter. Not thinking it proper to press the point, I left it to another opportunity. Now that the rainy season approaches, it is his Majesty's resolution to settle the surrounding countries and proceed to extirpate the Sikhs, and he will shortly return (to the Punjaub) from Cabool. As a long time must elapse ere an answer can be received, I give your highness this early intimation. If your highness be disposed to arrange this new system (of alliance), be pleased to let me know, that I may forward his majesty's rukkum. But I hope that your highness will honour me by transmitting your answer through *me*, as it will procure me consequence among my equals and with his majesty, and add to Sheer Mohammed Khan's confidence in me; or else be pleased to inform me, that I may act accordingly."

APPENDIX H H.—(pp. 218 & 222.)

Despatch of the Earl of Mornington, after his Arrival in India to assume the functions of Governor General, containing an Exposition of the State of Affairs at that time, and showing the importance of depriving the French of all Influence in the Councils of the Nizam and of Scindiah.

"I transmit you an authentic copy of a proclamation by the Governor General of the Isle of France, during the residence of two ambassadors from Tippoo Sultan on that island. The proclamation purports to be a declaration of certain propositions communicated to the French Government in the name of Tippoo Sultan by his ambassador then on the spot.

"2. It enumerates those propositions with a particularity of detail which would not have been hazarded in the presence of the ambassadors, had it not corresponded with the substance of the communication made by them to the French Government.

"3. In addition to the arguments founded on the nature of the proclamation, and to the fact of its promulgation under the eyes of the ambassadors, I am in possession of evidence which leaves no doubt on my mind of the concurrence of the ambassadors in every part of the proclamation, and I cannot suppose that they would have ventured to exceed the limits of their instructions from Tippoo Sultan in a matter of such serious importance as the conclusion of offensive and defensive engagements with the French Government. Under this proclamation, one hundred officers and fifty privates were actually raised in the Mauritius for the service of Tippoo and for the purposes avowed in the proclamation, and that force has since been landed at Mangalore, and received into Tippoo's army with peculiar marks of honour and distinction. This circumstance is sufficient to prove that the proceedings of the ambassadors have obtained the sanction of their sovereign, who has thus confirmed and avowed the propositions made through them to the enemy by a solemn public and personal act. Having thus entered into an offensive and defensive alliance with the French Government, having collected in conjunction with that Government a force openly destined to act against the British possessions, having avowed through his public ambassadors that he has actually made preparations of war for the express purpose of attempting the subversion of the British power in India, and having declared that he only waits the effectual assistance of France to prosecute his designs, Tippoo Sultan has violated the treaties of peace and friendship subsisting between him and the Company, and has committed a direct act of hostility against the British power in India.

"That he has yet obtained no formidable assistance from the enemy is undoubtedly a fortunate circumstance for the British interests; but the temerity and consequent ill-success of his councils in no degree palliates the offensive nature of an aggression so unprovoked, and of a violation of faith so public and so undisguised. It is not improbable that he may still expect to receive a more effectual succour from the French, but there is every reason to hope that any attempt to furnish him with assistance from that quarter would be frustrated by the vigilance and superior power of his Majesty's fleets.

"It is, however, difficult to ascertain the precise motives which may stimulate the violence of his temper to action, and his late embassy to the Mauritius is a sufficient proof that revenge against the British nation in India is an object he is capable of pursuing with more zeal than discretion.

"Under such circumstances it is prudent to be prepared to repel the attack which he has openly menaced, and as our future security, our reputation, and our honour demand that he should be reduced to the alternative of making such satisfaction to the allies as they may hereafter require for the injury he has committed, or of risking another contest with the British power, it is advisable to arm for the purpose of supporting whatever requisition we may deem it necessary to make to him, when our respective preparations shall be sufficiently advanced to enable us to act with effect.

"The 13th article of the Treaty of Poonah provides that if Tippoo should molest or attack either of the contracting parties, the others shall join to punish him, the modes and conditions of which shall be hereafter settled by the three contracting parties; and the declaration of the Durbar of Poonah of the 3rd July, 1793, explanatory of the article, states, if a breach of engagement occurs on the part of Tippoo with respect to either of the allies, let that ally advise the other allies thereof, when, having understood the said breach of engagement, he will admonish him. And if he does not attend to the admonition, then let the states act agreeably to the treaties which have been formed.

"Adverting to your letter of the 1st of June, I take the occasion to declare, that Bajee Row could not be justified in attempting to evade the obligation contracted by the Peishwa under this article. The defensive stipulations in the treaty of triple alliance must be presumed to have been intended by the contracting powers to operate, not as a personal but as real engagements binding the three states, and not merely the persons whose names are inserted in the treaty. Upon established principles of public faith, the obligations of the article in question must therefore be deemed to pass to the Peishwa for the time being, although the treaty does not expressly include the heirs and successors of the prince whose signature it bears. In 1796, when an application for co-operation against Tippoo was made under the same article by this Government to Chimna Appa, then holding the office of Peishwa, the idea of the defensive obligations of the treaty being merely personal to Madhoo Rao was never suggested, and Chimna Appa united without hesitation in the first representation then made to Tippoo by the allies.

" The objection, therefore, is unsupported by the practice of the court of Poonah in the only case which has yet arisen with relation to that court under the article in question. But even if the practice of the court of Poonah had been different in this instance, it never could be admitted to derogate from a known and fundamental maxim of the law of nations, 'that treaties of a defensive nature (unless limited in express terms) are not merely personal contracts with the reigning prince, but permanent obligations binding the faith of the state, into whatever hands the supreme power may devolve.' I therefore desire that you will immediately communicate to the Peishwa in a formal manner the accompanying proclamation, and explain to him the nature of the propositions which it contains. You will also notify to him the landing of the French force at Mangalore, and declare to him in my name that I consider the whole transaction as a violation of treaty, and a direct act of hostility on the part of Tippoo, and that I claim the assistance and co-operation of the Peishwa under the 13th article of the treaty of Poonah. You will, however, add, that although I should feel myself completely justified in making an immediate attack upon the territories of Tippoo, my disposition to preserve the tranquillity of India induces me in the first instance to afford him an opportunity of restraining the excess of his violence before it shall have involved him in the calamity of war. With this view, you will signify to the Peishwa my wish that he should now express his disposition to concur with the Nizam and with us in making a demand of satisfaction from Tippoo; the nature and extent of the demand, and the time of making it, to be hereafter concerted between the allies. You will inform him that a similar application has been made to the Nizam, and as soon as the Peishwa shall have signified his concurrence in the proposition made to him, on this part of the subject, you will notify the event by express to the Resident at Hyderabad. The Resident at Hyderabad will be directed to communicate to you the progress of his proceeding at that court, under the instructions which he will have received from me. For your full information and guidance, I transmit to you a copy of these instructions. If Tippoo, in the career of his ungovernable passions, should refuse to make the satisfaction which shall be demanded of him by the allies, hostilities will become inevitable, and you will signify to the Peishwa that I have already taken the necessary precaution of assembling the forces of the Company with a view to that event, entertaining no doubt that in such a contingency the Peishwa will be ready to afford to the common cause of the allies the effectual co-operation of the Mahratta force.

"Although I have thought it expedient to communicate my instructions to you in the foregoing order, I am sensible that their effectual execution will be impracticable unless some previous measures be taken for restoring the Government of Poonah to that degree of power which it possessed before the death of the late Peishwa, and I entirely concur with you in lamenting the distractions which, besides dividing and weakening the state, have subjected it to the undue influence of

Scindiah, and nearly disqualified it for affording us the assistance which we are entitled to claim by a treaty in any war with Tippoo.

"In considering the actual situation of the government of Poonah, it is necessary to advert also to that of the other ally, whose co-operation it was equally the object of the same treaty to secure to us in the same event.

"The present crisis demands a serious and dispassionate review of the relative interests of the powers united by treaty for the purpose of securing an effectual barrier against the inordinate ambition and implacable revenge of Tippoo Sultan.

"It has been painful to observe that since the conclusion of the treaty of Seringapatam, two great branches of the triple alliance have been engaged in mutual contests, the result of which has terminated in their mutual weakness, while the common enemy has remained at rest, improved his resources, and increased his strength. The unfortunate animosity between the courts of Poonah and Hyderabad, while it has tended to foment and aggravate the distractions in the former court, has contributed to reduce the latter to the lowest degree of weakness and humiliation. In the meanwhile the French faction at the court of Hyderabad has grown to so formidable a degree of power, as to control, on many important occasions, the councils of the state, and to menace an ascendant influence in the eventual succession to the throne of the Nizam. Although the death of Mons. Raymond, and the resumption of the Jaghire which had been granted to him, have in some degree reduced the political influence of the French army at Hyderabad, it now forms the only efficient part of the Nizam's military strength; its numbers have been lately increased, its discipline considerably improved, and it possesses sufficient activity and power to attempt and to accomplish objects of the most prejudicial nature to the interests of the court of Hyderabad, to the common interests of the Nizam and the Peishwa, as well as those of the British nation in India.

"In the event of a war with Mysore there can be no doubt that the wishes and interests of this part of the Nizam's army must be favourable to the cause of Tippoo Sultan, more especially under the actual circumstance of his having concluded an alliance with the French, and having admitted a body of French troops into his service.

"If the French troops of the Nizam did not afford Tippoo open assistance, at least they could not be brought into the field against him without the utmost danger to the cause of the allies, nor could they be suffered to remain in the Deccan during the continuance of the contest unless checked by the presence of an equally powerful force, which must in that case be diverted from the common object of the war, and must operate as a positive diminution of our effective strength in the field. It appears, however, nearly certain that in the present weak state of the Nizam's Government, the French corps in his service would openly join Tippoo Sultan, and by a sudden blow endeavour to seize the Nizam's territories, and secure them to the dominions of France under an alliance, offensive and defensive, with Tippoo Sultan. It is scarcely necessary to observe, that the success of such a design must be highly injurious to the interests of the court of Poonah, especially when it is considered that it must be the interest and inclination of Scindiah (who entertains a large body of infantry in his service under the command of French officers) to engage with Tippoo Sultan and the French, upon conditions fatal to the existence of the Peishwa's authority and even to his office; the junction which might thus be effected between the French officers with their several corps in the respective services of the Nizam, of Scindiah, and of Tippoo, might establish the power of the French in India, on the ruin of the states of Poonah and of the Deccan. The court of Hyderabad, therefore, in its present condition is more likely to prove the source of additional strength to the common enemy of the Nizam, of the Peishwa, and of the Company, than to afford useful assistance to any branch of the triple alliance.

"I rely upon your ability, experience, and zeal for the public service to state with every degree of advantage, the arguments of prudence and policy which should induce the Peishwa to view the restoration of the Nizam to a just degree of consideration and power, as an object intimately connected with the Peishwa's own emancipation from the undue influence by which he is now oppressed, as well as with his future security against the violence of Tippoo Sultan and of Scindiah.

"If the Peishwa can be made sensible of his real interest in the destruction of the French party at Hyderabad, he cannot view with jealousy or suspicion any assistance which I may think it advisable to afford to the court of Hyderabad for that desirable purpose. The same train of reflection will lead him to acknowledge the benefit which must result to all parties by accepting my arbitration between the courts of Poonah and Hyderabad and Scindiah, for the amicable adjustment of all subsisting difficulties upon the permanent basis of reciprocal interests and mutual advantage. In your letter No. 17, dated on the 1st June, you state your opinion, that 'the authority of the Peishwa would be restored by the appearance of a strong British force at Poonah, and that Scindiah, under the circumstance of Tippoo's recent aggression, could, on no pretence, object to such a movement of our troops, nor in his present condition be able to oppose it.' It is not my intention to give any just cause of offence to Scindiah, or to assist the Mahrattas in any hostile attempt against him, however I may disapprove his late violent and oppressive measures, and lament their injurious consequences to the strength of our ally, but it must be an essential part of our preparations for counteracting the avowed hostility of Tippoo, to place our allies in a condition to fulfil their engagements with us, and if the presence of a British force at Poonah be necessary to the accomplishment of this object, as far as it respects the Peishwa, it is my strict right to furnish him with such assistance, nor can Scindiah, with any colour of justice resist this step, although the consequences of it must be to compel him to retire from Poonah, for he cannot be ignorant that his present position obstructs the operations of the triple alliance, and thereby affords the most effectual aid to the cause of Tippoo.

"I therefore empower you to inform the Peishwa that you have my authority to furnish him with a strong force from Bombay whenever he shall require their presence at Poonah, provided he shall stipulate to secure the regular discharge of the expenses of the detachment in a manner satisfactory to you, and shall agree to certain other conditions stated in a certain part of this despatch. I have directed the government of Bombay to order the troops to march as soon as they shall receive a requisition from you to that effect. You will state to the government of Bombay the strength of the force necessary to secure the proposed objects, and if the force required should not exceed one regiment of native infantry, each battalion completed to one thousand men, a company of artillery and one regiment of Europeans, I should hope assistance to that extent might be immediately furnished from that presidency. To this force, they would probably be able to add another native regiment, after the breaking up of the Monsoon. The commanding officer will be ordered to obey your directions respecting the employment of the troops when arrived at Poonah. Before, however, you engage to furnish the Peishwa with the proposed force, you will take care to explain to him that it is my intention to increase the British detachment now in the service of the Nizam, with a similar view of enabling that prince to fulfil his engagements with us in the event of a war with Tippoo. You will add that the additional force to be furnished to the Nizam will be subject to the same restrictions and limitations with regard to its employment, as the detachment now in the service of his highness, and that no enlargement or alteration of those restrictions and limitations will be made without the previous knowledge and consent of the Peishwa; you will also make a formal tender to the Peishwa in my name of any arbitration between the courts of Hyderabad and Poonah and Scindiah, and you will declare to him my decided opinion that his own authority can neither be restored nor ultimately secured, without a cordial union between the two courts; nor can the union be firmly cemented by any other means than the arbitration of the British government, which must always feel an equal interest in the welfare, dignity, honour, and strength of both parties, and you will further state to the Peishwa the advantages which he would derive from a settlement of all contested points between him and Scindiah under my mediation. You will also declare my wish, that he should bind himself by treaty to exclude for ever all natives of France from his armies and from his dominions, a measure essentially necessary to the preservation of his own authority, which would be exposed to perpetual hazard from the admission of the agents of French intrigue. The state of the Nizam's government has for some time past afforded a sufficient example of the danger to be apprehended from the introduction of the natives of France into an Asiatic court. After having fully explained all these points to the Peishwa, you will consider his consent to the increase of the British detachment in the service of the Nizam, to my arbitration of the subsisting differences between the courts of Poonah and Hyderabad and Scindiah, and to the exclusion of the French from his armies and dominions, as a necessary preliminary to the measures which I have authorized you to take for restoring the Peishwa to his due authority and power in the Mahratta empire. I have already observed that the present position of the army of Scindiah operates as an effectual assistance to the cause of Tippoo.

"If an alliance, offensive and defensive, had been formally concluded between those two powers, Scindiah could not render a more effectual service to Tippoo than he now performs by holding in check both the allies of the Company. You will, however, omit no endeavour to conciliate the mind of

Dowlut Rao Scindiah to the measures which I have empowered you to take for restoring the authority of the Peishwa; and you will assure Dowlat Rao Scindiah that I feel the most genuine desire to maintain and improve the relations of amity and peace with him, and that it will always give me pleasure to receive accounts of his prosperity within his own dominions, and to witness the stability of his just authority and power over his own subjects.

"At the same time you will represent to him, that the continuance of his army in its present position renders our allies, the Peishwa and the Nizam (especially the former), unable to fulfil their defensive engagements with us in the actual crisis of Tippoo Sultan's preparations for offensive warfare, and that it, therefore, would be esteemed a testimony of friendship and good-will towards this Government, if Dowlut Rao Scindiah would return within the limits of his own dominions.

"You will at the same time deliver to Scindiah the accompanying letter from me, communicating a paper lately received by the Resident at Lucknow from a Vakeel of Zeman Shah. I forward to you a copy of my letter to Scindiah, and of that paper, by which you will perceive that Zeman Shah has announced his intention of invading Hindustan, and has demanded the aid of this Government, and of the Nawab Vizier, for the purpose of delivering Shah Allum from the hands of the Mahrattas, and of expelling them from their possessions on the north-western frontier of Oude.

"I authorize you to assure Scindiah that I will use every effort to counteract the designs of Zeman Shah, being resolved to resist to the utmost extent of the power vested in me the attempt of any invader, who shall endeavour to disturb the established states of India in their actual possessions. You will further suggest to Scindiah, that as soon as he shall arrive in his own dominions, he will find the British Resident at his durbar prepared to enter into defensive engagements with him for the mutual protection of his territories, and those of the

Nawab Vizier, and of the Company, against the threatened invasion of Zeman Shah, and that it is my intention to propose a similar defensive treaty to all the British allies in India. You will suggest to Scindiah, that if, contrary to my expectations, he should not return to Hindustan, for the purpose of assisting in person in the protection of his dominions against the menaced attack of Zeman Shah, I will take no concern in the security of a country abandoned by its own sovereign, and I will limit the operations of the British troops exclusively to the defence of our own territories and of those of the Vizier. In addition to whatever Scindiah may apprehend from Zeman Shah, he must be sensible, in the present disturbed state of his dominions and of his army, his fate is in our hands, but it would not be proper to make any direct intimation to him of our sense either of his danger or of our own power, with relation to the internal condition of his civil and military government. This instruction is not meant to apply to the cases of Scindiah's obstructing the march of the British detachment from Bombay, or of his entering into engagements with Tippoo either against the Peishwa, or the Company. In any of these cases, I empower you to state distinctly to Scindiah, that I shall deem myself justified in acting offensively against his dominions in Hindustan.

"The proposition to be made to Dowlut Rao Scindiah appears to be so reasonable, that I have formed a strong expectation of its success. If he should be induced by your representations to retire from Poonah, it is my intention, upon his arrival in his own dominions, to offer him my mediation between him, the Peishwa, and the Nizam, for the purpose of establishing peace between those powers. You will apprise him of my intentions in this respect, at the moment which shall appear to you most favourable to such a communication. I now proceed to give you my instructions with respect to the employment of the force which I have authorized you to require from Bombay. If Scindiah should disregard the representations which I have directed you to make to him, you will apprise him in the first instance, that you have power to employ the British force for the protection of the Peishwa's person and for the support of his authority; accordingly, if Scindiah should attempt to obstruct the march of the British detachment to Poonah, or if, after its arrival at Poonah, he should not conform to the orders of the Peishwa, enjoining him to retire to his own territories, or if (according to the suggestion stated in the 11th paragraph of your letter to me, No. 19 of the 13th of June), he should manifest any intention of soliciting the succour of Tippoo, in the prosecution of hostilities against the Peishwa, or if he should enter into any engagements with Tippoo of a nature dangerous to our safety, I authorize you, in each of these cases, to employ the British troops in active operations against Scindiah, provided that the force detached from Bombay shall, in the judgment of the commanding officer, be deemed adequate to the service required.

"You will communicate my letter to Scindiah to the Peishwa, at such time as you may think most proper.

"Although I have entered into so particular a detail with respect to the communications to be made to Dowlut Rao Scindiah, placing great reliance on your discretion, I authorize you either to vary the mode of those communications, or wholly to omit them, and to withhold my letter to Scindiah according to your judgment on all the circumstances of the case, and you may look with confidence to my approbation of any measures you shall pursue for the purpose of removing Dowlut Rao Scindiah from his present position, provided those measures be not inconsistent with the general tenor of my instructions. I concur with you in opinion that the treaty of triple alliance is very defective, inasmuch as it does not specify the amount of the aid to be furnished by each of the contracting parties in the event of hostilities with Tippoo Sultan. Your letter of 1st June states, 'that the Peishwa is very desirous of entering into new engagements with us, and that a new treaty with him might comprise many new objects.'

I am ready to enter into the conditions of a new treaty with the Peishwa, provided that it be founded on the basis of his present engagements with us, that it be consistent with the tenor of our treaties with other powers, and that it contain no stipulation of any offensive tendency or calculated to disturb the general peace of India. But before I can consent to contract any new engagements with the Peishwa, I must require his full and unqualified acknowledgment of the binding force of the treaty of Poonah upon him, and upon that state. Should he attempt to evade the obligations of that treaty, under the pretence stated in your letter of the 1st of June, I never will place any reliance on his faith, nor will I enter into engagements with him of any kind; but as I am persuaded that you will without difficulty convince him of the injustice and danger to his own interests of endeavouring to shake an acknowledged principle of public faith, I trust no obstacle will occur to the commencement of the proposed negotiations, which I authorize you to open under the reservations and exceptions already stated. I refer you to the correspondence in the years 1792 and 1793, the guarantee treaty, and those of Poonah and Hyderabad; and I desire that you will communicate to me such articles of a new engagement, as you think would be either acceptable to the Peishwa, or desirable for us, before you make any formal propositions to the ministers of the Peishwa.

"You will understand that I do not mean to prevent your opening conferences for the purpose of collecting the general sentiments of the court of Poonah respecting a new treaty, but merely to caution you against either making or receiving any formal propositions of detail, before you shall have apprised me of the nature and extent of the Peishwa's views and of your own.

"There is one point, however, upon which you may make a direct offer at the moment which may appear to you most favourable; you may inform the Peishwa, that I am disposed to enter into the same subsidiary engagements with him, which now exist, or shall hereafter be contracted between this Government and the Nizam.

"You will, however, take care in negotiating any subsidiary treaty, not to agree to furnish any European troops, excepting the requisite proportion of artillerymen, and also not to demand in any case, nor to accept, without previous reference to me, any assignment of revenue or territory, for defraying the payment of the troops to be furnished. It is entirely contrary to the whole object and policy of the arrangement proposed in this letter, to extend the territory of the Company at the expense of any of the parties concerned.

"It would be injurious to our character that any circumstance attending the negotiations should betray the symptoms of that species of irregular ambition, which is utterly repugnant to the disposition of this Government.

"It would be desirable that the Nizam should be made a party to any new engagements which we may contract with the Peishwa. The Nizam's participation might facilitate the restoration of harmony between the two states, tend to secure their future union and co-operation, and strengthen the revived authority of the Peishwa.

"You will communicate to the Resident at Hyderabad, with all practicable despatch, the result of your endeavours to obtain the Peishwa's consent to the several conditions proposed in this despatch.

"The Resident at Hyderabad will be directed to govern his conduct by the nature of the information which he shall receive from you with respect to these important points.

"The whole scope of my views is to re-establish our means of defence against the avowed designs of Tippoo by restoring to our allies that degree of consideration and strength which they possessed at the conclusion of the Treaty of Seringapatam, and which it was the object of that treaty to secure on solid and permanent foundations, an object inseparably connected with the security of the British possessions in India.

"Since the conclusion of the peace of Seringapatam, a material change has taken place in the situation of almost all the states of India, both with relation to each other, and to the interests of the British government. The revolutions at Poonah have impaired the influence of the constitutional head of the Mahratta empire, and deranged the whole system of the balanced powers and interests of the several confederate Mahratta states. Both the Peishwa and the Nizam, whose respective power it was the object of the Treaty of Seringapatam to strengthen and uphold, are now depressed and weakened, the former by the intrusion of Scindiah, and the latter by the threatened hostilities of the same chieftain, and by the establishment of a French faction in the centre of the Deccan. The co-operation of these two members of the triple alliance has been rendered impracticable by the progress of their mutual contentions, at the same time that the internal convulsions of each state have diminished the resources of both. In this scene of general confusion, the power of Tippoo Sultan alone (to restrain which was the policy of all our alliances and treaties) has remained undisturbed and unimpaired, if it has not been augmented and improved. The final result to the British Government is the entire loss of the benefit of the treaty of triple alliance against Tippoo Sultan, and the establishment of a French army of 14,000 men in the dominions of one of our allies, in the vicinity of the territories of Tippoo Sultan, and on the confines of the Carnatic and Northern Circars.

"It is now become an urgent duty to make an effort for the arrangement of a system, the disorders of which already menace our safety by exposing us to the hazard of a war without the aid of an ally, while, on the other hand, the influence of France acquires daily strength in every quarter of India, under the progressive system of introducing French officers into the armies of all the native powers. The principles of justice, good faith, and moderation, enjoined by Parliament, and by the orders of the Honourable the Board of Directors, must form the basis of these comprehensive measures, the execution of which is demanded by the exigency of our present situation, and is favoured by the peculiar circumstances of the moment.

"Pursuing no schemes of conquest or extension of dominion, and entertaining no projects of ambition or aggrandisement either for ourselves or our allies, it is both our right and our duty to give vigour and effect to our subsisting alliances and treaties, by restoring to our allies the power of fulfilling their defensive engagements with us. Through the means of moderate and specific representations, confirmed by the force of our own example, it must also be our policy to convince the several powers of India that their real interest consists in respecting the rights of their neighbours, and in cultivating their own resources within the limits of their several territories; to these efforts we must add a firm resistance against the intrusion of any foreign power which shall endeavour (to the prejudice of our allies and interests) to acquire a preponderating influence in the scale of Indian politics, either by force or intrigue, but the primary object of all our vigilance and care must be the destruction of every seed of the French party already grown to so dangerous a height, and still increasing in the armies and councils of the Nizam, of Scindiah, and of Tippoo. The exclusion of the influence of the French from the dominions of the native states, is not more necessary to the preservation of our own power, than to the happiness and prosperity of this part of the world.

"In this first communication with you, I thought it advisable to apprise you of the leading principles which will govern my conduct towards the native princes, and I have taken a general view of the actual state of our political relations, in order to enable you to act with more confidence and despatch upon such questions of detail as may occasionally call for the exercise of your judgment in promoting the objects of your mission.

"Having received overtures of a very friendly nature from the Rajah of Berar, who has requested the presence of a British Resident at his court, I have despatched an ambassador to Nagpore with full powers to ascertain the precise nature of the Rajah's views. You will make such use of your knowledge of this circumstance, as you may think most advantageous in the present state of affairs. Without deciding what benefit to the common cause of the allies may result ultimately from this embassy, it may be expected that the appearance of an established intercourse between this government and that of Berar, may lead Scindiah to form serious reflections upon his own situation, and may tend to give additional confidence to the adherents of the Peishwa and of the Nizam."

APPENDIX I I.—(p. 255).

Concluding portion of Colonel Low's Letter to the Governor General (cited above), relative to the Pecuniary Embarrassment of the Nizam's Government.

"The pecuniary affairs of this government are in a worse condition than they have ever been since the treaty of 1800. The Nizam in those days had large private treasures, and the amount of his debt was trifling. His highness's treasures have been since almost entirely exhausted. The debts now amount to 3 crores and a half of rupees: a large portion of this consists of arrears of pay long due to troops and other public servants, who cannot be discharged for want of ready money wherewith to pay them up. Another large portion of the debt is due to sowcars, which is running at a ruinous rate of interest, and upwards of 42 lacs of rupees are due to the British Government.

"The whole revenue of this state amounts only to about a crore and fifty lacs of rupees, and as public credit is altogether unknown, a debt of that magnitude, with heavy interest accruing on it, presses most severely upon the government, and causes a great ramification of evils throughout the country, the nature of which is too well known to render it of any use that I should here expatiate on them."

APPENDIX J J.—(p. 315).

Translation of a Placard alluded to by the Nizam on the occasion of his investiture as a Knight of the Most Exalted Order of the "Star of India."

[The original copies in Persian were placarded in the city of Hyderabad at the following places: One inside the Nizam's palace; others on each of the two mosques where Salar Jung and Shumsh-ool-oomrah usually say their prayers; one on the new bridge, and finally one on the gateway of the city.]

"The ruler of the Deccan and his officers are misinformed, and the veil of neglect is over their minds. May God Almighty grant His grace! The Dewan is intriguing and suggesting on behalf of the Company that it is advisable that the Star, Effigy, and the title of knighthood, which have been received from the Company for the ruler, should be accepted without objections. After a few days, in the event of their acceptance, a request will be made for the expulsion of the Afghans, Arabs, and Rohillas, and the disarming of the population of the city; and then it will be said that guards should be placed over the house of the prince (Moorshidzada), and a Company's Adawlut established for the improvement of the state. If these orders of the Company are disregarded, the ruler will be summoned to the presence of the Governor General, and orders personally given him. If even then he should decline them, some member of the ruler's family will be made to succeed him. All these measures are owing to the intrigues of the Dewan. Beware, and be on the alert!

or otherwise you will have to repent of your doings. The Ameer Kubeer (Shumsh-ool-oomrah) even does not point out any measures, as he thinks that he has nothing to do with the ruler or the state so long as his own house is in safety. It is a pity, and a hundred pities, that the love of the world has fixed itself in his heart, and that he is devoid of zeal for his faith and the religion of Islam! Curses on his worldly-mindedness! The Dewan also intends to take under his own control the Siri Khass and Jeki Khass (the private estates and income of the Nizam), and to exclude the ruler from all interference, to keep him in submission, and bring him under obedience and subjection to himself, and even to destroy him by poisoning his food. When the ruler consults his attendants or those who have access to him, these men, from fear of the Dewan, advise his highness to leave the matter to the judgment of the Dewan, and act according to his advice. They give such advice merely from the idea that if they said anything contrary to the wishes of the Dewan they would be ruined, as those four persons were who were expelled from the city. All who have access to his highness, and his attendants, from the noble to the female domestic, are under subjection and obedience to the Dewan, receive salaries from him, and support him.

"All these proceedings, namely the 'Star, Effigy, Title,' &c., are entirely the result of the Dewan's intrigues and instigations, and as formerly the ruler insulted the Dewan by the use of harsh language so now the Dewan, in retaliation, causes the ruler to be insulted, and conceives that he is to be made permanent in his Dewanee by rendering good service to the Company. It is owing to the advice of the Dewan that the Star, Effigy, &c. have been sent to other countries also, and he will make the ruler of the Deccan nominally such, and himself absolute in everything. The ruler of the Deccan is negligent of these things, and occupies himself in amusements, dancing, and jesting. May the Almighty remove the veil of neglect from the minds of these persons, and instil into them the zeal for the religion of Islam and for their faith.

"I have written all this. If it is wrong, see what will come to light in a few days. The ruler has given frequent orders for the cheapening of grain, but the Dewan will not give effect to them. The people are all ruined and in distress and trouble; it is therefore certain that in a short time all the people will get together and make a disturbance against the Dewan.

"If his highness the Nizam accept the Effigy and Star, notwithstanding this notice of ours, all of us Mussulmans will make a disturbance against his highness and the Dewan."

APPENDIX K K.—(p. 321).

Tradition concerning the Construction of the great Hoossain Saugor Tank near Secunderabad.

"The above Khajah Hoossain Shawullee Sahib was a resident of Goolburgah from his birth up to the time that he had attained the age of twenty-four years, when he married, and had issue two sons.

"It was the practice of the ancient sovereigns of the Deccan to have near their persons a descendant of Khajah Bundenewaz Hoossainee, the first or primeval Peerzadah of Goolburgah Shereef (or the holy), with a view to ensure the well-being and prosperity of the state.

"On the occasion of the accession of Ibrahim Kootab Shah to the throne of the Deccan, his highness sent for Khaja Hoossain Shawullee, and as the manners and disposition of the Peerzadah pleased his highness, he was thenceforth ordered to be in attendance on his highness's person.

"It happened one day that his highness sent for the Peerzadah, and after extolling his high qualities and superior judgment, requested he would undertake the formation of the tank above alluded to.

"The Peerzadah, in obedience to his highness's instructions, commenced preparations for the tank, which was completed in three years, seven months, and nineteen days, from date of commencement. Rs. 2,54,636-12-3 were expended upon this work, but the tank continued almost empty for four years succeeding its completion.

"His highness having been disappointed, and his expectations unrealized with respect to the filling of the tank, directed a nobleman of his court, of the name of Kijah Nek Nam Khan, to cause a channel to be made from the river Moossey to the Hoossain Saugor Tank, in order that it might be filled. Nek Nam Khan accordingly cut a small channel, paying the expenses out of his own private funds, and succeeded as an experiment in bringing the water into the Hoossain Saugor Tank. When the Ameer had thus far succeeded, he intended to enlarge the channel, and make it a complete work, but he unfortunately died.

"One day his highness went on a pleasure excursion to the Hoossain Saugor Tank, and inquired of the spectators what its name was. They replied that it was called "Hoossain Sahib Cherroo." His highness, indignant that his own name was not given to the tank, resolved that another should be sunk. His highness, accordingly, on leaving the tank, proceeded to Ibrahimpatam, when he marked out the outlines of a tank himself, in order that it should bear his own name.

"On this occasion the favourite of his highness, Hoossain Shawullee Peerzadah, was in attendance, when it so happened that a pigeon, which was perched on the tree under which the Peerzadah was resting, cast its excrements upon him, and soiled his robes. Thereupon the Peerzadah casting an indignant glance at the bird, it fell down dead. His highness, observing the sudden death of the bird, inquired who had killed it? The vizier explaining the cause, his highness directed that it should immediately be restored to life; upon which the Peerzadah put the bird into his vest, warmed, and brought it to life. His highness, struck with astonishment, fell down on his knees at the feet of the Peerzadah and exclaimed, "The miracle you have just performed has exceeded all I had heard or witnessed before."

"His highness, after a short interval (*i. e.* after marking out the outline of the tank), threw with his own hands five basketfuls of earth to inaugurate the commencement or foundation of the bund, and proceeded on to the fort of Golcondah.

"In a short time the tank was completed, and is known to this day by the name of "Ibrahim Cherroo."

"Subsequent to this, on the occasion of the festival of the Ramzan, the noblemen and others of the city presented nuzzurs to his highness; among the rest was the Peerzadah Khajah Hoossain Shawullee Sahib. When he had got as far as the door, the durbans prevented his entering, but the Peerzadah did not heed them, and went on. Conceiving his disciples were following, he drew his sword out of his belt, and handed it behind him, as it was not usual to go armed into the presence.

"The sword which had been dropped by the Peerzadah, instead of falling to the ground, remained suspended in mid air. The persons present at the durbar saw the miracle, and were astonished, as was his highness.

"The Peerzadah, finding that his highness's gaze was also directed towards the sword, looked back himself, and saw it still suspended. He then went on, and taking up the sword, advanced towards his highness.

"His highness stood before the Peerzadah, and paying his obedience to him, placed him on the musnud, and presented him with a nuzzur. His highness then, addressing the Peerzadah, said, "In reality I perceive that you are a saint. With my own eyes have I witnessed two miracles. My desire now is, that you will make my daughter your slave; in other words, take her to wife." The Peerzadah would not consent, but upon his highness persisting, he at last agreed, and Beermah Sahiba Beebee was accordingly given in marriage to the Peerzadah.

" The historian adds that the miracles performed by the Peerzadah Hoossain Shawullee Sahib were so numerous, that they were incapable of being noted down.

" Some time after the above occurrences, his highness being on the eve of his departure to Churchee Chinchawur with his army, and finding the health of the Peerzadah in a precarious state, directed that in case the Peerzadah died before his highness returned from the wars, he should be buried within the Fort of Golcondah.

After his highness's departure, the Peerzadah grew worse, and sending for his senior disciple, thus addressed him :—' It is true that his highness, in the event of my death, directed my remains to be interred within the Fort of Golcondah, but my desire is, that they should be interred in Kirnee Bagh *without* the fort : ' saying this, he expired.

" The Killadar on hearing of the Peerzadah's death, and the expression of his desire to be buried outside the fort, determined to oppose it, closed the gates, and was resolved that the remains of the deceased should be interred within the fort. After the usual ceremonies in such cases, the procession attempted to proceed, but in doing so the bier of itself moved on, and with such rapidity that it did not stop until it had reached the Puttencheroo gate. The people at the gate stopped the bier, and would not allow it to proceed, but those following the procession explained that it was the dying request of the Peerzadah to be buried outside the fort, and that they were determined to carry it into execution. An altercation ensued, when it was at last settled that the shroud of the deceased should be searched, and that they should abide by the result. Accordingly, Syud Ally Sahib, the favourite disciple of the deceased, put his hand into the shroud, when he found a paper with his highness's seal attached to it, and apparently in the court moonshee's handwriting; the document was to the effect that no hindrance was to be offered to the funeral procession. The Killadar of the fort placed the paper on his forehead, and had the gate immediately opened, when the funeral proceeded to Kirnee Bagh, where the remains were duly interred.

"His highness was in due time informed of the death of his favourite Peerzadah, together with all particulars connected with it. Finding his orders regarding the burial of the Peerzadah disregarded, he ordered the Killadar to be imprisoned. His highness, on his return to Golcondah from the war, sent for the Killadar, and inquired of him his reasons for disobeying his orders, and added that he would severely punish him for so doing. The Killadar replied that he was the slave of his highness's orders, and would not dare disobey them; that on seeing his highness's orders produced from the corpse of the Peerzadah, he could not but obey, and therefore placed the paper in question in his highness's hands. His highness on looking at the document was struck with astonishment, and sending for the court moonshee, was exceedingly enraged, and upbraided him for clandestinely attaching his highness's seal to the paper. The moonshee took his oath, saying that he was not acquainted in the least with the circumstances alluded to, but at the same time admitted that the handwriting resembled his own.

"His highness then carefully reflected on the matter, and exclaimed, 'It is no wonder that this should be a miracle after what I have myself witnessed.' His highness then ordered the release from custody of the Killadar, and restored him to his post."

APPENDIX L L.—(p. 321.)

Details of Road from Hyderabad to Sholapore, constructed from Funds provided by his Highness the Nizam, from the Revenues of the Assigned Districts, and from the Abkaree Revenue under the Resident's control.

"As shown in the subjoined plan, the road was constructed in three sections. Section No. 1—68 miles, by Candasamy

Moodliar, under the supervision of the chief engineer of Hyderabad, at a cost of 2,280 rs. per mile.

"Section No. 2.—70 miles under the superintendent of roads in the Nizam's dominions, at a cost per mile of 1,672 rs.

"Section No. 3.—39 miles, under the executive engineer, Dharaseo division, at a cost per mile of 3,750 rs.; a fourth section, it will be seen, falls under the direction of the Bombay presidency.

"The total length of the three sections is 177 miles, constructed at a cost of 4,15,937 rs. 8 a. The road was commenced in 1857 and completed in 1860." (*See plan*, p. 500.)

Section I.

"Length 68 miles; original estimate, 1,31,193 Company's rupees.

"The Nizam's government undertook to supply funds for this section of the road at the rate of 10,000 rs. per month.

"Candasamy Moodliar entered into a contract to construct the road for the amount of the estimate to the satisfaction of the chief engineer, binding himself down to complete the work within fifteen months from the 11th of August, 1857.

Section II.

"Length 70 miles, original estimate, Hyderabad, 74,893 rs. 15a. 2p.

"The money for this section was proposed by the Resident to be paid from the Abkaree and Bazaar Fund."

Section III.

"Length 39 miles, original estimate, Company's rs. 1,15,260. Payable from the revenue of the Assigned Districts."

[See Plan of Road next page.]

PLAN OF ROAD FROM HYDERABAD TO SHOLAPORE.

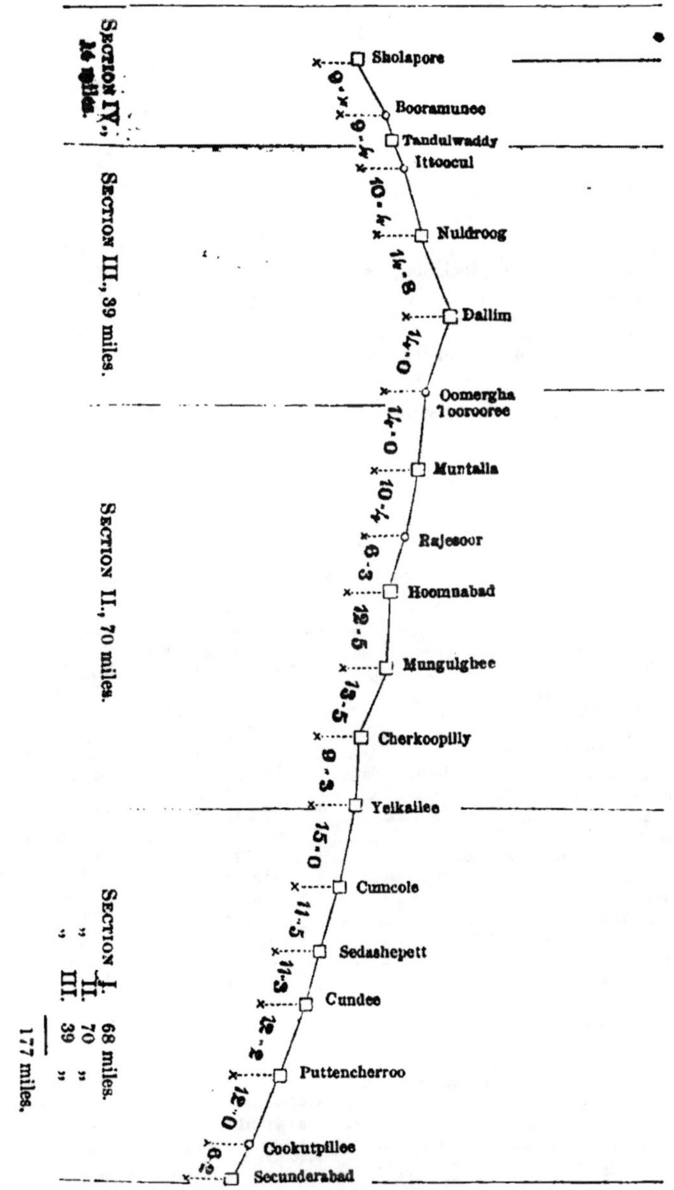

NOTE.—The figures in the above plan express the distance in miles and furlongs. For details of sections, see preceding page.

APPENDIX M M—(p. 323.)

Statement of Revenue in the Hyderabad Assigned Districts, from 1853-54 *to* 1860-61.

	1853–54.			1854–55.		
	RS.	A.	P.	RS.	A.	P.
Land Revenue	28,98,255	12	6	37,11,505	2	4
Customs	61,059	6	10	20,735	7	8
Abkarry	1,18,652	6	8	2,06,125	8	11
Frontier Duties	1,55,260	1	4	33,395	8	6
Salt	27,521	14	11	33,178	12	6
Saltpetre Beds	495	13	10	495	13	10
Miscellaneous Revenue, including Sayer	1,33,726	7	6	2,00,128	14	8
Postage Collections	1,182	2	8	1,091	6	0
Fines, &c.	9,354	8	4	15,936	5	7
Nuzzurs	1,705	11	3	2,312	1	1
Government Dues on a Mint for Copper Pice	363	13	4	—		
Gain in negotiating Homdees	50,597	5	9	1,21,429	12	8
Sale Proceeds of unclaimed Gold Pagodas	173	5	4	—		
Judicial Fees	2,390	11	6	14,525	0	8
Ferries	132	15	6	2,908	6	1
Miscellaneous Receipts	—			63	14	1
Interest on Sicceavic Advances	—			4,252	10	8
Total Rs.	34,60,872	9	3	43,68,084	13	3

	1855-56.			1856-57.		
	RS.	A.	P.	RS.	A.	P.
Land Revenue	36,62,935	3	0	41,14,963	6	4
Abkarry	2,29,649	4	5	2,36,199	12	11
Frontier Duties	29	5	11	—		
Salt	341	4	6	—		
Saltpetre Beds	2,385	9	2	1,500	0	0
Miscellaneous Revenue, including Sayer	1,64,599	9	4	63,839	14	11
Postage Collection	35	15	6	225	6	11
Fines, &c.	21,501	8	5	40,707	9	11
Nuzzurs	1,327	7	2	1,059	8	0
Gain in negotiating Homdees	29,231	10	10	4,983	4	11
Judicial Fees	11,075	1	9	6,741	4	3
Ferries	4,850	12	11	—		
Miscellaneous Receipts	358	0	2	3,946	6	5
Interest on Sicceavic Advances	3,866	1	2	7,143	6	1
Salt Pans	2,626	2	11	7,895	12	9
Salt Wells	35,651	4	5	17,823	2	2
Sale Proceeds of Judicial Stamps	—			8,886	3	11
Sale Proceeds of Articles disposed of in the Parinda Fort, belonging to former Government	447	1	0	21	10	4
Sale Proceeds Jail Manufactures	—			386	14	8
Total Rs.	41,70,911	7	7	45,16,323	12	6

Statement of Revenue in the Hyderabad Assigned Districts—*continued.*

	1857–58.			1858–59.		
	RS.	A.	P.	RS.	A.	P.
Land Revenue	44,58,231	10	10	39,96,984	7	7
Abkarry	2,77,803	5	6	3,14,247	10	8
Salt	36,299	1	5	21,092	10	5
Saltpetre Beds	1,207	0	0	1,821	0	0
Miscellaneous Revenue, including Sayer	22,847	4	5	16,448	10	9
Postage Collection	21	14	0	51	11	0
Fines, &c.	42,814	10	9	38,258	6	10
Nuzzurs	789	10	1	824	0	0
Gain in negotiating Homdees	7,796	0	11	2,917	13	3
Judicial Fees	650	8	9	806	11	10
Miscellaneous Receipts	3,515	0	7	672	11	11
Interest on Siccavie Advances	1,811	6	5	4,492	2	0
Sale Proceeds of Judicial Stamps	32,350	13	7	19,815	1	6
Sale Proceeds Jail Manufactures	85	9	10	996	8	4
Alkali		—		8	0	0
Penalty in lieu of Stamps		—		442	1	0
Interest on Grazing Ground Contract	20	4	9	616	1	0
Total Rs.	48,86,244	5	10	44,20,495	12	1

	1859-60.			1860-61.		
	RS.	A.	P.	RS.	A.	P.
Land Revenue	39,02,269	10	0	43,67,008	0	0
Abkarry	3,84,644	14	3	5,39,399	5	1
Salt	27,728	6	0	30,703	1	8
Saltpetre Beds	1,954	12	0	1,462	0	0
Miscellaneous Revenue, including Sayer	3,218	13	5	1,088	9	0
Fines, &c.	24,249	11	10	30,053	5	6
Nuzzurs		—		861	0	0
Gain in negotiating Homdees	8,467	0	6	515	12	3
Ferries		—		8,706	0	0
Miscellaneous Receipts	2,749	0	11	56,048	10	1
Interest on Siccavie Advances	1,645	5	4	445	6	10
Salt Pans	5,503	6	11	5,339	4	0
Sale Proceeds of Judicial Stamps	28,055	11	0	51,531	1	6
Sale Proceeds of Jail Manufactures	1,351	4	10	2,351	2	5
Alkali	4	0	0	7	0	0
Penalty in lieu of Stamps	770	4	0	812	4	0
Lonar Lake	1,000	0	0	1,000	0	0
Sale Proceeds of Intestate Property	23,370	13	9	11,253	7	2
Gain on serving Processes	3,788	6	9	13,414	13	7
Fee in lieu of Judicial Stamps	547	9	6	5	12	0
Grazing	24,412	6	0	21,0 3	0	9
Orchards	11,288	10	0	4,203	8	6
Total Rs.	44,56,970	3	0	51,47,292	8	4

APPENDIX N N.—(p. 323.)

Statement of Receipts and Expenditure in the Hyderabad Assigned Districts, from 1853-54 *to* 1859-60.

	RECEIPTS.			EXPENDITURE.				
	Land and other Miscellaneous Revenue.	Balance of Accounts of Paymaster Hyderabad Contingent prior to reorganization, and value of Ordnance and Medical Stores in hand.	Total Receipts.	Civil Payments or Charges for Administration.	Public Works Charges.	Military Payment under Treaty.	Interest on Debt, Mahratta Choute, and Mahiput Ram's Family Allowance.	Total Disbursements.
	Rs. A. P.	Rs. A. P.	Rs. A. P.	Rs. A. P.	Rs. A. P.	Rs. A. P.	Rs. A. P.	Rs. A. P.
1853–54	35,82,285 14 2	3,89,392 4 10	39,71,678 3 0	4,56,726 12 11	.. ..	38,49,838 9 10	3,59,8[illegible] 5 9	46,66,423 12 6
1854-55	40,83,034 5 2	17,057 11 4	41,00,092 0 6	10,78,942 8 1	.. ..	27,56,973 3 0	3,7[illegible]215 2 0	42,09,130 13 1
1855-56	39,73,129 6 11	17,839 8 8	39,90,968 15 7	10,46,252 8 4	.. ..	26,32,659 11 0	3,74,1[illegible] 7 9	40,53,062 11 1
1856-57	41,85,542 8 2	.. ..	41,85,542 8 2	11,25,800 5 5	52,890 1 9	25,58,389 13 0	3,74,1[illegible] 7 9	41,10,730 11 11
1857-58	43,71,975 8 6	.. ..	43,71,975 8 6	13,57,057 13 2	1,29,969 7 6	27,02,331 12 8	3,74,150 7 9	45,63,509 9 1
1858-59	44,02,289 10 1	157 3 9	44,02,446 13 10	12,38,512 9 8	3,34,696 15 11	26,74,826 11 6	3,74,150 7 9	46,17,186 12 5
1859-60	44,76,786 5 3	25,963 1 2	45,02,749 6 5	12,37,790 2 1	4,58,036 3 10	27,36,578 6 11	3,74,150 7 9	48,06,555 4 7
Total	290,75,043 10 3	4,50,409 13 9	295,25,453 8 0	75,35,582 11 3	9,75,592 13 0	199,11,598 3 11	26,03,825 14 6	310,26,599 10 8

Per-centage of civil payment or administrative charges to revenue in first column of receipts .. .. 25rs. 14a. 8p.

APPENDIX O O—(p. 330).

Hyderabad Assigned Districts: Abstract of the General Budget of Receipts and Disbursements.

RECEIPTS.	Actuals.	Estimate.		DISBURSEMENTS.	Actuals.	Estimate.	
	1861-62.	1862-63.	1863-64.		1861-62.	1862-63	1863-64.
	RS.	RS.	RS.		RS.	RS.	RS.
Estimated Receipts of East and West Berar, and the Resident's Civil Treasury, as per Abstract of the Budget	36,86,318	40,37,415	39,75,780	Estimated Disbursements of East and West Berar, and the Resident's Civil Treasury, as per Abstract of Budget	9,49,616	965,803	10,61,460
				Payments to Hyderabad Contingent, as per Budget appended	23,30,180	23,71,653	23,90,569
				Military Stores, ditto	12,142	54,000	54,000
				Medical Stores, ditto	8,275	9,412	7,100
				Clothing, ditto	—	17,000	36,341
				Pensions of the Hyderabad Contingent residing in Hindustan	*	2,550	19,150
				Total	23,50,597	24,64,615	25,07,160
				Public Works Department	.....	.....	2,00,000
				Total Disbursements	.....	.....	37,68,620
				Estimated Receipts over Expenditure	.....	.....	2,07,160
Grand Total	.....	..... Rs.	39,75,780	Grand Total ..... Rs.	.....	..... Rs.	39,75,780

* Accounts not received from Calcutta.

GLOSSARY.

Ackbar, a paper containing news.

Adawlut, a court of justice.

Ameen, Aumeen, a commissioner or collector appointed for special reasons, generally of a temporary nature; for example, to make some local investigation or necessary arrangement of affairs.

Ameer, a nobleman.

Amil, a native collector of revenue, the superintendent of a district.

Banyan, a Hindoo merchant or tradesman. In Bengal a banyan often acts as an interpreter, and manages the money affairs of Europeans.

Bega, a measure of land, equal to about the third part of an acre.

Begaries, low-class natives, labourers, guides to travellers. Usually they receive a small gratuity for rendering this service; the payment is optional with the traveller.

Bhonsla, Bhoonsla, the title of the Rajah of Nagpore, or Berar.

Brinjarah, Brinjarries, a class of people who carry grain from one part of the country to another.

Chaoos, an Arab chief.

Choute, a fourth part, frequently applied to the tribute exacted by the Mahrattas.

Chowk, a space generally in the centre of a native town.

Circar, a government or large division of a province.

Crore, ten millions.

Cutwal, *see* Kotwal.

Darogah, a superintendent.

Darool-in-Sha, officer of correspondence.

Dawks, posts.

Deccan, the south.

Dewan, a minister similar to our First Lord of the Treasury.

Dewannee, the office or jurisdiction of a dewan.

Doab, a tract of country between two rivers.

Droog, a hill or rock fortress.

Dufterdar, a keeper of records.

Durbar, the court of the sovereign.

Feelkhana, the elephant department.

Fowjdarry, the office of a Fowjdar or police magistrate, who was sometimes employed under the Mogul Government as receiver-general of the revenue, as well as administrator of criminal justice.

Ghaut, a pass.

Hircarra, Hurkurrah, a messenger, literally a man of all work.

Holkar, the Rajah of Indore.

JAGHIRE. See JAGHEERDAR.

JAGHEERDAR, the person to whom a Jaghire, or portion of territory, is assigned, from which he draws the revenue due to the Government, either for his own personal use or for the maintenance of troops.

JEMADAR, a military officer, a chief of the Hurkurrahs.

KAZY, CAZY, CAWZI, a Mohammedan judge, who also officiates as a public notary, the same as the Turkish cadi.

KHALSA, the office of the revenue department of state.

KHILLAT, KHILAUT, a dress of honour, worn when a dignity is conferred.

KHUREETA, a despatch.

KIST, the sum stipulated to be paid by way of instalment.

KOTWAL, a magistrate's deputy, acting as chief officer of police, superintendent of markets, &c.

LAC, one hundred thousand.

MEHAL, an estate or district, considered as a source of revenue.

MOOLLAHS, priests.

MOONSHEE, a Mohammedan letter-writer, or secretary, a learned teacher, the griffin's preceptor.

MOOTASUDDIES, Hindoo writers or clerks.

MUSNUD, a seat of state for sovereigns below the rank of king. It consists of the ordinary mattress, raised higher, and covered with a small carpet of embroidered silk, and has an embroidered bolster behind.

NABOB. See NAWAB.

NAIK. A military officer.

NAWAB, equivalent to viceroy; under the Mogul Government, the ruler of a province.

NAZIM, a minister of criminal justice, literally an arranger, an adjuster.

NIZAM-OOL-MOOLK, literally, a Nizam is one who arranges or puts in order. Nizam-ool-Moolk is the orderer or administrator of the empire.

NUZZER, NUZZERANAH, a present, usually an offering from an inferior to a superior.

PESHCAR, the minister's assistant.

PESHCUSH, tribute money.

PEISHWA, a leader; the title of the head of the Mahratta nation when it existed.

POLYGAR, a military chief, the head of a village district.

RAJAH, a prince or king, a great nobleman.

ROY ROYAN, the chief treasurer of the exchequer, or Khalsa.

RYOT, a peasant, the tenant of a house or land.

SERISHTADAR, an accountant to a corps.

SIRCAR, see CIRCAR.

SIRPESH, an ornament for the head.

SOWKAR, a banker or merchant, who is also a money-lender.

SUBAH, a province, a larger division of the country than a circar. The whole empire under Akbar was divided into fifteen subahs.

SUBAHDAR, SOUBADAR, a governor or viceroy, the ruler of a subah.

SEBUNDY, troops employed in the collection of revenue.

SHROFFS, money-changers.

SUDDER TOWN, the capital of a province.

SUMESTHAN, a small principality.

SUNNUD, a written authority, charter, letters patent.

TALOOK, TALOOG, a small portion of land.

TALOOKDAR, a local governor, the holder of a talook.

TUNCAH, TUNCAW, TUNKHA, an assignment on the revenue.

URUZKHANA, an office where petitions are given in.

VAKEEL, a confidential agent, commissioner or ambassador; one acting confidentially for another.

WAHABEES, a warlike sect of Mohammedans who arose in Arabia about the middle of last century, and in 1803, under the command of Saoud, conquered Mecca and Medina. From that time their influence increased considerably till the defeat and capture of their chief, Abdallah, by Ibrahim Pacha. We are occasionally reminded of their existence in a scattered state by their readiness to enter into political plots and resort to violence.

ZEMINDAR, literally a landholder; the designation of an officer charged with the superintendence of the lands of a district, and with the realization of the Government revenue arising from them. Apart from this official employ, the Zemindar was usually, as a land-owner, the representative of the agricultural class in his district. Their right under the Mohammedan empire, was restricted to the Government share of the soil.

ZILLAH, a division or district, hence the designation of Zillahdar, given to the commanders of bodies of police.

THE END.

ERRATA.

Page 47, line 9, *for* "Dewahe" *read* "Dewale."
" 108, " 20, *for* "Bey" *read* "Beg."
" 204, " 23, *for* "Crosah" *read* "Owsah."
" 217, " 1, *for* "at Mortsuddy" *read* "a Mootsuddy."
" 229, " 15, *for* "Goorud" *read* "Govind."
" 233, last line, *for* "presidency" *read* "Residency."
" 264, line 13, *for* "Gunerish Rao" *read* "Guneish Rao."